"If this volume is an indication of the next generation of fit research, then we're in for an exciting ride! The authors represent a wide variety of viewpoints on fit, and provide relevant suggestions on how research in this domain can continue to thrive."

Dan Cable
Professor of Organisational Behaviour, London Business School

"This book represents a fine compendium of thinking about what fit is, the motivations of people to seek it, the antecedents of achieving it, and the consequences of having – and not having it – at work. The consequences, indeed, extend to performance of the individual and the organizations in which people work. The chapters offer a broad range of insights into the fit process and contain many useful suggestions for – indeed pleas for – future research efforts on this important psychological phenomenon."

Benjamin Schneider
Senior Research Fellow, CEB Valtera
Professor Emeritus, University of Maryland

"The idea of "fit" is central to every aspect of every employee's worklife. An employee who says to her or himself, "I just don't fit in here" is expressing a view that s/he would prefer to be somewhere else. In other words, working in an organization that does not fit can be like wearing a shoe size that does not fit; it's great to get out of. In this situation, it is most pleasing to see publication of a volume that offers such a wide range of different views on the topic of fit. An especial strength of the volume is that it is not restricted to one epistemological view, thus enabling a broader coverage of the field than has been the case in the literature to date. Thus, while readers might not agree with the views of one particular chapter's authors, there is sure to be at least one other model or perspective with which they will feel comfortable. As such, and as is reflected in the title, this is a volume for the future of research in this field. I have little doubt that it will serve to generate a surge of interest in the concept and importance of fit in organizational research."

Neal Ashkenasy
Professor of Management, University of Queensland
Editor-in-Chief of the Journal of Organizational Behavior

"This book pushes the boundaries of research on and thinking about fit in organizations. Throughout the chapters, the authors tackle a broad array of underexplored topics, and in doing so, provide new understanding about the process of how people fit into organizations. Anyone interested in fit will want to read this book."

Cheri Ostroff
Professor of Industrial/Organizational Psychology, University of Maryland

Organizational Fit

Key Issues and New Directions

Edited by

Amy L. Kristof-Brown and Jon Billsberry

WILEY-BLACKWELL

A John Wiley & Sons, Ltd., Publication

This edition first published 2013
© 2013 John Wiley & Sons, Ltd

Wiley-Blackwell is an imprint of John Wiley & Sons, formed by the merger of Wiley's global Scientific, Technical and Medical business with Blackwell Publishing.

Registered Office
John Wiley & Sons Ltd, The Atrium, Southern Gate, Chichester, West Sussex, PO19 8SQ, UK

Editorial Offices
350 Main Street, Malden, MA 02148-5020, USA
9600 Garsington Road, Oxford, OX4 2DQ, UK
The Atrium, Southern Gate, Chichester, West Sussex, PO19 8SQ, UK

For details of our global editorial offices, for customer services, and for information about how to apply for permission to reuse the copyright material in this book please see our website at www.wiley.com/wiley-blackwell.

The right of Amy L. Kristof-Brown and Jon Billsberry to be identified as the authors of the editorial material in this work has been asserted in accordance with the UK Copyright, Designs and Patents Act 1988.

Library of Congress Cataloging-in-Publication Data

Organizational fit : key issues and new directions / Edited by Amy L. Kristof-Brown and Jon Billsberry
    pages cm
  Includes bibliographical references and index.
  ISBN 978-0-470-68361-3 (print)
  1. Organizational behavior.   2. Corporate culture.   I. Kristof-Brown, Amy L., editor.
II. Billsberry, Jon, editor.
  HD58.7.O7367 2013
  302.3′5–dc23

                                      2012021975

A catalogue record for this book is available from the British Library.

Set in 10.5/13pt Minion by Aptara Inc., New Delhi, India
Printed and bound in Malaysia by Vivar Printing Sdn Bhd

1   2013

This book is dedicated to Benjamin Schneider whose work on organizational fit inspired us to work in this field and continues to do so today.

Amy and Jon

Contents

About the Editors

Jon Billsberry is a Professor of Management at Deakin University. He received his PhD in Applied Psychology from the Institute of Work, Health and Organisations (I-WHO) at the University of Nottingham. Jon's research interests are in organizational fit with an emphasis on perceived fit approaches and misfit. He also is interested in the cinematic portrayal of work and working life and has written extensively on the use of film in the management and leadership classrooms. Jon's published work has appeared in *Journal of Business Ethics, Journal of Managerial Psychology, Journal of Business and Psychology, Journal of Management Education, New Technology Work and Employment*, and *Higher Education*, and in a number of other journals. In addition, Jon has authored three books: *Person–Organisation Fit: Value Congruence in Attraction and Selection Decisions* (2010; Lambert Academic Publishing), *Experiencing Recruitment and Selection* (2007; John Wiley and Sons, Ltd), and *Finding and Keeping the Right People* (2000; Prentice Hall). He has edited four other books: *Moving Images: Effective Teaching with Film and Television in Management* (Billsberry, J., Charlesworth, J. A., and Leonard, P., 2012; Information Age Publishing), *Discovering Leadership* (Billsberry, J., 2009; Palgrave Macmillan), *Strategic Human Resource Management: Theory and Practice* (Salaman, J. G., Storey, J., and Billsberry, J., 2005; Sage), and *The Effective Manager: Perspectives and Illustrations* (Billsberry, J., 1996; Sage).

Jon is the Editor-in-Chief of the *Journal of Management Education*. He serves on the editorial boards of *Academy of Management Learning and Education, International Journal of Management Reviews*, and *Organization Management Journal*. He has also served as the Chair of the Management Education and Development division of the Academy of Management (2011–2012). He was the Inaugural Chair of the Organisational Psychology Special Interest Group and a Council Member of the British Academy of Management. In 2007, Jon launched and organized the first Global e-Conference on fit (see www.fitconference.com), the world's only conference dedicated to organizational fit, and chaired the organizing committee for subsequent conferences.

Amy L. Kristof-Brown is the Henry B. Tippie Research Professor of Management in the Henry B. Tippie College of Business at the University of Iowa. She received her PhD in Organizational Behavior and Human Resource Management from the Robert E. Smith College of Business at the University of Maryland. Amy's research seeks to explore and integrate the many conceptualizations of person–environment fit, particularly in the context of organizational entry. Her recent research has emphasized person–group fit and goal-based fit. Incorporating a mix of experiments, field studies, and quantitative and qualitative reviews, her research has been published in *Journal of Applied Psychology*, *Academy of Management Journal*, *Personnel Psychology*, *Organizational Behavior and Human Decision Processes*, *Journal of Management*, *Journal of Vocational Behavior*, and a number of other journals. She recently co-authored the American Psychological Association's *Handbook of Industrial and Organizational Psychology* (2011) chapter on person–environment fit, and has written entries on person–environment, person–job, and person–organization fit for the *Encyclopedia of Industrial and Organizational Psychology* (2007) and *The Blackwell Encyclopedia of Management* (2005). Although she has co-authored several book chapters, this is her first edited book.

Amy has been an Associate Editor at *Journal of Applied Psychology* (2005–2008), currently serves on the editorial teams of *Journal of Applied Psychology*, *Academy of Management Journal*, *Personnel Psychology*, and *Organization Management Journal*, and has served as an ad hoc reviewer for more than 20 journals. Amy is a Fellow of the Society of Industrial and Organizational Psychology and the American Psychological Association, and a member of the Academy of Management, where she served as a member of the Executive Committee of the Human Resources Division.

About the Contributors

Véronique Ambrosini is a Professor of Management at Monash University. She earned her PhD in Strategic Management from Cranfield University. She was previously a Professor of Strategic Management at Birmingham and Cardiff universities. Her research is conducted essentially within the resource-based and dynamic capability view of the firm. She has articles published in internationally recognized academic journals such as *Journal of Management Studies, British Journal of Management,* and *Human Relations,* and practitioner-oriented journals such as *European Management Journal* and *Management Decision.* She is the author of *Tacit and Ambiguous Resources as Sources of Competitive Advantage* (2003; Palgrave Macmillan), the editor of *Exploring Techniques of Analysis and Evaluation in Strategic Management* (1998; Financial Times/Prentice Hall), and a co-editor of *Advanced Strategic Management: A Multiple Perspectives Approach* (2007; Palgrave Macmillan). Véronique is an associate editor of the *Journal of Management and Organization* and a council member of the British Academy of Management. She is also on the editorial board of the *Journal of Management Studies* and the *Organization Management Journal.*

Linda M. Bajdo is a Professor of Psychology at Macomb Community College. She teaches Introduction to Psychology, Industrial and Organizational Psychology, Psychological Statistics, Psychology of Gender, and Human Sexuality. She received her BA in marketing from Michigan State University, MBA from Northwood University, and PhD in Industrial and Organizational Psychology from Wayne State University. Her research on cultural issues relating to women's advancement in organizations has appeared in *Sex Roles.*

Chu-Hsiang (Daisy) Chang is an Assistant Professor in the Department of Psychology at Michigan State University. Prior to joining Michigan State, she was a faculty member in the Department of Environmental and Occupational Health at the University of South Florida, and in the Department of Psychology at Roosevelt University. She received her PhD in Industrial and Organizational Psychology from the

University of Akron in 2005. Her research interests focus on occupational health and safety, leadership, and motivation. Specifically, she studies issues related to occupational stress, workplace violence, and how employee motivation and organizational leadership intersect with issues concerning employee health and well-being. Her work has been published in *Academy of Management Review, Academy of Management Journal, Journal of Applied Psychology, Journal of Organizational Behavior, Organizational Behavior and Human Decision Processes, Psychological Bulletin*, and *Work and Stress*.

Marije E. E. De Goede is researcher at the Rathenau Institute in The Hague, the Netherlands, an institute that studies the organization and development of science systems. She received her PhD in Work and Organizational Psychology from the University of Amsterdam, the Netherlands. Her current research concerns the career paths of researchers and the factors that affect these *paths*. Furthermore, she is interested in the antecedents and consequences of person–organization fit. Marije received her PhD at the University of Amsterdam in 2012 with a dissertation titled "Searching for a match. The formation of person–organization fit perceptions." Her research has been published in the *International Journal of Selection and Assessment*.

Marcus W. Dickson is a Professor of Organizational Psychology at Wayne State University in Detroit, Michigan, USA. He completed his graduate studies in Industrial and Organizational Psychology at the University of Maryland, studying with Paul Hanges and Rick Guzzo. He completed his undergraduate studies at West Virginia Wesleyan College. Dr Dickson was formerly Co-PI of Project GLOBE, the largest study of leadership and culture conducted to date. His research on leadership has been published in several major outlets, including *The Leadership Quarterly, Journal of Applied Psychology*, and *Sex Roles*, as well as in edited books such as *Advances in Global Leadership, The Nature of Leadership*, and *The Handbook of Teaching Leadership*. He has been recognized for teaching excellence by Wayne State University and the Society for I/O Psychology. When he is not at school, he is probably either playing or researching nineteenth-century baseball.

Tomas R. Giberson is an Associate Professor and Chair of the Department of Human Resource Development at Oakland University in Rochester, Michigan. He received his PhD in Organizational Psychology from Wayne State University. His primary research interest is in person–organization fit, particularly as it relates to organizational culture and leadership. His work has appeared in several journals, including *Journal of Applied Psychology, Journal of Business and Psychology, Journal of Physical Therapy Education*, and *Performance Improvement Quarterly*. He is also the lead editor of an international, interdisciplinary book regarding the current status and potential future of the Academy, entitled *The Knowledge Economy Academic and the Commodification of Higher Education*.

Jonathon R. B. Halbesleben is the HealthSouth Chair of Health Care Management and Associate Professor in the Department of Management and Marketing at the University of Alabama. He received his PhD in Industrial and Organizational

Psychology from the University of Oklahoma. Dr Halbesleben has published in such journals as the *Journal of Applied Psychology, Journal of Management, Journal of Organizational Behavior*, and *Journal of Occupational Health Psychology*, among others. His research interests include employee well-being and work–family issues.

Karen J. Jansen is an Assistant Professor of Management in the McIntire School of Commerce at the University of Virginia. She obtained her PhD in Strategic HRM and Organizational Change from Texas A&M University. Her research broadly explores the process and impact of change on an organization's employees, including how perceptions of person–environment fit change and evolve over time and how change processes gain, sustain, and lose momentum. Her research has appeared in *Academy of Management Review, Organization Science, Organizational Behavior and Human Decision Processes, Journal of Applied Behavioral Science*, and *Journal of Applied Psychology*. She serves as an associate editor of the *Journal of Applied Behavioral Science*. Before becoming an academic she worked as a systems engineer for IBM.

Russell E. Johnson is an Assistant Professor in the Department of Management within the Eli Broad College of Business at Michigan State University. He joined the Department of Management in 2010 after spending 4 years as an Assistant Professor of Industrial and Organizational Psychology at the University of South Florida. He received his PhD in Industrial and Organizational Psychology from the University of Akron. His research examines the role of motivation- and leadership-based processes that underlie employee attitudes and behavior. His research has been published in *Academy of Management Review, Journal of Applied Psychology, Organizational Behavior and Human Decision Processes, Personnel Psychology, Psychological Bulletin*, and *Research in Organizational Behavior*. Originally from Canada, Dr Johnson still dreams of one day playing in the National Hockey League.

John D. Kammeyer-Mueller is an Associate Professor in the Department of Management, Warrington College of Business, University of Florida. He received his PhD in Human Resources and Industrial Relations from the University of Minnesota. John's primary research interests include the areas of organizational socialization and employee adjustment, personality and the stress process, longitudinal research methodology, employee retention, and career development. His work has appeared in the *Journal of Applied Psychology, Personnel Psychology, Journal of Management*, and *Annual Review of Psychology*, among other outlets. In addition to his scholarly work, John has performed consulting work in the areas of employee satisfaction, retention, and workplace safety for 3M Corporation, Allegiance Healthcare, the State of Minnesota, and the Florida Bar.

Cristina K. Kawamoto is a doctoral candidate in the Industrial and Organizational Psychology program at the University of South Florida. She is also a trainee in the Occupational Health Psychology program, which is part of the Sunshine Education and Research Center at the University of South Florida funded by the National Institute for Occupational Safety and Health. Her research interests include person–environment fit, non-work stressors and demands, emotional exhaustion, and employee health and overall well-being.

Yih-teen Lee is Assistant Professor at IESE Business School, University of Navarra (Spain). He obtained his PhD from HEC, University of Lausanne (Switzerland). He teaches leadership, cross-cultural management, and strategic human resource management in MBA as well as executive programs. His research topics include person–environment fit and its variation in different cultural contexts, intercultural competences (cultural intelligence), multiple cultural identities, and leadership in multicultural teams. His papers appear in scientific journals such as *Journal of Management, Personality and Individual Differences*, and *International Journal of Cross-Cultural Management*. His article on culture and person–environment fit has won the Best International Paper Award of the OB Division of Academy of Management 2006 Annual Meeting, and is finalist for the academy-wide Carolyn Dexter Award.

Aarti Ramaswami is an Assistant Professor in the Department of Management at ESSEC Business School, France. She received her PhD in Organizational Behavior and Human Resource Management from the Kelley School of Business at Indiana University Bloomington, USA. At ESSEC, Aarti teaches the organizational behavior and human resource management courses in Master's, Global MBA, and PhD programs. Her research focuses on (a) mentoring, developmental relationships in organizations, and their association with diversity issues and career attainment, (b) person–environment fit, its conceptualization and measurement, and its influence on individual and group attitudes, behavior, and performance, and (c) cross-cultural organizational behavior and human resource management, specifically the generalizability of concepts and hypotheses supported in Anglo/Western settings to other cultural settings. Her work has been published in *Personnel Psychology, Human Resource Management*, and *Journal of Career Development*.

Christian J. Resick is an Assistant Professor of Management and Organizational Behavior with the LeBow College of Business at Drexel University in Philadelphia, Pennsylvania. He received his PhD in Organizational Psychology from Wayne State University. His research broadly examines the social-cognitive psychological processes linking people with their environments. More specifically, his work focuses on four primary areas, comprising organizational culture and fit, executive leader influence, ethics-based leadership and employee cognition, and team cognition and performance. Christian's research has appeared in leading journals such as *Journal of Applied Psychology, Human Relations, Group Dynamics*, and *Journal of Business Ethics*.

Alex L. Rubenstein is a doctoral student in the Department of Management, Warrington College of Business, University of Florida. Alex's primary research interests include individual differences in intelligence and personality, newcomer socialization and adjustment, employee retention, and research methodology. His work has appeared in *Journal of Business Ethics* and *Multivariate Behavioral Research*.

Pauline Schilpzand is an Assistant Professor in the College of Business at Oregon State University. She earned a PhD in Management from the Warrington College of Business at the University of Florida. Her research focuses on business ethics, interpersonal processes, and incivility in the workplace. Her research has appeared in the *Academy of Management Journal.*

Kristen Shanine is a management doctoral student in the Department of Management and Marketing at the University of Alabama. She received her MBA at Bradley University. She has presented research at the Academy of Management Annual Meetings and at the Southern Management Association's Annual Conference; and she has published research in *Business Horizons.* Her research interests include employee well-being and counterproductive behavior issues.

Abbie J. Shipp is an Assistant Professor at Texas A&M. She received her PhD in Organizational Behavior from the Kenan-Flagler Business School at the University of North Carolina Chapel Hill. Her research focuses on the psychological experience of time at work including: how the trajectory of work experiences over time affects attitudes and behaviors, how time is spent on work tasks, and how individuals think about the past/present/future. Dr Shipp has articles published or in press at *Academy of Management Review, Journal of Applied Psychology, Organizational Behavior and Human Decision Processes,* and *Journal of Management.* She is on the editorial boards of *Academy of Management Journal* and *Journal of Management,* as well as a Principal Reviewer for *Journal of Applied Psychology* and an adhoc reviewer for *Personnel Psychology* and *Organization Science.*

J. W. (Jan-Willem) Stoelhorst is an Associate Professor of Strategy and Organization at the Amsterdam Business School, University of Amsterdam, the Netherlands, where he coordinates the strategy teaching in the school's MSc and MBA programs. He received his PhD (cum laude) from the University of Twente, the Netherlands. His research interests include the application of evolutionary theory in the social sciences (in particular, economics) and the application of evolutionary and economic theory in management (in particular, the field of strategy). His work on these and related issues has been published in *California Management Review, Journal of Business Research, Journal of Economic Methodology,* and *Journal of Management Studies,* among others. He is coordinator of the research area "The ontological foundations of evolutionary economics" for EAEPE (the European Association of Evolutionary Political Economy).

Meng U. Taing is a doctoral candidate in the Industrial and Organizational Psychology program at the University of South Florida. He completed his undergraduate degree in psychology at the University of Washington. His research interests include organizational commitment, work motivation, and leadership. For his dissertation, he is forging connections between his research interests by examining the possible mediating role of autonomous motivation in the relationship between transformational leadership and commitment to one's organization and supervisor. To help complete his dissertation, he was awarded a grant from The Forum for People

Performance Management and Measurement, which is an affiliate of Northwestern University.

Danielle L. Talbot is a Senior Lecturer in Leadership and Management at Coventry University. Dannie gained her PhD from the Open University in the UK. Her research interests lie in person–environment fit and misfit: in particular, how employees experience fit and misfit at work and the multidimensionality of fit. She is a member of the Academy of Management (AoM) and the British Academy of Management (BAM) where she is the treasurer of the Organisational Psychology special interest group. Dannie has been a regular reviewer for the AoM and BAM conferences as well as the *Journal of Management Education* and *Organization Management Journal*. Dannie is the incoming Associate Editor of the *Journal of Management Education*'s Resource Review Section.

Annelies E. M. Van Vianen is Full Professor in Organizational Psychology, and Chair of the Department of Work and Organizational Psychology at the University of Amsterdam. She received her PhD in psychology from the University of Leiden, the Netherlands. Her research interests are person–environment fit, career development, aging, organizational culture, and leadership. Her work has been published in journals such as *Personnel Psychology, Academy of Management Journal, Journal of Organizational Behavior, Group and Organization Management, Journal of Vocational Behavior, International Journal of Selection and Assessment, Leadership Quarterly*, and *Psychological Science*. She served as a member of several journal review boards, as guest editor, and as editor of the Dutch journal *Gedrag and Organisatie* (Behavior and Organization).

Anthony R. Wheeler is an Associate Professor of Human Resources Management in the Schmidt Labor Research Center and the College of Business Administration at the University of Rhode Island. He received his PhD in Industrial and Organizational Psychology from the University of Oklahoma. His research has been published in journals such as *Journal of Organizational Behavior, Journal of Business Research, Journal of Occupational and Health Psychology*, and *Journal of Business Logistics*. His research interests include person–organization fit and employee turnover.

Kevin T. Wynne is a doctoral student in Industrial and Organizational Psychology at Wayne State University. He graduated cum laude from The Ohio State University with a BA in Psychology, and subsequently earned an MS in Management from the Mays Business School at Texas A&M University. Kevin's research interests fall into three primary domains: (a) social identification in the workplace, (b) leadership effectiveness, and (c) work–family conflict/balance. Kevin has also consulted with organizations on issues related to organization and leadership development, and talent assessment.

Kang Yang Trevor Yu is an Assistant Professor at the Nanyang Business School of the Nanyang Technological University. He received his PhD in Organizational Behavior from the Kenan-Flagler Business School at the University of North Carolina

Chapel Hill. His research involves applying person–fit frameworks to understand psychological experiences during job search, recruitment, organizational entry, and socialization. He has published in *Journal of Applied Psychology*, *Human Resource Management Journal*, and *Team Performance Management*. He is also co-editing the upcoming *Oxford Handbook of Recruitment* with Dr Daniel M. Cable. He serves as an ad hoc reviewer for *Human Relations*, *Human Resource Management Review*, *Human Resource Management Journal*, and *Group and Organizational Management*.

Preface

This book is about organizational fit, which is also commonly referred to as person–organization (PO) fit. More precisely, this book is about how we might rethink, develop, and expand our existing notions of organizational fit. It contains chapters from leaders in the field who have stepped back from their empirical work on the topic, and tried to reconceptualize our ways of thinking about fit. Some authors have focused on how we might find new directions within existing paradigms, whilst others have addressed the field as a whole and suggested expanding into new directions.

The tone of this book is generally positive, in which the contributors describe organizational fit as a topic that should and will continue to thrive. This is an important consideration, as some recent critical reviews have seemed to question the continued viability of research on organizational fit. Despite a longstanding tradition, based in interactional psychology, which asserts that behavior is best understood as the interaction of person and situation variables, fit research has been plagued by definitional and conceptual ambiguity. Some have questioned whether the domain is so rife with differing, poorly defined, and overly ambitious definitions that it is beyond interest. The authors of the chapters in this book have responded to this challenge and developed compelling arguments about why fit matters, and why more, rather than less, research on fit is necessary. Still believing that fit offers one of the best explanations of human behavior in the workplace, these contributors have advanced arguments that are likely to shape future organizational fit research for years to come.

The chapters in this book had a relatively unorthodox gestation. During a sabbatical visit to Europe, Amy visited with various fit scholars and discussed the recent publication of Ostroff and Judge's (2007) book, *Perspectives on Organizational Fit*. We were energized by the strength of ideas in that book, but also reflected on the widely differing views of fit in the United States and other parts of the world. We began to discuss ways to better integrate these different approaches, and to respond

Process for vol, for devel.

to some of the challenges raised in the 2007 book. We began by holding a caucus at the Academy of Management meeting in Chicago (2009), which about 30
fit scholars from around the world attended. At the caucus we discussed the idea
for this book, and clarified the competitive process by which we would solicit and
select chapters. We next widely distributed a Call for Papers to ask for contributions
of a 2000-word extended abstract to the 3rd Global e-Conference on Fit. Jon had
established the e-conference in 2007, to allow scholars around the world to meet
virtually to discuss their fit-related research, teaching, and practice ideas. Eighteen
papers were received and discussed at the conference. After the conference we made
an initial selection of the papers that we thought might be developed into full papers
within the book's theme of "New Directions in Fit," and we invited those authors
to submit a full version of their papers. We each evaluated all the papers that were
submitted, reduced the set to nine chapters that we felt best matched the book's
theme, and began a two-round feedback and editing process with the authors. Most
of these papers were presented and discussed at a symposium titled "New Directions
in Organizational Fit" at the Academy of Management meeting in San Antonio. This
additional feedback resulted in the final set of nine chapters, which you find contained
in this book.

Reflecting upon this process, we think it has a lot to commend it, and it is certainly
an approach we should use again. By using a widely distributed and competitive call
for papers, the process moves away from the traditional model in which contributors
of book chapters are generally friends and colleagues of the editors. At a minimum
this casts a small net for good ideas, and more detrimentally it can constrain thinking by preventing new and radical ideas from being heard. Our Call for Papers was
truly global in scope, and contributors from across the globe competed for inclusion. The process of presenting extended abstracts at the e-conference had several
benefits. First, it got people writing about new ways to study fit, with a relatively
small initial investment. Second, it tested the strength of these initial ideas as the
various participants from around the globe could engage in debate on each submitted abstract. By sharing these ideas publicly, authors could better understand how
their submissions would sit against the others that eventually would be contained
in the book.

Editing the chapters has been both an exhilarating and a learning experience for
us. Not only have we enjoyed being part of the development of these new ideas, but it
has helped us reflect on our own understanding of organizational fit. For Jon, it has
cemented two notions. First, he thinks that we should be focusing on misfit rather
than fit, which he now sees "as the absence of misfit." Given the negative implications
of misfit (e.g., alienation, anxiety, stress, exit, depression), he now argues that whilst
studying fit is interesting, studying misfit is important. Second, he views perceived fit
as the "real fit" and argues that we should focus exclusively on fit as a psychological
construct in people's heads in a similar manner to the way we think about job
satisfaction, stress, or motivation. Such an approach would, once and for all, end our
definitional and conceptual issues and allow us to develop a research agenda with
the prospect of helping people make the most of their organizational lives (e.g., to

choose organizations where they will fit and to avoid organizational environments where they may become misfits). These are ideas that crystalized for Jon in the editing of this book.

For Amy, she has become convinced that much of the interesting work to be done on fit has to do with the motivations behind people's striving for fit. The process of seeking fit, finding it, losing it, and then moving on to seek it again provides a backdrop against which we can understand most of the transitions that people make in their work lives. How individuals make sense of fit – perceiving it and then taking actions to manage it – is a process that bridges the gap between objective reality and individuals' experienced work lives. These are the ideas that Amy is most enthusiastic to begin exploring in empirical work.

We should like to end this Preface by thanking a number of people. First, we want to thank everyone who took the time to contribute papers to the 3rd Global e-Conference on Fit. Submitting papers in open forum is a scary thing to do, particularly when they are going to be competitively evaluated. It is important to note that the papers that did not make it into the book were not necessarily poor ideas. It was more common for us to assess them as ideas that had too far to travel to make it into the book in time. We hated turning away some of these exciting ideas and we want to thank those people for their good humor and positive reactions. Second, we want to thank the over 200 people who contributed in other ways to the e-conference, either through commentaries, asking questions, or even just socializing at Fit Island in Second Life. Participating with students and scholars from around the world made this conference a rich and rewarding experience. Third, we want to thank everyone at Wiley-Blackwell for helping us produce this book. Without their courteous professionalism and patience, we fear we would not have made it to the end of this project. Everyone with whom we have worked on this project has been a joy to work with and this has helped us greatly to produce what we hope you will find a top-notch book. Finally, we thank our spouses – Véronique Ambrosini and Ken Brown – for their patience, support, and very often brilliant ideas that helped us push through roadblocks when they emerged. We thank you both from the bottom of our hearts.

Jon Billsberry
Deakin University

Amy L. Kristof-Brown
University of Iowa

1

Fit for the Future

Amy L. Kristof-Brown
University of Iowa

Jon Billsberry
Deakin University

This is a time of change for scholars of organizational fit (Judge, 2007). Although organizational fit has been shown to influence employees' motivation, job satisfaction, organizational commitment, tenure, and performance (Arthur *et al.*, 2006; Kristof-Brown *et al.*, 2005; Verquer *et al.*, 2003), it remains questionably defined and often misunderstood. Yet, it is one of the most widely used psychological constructs in industrial and work psychology. The great irony is that the breadth of fit definitions that entices a wide range of scholars to the topic is what also generates the most criticism (e.g., Edwards, 2008; Harrison, 2007; Judge, 2007). It has been suggested that there are as many ways to conceptualize and measure fit as there are scholars who study it. Yet, we believe that criticisms of conceptual ambiguity are a side-effect of rich methodological variety and distinctly different approaches to the compelling concept of compatibility of individuals and their organizations.

When we review the fit literature we see two dominant, and increasingly distinct, portrayals of organizational fit. This divide is between those researchers who focus on fit as an internal feeling of "fitting in" or of "feeling like a misfit" (usually referred to as "perceived fit"), and those who view fit as the interplay or interaction of internal and external factors. This may take the form of objective or actual fit, when the person and environment are measured from distinct sources, or subjective fit, in which a person reports separately about him or herself and the environment. In both cases, fit is assessed by the explicit comparison of person and environment characteristics to determine whether or not there is a match.

The debate has been vigorous over which type of fit is more meaningful, with strong arguments existing for both perceived fit and the more calculated forms of fit. However, we view them as distinctly different domains that should be treated as

Organizational Fit: Key Issues and New Directions, First Edition.
Edited by Amy L. Kristof-Brown and Jon Billsberry.
© 2013 John Wiley & Sons, Ltd. Published 2013 by John Wiley & Sons, Ltd.

separate concepts, rather than a competition over which is a more accurate portrayal of the fit construct. It is our belief that the conflation of these two types of fit is a large factor underlying people's uneasiness with the term "organizational fit." By recognizing that this field of study contains two distinctly different paradigms, and that both have valid interpretations and measurement approaches, forward progress can be made. We review each of these paradigms in turn, beginning with the more interactionist form of organizational fit.

Person–Environment (PE) Fit Paradigm

The bedrock of organizational fit research is person–environment (PE) fit theory (e.g., Caplan, 1983; French *et al.*, 1974; Pervin, 1987). Researchers following this paradigm take a more interactionist approach to assessing fit than those who study perceived fit. They attempt to understand and predict employees' attitudes and behavior by comparing internal aspects of the person (e.g., values, personality, goals, abilities) to commensurate, or at least conceptually relevant, elements of the external environment (e.g., values, culture, climate, goals, demands). Based firmly in the tradition of interactional psychologys where behavior is a function of the interplay between person and situational factors (e.g., Cable and Judge, 1996, 1997; Chatman, 1989; Krahé, 1992; Pervin, 1968, 1987; Schneider, 1987), researchers capture these two distinct elements to calculate a measure of PE fit. The key difference from perceived fit, which we discuss shortly, is that individuals are never asked directly to report their feelings or cognitions about how well they fit. Instead, they report various sets of data about themselves and/or the environment, which researchers then use to *calculate* a measure or index of fit.

This calculated form of fit is subdivided into two main streams of research. The first, called subjective fit, is assessed when the individual whose fit is being measured is asked to report regarding internal and external elements. For example, respondents might be asked to report their own values and also their perceptions of their organizations' values. The distinguishing characteristic is that both assessments originate in the views of the respondent. The second, called objective or actual fit, uses different sources to report the characteristics of the person and the environment. Most typically, the internal dimensions (i.e., personal values or personality) are self-reported by the person whose fit is being calculated, and the external dimensions (i.e., organizational values or climate) come from another source. These external sources may still include perceptions – for example, senior managers' perceptions of the organizations' values – but the observation is considered more objective because it is reported by someone else. In other cases, the environment may be measured truly objectively, as when structural characteristics or reward system elements are used as the environment measure.

Researchers of both the subjective and objective approaches use the word "fit" as a noun: a tangible concept that can be calculated by the sum of its parts. The underlying assumption of these approaches is that the more precise the fit or closer the match between the two set of variables, the better the outcomes (Ostroff, 2012). What a match means, however, can be interpreted widely (Edwards *et al.*, 2006; Edwards and Shipp, 2007). Typically, it is interpreted to mean that when person and environment are in perfect alignment (i.e., high P–high E fit, low P–low E fit), or when the differences between an individual's profile and the environmental profile are minimized, positive outcomes should result. Kristof-Brown and Guay (2011) term this condition of perfect alignment "exact correspondence."

Results of early fit studies using profile similarity indices and other types of difference scores (e.g., Chatman, 1991; O'Reilly *et al.*, 1991) appeared to support this prediction. However, as the field transitioned to using more precise methods of calculating congruence, such as polynomial regression and surface plot analysis (Edwards, 1993, 1994; Edwards and Parry, 1993), only a handful of studies supported exact correspondence as predictive of optimal outcomes (i.e., Jansen and Kristof-Brown, 2005; Kristof-Brown and Stevens, 2001; Slocombe and Bluedorn, 1999). In most cases, the functional forms of fit relationships followed a pattern in which fit at high levels of the person and environment is more strongly associated with positive outcomes than fit at low levels of these entities. Moreover, various types of misfit (assessed as points of incongruence) are typically found to have asymmetrical effects, with the effects of the environment generally outweighing those of the person. For example, several studies have found that having inadequate environmental supplies is a more detrimental condition of misfit than is having excess supplies (e.g., Edwards, 1993, 1994; Edwards and Harrison, 1993; Edwards and Rothbard, 1999). Thus, as analytic methods evolved to allow closer investigation of the exact functional form of fit relationships, the simplistic assumption that congruence is always optimal, and that any kind of incongruence is equally suboptimal, has been mostly abandoned. This leaves scholars with the troublesome conclusion that fit may take any number of functional forms, depending on what variables are under consideration.

PE fit is recognized as an umbrella term that allows three major variations. First, scholars can choose which internal or personal factors are most relevant to their research questions. Second, they can then select which environmental variables are most relevant for assessing fit. In many cases they pursue commensurate variables, but sometimes other theoretically justifiable variables of anticipated compatibility suffice (e.g., pay-for-performance systems are considered a good fit for people with a high value for achievement; Cable and Judge, 1994). Such variations in the environment variables have produced different types or dimensions of fit: person–job (PJ) fit, person–organization (PO) fit, person–group (PG) fit, person–vocation (PV) fit, and person–supervisor (PS) fit. Within each of these types of fit, there is a further diversity of characteristics on which fit can be assessed (i.e., values, goals, abilities). Edwards and Shipp (2007, p. 218) present a multifaceted cube in which all of the varieties of possible fit types and characteristics are crossed, producing an almost infinite range of possible fit types.

The third variation in defining PE fit is the flexibility that researchers have for determining what underlies compatibility on the personal and environmental characteristics of choice. Those in the *supplementary* tradition focus on a compositional view of similarity and congruence; whereas, the *complementary* tradition emphasizes more of a compilational view, in which one entity completes the other (Muchinsky and Monahan, 1987; Ostroff and Schulte, 2007). Still others do not calculate fit at all, but instead interpret the statistical interaction of meaningfully related person and environment variables (e.g., Cable and Judge, 1994; Chatman *et al.*, 2008). Even with this wide variety of fit conceptualizations, the underpinning idea of the PE fit paradigm is the notion that an appropriate alignment or interaction of internal and external factors (whatever that might be) will shape individuals' attitudes and behaviors.

Despite its richness, this is a rather troubled paradigm in the sense that there are many different conceptualizations of PE fit, but little integration in how the various findings knit together. As scholars in this area, we can conclude that some type of interaction between person and environment influences outcomes, typically in a positive direction. However, this gives us little insight into the actual *experience* of fit by individuals. For example, when Chatman (1991) reported that value congruence as measured by the Organizational Culture Profile (O'Reilly *et al.*, 1991) led to increased job satisfaction, she informed us about the relationship of values to job satisfaction through an interactional lens. Arguably, however, we learned little about how people experience the state of fit or misfit. This is why the second paradigm, which focuses on perceived fit, is burgeoning.

Perceived Fit Paradigm

Some consider organizational fit as a psychological construct, similar to job satisfaction or organizational commitment: as something inside a person's mind that influences their thoughts and feelings towards their job or organization (e.g., Billsberry *et al.*, 2005; Cooper-Thomas *et al.*, 2004; Kristof-Brown, 2000; Ravlin and Ritchie, 2006; Wheeler *et al.*, 2007). As mentioned above, in common parlance, this perspective portrays fit as an individual's sense of "fitting in" or, alternatively when it does not exist, "feeling like a misfit." Kristof-Brown and Guay (2011) refer to this conceptualization of fit as "general compatibility," and provide examples of how it is typically measured directly with questions that ask an individual to report the fit that he or she believes exists. Questions such as "How well do you think you fit in the organization?" and "How well do your skills match the requirements of your job?" are examples of these kinds of direct measures of perceived fit. This perspective of fit as a psychological experience of the individual has been described further in the following way:

> Perceived fit allows the greatest level of cognitive manipulation because the assessment is all done in the head of the respondents, allowing them to apply their own weighting scheme to various aspects of the environment. This permits individual differences in importance or salience of various dimensions to be captured in their ratings. (Kristof-Brown *et al.*, 2005, pp. 291–292)

Although perceived fit is arguably most proximal to individuals' decision making and has been shown to offer the strongest relationships to expected outcomes such as job satisfaction and organizational commitment (Kristof-Brown *et al.*, 2005; Verquer *et al.*, 2003), it has attracted comparatively little research and has been criticized for being "just another attitude" and heavily influenced by affect (e.g., Edwards *et al.*, 2006; Harrison, 2007). The longstanding presumption has been that perceived fit is simply the cognitive representation of the person–environment interactions described previously. Therefore, perceived fit and PE calculated interactions should be closely related. Most evidence, however, suggests that there are only low to moderate correlations between these more calculated forms of fit and an individual's experience of perceived fit (Edwards *et al.*, 2006). Very little is known, then, about how these perceptions form, or why they influence attitudes and behaviors as strongly as they do. This is fertile ground for new organizational fit research, and not surprisingly many of the chapters in this book advocate studies in this area.

The Epistemology of Fit

Although these two paradigms reflect a methodological distinction of indirect (PE interaction) versus direct (perceived) measurement, their differences also suggest distinct epistemological underpinnings. Although few researchers have explicitly stated their epistemological leanings, it is clear to us that positivism, or perhaps more accurately post-positivism, underpins PE fit research, whereas interpretivism is the spirit underpinning the perceived fit paradigm.

These epistemologies differ in the way that researchers position themselves regarding what counts as knowledge. A positivist believes that knowledge is objective. It is an extrapolation from "pure science," in which the researcher is thought of as a scientist in a white coat carrying a clipboard, who takes measurements to capture the nature of the "real world" to produce universal truths and laws (Blaikie, 2007). It is what many regard as "true" scientific knowledge. A post-positivist relaxes the strict conditions of measurement and accepts that people's reports of their psychological states constitute objective knowledge, even though such phenomena cannot be seen and objectively measured (Johnson *et al.*, 2007). Alternatively, an interpretivist believes that knowledge is constructed in people's minds and influenced by their social interactions with others. Discovering what is "real" to the individual is most important, because it is those perceptions that influence their behavior. Interpretivists may also look for general patterns, but their attention is on people's perceptions and they recognize that these will differ. The goal of interpretive research is not to discover universal rules, but to understand the phenomena under scrutiny more fully. Although there are certainly exceptions, positivists in general look for similarity and interpretivists look for differences to illuminate understanding of a subject.

Relating these approaches to organizational fit, we see that many of the principles of positivism and post-positivism underpin the PE fit paradigm. This approach involves the researcher looking in on the subjects, taking measurements, calculating fit, and drawing general lessons. In these studies, the researchers make predictions about what they expect to see (in the tradition of positively phrased hypotheses), develop studies that gather relevant data to test the hypotheses, and then draw conclusions in the form of universal propositions. For example, in the classic PO fit study by Chatman (1991), hypotheses were set out predicting relationships between PO fit and psychological outcomes, data on newcomers' values were captured from them, and data on their employing organizations were gathered from senior executives, allowing the researcher to calculate a measure of PO fit for every newcomer to test the hypotheses. Chatman (1991) was able to conclude with a general rule saying that newcomers' PO fit is positively related to their levels of job satisfaction and organizational commitment, and negatively related to their intent to quit. This is a finding that has been replicated in many subsequent studies (Kristof-Brown *et al.*, 2005; Verquer *et al.*, 2003).

In the perceived fit paradigm, researchers seek to understand how people make sense of their organizational lives and, in particular, how their sense of fit or misfit is formed and changes over time. They seek an understanding of people's perceptions and the impact these thoughts have on their behavior. This is a direct correlate of the interpretivist approach, in which researchers want to understand the complexity of people's thoughts, feelings, and desires, and the impact these have on their work and life experiences. They want to understand the world from the subject's perspective, allowing people to describe fit in their own ways that are meaningful to them. The perceived fit researcher may then look for similarities or differences across these accounts to draw universal or general rules. Thus, this approach does not have to go to the extreme of idiographic approaches, which seek to understand the richness of a small subset of individuals' experiences. General conclusions can be drawn, but the impetus for what is included in the measures and experiences of fit is generated by the participants themselves, rather than by the researchers. At the present time, the interpretivist approach to perceived fit is best represented in theoretical work (e.g., Billsberry *et al.*, 2005; Kammeyer-Mueller, 2007). However, we would also include in this category studies that seek to understand the relationship between PE fit interactions and perceived fit (e.g., Edwards *et al.*, 2006).

We have deliberately set out these paradigms and their underpinning epistemology because we believe that they can help define the field, remove confusion about what fit is, and give guidance to researchers about how to operate in these domains. However, we note that our categorization of the paradigms and elaboration of the epistemologies is new and not yet fully represented in empirical work. In particular, whilst the PE fit paradigm and its underlying post-positivist epistemology is well established, much of the work conducted in the perceived fit paradigm has also adopted a post-positivist, rather than an interpretivist, epistemology. In these studies, researchers are concerned with individuals' experience of fit, but use it as a predictor of other outcomes, rather than seeking to understand what underlies it (e.g., Edwards and Billsberry, 2010; Lauver and Kristof-Brown, 2001; Schmitt *et al.*, 2008). Thus, these studies reflect interests in individuals' perceptions, but embrace a post-positivist epistemology regarding what counts as knowledge. Recent studies (Seong and Kristof-Brown, in press; Seong *et al.*, in press) have begun to examine how superordinate perceptions of overall fit underlie more specific dimensions of fit. These types of studies help us better understand what underlies people's perceptions of fit. They remind us that understanding people's experiences of fit can help us make better predictions about how fit relates to attitudes and behavioral outcomes.

In practice, however, research attempting to subvert paradigmatic boundaries is often fraught with definitional, theoretical, and ontological problems. The reality is that epistemologies have considerable difficulty talking to each other. This is not just because the understanding of what constitutes knowledge is fundamentally different; it is also because the approaches construct markedly different conceptualizations to study. In this case, one approach is concerned with a person's feelings and thoughts about how they do or do not fit in, and how this links to their sense of belonging, inclusion, engagement, and mental well-being. The other approach regards fit as a theoretical underpinning in which forms of similarity (i.e., supplementary approaches) and difference (i.e., complementary approaches) drive behavior. In perceived fit, it is the sense of fit driving behavior; whereas in PE fit it is similarity, interaction, or difference between relevant internal and external factors that are the compelling factors.

Understanding the different epistemologies underpinning the two fit paradigms is crucially important because it explains some of the frustration that researchers have had in appreciating each other's work. Researchers interested in fit from an interpretivist slant have difficulty understanding how the alignment of particular (or even sets of) values, for example, relates to people's overall sense of fit. They may see values as one component, perhaps even an important one, influencing people's fit perceptions. However, separating it from other influences on fit perceptions seems overly simplistic and inappropriate from the interpretivist's standpoint. Conversely, researchers viewing fit from a positivist slant are aghast at what they see as weakly defined concepts, overly general measures, small sample sizes, and often atheoretical approaches to data generation in perceived fit research. Anyone who has submitted a fit paper to a journal and had reviewers from a different epistemological leaning will know full well how extreme these cross-epistemological reactions can be!

Nevertheless, changing or blending epistemology could be a particularly useful way to find new directions in the organizational fit literature, as we have already noted. We imagine that researchers taking an interpretivist approach to the thorny problem of how the various forms of PE fit (e.g., PJ, PO, PV, and PG) interweave in people's minds could be very useful. Conversely, a post-positivist approach to perceived fit issues could help us understand to what extent individuals' perceptions of fit are generic. We do not propose that one view is superior to another, or seek to draw conclusions about the direction in which fit research should proceed – that would do a disservice to a field in which the diversity of views and an intuitive sense that *fit does matter* motivates a rich, heterogeneous field of inquiry. Theoretical parsimony may never be achieved by organizational fit researchers, but compelling investigations of a meaningful concept will hopefully continue to thrive.

The Chapters

In the Call for Papers for this edited volume, we invited people to submit chapters that would offer new directions for organizational fit research. This was a response to the various criticisms and concerns that had been voiced over the domain of organizational fit. When we reviewed these papers, we noticed that five of them were arguing for new research within the existing fit paradigms. The other four papers offer quite different takes on organizational fit and offer new ways to approach the subject. Therefore, we decided to separate these two different types of submission into two parts – one looking at new directions within existing fit paradigms and the other looking at new directions for the paradigms themselves.

Part 1: New directions within the fit paradigms

In the first chapter in Part 1, **Yu** addresses the motivations that lead individuals to strive for perceived fit, and a set of agentic behaviors that they will use to establish and maintain this sense of fit. As such, this chapter delivers on the call for additional research on perceived fit antecedents, and does so by addressing why fit is pursued at a basic motivational level. Yu proposes a variety of fundamental needs that are addressed by maximizing fit. These include a need for consistency, hedonism, and uncertainty reduction, a need for mastery or control over the environment, and a need for belonging. He explores how various types of fit fulfill each of these basic motivations. He then proceeds to describe an individually focused and proactive set of strategies that people intentionally, and perhaps more likely unintentionally, engage in to increase their subjective experience of fit.

Building on Caplan's (1983) distinction between subjective and objective fit, he argues that people's biases and heuristics will lead them to manipulate their perceptions of PE fit in a way that allows them to fulfill the motivations previously described. Through social projection (i.e., putting one's own attitudes and views on others), affective-consistency (i.e., modifying perceived fit in such a way that it is consistent with work-related attitudes), and social information processing (i.e., using social information to engage in sense making about person and environment), Yu argues that people are unconsciously managing their perceptions of PE fit through their basic interpretations of people, events, and the situations they encounter. The disconnect between objective fit and subjective fit can thus be explained by the natural tendency to engage in these biases and heuristics. A second set of strategies for managing fit is through the responses of approach and avoidance (through exit, voice, loyalty, or neglect) made to job satisfaction and dissatisfaction, respectively. Coping behavior is reviewed as another set of efforts to change both subjective (through thoughts and cognitions) and objective (through behaviors) elements of PE fit. Yu briefly reviews the negative feedback loops of the cybernetic models of stress (for more detail, see Chapter 4 in this volume) as an additional, natural set of tactics used to establish and maintain levels of PE fit. And finally, he reviews the proactive strategies of job crafting, role adjustment, and deal making as well as information seeking as ways in which people actively and intentionally maintain high levels of fit.

Yu concludes his chapter by proposing several areas for future research on these motivations for fit, including individual differences and environmental conditions that may influence the degree to which people have a strong desire to attain and maintain fit, and how they might go about actively managing it. A brief set of ideas on conditions that might prompt the desire for lesser levels of fit are presented, but the primary emphasis is on understanding individuals as agentic creators and maintainers of perceived fit.

Kammeyer-Mueller, Schilpzand, and Rubenstein outline a comprehensive model of how perceived fit develops in the course of social interactions among established organizational members and organizational newcomers. They begin by focusing on the process of organizational socialization to emphasize the critical moments for fit development that occur during the initial acquaintance phase. From that point forward they build on the relationship science perspective (e.g., Berscheid, 1999; Kelley *et al.*, 1983) to address how fit evolves as a dyadic process by individuals coming to know one another better. By invoking the relationship literature, they present an in-depth perspective on the development of affective bonds between people and the processes of social acceptance and rejection that occur over time. Thus, the authors emphasize the distinctly "interpersonal side" of fit that emanates from dyadic relationships formed with others in the workplace. They describe three types of interpersonal bonds that can be viewed as the basis for fit relationships: affective bonds, instrumentality/exchange, and animosity. The first becomes the emphasis of a supplementary fit relationship in which the similarities of the two parties create a strong emotional connection and basis for liking. The instrumental bonds, in which one party has something the other values and vice versa, are described as the basis for complementary fit relationships. And the final connection, animosity, is presented as a basis for misfit, in which two parties are so different on fundamental attributes that they form an antagonistic relationship. This view of interpersonal perceived fit as a collection of unique dyadic ties has implications for measures of fit, and PG fit specifically. For example, it provides a rationale for how a single negative interpersonal relationship can create an overall assessment of misfit in the work environment, particularly if that person is the individual's supervisor.

Building on this notion of dyadic fit, the authors propose a model of how interpersonal fit develops during socialization. The model begins by suggesting that certain personal and environmental conditions can either foster or inhibit dyadic fit for newcomers. If certain dyadic fit conditions are met, a number of self-reinforcing processes are set into motion that build relationships and increase the strength of ties in a reciprocal fashion, resulting in an overall level of increased fit and subsequent positive outcomes. Multiple propositions are set forth, which show dyadic fit as a dynamic process evolving from an original emphasis on surface characteristics to deeper-level characteristics over time. Team and organizational climate as well as organizational socialization processes are included as means to strengthen these interpersonal processes. As the dyadic relationships develop, additional processes that stem from the social nature of the fit relationship will continue to influence fit. On the positive side, these include personal disclosure, social support, proactivity, and the exchange of goods and services; whereas, on the negative side, the process of social undermining can occur. Concluding their model, they expand traditional affective outcomes of PE fit to include organizational knowledge, turnover, citizenship behaviors, deviance and resilience. Taken together, their chapter presents a holistic view of the development and maintenance (or destruction) of perceived interpersonal fit in the workplace.

The emphasis of **Johnson, Taing, Chang, and Kawamoto** is on how self-regulation processes may underlie the striving for and attainment of fit. Viewing PE misfit as a discrepancy between people's ideal conditions and those that they experience, these authors apply self-regulation theory (Latham and Pinder, 2005; Lord *et al.*, 2010) to conceptualize the attainment and preservation of a certain standard of fit as a goal-related process. Through inputs, comparators, feedback loops, and outputs, individuals are proposed to ascertain and work to reduce perceived discrepancies (or misfit). If these feedback loops are organized hierarchically, with some being more central to people's self-concepts than others, then an interconnected set of feedback loops emerges. Thus, they present a hierarchical model of PE fit in which entity-level fit – that is, across multiple types of fit (PV, PO, PG, and PJ), and labeled "multidimensional fit" in Jansen and Kristof-Brown (2006) and Edwards and Billsberry (2010) – is the highest level, followed by person-level fit (based on needs–values and traits), and then by task-level fit at the most basic level (based on knowledge, skills, abilities, and task goals).

Viewing PE fit as the result of a self-regulation process that unfolds over time prompted these authors to consider both the magnitude of discrepancy involved in fit and also the velocity. They define "velocity" as the direction and rate of change in the size of the discrepancy that underlies fit or misfit. With successful self-regulation depending on both discrepancy and velocity information, these authors assert that prediction of various outcomes can be improved by considering both. Thus, it is not just the current level of fit that predicts an outcome, but also the rate at which this level is perceived to be changing, and in which direction. In fact, these authors go so far as to suggest that velocity may be even more predictive of outcomes than is the magnitude of the discrepancy itself.

Finally, drawing on the rich history of self-regulation theory, these authors propose several individual differences that may influence how fit is perceived and also how it relates to important outcomes. One example is self-consciousness and self-focus, which have been found to influence people's sensitivities to perceived discrepancies, making them more or less attuned to levels of misfit. Another is individuals' level of action identification, or the hierarchical level of abstraction at which they typically relate to their behaviors (i.e., concrete, immediate behaviors versus abstract, long-term, goal-oriented ones). This is proposed to influence the strength with which fit at the entity, person, and task levels influences outcomes for those individuals. Finally, individuals' past versus future orientation is proposed as an influence on the effects of both discrepancy magnitudes and velocities on fit–outcome relationships. Thus, by building on self-regulation theory, these authors shed insight into the motivational processes underlying fit, and provide several new directions for research to examine how to strengthen fit–outcome relationships.

Shifting from the perspective of what motivates people to seek fit, **Resick, Giberson, Dickson, Wynne, and Bajdo** focus instead on what fit motivates people to do. In particular, they explore the oft-reported finding that people who form a strong sense of fit with their organizations also tend to be good organizational citizens. They present a theoretical model examining the social-cognitive psychological processes that are triggered by a person's conscious perception of fit with an organization, and which then motivates that person to engage in discretionary, prosocial work performance.

They base their model on Mischel and Shoda's (1995) cognitive-affective personality system (CAPS) theory, which proposes that people have cognitive and affective reactions to features of their environments that are relevant to an existing schema. Applying this logic to fit, Resick and colleagues argue that individuals create personally held schemas for what makes a "good organizational fit." These schemas are based on personal characteristics, such as values and goals, and may be intensified or clarified by past experience. They propose that individuals attend to features of their work environment to assess whether they match their fit-related schema. If they perceive fit, then four cognitive-affective processes are stimulated. These include the incorporation of organizational membership into one's self-identity, the experience of positive emotion as a result of perceived fit, the formation of motivational strivings that are aligned with organizational success, and the development of specific expectancies that personal efforts can help the organization succeed and thereby preserve employment with that company. These four psychological mechanisms combine to form a processing disposition that inclines people toward engaging in citizenship performance. Building on the logic of self-regulation theory, they then close the loop by proposing that feedback received as a result of citizenship performance will lead to alterations in the intensity of the cognitive and affective reactions, the strength of fit perceptions, and the content of fit-related schema over time. In this way, this chapter views perceived fit as a motivator of other actions at work.

Billsberry, Talbot, and Ambrosini approach organizational fit from a perceived fit perspective, with strong interpretivist underpinnings. They are interested in discovering the nature of people's perceptions of fit and misfit, how they are formed, and how they influence behavior. However, this chapter is very different from other chapters in this book because, rather than extend fit theory or look at how fit may influence other factors, the authors recognize that perceived fit research is in its infancy and focus their attention on how researchers might develop theories about perceived fit. Their conceptual investigation begins with the nomothetic–idiographic divide that PE fit researchers (e.g., Chatman, 1989) examined in the early days of organizational fit research. The primary insight in this chapter is the realization that the research stages of data generation and data analysis might be considered differently from nomothetic and idiographic perspectives. From a perceived fit perspective this is important because it suggests that researchers might be able to take idiographic approaches to data generation and thereby gain an in-depth understanding of the individual, but use nomothetic data analysis approaches to look for similarities and differences between people and thereby generate testable propositions.

In the second part of this chapter, the authors look at cognitive mapping as a means to conduct idiographic data gathering that explores individuals' deep-seated perceptions of fit. They also show some of the different ways in which such data might be analyzed. By focusing on this research method, they illustrate how data gathering and data analysis are two separate phases that can be conducted separately. Through their analysis of data generation and analysis, the authors illustrate how different empirical research in perceived fit will be from PE fit when an interpretivist approach is taken.

Part 2: New directions for the fit paradigms

Building on the idea that individuals hold fit-related schemas or mental models, **Van Vianen, Stoelhorst, and De Goede** emphasize the construal process by asking what people "have in mind" when they assess fit. They begin by arguing that people experience a fundamental need to belong, from both evolutionary and psychological perspectives. These perspectives may differ on why people have this need, but they are consistent in asserting people's natural tendency to strive for belonging, often with similar others. Asking the fundamental question of what people consider when they assess fit, these authors argue that despite the multidimensional nature of fit, people are likely to use only a limited set of cues on which to determine fit. In terms of sources, they emphasize that people are likely to focus on only a few cues from important (and concrete) others regarding what the organization is like. And in terms of focal referent, they suggest that psychological theories emphasize the individual as the primary reference for fit, whereas the evolutionary theories suggest that the environment will be the focal reference. Finally, in keeping with a dynamic view of fit, these authors suggest that this construal process is likely to change over time depending on what stage (attraction, selection, or post-organizational entry) of the work relationship the person is in.

Using Construal Level Theory (CLT; Liberman et al., 2002; Trope and Liberman, 2003), these authors suggest that people will construct mental models of fit differently as their "distance" from the organization changes. At the beginning of the process – for example, when novice job seekers are just beginning to look at companies to join – their fit schema should be based on a few, abstract dimensions. Furthermore, those dimensions will stem from self-rooted perceptions about what is desirable in an organization. As such, they portray initial fit perceptions as a relatively ego-centric and content-deficient assessment. As the selection stage begins, individuals begin to interact more closely with organizational insiders, particularly recruiters. This, combined with pre-interview perceptions of fit, and perceived fairness of the selection system, contributes to the establishment of organizational fit perceptions during selection. Then during the first 4 to 6 months of the employment relationship, individuals focus on particular groups of insiders as the focal reference for organizational fit assessments. These salient individuals become the ultimate source of organizational fit perceptions post-hire, implying that only "some people make the place." Newcomers' fit perceptions therefore depend primarily on similarity with the salient and shared features of prototypical members. Lower levels of similarity with such members make it more difficult for newcomers to behave like insiders, and these discrepant behaviors then feed into perceptions of organizational misfit and feelings of social exclusion.

Wheeler, Halbesleben, and Shanine shed further light on the underlying mechanisms through which individuals react to a lack of fit. Using conservation of resources (COR) theory (Hobfoll, 1988, 1998), these authors elaborate on four motivational mechanisms that underlie the pursuit and maintenance of fit. Viewing individuals as resource seekers and their environments as resource providers, these authors describe four paths by which individuals will seek to accumulate, protect, and invest resources, all resulting in sustaining a desired level of fit. First, individuals experience stress when they are faced with resource losses, and satisfaction when they experience resource gain. Second, they are motivated to invest their current resources in order to gain others, resulting in a cyclical process of resource expenditure and replenishment. People who have more resources to begin with are generally better able to gain more by relying on social support and also by hoarding excess resources for investment. These processes can result in a resource gain spiral, by which excesses result in additional gains. Alternatively, those who have fewer resources initially to invest will end up in a downward spiral of resource loss or conservation.

The authors argue that COR as a theory can be used to explain multidimensional fit and the diverse conceptualizations of fit that exist. This includes supplementary fit, in which an individual matches with the environment, as well as complementary fit, in which one party adds something new to the other. The key is whether or not individuals have, or can work to attain, sufficient resources to meet the demands of the environment and vice versa. One of the benefits of this resource-based perspective is that it blurs the lines between the traditional domains of supplementary and complementary fit. Needs and values and traits and skills all become resources that are interchangeable. The authors use COR to explain five distinct streams of research on fit, comprising stress, job satisfaction, person–vocation matching, recruitment and selection processes, and culture and climate matching processes, including the ASA model (Schneider, 1987). Additionally, these authors suggest that individuals will not engage in constant assessments of fit because the assessment itself requires cognitive resources. Instead, they suggest that environmental events or shocks will trigger assessments of fit. Because shocks activate a threat of resource loss, they push people to reevaluate how their fit may be changing.

Wheeler and colleagues build these ideas of resource-based fit to address the relatively unexplored topic of misfits, and what they do in reaction to the recognition that they are misfits in their work environments. In earlier work, Wheeler and colleagues (Wheeler *et al.*, 2007) offered five reactions to misfit: adapt to the environment, withdraw from the environment, become vocal as a means of changing the environment, engage in passive–aggressive behavior designed to hide their misfit, and try and ignore it as best they can. Using a resource-based theory such as COR, these authors argue that individuals will select the reaction that is most likely to convert them from a resource-loss mode to one in which new resources will be gained. In sum, Wheeler and colleagues propose COR theory as a mid-range theory that helps to explain how the various conceptualizations interact with each other, and the types of behavior that people will engage in over time to work to restore desired levels of fit.

Despite early research that incorporated time into assessments of PE fit (Caplan, 1983; French *et al.*, 1974), the majority of recent fit research has been contemporaneous – focusing on a person's current fit in the current moment. In response, **Jansen and Shipp** focus explicitly on the topic of *temporal fit*, which they define as fit assessments that explicitly or implicitly incorporate time in terms of three conceptual dimensions: *context* (i.e., the temporal setting in which fit is perceived or experienced), *impact* (i.e., the temporal effects of fit on outcomes), and *process* (i.e., how fit unfolds over time and influences subsequent fit or outcomes). In terms of context, they propose how both person and environment may change over "clock" time, resulting in shifting levels of fit. They also discuss the notion of "psychological" time and how people construct fit narratives that incorporate their past and anticipated fits (Shipp and Jansen, 2011), when evaluating their levels of fit in the current moment. In terms of impact, they present how changes in fit, the duration of fit, and the salience of fit can impact upon a variety of individual outcomes over clock time. In terms of psychological time, they assert how retrospected and anticipated fit can be "lived" in the present moment (i.e., through nostalgia or dread) to influence outcomes, and how comparisons with past and anticipated fit can moderate the relationships between current fit and outcomes. Finally, they discuss the process of "fitting" over time, as one in which fit evolves through socialization, coping, attrition, sense making, and recrafting fit narratives. Spillover and spiraling processes are described as additional processes in which people's fit at one point in time can prompt modifications to future experiences of fit. Taken as a whole, their model provides a richer and more complex understanding of an individual's experience of fit in the present, and how that fit will evolve over time through natural individual and organizational processes. They conclude their chapter by introducing a systematic research agenda that includes a number of specific and actionable recommendations for future projects on fit. This chapter, in conjunction with their earlier piece (Shipp *et al.*, 2011), lays the foundation for expanding fit theory, conducting empirical research, and informing management practice around the neglected topic of fit situated in time.

In the final chapter, **Lee and Ramaswami** introduce an important boundary condition to the concept of organizational fit by addressing whether the concept of fit is equivalent across cultures or societies. They point out that, although many studies of fit have occurred using non-US samples, few if any of these have emphasized culture as a meaningful contextual variable. Therefore, in this chapter the authors propose three primary ways in which cultural values can influence the concept of organizational fit. First, they suggest that cultural values are a strong determinant of the way in which individuals think about themselves and the environment. Because culture provides a frame of reference for interpreting the world, they assert that culture will influence sense-making, regarding both self and the environment. Moreover, culture may influence the process by which people combine assessments of person and environment to generate perceptions of compatibility. Second, Lee and Ramaswami argue that cultural differences exist concerning the emphasis that people will place on fit as a desired and expected outcome. Finally, they address ways in which culture influences how fit and misfit are tolerated and managed.

Following the temporal sequence of the ASA model (Schneider, 1987), they present empirical and theoretical arguments for how cultural values including individualism/collectivism, uncertainty avoidance, and power distance can influence the particular types of fit that people attend to during organizational entry. Shifting to post-hire time periods, they also describe how people's reactions to misfit are likely to be sifted through a cultural lens. Specifically, they argue that attrition due to misfit may be more prevalent in individualistic cultures than in collectivistic ones. Thus, these authors raise important contextual conditions that influence not only the meaning of organizational fit, but also its relationship with relevant work-related outcomes. Their call for culturally sensitive theory development in the field of organizational fit forces researchers to take a hard look at the context in which they are conducting their research.

Conclusion

Together, these chapters represent varied and intellectually stimulating considerations of organizational fit. Rather than be perplexed and stymied by the lack of consensus on the construct definition of organizational fit, we suggest that this variety be embraced and explored by fit scholars. Within the construct of organizational fit reside many concepts worthy of investigation. We hope that the chapters contained in this book offer new insights and provide the impetus for new and existing scholars to research, theorize, and write about the topic that has fascinated so many of us for so long – organizational fit.

References

Arthur, W., Jr., Bell, S. T., Villado, A. J., and Doverspike, D. (2006) The use of person–organization fit in employment decision making: An assessment of its criterion-related validity. *Journal of Applied Psychology*, 91, 786–801.

Berscheid, E. (1999) The greening of relationship science. *American Psychologist*, 54, 260–266.

Billsberry, J., Ambrosini, V., Moss-Jones, J., and Marsh, P. J. G. (2005) Some suggestions for mapping organizational members' sense of fit. *Journal of Business and Psychology*, 19, 555–570.

Blaikie, N. (2007) *Approaches to Social Enquiry: Advancing Knowledge*, 2nd edn. London: Polity Press.

Cable, D. M., and Judge, T. A. (1994) Pay preferences and job search decisions: A person–organization fit perspective. *Personnel Psychology*, 47, 317–348.

Cable, D. M., and Judge, T. A. (1996) Person–organization fit, job choice decisions, and organizational entry. *Organizational Behavior and Human Decision Processes*, 67, 294–311.

Cable, D. M., and Judge, T. A. (1997) Interviewers' perceptions of person–organization fit and organizational selection decisions. *Journal of Applied Psychology*, 82, 546–561.

Caplan, R. D. (1983) Person–environment fit: Past, present, and future. In C. L. Cooper (ed.), *Stress Research* (pp. 35–78). New York: John Wiley & Sons, Inc.

Chatman, J. A. (1989) Improving interactional organizational research: A model of person–organization fit. *Academy of Management Review*, 14, 333–349.

Chatman, J. A. (1991) Matching people and organizations: Selection and socialization in public accounting firms. *Administrative Science Quarterly*, 36, 459–484.

Chatman, J. A., Wong, E. M., and Joyce, C. (2008) When do people make the place?: Considering the interactionist foundations of the attraction–selection–attrition model. In D. B. Smith (ed.), *The People Make the Place: Dynamic Linkages Between Individuals and Organizations* (pp. 63–86). New York: Lawrence Erlbaum Associates.

Cooper-Thomas, H. D., Van Vianen, A., and Anderson, N. (2004) Changes in person–organization fit: The impact of socialization tactics on perceived and actual P-O fit. *European Journal of Work and Organizational Psychology*, 13, 52–78.

Edwards, J. A., and Billsberry, J. (2010) Testing a multidimensional theory of person–environment fit. *Journal of Managerial Issues*, 22, 476–493.

Edwards, J. R. (1993) Problems with the use of profile similarity indices in the study of congruence in organizational research. *Personnel Psychology*, 46, 641–665.

Edwards, J. R. (1994) The study of congruence in organizational behavior: Critique and a proposed alternative. *Organizational Behavior and Human Decision Processes*, 58, 51–100.

Edwards, J. R. (2008) Person–environment fit in organizations: An assessment of theoretical progress. *Academy of Management Annals*, 2, 167–230.

Edwards, J. R., and Harrison, R. V. (1993) Job demands and worker health: Three-dimensional reexamination of the relationship between person–environment fit and strain. *Journal of Applied Psychology*, 78, 628–648.

Edwards, J. R., and Parry, M. E. (1993) On the use of polynomial regression equations as an alternative to difference scores in organizational research. *Academy of Management Journal*, 36, 1577–1613.

Edwards, J., and Rothbard, N. (1999) Work and family stress and well-being: An examination of person–environment fit in the work and family domains. *Organizational Behavior and Human Decision Processes*, 77, 85–129.

Edwards, J. R., and Shipp, A. J. (2007) The relationship between person–environment fit and outcomes: An integrative theoretical framework. In C. Ostroff and T. A. Judge (eds), *Perspectives on Organizational Fit* (pp. 209–258). New York: Lawrence Erlbaum Associates.

Edwards, J. R., Cable, D. M., Williamson, I. O., Lambert, L. S., and Shipp, A. J. (2006) The phenomenology of fit: Linking the person and environment to the subjective experience of person–environment fit. *Journal of Applied Psychology*, 91, 802–827.

French, J. R. P., Jr, Rodgers, W., and Cobb, S. (1974) Adjustment as person–environment fit. In G. Coelho, D. Hamburg, and J. Adams (eds), *Coping and Adaptation* (pp. 316–333). New York: Basic Books.

Harrison, D. A. (2007) Pitching fits in applied psychological research: Making fit methods fit theory. In C. Ostroff and T. A. Judge (eds), *Perspectives on Organizational Fit* (pp. 389–416). New York: Lawrence Erlbaum Associates.

Hobfoll, S. E. (1988) *The Ecology of Stress.* New York: Hemisphere.

Hobfoll, S. E. (1998) *Stress, Culture, and Community.* New York: Plenum Press.

Jansen, K. J., and Kristof-Brown, A. (2006) Toward a multidimensional theory of person–environment fit. *Journal of Managerial Issues*, 18, 193–212.

Johnson, G., Langley, A., Melin, L., and Whittington, R. (2007) *Strategy as Practice: Research Directions and Resources.* Cambridge, UK: Cambridge University Press.

Judge, T. A. (2007) The future of person–organization fit research: Comments, observations, and a few suggestions. In C. Ostroff and T. A. Judge (eds), *Perspectives on Organizational Fit* (pp. 417–445). New York: Lawrence Erlbaum Associates.

Kammeyer-Mueller, J. D. (2007) The dynamics of newcomer adjustment: Dispositions, context, interactions and fit. In C. Ostroff and T. A. Judge (eds), *Perspectives on Organizational Fit* (pp. 99–122). New York: Lawrence Erlbaum Associates.

Kelley, H. H., Berscheid, E., Christensen, A., Harvey, J. H., Huston, T. L., Levinger, G., McClintock, E., Peplau, L. A., and Peterson, D. R. (1983) Analyzing close relationships. In H. H. Kelley, E. Berscheid, A. Christensen, J. H. Harvey, T. L. Huston, G. Levinger, E. McClintock, L. A. Peplau, and D. R. Peterson (eds), *Close Relationships* (pp. 20–67). New York: W. H. Freeman.

Krahé, B. (1992) *Personality and Social Psychology.* London: Sage.

Kristof-Brown, A. (2000) Perceived applicant fit: Distinguishing between recruiters' perceptions of person–job and person–organization fit. *Personnel Psychology*, 53, 643–671.

Kristof-Brown, A. L., and Guay, R. P. (2011) Person–environment fit. In S. Zedeck (ed.), *APA Handbook of Industrial and Organizational Psychology* (Vol. 3, pp. 3–50). Washington, DC: American Psychological Association.

Kristof-Brown, A. L., and Stevens, C. K. (2001) Goal congruence in project teams: Does the fit between members' personal mastery and performance goals matter? *Journal of Applied Psychology*, 86, 1083–1095.

Kristof-Brown, A., Zimmerman, R. D., and Johnson, E. C. (2005) Consequences of individuals' fit at work: A meta-analysis of person–job, person–organization, person–group, and person–supervisor fit. *Personnel Psychology*, 58, 281–342.

Latham, G. P., and Pinder, C. C. (2005) Work motivation theory and research at the dawn of the twenty-first century. *Annual Review of Psychology*, 56, 485–516.

Lauver, K., and Kristof-Brown, A. (2001) Distinguishing between employees' perceptions of person–job fit and person–organization fit. *Journal of Vocational Behavior*, 59, 454–470.

Liberman, N., Sagristano, M. D., and Trope, Y. (2002) The effect of temporal distance on level of mental construal. *Journal of Experimental Social Psychology*, 38, 523–534.

Lord, R. G., Diefendorff, J. M., Schmidt, A. M., and Hall, R. J. (2010) Self-regulation at work. *Annual Review of Psychology*, 61, 543–568.

Mischel, W., and Shoda, Y. (1995) A cognitive-affective system theory of personality: Reconceptualizing situations, dispositions, dynamics, and invariance in personality structure. *Psychological Review*, 102, 246–268.

Muchinsky, P. M., and Monahan, C. J. (1987) What is person–environment congruence? Supplementary versus complementary models of fit. *Journal of Vocational Behavior*, 31, 268–277.

O'Reilly, C. A., Chatman, J., and Caldwell, D. F. (1991) People and organizational culture: A profile comparison approach to assessing person–organization fit. *Academy of Management Journal*, 34, 487–516.

Ostroff, C. (2012) Person–environment fit in organizations. In S. W. J. Kozlowski (ed.), *Handbook of Organizational Psychology* (Vol. 1, pp. 373–408). Oxford: Oxford University Press.

Ostroff, C., and Schulte, M. (2007) Multiple perspectives of fit in organizations across levels of analysis. In C. Ostroff and T. A. Judge (eds), *Perspectives on Organizational Fit* (pp. 3–69). New York: Lawrence Erlbaum Associates.

Pervin, L. A. (1968) Performance and satisfaction as a function of individual–environment fit. *Psychological Bulletin*, 69, 56–68.

Pervin, L. A. (1987) Person–environment congruence in the light of the person–situation controversy. *Journal of Vocational Behavior*, 31, 222–230.

Ravlin, E. C., and Ritchie, C. M. (2006) Perceived and actual organizational fit: Multiple influences on attitudes. *Journal of Managerial Issues*, 16, 175–192.

Schmitt, N., Oswald, F., Friede, A., Imus, A., and Merritt, S. (2008) Perceived fit with an academic environment: Attitudinal and behavioral outcomes. *Journal of Vocational Behavior*, 72 (3), 317–335.

Schneider, B. (1987) People make the place. *Personnel Psychology*, 40, 437–453.

Seong, J. Y., and Kristof-Brown, A. L. (in press) A multidimensional model of person–group fit on individual outcomes. *Journal of Managerial Psychology*.

Seong, J. Y., Kristof-Brown, A. L., Park, W., Hong, D., and Shin, Y. (in press) Person–group fit: Relationships with diversity, emergent states and performance. *Journal of Management*.

Shipp, A. J., and Jansen, K. J. (2011) Reinterpreting time in fit theory: Crafting and recrafting narratives of fit in *Medias Research*. *Academy of Management Review*, 36, 76–101.

Slocombe, T. E., and Bluedorn, A. C. (1999) Organizational behavior implications of the congruence between preferred polychronicity and experienced work-unit polychronicity. *Journal of Organizational Behavior*, 20, 75–99.

Trope, Y., and Liberman, N. (2003) Temporal construal. *Psychological Review*, 110, 403–421.

Verquer, M. L., Beehr, T. A., and Wagner, S. H. (2003) A meta-analysis of relations between person–organization fit and work attitudes. *Journal of Vocational Behavior*, 63, 473–489.

Wheeler, A. R., Coleman-Gallagher, V., Brouer, R. L., and Sablynski, C. J. (2007) When person–organization (mis)fit and (dis)satisfaction lead to turnover: The moderating role of perceived job mobility. *Journal of Managerial Psychology*, 22, 203–219.

Part 1

New Directions within the Fit Paradigms

2

A Motivational Model of Person–Environment Fit: Psychological Motives as Drivers of Change

Kang Yang Trevor Yu
Nanyang Technological University

It is commonly accepted that person–environment (PE) fit leads to positive outcomes ranging from behavior to attitudes. As such, organizations are typically encouraged to attract, hire, and socialize individuals so as to create and develop PE fit (Cable and Parsons, 2001; Chatman, 1989; Kristof, 1996; Yu and Cable, 2009). Similarly, job seekers are advised to choose jobs and organizations where they think they will fit (Cable and Judge, 1996; Judge and Cable, 1997). These ideas about its potential benefits have created a paradigm where PE fit is usually conceptualized as an exogenous variable that simply exists due to individual job choice or organizational human resource practices (e.g., recruitment, selection, and socialization). This view of the antecedents of PE fit is limited because it ignores the *motivation* and *ability* of individuals to *actively manage* fit-based relationships. In a recent article, I called attention to the ability of individuals to change PE fit in response to their affective experiences (Yu, 2009). This chapter expands on this idea by examining the motivational basis behind attempts to manage PE fit. In other words, I ask the fundamental question: "*Why* do people want to fit?" To answer this question, I first develop a model that identifies several motivations that drive individuals to manipulate both self (P) and environment (E) in order to achieve PE fit. I then proceed to review literature to show exactly how people respond to these motivations by changing fit-based relationships. This motivational model of PE fit is illustrated in Figure 2.1.

Kristof-Brown, Zimmerman, and Johnson (2005) identify several limitations in our current understanding of PE fit. One of these deals with the lack of research treating PE fit as an outcome. Thus, we still need a better understanding of what drives individuals toward fit or misfit. Second, there is a lack of theory explaining how individual actions and the organizational context impact both subjective and

Organizational Fit: Key Issues and New Directions, First Edition.
Edited by Amy L. Kristof-Brown and Jon Billsberry.
© 2013 John Wiley & Sons, Ltd. Published 2013 by John Wiley & Sons, Ltd.

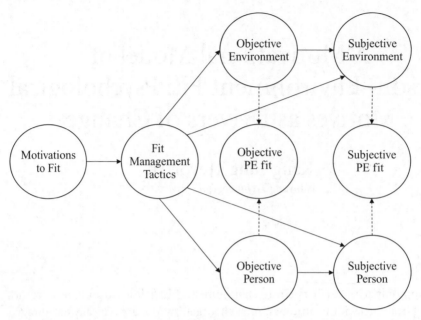

Figure 2.1   A motivational model of PE fit

objective experiences of fit. Third, understanding of the dynamic nature of fit is severely limited (Kristof-Brown and Jansen, 2007). This chapter aims to address these issues by bolstering the theoretical foundations for further research to explore the dynamism of PE fit. It specifically contributes to current understanding of the PE fit phenomenon by (a) outlining the motivational implications behind PE fit experiences; (b) highlighting human agency when it comes to understanding antecedents to PE fit; and (c) facilitating investigations into the dynamic nature of fit, where fit changes in tandem with individuals' organizational experience.

Fundamental Motivations to Fit

The first key to understanding how people manage PE fit is to appreciate *why* they would want to fit in the first place. Behavior is determined by how a person relates to his or her environment (Lewin, 1935; Pervin, 1981, 1989), and most individuals are aware of the importance of their relationship with their environments (Folkman and Moskowitz, 2004; Pervin, 1981). Hence, PE fit may become the target of certain fundamental drives that impact overall well-being. The motivations to fit identified in this chapter are largely derived from research outside the PE fit domain. Originating from areas such as social cognition (e.g., social projection) and human resource management (e.g., socialization), these motivations treat PE fit as a tool by which underlying needs can be fulfilled.

Drive for consistency

Previous research has argued that individuals strive for consistency among aspects of the self, such as attitudes, beliefs, and behavior. The drive to be consistent features prominently in several theories that deal with individuals and their relationships with the social environment. For example, the basic premise of self-consistency theory (Lecky, 1968) is that people's self-concepts comprise an organized set of congruent self-perceptions integrated into a coherent whole. People are thus motivated to act in ways that are congruent with their understanding of themselves in order to maintain self-consistency (Elliott, 1986, pp. 207–208). Similarly, balance theory (Insko, 1981) posits that inconsistency among any one of the following three components gives rise to an imbalanced state which triggers feelings of "tension": (a) a person's attitudes toward an object, (b) the perceived attitudes of a significant other toward the same object, and (c) the person's relationship with the significant other. This tension in turn produces a motivational drive to establish balance via either a change of attitude toward the object or a change of attitude toward the significant other (Eagly and Chaiken, 1993; Heider, 1958; Insko, 1981). Finally, cognitive dissonance theory argues that incompatibility between cognitions and behavior gives rise to a negative affective state. Actors in such situations are thus motivated to reduce this dissonance by engaging in some form of cognitive adjustment such as changing one's attitudes (Cooper and Fazio, 1984; Eagly and Chaiken, 1993; Festinger, 1957).

Recently Cialdini, Trost, and Newsom (1995) defined a *preference for consistency* as a trait that differentiates the degree to which individuals prefer to have consistency among elements involving individual attitudes and behavior. The implications of this consistency preference could be significant for individuals and how they manage PE fit, especially when it is commonly assumed that experiencing positive outcomes is consistent with good PE fit (Chatman, 1989; O'Reilly et al., 1991). Thus, it is possible for someone to infer that he or she must fit the environment simply because a positive attitude or behavior is experienced (e.g., "I am happy with my job. Therefore I must fit!"). Similarly, a negative affective experience could also be easily attributed to the presence of misfit with one's environment (e.g., "I feel lousy about my job. Therefore, my job does not fit me") (Yu, 2009). Therefore, the consistency motivation is relevant for understanding why people will seek to manage PE fit so that they can have consistency with other types of organizational experience like affect (e.g., job-based emotions) and attitudes (e.g., job satisfaction and organizational commitment).

Drive for hedonism

In contrast to a motive for consistency, in which people may manipulate PE fit to be concordant with affect, the hedonistic motive posits that individuals use PE fit as a tool for achieving such positive affective states. Hedonism is widely assumed to be a basic and universal motive. Many of our daily activities are characterized by hedonistic pursuits that involve avoiding or rectifying situations that make us feel bad, and similarly approaching or maintaining situations that make us feel good (Buss, 2000; Larsen, 2000). Diener (2000) has provided powerful evidence attesting to the universality of hedonistic motivation. Results from surveys conducted in 42 different countries around the world suggest that happiness and life satisfaction were very important to most people, even in societies that are not fully westernized (e.g., Indonesia and Bahrain). This hedonistic motivation has significant implications for PE fit because it implies people will seek fit in order to enjoy the positive consequences that result from it. This idea is a recurring theme in many theories of self-regulation, stress and job satisfaction. For instance, cybernetics argues that human behavior exists as part of a self-regulating system that is constantly involved in the detection and subsequent minimalization of misfit between aspects of the person (i.e., the individual's desires) and his or her environment (Carver and Scheier, 1982; Edwards, 1992). Therefore, a hedonistic motive can cause people to alter aspects of both themselves and their environment, to achieve PE fit and the resulting positive states (Lazarus and Folkman, 1984).

Drive for uncertainty reduction

Past research has indicated that people generally want to reduce uncertainty in their lives (Festinger, 1957; Webster and Kruglanski, 1994). The motivation to reduce uncertainty derives from our need for cognitive closure, which is manifested through desires for predictability, structure, and intolerance for ambiguity (Webster and Kruglanski, 1994). This motivation would lead people to seek PE fit because it is seen as a way to reduce uncertainty. Uncertainty can be reduced by achieving several different types of PE fit. Being around similar others (i.e., having person–organization fit) allows one to better predict and understand the motives and actions of co-workers and the organization (Edwards and Shipp, 2007; Schein, 1990). People with similar values often share similar goals and thought processes. Sometimes, they even respond to situations in similar ways (O'Reilly *et al.*, 1991). Recent research also suggests that similarity-based fit facilitates trust and interpersonal communication, which can reduce uncertainty in social interactions (Edwards and Cable, 2009). There is also less uncertainty on the job when people have the abilities to meet job demands because they have the knowledge, skills, and abilities to deal with the ambiguities and complexities of their jobs. Furthermore, the improved job performance that demands–abilities fit produces is likely to be rewarded in terms of power and influence at the workplace, which in turn can be used to acquire information that reduces future uncertainty (Cable and DeRue, 2002; Edwards and Shipp, 2007). Hence, both value congruence and demands–abilities fit can reduce uncertainty.

Drive for control

Being in control of one's environment is another fundamental human need (Adler, 1930). White (1959) referred to this need for control as an "instinct to master," which describes an innate drive "to do and to learn how to do" (p. 307). He further notes that this instinct drives behavior to attain a state where an individual can control and alter his or her circumstances. Thus, individuals are motivated to seek jobs where they have demands–abilities fit so that they will be in a position to exert more control over their work roles and responsibilities (Nicholson, 1984; Wrzesniewski and Dutton, 2001). Similarly, people also try to adapt their work-related values to fit into their employer's culture so that they can enjoy feelings of control in order to maximize performance and satisfaction on the job (Ashford and Black, 1996).

Drive for belonging

Most individuals are also driven by a motivation to form and maintain strong and stable relationships (Baumeister and Leary, 1995). The need for affiliation and relationships has long been recognized as a key motivation behind human behavior (Maslow, 1968); so much so that Baumeister and Leary (1995) posit that "much of what human beings do is in the service of belongingness" (p. 498). They further argue that the need for belonging goes beyond a simple need for intimate attachment to require frequent and pleasant interactions with others, and for these interactions to occur within relationships characterized by stable and enduring affective concern for each party's well-being.

Belonging accrues significant benefits to individuals. In fact, it appears have an evolutionary basis, where the motivation to form and maintain positive relationships has both survival and reproductive benefits (Ainsworth, 1989; Baumeister and Leary, 1995; Moreland, 1987). Research identified a wide range of consequences that positive and stable relationships, or the lack of them, can have for individual well-being. Thus, Baumeister and Leary (1995) conclude that people who lack belongingness not only suffer from more mental and physical ailments, but are also more susceptible to behavioral problems (e.g., criminality and suicide). Past research on turnover has argued that improving PE fit is crucial to enjoying longer organizational tenures because fit accrues a sense of belonging to individuals (Mitchell *et al.*, 2001). Similarly, Edwards and Shipp (2007) argue that types of supplementary fit such as value congruence serve to satisfy needs for affiliation and belonging.

Fit Management Tactics

Model of PE fit

Before discussing how the above motivations may influence a person to change their experience of fit, it is important to review the PE fit construct. Figure 2.1 illustrates an expanded model of PE fit built upon one of the most contemporary conceptual-izations of the phenomenon (Edwards *et al.*, 1998; Harrison, 1978; Yu, 2009). This model presents PE fit as a relationship between separate constructs of the person (P) and his or her environment (E). Originating from a positivist approach, it further distinguishes between objective and subjective P and E. The objective person refers to characteristics of the individual such as abilities, needs, and values, while the subjec-tive person refers to the individual's perception of these characteristics. The objective environment refers to physical and social attributes that exist independently from perception, such as actual amounts of autonomy and authority contained in a job. In contrast, the subjective environment describes people's experiences and perceptions of these attributes, such as perceptions of how much autonomy and variety a job entails (Caplan, 1987; Edwards *et al.*, 1998). Two types of PE fit exist due to the relationships between subjective and objective P and E. *Objective PE fit* is present when there is fit between objective P and objective E, while *subjective PE fit* consists of the fit between subjective P and subjective E. This model also places objective P and E as antecedents of their subjective counterparts. Thus, subjective PE fit mediates the relationship between objective fit and individual outcomes (Edwards *et al.*, 1998; Kristof, 1996).

The strength of this model lies in both its unambiguous definition of the person and environment, and also its clear distinction between the objective and subjective forms of fit (Edwards, 2008; Yu, 2009). The model is thus best suited to accurately describe and explain how the various motivations to fit impact objective and/or subjective PE fit. Specifically, each motivation can be discussed in terms of which component of fit it affects (i.e., P or E) and also whether this impact operates through objective or subjective phenomena. Hence, the following sections review the broad categories of cognitions and behaviors, and the theories that describe how they impact PE fit. This information is summarized in Table 2.1.

Biases and heuristics

Several of the above motivations cause heuristics that may bias perceptions of PE fit. Several prominent heuristics that people engage in as a result of these motivations include: social projection, affective-consistency, and social information processing.

Social projection. Social projection refers to the tendency for individuals to assume that others think, want, and feel the same way that they think, want, and feel (Ames, 2004a; Marks and Miller, 1987). This tendency creates a "fundamental asymmetry" in decision making, where people attach more importance to self-based information and are similarly relatively insensitive to social information (Robbins and Krueger, 2005, p. 40). This phenomenon is particularly relevant for individuals looking to infer qualities about the group to which they belong (Clement and Krueger, 2002; Robbins and Krueger, 2005).

Table 2.1   Relationships between fit motivations and their associated fit-modifying tactics

| | Strategies | | | | | | | |
| | Biases and heuristics | | | Responses to job satisfaction | Coping, stress, and regulation | | Proactive behaviors | |
Motives	Social projection	Affective-consistency	Social information processing	Job satisfaction theory	Coping	Cybernetics	Job crafting, role adjustment, and deal making	Information seeking
Consistency	SE	SP; SE	SP; SE					
Hedonism				OP; OE	SP; OP; SE; OE	SP; OP; SE; OE	OP; SE; OE	SP; SE
Uncertainty reduction	SE	SP; SE	SP; SE					SP; SE
Control				OP; OE			OP; SE; OE	SP; SE
Belonging	SE		SP; SE				OP; SE; OE	SP; SE

Note: **SP** denotes changes to subjective perceptions of the person; **OP** denotes changes to objective aspects of the person; **SE** denotes changes to subjective perceptions of the environment; **OE** denotes changes to aspects of the objective environment.

The most obvious motivation that drives social projection is uncertainty reduction. The social projection heuristic functions as a way for individuals to use their own traits and preferences as a lens to interpret aspects of their social environment which are uncertain and not readily apparent. It thus serves as an egocentric heuristic for inductive reasoning to make sense of those around us. People try to understand the goals and values of members of their social collective (e.g., group, department, and organization) by using their own attributes as part of a heuristic mental simulation and anchoring process. Interestingly, meta-analyses have shown that this heuristic process of induction often produces relatively accurate inferences (Krueger, 1998; Robbins and Krueger, 2005).

Social projection can also satisfy needs for belonging. For instance, individuals have been observed to engage in more of this heuristic in response to having their mortality made salient, presumably to enhance fit and social connectedness (Arndt *et al.*, 1999). This finding reinforces the idea that social projection, with its assumptions of similarity, serves to create accompanying perceptions of cohesion, attraction, and attachment to one's social environment, thus satisfying one's need to belong (Robbins and Krueger, 2005).

Evidence also suggests that social projection can satisfy needs for consistency. For example, Ames (2004a, 2004b) found that people use more of this heuristic when they perceive the target to be generally similar to themselves. Thus, a person assumes that others who initially appear similar on a particular dimension will also share his or her thoughts, desires, and feelings (Ames, 2004a). Hence, social projection may also be construed as a tactic that people employ to align the attributes of others with their initial general judgments of similarity.

Social projection is an egocentric heuristic that impacts perceptions of the subjective environment. This process should be relevant for types of PE fit that deal with supplementary relationships between individuals and the people with whom they work (Muchinsky and Monahan, 1987). Specifically, projection occurs when people use their own attributes as approximations of the goals, values, and preferences of social collectives (e.g., organizations) when these phenomena are not readily apparent.

Affective-consistency.   The affective-consistency model was developed to explain why people make changes to PE fit based on experienced affect at work (Yu, 2009). It draws from a variety of social-cognitive theories dealing with affective influence on social judgment to propose that people will adjust P and E so as to have a PE fit consistent with experienced work-based affect. Such changes to subjective P and E are largely heuristic because they require little or no cognitive processing (Schwarz, 1990). Also outlined in this model is the notion that PE fit becomes the dependent variable that is influenced in response to affect because affective experience is assumed to occur before any cognitive awareness of P, E, and their fit relationship (Yu, 2009; Zajonc, 1980). Thus, based on the common assumption that PE fit and positive affect are positively correlated (Chatman, 1989; O'Reilly *et al.*, 1991), people who experience positive affect would be inclined to perceive a good fitting relationship between P and E. Similarly, as poor PE fit is normally associated with negative affect, people experiencing negative affect would be biased toward perceiving a misfit between P and E.

Heuristics based on affective-consistency satisfy the need for consistency. Explanations for exactly *why* this occurs can be inferred from past research on mood congruency and associative networks, which focus on the ability of affective experience to influence various steps of information processing from selective attention and encoding of certain information to its later recall from memory (Bower, 1981; Bower and Forgas, 2001). Owing to the need for consistency, people are sensitized to select and process information about the self and the environment so that the resulting PE fit relationship is congruent with the valance of experienced affect (Bower and Forgas, 2001; Yu, 2009). Therefore, consistency is achieved by means of affect acting as a "cognitive filter" that causes people to think about PE fit in ways that are consistent with affective experience (James and Jones, 1980; James and Tetrick, 1986).

Affect-based heuristics also help deal with the need to reduce uncertainty about the desirability of a person's situation with respect to work. Specifically, affect serves as a signal for the nature of an individual's psychological condition (Frijda, 1988). Positive affect indicates that a situation is safe and free from danger of negative outcomes, while negative affect signals the presence of a problematic situation and risk of negative outcomes (Clore *et al.*, 1994). Thus, the informative function of affect also serves to reduce uncertainty about work situations and PE fit with respect to a particular job and organization (Schwarz and Clore, 2003).

With regard to PE fit, affect-based heuristics impact perceptions of both the self and the environment. In particular, affect can have a significant biasing impact on PE fit when aspects of the environment such as organizational culture and job supplies are less than certain, or when self-based attributes are similarly unclear (Forgas *et al.*, 1984; Sedikides, 1992, 1995). Evidence for this idea can be seen in the biasing effect of affect on self-cognitions, where the positivity of self-cognitions is emphasized when positive affect is experienced and vice versa (Sedikides and Green, 2001). Similar relationships have also been detected for work environments, where positive affect was responsible for tasks being rated higher on generally positive qualities like feedback, variety, and significance (Kraiger *et al.*, 1989). Therefore the impact of affective-consistency heuristics on PE fit can occur through subjective perceptions of both person and environment.

Social information processing. The social information processing (SIP) paradigm assumes that characteristics of job and organizational environments such as the amount of autonomy and organizational culture are constructed by individuals making sense of their experiences (Salancik and Pfeffer, 1978; Weick, 1979). SIP impacts upon subjective assessments of P and E because perception is a retrospective process where perceptions of self-attributes (e.g., values and goals) and work environments (e.g., culture and job supplies) are subject to recall and reconstruction. Since the processes of memory and recall are not perfect, it is thus likely that a fair bit of reconstruction and sense making would be required to derive judgments of PE fit based on information from one's social environment (e.g., co-workers).

The impact of social information extends beyond recollections of the past. The social context can also introduce bias into judgments of job (e.g., design) and organizational (e.g., culture) attributes via social influence processes (Morgeson and Campion, 1997). Strong organizational norms and expectations may bias perceptions of job attributes by making information on these attributes more salient or highlighting their desirability. For example, an organization that has embraced flexible work schedules invariably creates a climate whereby employees recognize the importance of such practices and are thus sensitized to pay extra attention to them during job evaluations. Coupled with their increased salience, the apparent social desirability of such practices serves as a motivating factor for people to give additional weight to flexibility and autonomy in their perceptions of the job environment (Arnold and Feldman, 1981; Dipboye, 1985; Smith and Hakel, 1979).

People derive meaning from their organizational experiences through their interactions with the people around them. Thus, the use of social information to construct perceptions of person and environment fulfills the need to reduce uncertainty. SIP also satisfies the need for consistency because when constructing their perceptions of person and environment people seek to be consistent with the signals that they receive from others in their social environment as well as with their own past behavior. For example, a person may be biased to perceive a higher need for relationships if his or her organization's culture strongly emphasizes the importance of teamwork and cooperation. Similarly, this person may infer that his or her need for relationships is high simply based on the fact that the majority of time is spent working closely in teams. The SIP paradigm argues that the social context affects perceptions of personal needs (subjective P) through pressures for conformity. Salancik and Pfeffer (1978) argue that individual perceptions of needs are subject to social information that is directly available from the job environment. For instance, certain organizational environments may cue individuals to perceive high needs for variety by emphasizing the desirability and appropriateness of job variety through the pervasiveness of job rotation. Similarly, individuals may perceive high needs for autonomy when a company emphasizes individual choice and flexibility over work arrangements.

Responses to job satisfaction

Job satisfaction theory. The second category of tactics that can be employed to manage PE fit concerns the various ways that people act in response to job satisfaction. Job satisfaction is widely considered as an individual's affective reaction to his or her job (Cranny *et al.*, 1992; Locke, 1969). This affective experience serves as an incentive for future actions (Locke, 1970). Drawing on ideas from goal-setting research as well as work by Arnold (1969), Locke (1970, p. 490) further argues that certain action tendencies are inherent in the experience of job satisfaction. These action tendencies can be categorized according to two basic types: (a) a tendency to *approach* a positively appraised object that causes satisfaction; and (b) a tendency to *avoid* a negatively appraised object that causes dissatisfaction. These actions do not refer only to actual observable behaviors because satisfaction acts as a catalyst for both cognitive and behavioral attempts to change one's job situation (Locke, 1976). For instance, Henne and Locke (1985) argue that "job satisfaction and dissatisfaction are psychological states which allow for numerous and varied action alternatives" (p. 221), where such responses can be either psychological or behavioral. Similar ideas can also be found in other job satisfaction theories such as the exit, voice, loyalty, and neglect (EVLN) model, which proposes four approach and avoidance-based actions as possible responses to job satisfaction (Farrell, 1983).

Locke (1970) further proposed that approach-based reactions to positive job satisfaction experience could entail either getting more involved in one's job or switching goals and the activities associated with them. The latter action occurs when a person feels that there is little positive satisfaction left to be gained from performing the same job task or activity. Hence, motivated by a need to master the unfamiliar, a person will respond to dissatisfaction by changing the nature of the job, where the tasks chosen will become more challenging as his or her knowledge, skills, and abilities increase (p. 491). This tactic of changing job tasks and goals is equivalent to changing the objective environment to obtain a better PE fit.

In contrast, four types of avoidance-based action were proposed to follow the negative experience of dissatisfaction. First, people could simply avoid their jobs entirely, as evidenced by turnover and absenteeism. This link between job satisfaction and behavioral withdrawal has garnered a significant amount of empirical support (Hanisch and Hulin, 1990, 1991; Hulin, 1991). Secondly, one could also try to change aspects of the job through change-directed voice (Van Dyne and LePine, 1998). For instance, job change could be achieved through persuading, complaining to, and convincing one's superior to modify the requirements of a task. Since they involve either removing or changing unpleasant aspects of the job, these two responses to dissatisfaction are essentially attempts to change the objective environment. Thirdly, people can also change their needs and values (i.e., objective P) in response to dissatisfaction. They do this by self-persuasion and rationalizing that certain aspects of the job that are responsible for the negative affect (e.g., relationships with co-workers and/or level of autonomy) are actually not all that important (Locke, 1970). Lastly, people can also choose to tolerate job dissatisfaction if changing aspects of the person and environment is not possible. The type of action that is enacted in response to job satisfaction depends on the individual's perception of the job situation, available job alternatives, and his or her own abilities and aspirations (Henne and Locke, 1985; Locke, 1984).

According to job satisfaction theory, people respond to satisfaction by behaving in ways that emphasize the current desirable job situation. Similarly, people respond to dissatisfaction by either rectifying the unpleasant job situation or preventing it from having a negative impact on their overall well-being. These actions are characteristic of attempts to satisfy hedonistic desires. In addition, the need for control is also fulfilled because people may seek out or create new opportunities in their jobs to develop mastery over new challenges once satisfaction is attained at a particular time (Locke, 1970, 1976).

Overall, though these perspectives do not explicitly draw a link between job satisfaction and PE fit, they essentially view satisfaction as a product of the need fulfillment form of PE fit. This point is emphasized by Locke's (1976) statement that job satisfaction is an emotional reaction to the perception of whether or not the environment facilitates the fulfillment of one's values. It also follows that most of the proposed reactions to satisfaction involve altering some aspect of the person or environment, and hence the PE fit relationship. Hence, more explicit integration between job satisfaction and PE fit theories may yield a better understanding of the interrelationships between these constructs.

Coping, stress, and regulation

Theories of coping, stress, and regulation provide insight into how people react to stressful situations by managing their PE fit. Specifically, these theories outline how and why people deal with unpleasant circumstances by utilizing mechanisms designed to achieve or maintain PE fit.

Coping. Coping is "a complex, multidimensional process that is sensitive to the environment (i.e., its demands and resources), and to personality dispositions that influence the appraisal of stress and resources for coping" (Folkman and Moskowitz, 2004, p. 747). Lazarus and Folkman (1984) highlight the integral roles of both the person and the environment in the coping process by defining coping as the thoughts and behaviors that people employ to manage the internal and external demands of situations that are appraised as stressful. Though PE fit is seldom mentioned in coping research, people use a variety of cognitive and behavioral responses to manage stressful situations that impact PE fit. For instance, problem-focused coping refers to attempts to improve fit between people and their environments (Folkman and Lazarus, 1980). Likewise, alloplastic coping refers specifically to coping directed at changing a person's environment (e.g., finding a more suitable job), while autoplastic coping describes coping directed at changing aspects of the self (e.g., setting more achievable goals) (Perrez and Reicherts, 1992). Thus, when viewed through a PE fit lens, coping behavior involves efforts to change both subjective (through thoughts and cognitions) and objective (through behavior) elements of PE fit.

Cybernetics and control theory. Cybernetics or control theory presents an alternative but complementary view of how attempts to maintain or improve well-being involve altering PE fit (Edwards, 1992; Powers, 1978). Key to this theory is the *negative feedback loop*, which serves to minimize discrepancies between environmental attributes and reference criteria derived from the individual (Edwards, 1992). The feedback loop consists of several components: The *input function* operates by monitoring and sensing the person's current situation. The *comparator* mechanism in turn evaluates this perception against a relevant point of *reference* such as a person's goal, values, or self-assessed needs. If a discrepancy is detected between the current state and the reference criteria, the *output function* is employed to try to reduce or remove the discrepancy. The main purpose of the feedback loop is thus to create and maintain the perception of a specific desired condition, where conditions in the environment fit with individual standards of reference (Carver and Scheier, 1982).

Edwards' (1992) cybernetic theory of stress, coping, and well-being builds on these self-regulatory principles to highlight the relationship between regulation, coping, and PE fit. This model views stress, coping, and well-being as key components of a cybernetic feedback loop. It essentially argues that stress, defined as the discrepancy between an individual's perceived state and desired state, leads to two types of outcome: well-being and coping. More importantly, stress may indirectly activate coping, or "efforts to prevent or reduce the negative effects of stress on well-being" (p. 245), through its influence on well-being.

According to Edwards (1992), coping behavior is initiated in response to the detection of a discrepancy, which may also be considered a misfit between P and E. Such behavior can reduce stress by improving fit in several ways. First, coping can involve attempts to improve well-being directly, such as meditation and relaxation (Newman and Beehr, 1979). Secondly, coping can also involve reducing the importance associated with the perceived source of stress. This behavior is equivalent to adjusting the objective person, and one's values in particular. Next, coping also consists of efforts to alter the objective and subjective work environment. These efforts can include changing the physical and social environment, which essentially alters objective work environments. Likewise, activities that involve altering social information (i.e., deemphasizing negative information and seeking out new sources of information) and cognitive reconstruction (i.e., repressing, denying, or distorting negative aspects of the situation) describe attempts to modify perceptions of the subjective work environment. Fourthly, people may also adopt a less proactive way of coping by avoiding a stressful situation. Such efforts may include directing one's attention away from a stressful discrepancy (Edwards, 1992; Edwards and Baglioni, 1993). The last mechanism via which coping influences stress is by changing objective aspects of the person and desires in particular to conform to situational feedback. Such activity is evidenced in attempts to adjust personal goals or standards in response to positive or negative feedback (Campion and Lord, 1982; Taylor *et al.*, 1984). Overall, ideas from cybernetics suggest that coping may be directed toward changing both objective aspects and subjective perceptions of the person and environment as part of the regulatory process to deal with stress. Furthermore, as these processes are chiefly governed by the need to maintain or improve experienced affect and well-being, they are primarily motivated by hedonistic concerns (Yu, 2009).

Proactive behaviors

Proactive behavior refers to a broad class of anticipatory behaviors aimed at bringing about change to individuals themselves and their environments (Grant and Ashford, 2008). Grant and Ashford (2008) highlight two key characteristics of proactive behavior. First, such behavior is conscious and planned. Thus, people engage in proactive behavior when they have calculated and anticipated the impact of their actions on their future situation. Next, proactive behavior is also specifically intended to enact change on the self and/or the environment. Parker and Collins (2009) highlighted that two broad goals for proactive behavior were either to change the organizational work environment (E) by changing the nature of one's job responsibilities and tasks, or to modify aspects of the self (P) by obtaining information and seeking feedback so as to improve the PE fit between oneself and the organization. This present review highlights two general classes of proactive behavior that are considered to have relevant implications for the management of PE fit.

Job crafting, role adjustment, and deal making. Grant and Parker (2009) identify three types of proactive behavior that can have significant implications for the way jobs are designed in today's organizations. People engaging in these behaviors take the initiative to make changes to their jobs, roles, and responsibilities. These ideas draw from early discussions about how employees engage in role innovation by changing their job roles in novel ways (Katz and Kahn, 1966; Van Maanen and Schein, 1979), and adjust to their work by changing their job environments (Bretz and Judge, 1994; Dawis and Lofquist, 1984).

The first type of behaviors refers to the concept of job crafting. Wrzesniewski and Dutton (2001) outlined several characteristics of this process. First, job crafters change the task boundaries of their jobs by modifying either the type of job tasks that they engage in or the number of these tasks that they undertake. For instance, customer service employees can add more variety into their jobs by taking on more responsibilities, such as marketing new products and services.

Second, job crafters also change the relational boundaries of their work by adjusting whom they interact with and how they interact with them. Such job crafting focuses on the social context of work, which consists of interpersonal interactions and relationships that are woven into the job tasks and responsibilities present in one's job (Grant and Parker, 2009). Reichers (1987) pointed out that employees proactively seek out opportunities to interact with co-workers by engaging in behavior such as stopping by others' offices, frequenting common areas, planning social opportunities, and participating in formal social events. These behaviors help in the acquisition of appropriate skills and knowledge and also accurate views of organizational policies and norms (Ashford and Black, 1996). Furthermore, friendship and mentoring networks that result from these behaviors also provide social support and guidance for the advancement of one's career (Higgins and Kram, 2001). Therefore, employees enhance their PE fit by becoming closely integrated into the culture and workflow of their environment through networking and developing close relationships with people from other departments within the organization (Wolff and Moser, 2009).

Third, job crafting also involves cognitively changing task boundaries. This action encompasses manipulating how one views responsibilities and tasks that are inherent in the job. For example, one could adopt a more expansive view about his or her role as a teacher by thinking of responsibilities such as counseling as part of the job, in addition to the more conventional mindset of teachers as simply providers of information. With regard to PE fit, the first two forms of job crafting described here depict individuals as proactive shapers of their objective organizational environments, while the third form involves cognitively adjusting subjective perceptions of E.

Similar to job crafting, role adjustment occurs when employees' high performance creates perceptions of competence, which stimulates increased trust from their supervisors (Clegg and Spencer, 2007). This trust causes supervisors to expand the roles of these high-performing employees by assigning them more responsibilities. At the intrapersonal level, high performance also signals to employees themselves that they are capable and competent. This form of trust in oneself can also act as a motivator to expand one's roles by engaging in job crafting. These two processes further increase the experience and knowledge of these already high-performing employees, which in turn sets in motion an upward spiral of increasing high performance and expanded work roles (Lindsley *et al.*, 1995). A similar logic applies to poor performers who get caught in a downward spiral characterized by poor performance and shrinking role responsibilities, due to the reduced trust that supervisors have in them, and that poor-performing employees have in themselves.

Another form of proactive practice that has significant implications for PE fit is job negotiation (Grant and Parker, 2009). This practice highlights the role that supervisors play in bringing about change in people's jobs. Building on earlier findings of how employees negotiate changes in roles with leaders (Graen and Scandura, 1987), Rousseau, Ho, and Greenberg (2006) developed the concept of idiosyncratic deals (*i-deals*) to describe unique and customized employment terms that are the product of negotiation between employees and their supervisors. Negotiated as an attempt to satisfy the unique needs of employees, i-deals are formed when employees have either valuable specialized skills that deserve special consideration, or unique life circumstances that necessitate flexible working arrangements (Greenberg *et al.*, 2004). These i-deals are negotiated on the premise that such arrangements benefit both the employer and employee. The employer gets to satisfy and retain a valued human resource asset, while the employee has his or her individual needs fulfilled (Rousseau *et al.*, 2006).

In all, the three practices of job crafting, role adjustment, and job negotiation target change to the objective work environment by modifying the nature of people's actual jobs. Furthermore, job crafting through relationship and social network building also brings about change to objective person attributes and subjective perceptions of the environment. Actual attributes of the self, such as knowledge, skills, and abilities, are enhanced through improved access to resources and information, while environment perceptions are influenced through social and normative information on job requirements and organizational culture that are obtained through interpersonal relationships.

These proactive behaviors satisfy several of the aforementioned motivations to fit. Perhaps most prominently, such proactive behaviors satisfy individuals' needs to have control over their job environments. Being able to negotiate job changes and effectively playing a role in determining how their jobs are designed allows people to achieve behavioral control over their work behavior (Ashford and Black, 1996; Bell and Staw, 1989; Nicholson, 1984). Such behaviors also satisfy hedonistic concerns because they bring about positive feelings regarding the self. People engage in job crafting because they want to create a positive self-image of having high autonomy and being in control. Lastly, changing the relational aspects of one's job by job crafting can also be motivated by one's need to have deeper connections and a sense of belonging with the social environment (Reichers, 1987; Wrzesniewski and Dutton, 2001).

Information seeking. The second set of proactive behaviors deal with actions taken to gather information about aspects of both the person and his or her environment. Such behavior has a significant impact on subjective PE fit. Information seeking's impact on perceptions of the self is most evident in the large body of research on feedback seeking (Ashford *et al.*, 2003). Two common feedback-seeking behaviors are inquiry and monitoring. Inquiry involves asking directly for feedback on one's attributes, while monitoring involves observing the behavior of other people in the environment for clues on how they perceive the individual and his or her characteristics. These actions influence self-perceptions by providing information that improves a person's own awareness of his or her knowledge, skills, and abilities. It has been argued that such information is instrumental to helping people adapt and flourish in their jobs because it facilitates the regulation of one's behavior with respect to the achievement of all types of goal (Ashford, 1986; Ashford and Tsui, 1991).

Information seeking also has a powerful impact on perceptions of job and organizational environments. Morrison (1993a, 1993b) argues that people seek information about job requirements and other expected behaviors in order to clarifying their role within the organization. Such information facilitates the adaptation process to one's job by highlighting the fit between one's knowledge, skills, and abilities (KSAs) and job demands (Ashford and Taylor, 1990). People can also use information seeking to improve their understanding of a firm's culture by finding out about desired behaviors, attitudes, values, and other norms. The normative information gathered from this social feedback aids in the acculturation and integration of people into the social fabric of an organization (Morrison, 1993b). Furthermore, information seeking can also change objective person attributes by allowing employees to acquire job-related KSAs. People direct information-seeking behaviors toward supervisors and more experienced co-workers in order to learn technical and procedural information that allows them to perform their jobs more effectively (Morrison, 1993a). Therefore, these proactive behaviors also have a positive impact on demands–abilities (DA) fit through improving task mastery (Morrison, 1993b).

Information seeking is linked to several of the fundamental motivations to fit. Given that such behavior provides information that clarifies job demands, role requirements, and organizational norms, reducing uncertainty is often seen as one of the primary goals of information seeking (Grant and Ashford, 2008). In fact, research indicates that feedback seeking is more frequent under conditions of role ambiguity and uncertainty (Ashford *et al.*, 2003). Information seeking is also subject to hedonistic motivations, particularly when it comes to feedback seeking. Ashford,

Blatt, and Walle (2003) highlight that feedback seeking has a self-protection motive, which protects and enhances pride and ego-based considerations. For instance, Morrison and Bies (1991) argue that feedback seeking serves the need to feel good about oneself by creating and bolstering a positive image for the individual. Such behavior enhances one's image by creating a positive impression of a motivated and conscientious employee who is interested in finding out how he or she is performing at work. Furthermore, the verbalization of positive feedback can also help to solidify a positive impression about the target person in the mind of the feedback provider. Last but not least, information seeking can also be motivated by the need to gain control over the complexities of one's job. For example, Ashford and Black (1996) found that the desire for control was related to increased feedback-seeking behavior among individuals who were new to their organization.

Discussion

Despite PE fit's prominence in organizational research, little is understood about the role of human agency when it comes to influencing fit. This chapter seeks to address these concerns by forwarding the view that individuals are not passive slaves to their environments. Instead, there are multiple motives for actively managing subjective and objective PE fit. Drawing from research in social psychology and organizational behavior, I argue that people can actively seek to manage their PE fit in order to satisfy innate needs for consistency, hedonism, uncertainty reduction, control, and belongingness. Each of these motivations is a potential driver for individual behavior targeting change in PE fit.

In the second section of this chapter, I discussed the types of behavior initiated by each of these motives, and how such behavior would increase PE fit. These ideas are specifically based around Harrison's (1978) conceptualization of PE fit as the combination of subjective and objective forms of both the person and the environment (also see Edwards *et al.*, 1998). Hence, biases and heuristics, responses to job satisfaction, coping, and proactive behaviors alter PE fit by influencing one or more of the aforementioned components of fit. Overall, the ideas presented in this chapter set the foundation for further research into the causes of PE fit change by highlighting the motivational implications behind changes to fit, and identifying what sort of cognitive and/or physical behavior can be used to bring about this change.

Expanding the motivational model

As the main purpose of this chapter is to put forward the relatively novel view of individuals as active managers of PE fit, the current motivational model of PE fit adopts a somewhat narrow focus on individual motivation and the behaviors stemming from it that impact PE fit. Therefore, there are several areas for development in the model. First, important boundary conditions that govern the relationships proposed here need to be established. Past research on the fit management tactics discussed in this chapter suggests several important types of boundary condition that could influence the strength of fit-based relationships. Grant and Ashford (2008) highlight the role of several dispositions that moderate the impact of certain motivations on the enactment of proactive behavior. For instance, the motivation to reduce uncertainty could be affected by neuroticism. Neurotic individuals tend to be especially anxious and worried by ambiguous situations characterized by uncertainty (Organ, 1975). This heightened discomfort leads neurotics to engage in more proactive behaviors, such as anticipating and planning. Therefore, neuroticism may strengthen the relationship between the motivations to reduce uncertainty and proactive behavior. Similarly, individuals who are more open are more likely to explore a wider range of possibilities for action when dealing with uncertainty (Grant and Ashford, 2008). Thus, openness to experience could also increase the likelihood that the motivation to reduce uncertainty will impact PE fit through proactive behavior. Core self-evaluations could also moderate the influence of fit-based motivations on proactive behavior because people with favorable core self-evaluations carry with them the belief that they have the ability to anticipate, plan, and successfully execute intended behaviors (Erez and Judge, 2001; Grant and Ashford, 2008; Judge *et al.*, 2002). Therefore, people with favorable core self-evaluations should be more able to use proactive behavior as a means to respond to the various fit motivations that are related to proactive behaviors compared to those with unfavorable self-evaluations.

Individuals' ability to manage PE fit is also dependent on the job and organizational context. Initial job design could play a crucial role in providing situations that either encourage or inhibit the changes to PE fit. For example, the amount of autonomy on the job invariably affects the ability of employees to engage in proactive behaviors (Grant and Ashford, 2008; Karasek, 1979). Furthermore, the amount of feedback that is built into one's job system could not only negate the need for proactive information seeking, but also increase the ability of people to regulate their coping behavior in the pursuit of individual or organizational goals (Edwards, 1992). The social nature of jobs also impacts the link between motivations and subsequent changes to fit. For one, jobs vary in the amount of social support they offer (Grant and Parker, 2009). Jobs that provide more access to social support such as peer support groups and mentoring arrangements may act as a substitute for the need to cope through improving PE fit, hence weakening the relationship between fit motivations and coping. Task interdependence also could have a negative impact on individuals' ability to bring about change in job environments because the interconnectedness of their jobs makes it difficult to act upon PE fit in the service of selfish interests (Sprigg *et al.*, 2000). Finally, organizational climates also play a role in encouraging or discouraging some of the above behaviors that impact PE fit. For instance, organizational climates that encourage autonomy could facilitate proactive behaviors aimed at improving fit (Grant and Ashford, 2008).

It is important to note that the current discussion assumes that PE fit is perceived as a desirable phenomenon. In other words, though there is a strong theoretical rationale for the previously mentioned relationships involving fit motivations, little solid empirical evidence exists to support the idea that strivings for consistency, uncertainty reduction, control, and belonging are actually maximized when PE fit exists. Even more intriguing should be the possibility that misfit might actually in certain circumstances prove to be more desirable than fit. Edwards, Caplan, and Harrison (1998) identify some situations where positive outcomes may actually be maximized at certain levels of misfit. For instance, excess supplies compared to individual needs may either be used to attain other different types of desired supplies (i.e., carryover) or conserved for future use (i.e., conservation). Similarly, excess abilities compared to job demands may be desirable because it can allow people to conserve time and energy for future tasks. Several more recent empirical investigations have also found some evidence for misfit to be associated with the maximization of satisfaction, trust, intent to stay, and organizational identification across different types of fit including demands–abilities, needs–supplies, and person–organization (PO) fit (Cable and Edwards, 2004; Edwards, 1996; Edwards and Cable, 2009). Furthermore, people may also set future goals that exceed and thus do not fit with their present ability, so as to achieve high self-efficacy (Phillips *et al.*, 1996). Thus, considering the possible carryover and conversation effects of excess supplies and abilities, people may actually be motivated to strive for a certain amount of misfit with regard to particular aspects of the environment. Further work on this model should incorporate different relationship forms that relate misfit to desirable experiences.

Finally, this chapter is also silent on the possible relationships between the different types of fit motivation. Indeed the hedonistic motivation in particular may be considered more primary than the other motivations, where motivations for consistency, uncertainty reduction, control, and belonging simply serve as means or subgoals to satisfy an overarching hedonistic desire (Locke, 1970, 1976). Similar arguments have been made in research on the self-concept, where consistency has been viewed as one of several interchangeable mechanisms (the others being social comparison and self-affirmation) that can be used to regulate and maintain positive feelings about the self (Steel and Liu, 1983; Tesser, 2000; Tesser *et al.*, 2000). Thus, future research should also investigate the relative primacy of the five fit motivations.

Implications for PE fit research

The model presented in this chapter has important implications for PE fit research, most notably in the design, theorizing, and integration of fit with different streams of research. First, more longitudinal research designs capable of tracking changes to PE fit need to be employed. Thought also needs to be given to the appropriate time lags between self-assessed motivations and subsequent fit management behaviors. Some tactics like biases and heuristics may be employed almost instantaneously or within a relatively short period of time, while others like job satisfaction reactions and proactive behaviors require more time to be planned and executed. In addition, PE fit should be assessed using atomistic measures that clearly distinguish between elements of the person and environment (Edwards *et al.*, 2006). This measurement strategy facilitates investigations into not only which components of PE fit are being affected, but also how each component is being altered with respect to the other. Thus, we can have a more complete understanding of how individual motivations drive changes in both P and E and how the PE fit relationship is altered as a result. Finally, the existing PE fit relationship must be taken into account whenever subsequent changes to PE fit are analyzed because the amount of change in PE fit that can be achieved invariably depends on how much fit already exists (Yu, 2009). Hence, a person might have to explore other ways of improving feelings of belonging if PO fit already exists with the organization.

Edwards' (1995) multivariate multiple regression (MMR)-based framework for analyzing the effects of one or more independent variables on the fit between two dependent variables is well suited for analyzing the present relationships involving PE fit as an outcome. There are two main advantages of using this method of analysis. First, it retains the conceptual difference between person and environment components of PE fit. Secondly, it also facilitates the estimation of the direction and relative magnitudes of the relationships between motivations and changes to person and environment constructs respectively (Yu, 2009).

The current model also has implications for the continued development of PE fit theory. Namely, the need for more research integrating across the different types of PE fit (i.e., demands–abilities, needs–supplies, and all forms of supplementary fit) has become more urgent with our improved understanding of the multidimensional nature of the construct (Kristof-Brown *et al.*, 2005; Ostroff and Schulte, 2007). The current motivational fit model suggests that the needs–supplies type of fit, or the degree to which environmental supplies satisfy individual needs, may be the most primary when it comes to the actual experience of fit. This is because the various motivations to fit can also be essentially considered innate needs to be fulfilled. Hence, the use of biases and heuristics to perceive PE fit essentially satisfies one's need for consistency. Similarly, employing proactive behavior to change job demands to match one's abilities is also driven by the goal of satisfying one's need to reduce uncertainty. This idea about the primacy of needs–supplies fit (or need fulfillment) as the most basic or proximal type of fit when it comes to individual experience mirrors those of Edwards and Shipp (2007), who argue that demands–abilities and value congruence fit influence job attitudes like satisfaction and commitment through needs–supplies fit (Yu, 2008). Thinking of needs–supplies fit as the primary motivator and predictor behind both changes and reactions to fit provides better insight into difficult but important questions of how fit is experienced and what fit actually means to individuals (Billsberry *et al.*, 2005). The current motivational fit model suggests that people see fit as a tool that can be managed to satisfy basic needs of consistency, hedonism, uncertainty reduction, control, and belongingness.

Another implication involves rethinking the dynamism of fit as being driven by *both* individual and organizational factors. In line with recent calls for theory that is more capable of explaining the dynamic nature of fit (Kristof-Brown and Jansen, 2007), the current model suggests that individual factors should not be ignored as omnipresent predictors of PE fit. Up to this point, most research has focused on explaining how macro-level human resource processes like recruitment, selection, and socialization determine the fit of employees (Cable and Parsons, 2001; Cable and Yu, 2006; Chatman, 1991). The current view on fit motivations complements this existing research by focusing on individual behaviors that take place not only during these processes but also throughout the entire employment relationship. For instance, proactive socialization, or the process where individuals engage in their own attempts at information seeking, job negotiation, and relationship building (Ashford and Black, 1996), can complement more formalized socialization practices in establishing person–organization (PO) fit by bringing person-based attributes like values and goals in line with organizational culture (Bauer, Morrison, and Callister, 1998; Jones, 1986; Van Maanen and Schein, 1979). Additionally, changes to PE fit should not only occur during the earlier phases of the employment relationship. The current model implies that any form of organizational or job change that impacts fulfillment of the five motivations to fit can result in the highlighted array of fit management tactics, regardless of employee tenure (Caldwell *et al.*, 2004).

Finally, the scope of this chapter and the fact that it draws liberally from adaptation and socialization research suggests that there is considerable room for integration between these literatures and PE fit. One such point of integration would be for the former stream of research to adopt PE fit more explicitly as an outcome of the socialization and adaptation process. Despite the fact that the majority of research views the learning of job tasks and adoption of organizational values as part of the socialization process (Bauer *et al.*, 1998; Van Maanen and Schein, 1979), the majority of such research has not specifically focused on changes in KSAs or organizational values as outcomes of the socialization process (Bauer *et al.*, 2007). Instead, such research has tended to examine other variables including role clarity, self-efficacy, social acceptance, job performance, job attitudes, and turnover as socialization out-comes (Bauer *et al.*, 1998; Bauer *et al.*, 2007). Although these outcomes may be products of the socialization experience, they do not capture the essence of the so-cialization construct that is based on learning and adaptation. Bauer *et al.* (2007) seem to refer to role clarity, self-efficacy, and social acceptance as only indicators of a successful adjustment process, and even call for more proximal outcomes like the learning of job tasks and organizational values to be investigated in socialization research. Thus, using PE fit as an outcome of socialization more accurately reflects the theoretical treatment of the construct, where socialization as the learning of job tasks can be viewed as the development of demands–abilities fit, while the adop-tion of values is equivalent to building value congruence or PO fit. In addition, more integration of PE fit theory into socialization research can also facilitate re-search that provides more clarity to how fit as a socialization outcome is achieved.

Specifically, such research would be able to identify whether socialization or adaptation is being affected via a change in subjective or objective person and/or environment attributes.

Conclusion

For too long PE fit research has overlooked the potential of innate motives as drivers of changes in fit. The PE relationship carries important ramifications for individual well-being such that, far from being indifferent captives to their PE fit status, people see it as a tool to be managed in pursuit of consistency, hedonism, clarity, control, and belonging. It is hoped that the present discussion of these motivations and their respective tactics taken to manage fit will not only help illuminate our understanding of how people experience fit, but also set the foundation for future investigations into the dynamic nature of the PE fit construct.

References

Adler, A. (1930) Individual psychology. In C. Murchinson (ed.), *Psychologies of 1930* (pp. 395–405). Worcester, MA: Clark University Press.

Ainsworth, M. S. (1989) Attachments beyond infancy. *American Psychologist*, 44, 709–716.

Ames, D. R. (2004a) Strategies for social inference: A similarity contingency model of projection and stereotyping in attribute prevalence estimates. *Journal of Personality and Social Psychology*, 87, 573–585.

Ames, D. R. (2004b) Inside the mind reader's tool kit: Projection and stereotyping in mental state inference. *Journal of Personality and Social Psychology*, 87, 340–353.

Arndt, J., Greenberg, J., Pyszczynski, T., Solomon, S., and Schimel, J. (1999) Creativity and terror management: Evidence that creative activity increases guilt and social projection following mortality salience. *Journal of Personality and Social Psychology*, 77, 19–32.

Arnold, H. J., and Feldman, D. C. (1981) Social desirability response bias in self-report choice situations. *Academy of Management Journal*, 24, 377–385.

Arnold, M. B. (1969) Human emotion and action. In T. Mischel (ed.), *Human Action* (pp. 167–197). New York: Academic Press.

Ashford, S. J. (1986) Feedback-seeking in individual adaptation: A resource perspective. *Academy of Management Journal*, 29, 465–487.

Ashford, S. J., and Black, J. S. (1996) Proactivity during organizational entry: The role of desire for control. *Journal of Applied Psychology*, 81, 199–214.

Ashford, S. J., and Taylor, M. S. (1990) Adaptation to work transitions: An integrative approach. In G. R. F. K. M. Rowland (ed.), *Research in Personnel and Human Resource Management* (Vol. 8, pp. 1–41). Greenwich, CT: JAI Press.

Ashford, S. J., and Tsui, A. S. (1991) Self-regulation for managerial effectiveness: The role of active feedback seeking. *Academy of Management Journal*, 34, 251–280.

Ashford, S. J., Blatt, R., and Walle, D. V. (2003) Reflections on the looking glass: A review of research on feedback-seeking behavior in organizations. *Journal of Management*, 29, 773–799.

Bauer, T. N., Bodner, T., Erdogan, B., Truxillo, D. M., and Tucker, J. S. (2007) Newcomer adjustment during organizational socialization: A meta-analytic review of antecedents, outcomes, and methods. *Journal of Applied Psychology*, 92, 707–721.

Bauer, T. N., Morrison, E. W., and Callister, R. R. (1998) Organizational socialization: A review and directions for future research. In G. R. Ferris (ed.), *Research in Personnel and Human Resources Management* (Vol. 16, pp. 149–214). Greenwich, CT: Elsevier Science/JAI Press.

Baumeister, R. F., and Leary, M. R. (1995) The need to belong: Desire for interpersonal attachments as a fundamental human motivation. *Psychological Bulletin*, 117, 497–529.

Bell, N. E., and Staw, B. M. (1989) People as sculptors vs sculpture: The role of personality and personal control in organizations. In M. B. Arthur, D. T. Hall, and B. S. Lawrence (eds), *The Handbook of Career Theory* (pp. 232–251). Cambridge, England: Cambridge University Press.

Billsberry, J., Ambrosini, V., Moss-Jones, J., and Marsh, P. (2005) Some suggestions for mapping organizational members' sense of fit. *Journal of Business and Psychology*, 19, 555–570.

Bower, G. H. (1981) Mood and memory. *American Psychologist*, 36, 129–148.

Bower, G. H., and Forgas, J. P. (2001) Mood and social memory. In J. P. Forgas (ed.), *Handbook of Affect and Social Cognition* (pp. 95–120). Mahwah, NJ: Lawrence Erlbaum Associates.

Bretz, R. D., and Judge, T. A. (1994) Person–organization fit and the theory of work adjustment: Implications for satisfaction, tenure, and career success. *Journal of Vocational Behavior*, 44, 32–54.

Buss, D. M. (2000) The evolution of happiness. *American Psychologist*, 55, 15–23.

Cable, D. M., and DeRue, D. S. (2002) The convergent and discriminant validity of subjective fit perceptions. *Journal of Applied Psychology*, 87, 875–884.

Cable, D. M., and Edwards, J. R. (2004) Complementary and supplementary fit: A theoretical and empirical integration. *Journal of Applied Psychology*, 89, 822–834.

Cable, D. M., and Judge, T. A. (1996) Person–organization fit, job choice decisions, and organizational entry. *Organizational Behavior and Human Decision Processes*, 67, 294–311.

Cable, D. M., and Parsons, C. K. (2001) Socialization tactics and person–organization fit. *Personnel Psychology*, 54, 1–23.

Cable, D. M., and Yu, K. Y. T. (2006) Managing job seekers' organizational image beliefs: The role of media richness and media credibility. *Journal of Applied Psychology*, 91, 828–840.

Caldwell, S. D., Herold, D. M., and Fedor, D. B. (2004) Toward an understanding of the relationships among organizational change, individual differences, and changes in PE fit: A cross-level study. *Journal of Applied Psychology*, 89, 868–882.

Campion, M. A., and Lord, R. G. (1982) A control systems conceptualization of the goal-setting and changing process. *Organizational Behavior and Human Performance*, 30, 265–287.

Caplan, R. D. (1987) PE fit in organizations: Theories, facts, and values. In A. W. Riley and S. J. Zaccaro (eds), *Occupational Stress and Organizational Effectiveness* (pp. 103–140). New York: Praeger.

Carver, C. S., and Scheier, M. F. (1982) Control theory: A useful conceptual framework for personality-social, clinical, and health psychology. *Psychological Bulletin*, 92, 111–135.

Chatman, J. A. (1989) Improving interactional organizational research: A model of person–organization fit. *Academy of Management Review*, 14, 333–349.

Chatman, J. A. (1991) Matching people and organizations: Selection and socialization in public accounting firms. *Administrative Science Quarterly*, 36, 459–484.

Cialdini, R. B., Trost, M. R., and Newsom, J. T. (1995) Preference for consistency: The development of a valid measure and the discovery of surprising behavioral implications. *Journal of Personality and Social Psychology*, 69, 318–328.

Clegg, C., and Spencer, C. (2007) A circular and dynamic model of the process of job design. *Journal of Occupational and Organizational Psychology*, 80, 321–339.

Clement, R. W., and Krueger, J. (2002) Social categorization moderates social projection. *Journal of Experimental Social Psychology*, 38, 219–231.

Clore, G. L., Schwarz, N., and Conway, M. (1994) Affective causes and consequences of social information processing. In R. S. Wyer and T. K. Srull (eds), *Handbook of Social Cognition* (2nd edn, Vol. 1, pp. 323–417). Hillsdale, NJ: Lawrence Erlbaum Associates.

Cooper, J., and Fazio, R. H. (1984) A new look at dissonance theory. In L. Berkowitz (ed.), *Advances in Experimental Social Psychology* (Vol. 17, pp. 229–266). New York: Academic Press.

Cranny, C. J., Smith, P. C., and Stone, E. F. (1992) *Job Satisfaction: How People Feel about their Jobs and How it Affects their Performance.* New York: Lexington Books.

Dawis, R. V., and Lofquist, L. H. (1984) *A Psychological Theory of Work Adjustment.* Minneapolis: University of Minnesota Press.

Diener, E. (2000) Subjective well-being: The science of happiness and a proposal for a national index. *American Psychologist*, 55, 34–43.

Dipboye, R. L. (1985) Some neglected variables in research on discrimination in appraisals. *Academy of Management Review*, 10, 116–127.

Eagly, A., and Chaiken, S. (1993) *The Psychology of Attitudes.* Fort Worth, TX: Harcourt Brace Jovanovich.

Edwards, J. R. (1992) A cybernetic theory of stress, coping, and well-being in organizations. *Academy of Management Review*, 17, 238–274.

Edwards, J. R. (1995) Alternatives to difference scores as dependent variables in the study of congruence in organizational research. *Organizational Behavior and Human Decision Processes*, 64, 307–324.

Edwards, J. R. (1996) An examination of competing versions of the PE fit approach to stress. *Academy of Management Journal*, 39, 292–339.

Edwards, J. (2008) PE fit in organizations: An assessment of theoretical progress. *Academy of Management Annals*, 2, 167–230.

Edwards, J. R., and Baglioni, A. J. (1993) The measurement of coping with stress: Construct validity of the Ways of Coping Checklist and the Cybernetic Coping Scale. *Work and Stress*, 7, 17–31.

Edwards, J. R., and Cable, D. M. (2009) The value of value congruence. *Journal of Applied Psychology*, 94, 654–677.

Edwards, J. R., and Shipp, A. J. (2007) The relationship between PE fit and outcomes: An integrative theoretical framework. In C. Ostroff and T. A. Judge (eds), *Perspectives on Organizational Fit* (pp. 209–258). New York: Lawrence Erlbaum Associates.

Edwards, J. R., Cable, D. M., Williamson, I. O., Lambert, L. S., and Shipp, A. J. (2006) The phenomenology of fit: Linking the person and environment to the subjective experience of PE Fit. *Journal of Applied Psychology*, 91, 802–827.

Edwards, J. R., Caplan, R. D., and Harrison, R. V. (1998) PE fit theory: Conceptual foundations, empirical evidence, and directions for future research. In C. L. Cooper (ed.), *Theories of Organizational Stress* (pp. 28–67). Oxford: Oxford University Press.

Elliott, G. C. (1986) Self-esteem and self-consistency: A theoretical and empirical link between two primary motivations. *Social Psychology Quarterly*, 49, 207–218.

Erez, A., and Judge, T. A. (2001) Relationship of core self-evaluations to goal setting, motivation, and performance. *Journal of Applied Psychology*, 86, 1270–1279.

Farrell, D. (1983) Exit, voice, loyalty, and neglect as responses to job dissatisfaction: A multidimensional scaling study. *Academy of Management Journal*, 26, 596–607.

Festinger, L. (1957) *A Theory of Cognitive Dissonance.* Stanford, CA: Stanford University Press.

Folkman, S., and Lazarus, R. S. (1980) An analysis of coping in a middle-aged community sample. *Journal of Health and Social Behavior*, 21, 219–239.

Folkman, S., and Moskowitz, J. T. (2004) Coping: Pitfalls and promise. *Annual Review of Psychology*, 55, 745–774.

Forgas, J. P., Bower, G. H., and Krantz, S. E. (1984) The influence of mood on perceptions of social interactions. *Journal of Experimental Social Psychology*, 20, 497–513.

Frijda, N. H. (1988) The laws of emotion. *American Psychologist*, 43, 349–358.

Graen, G. B., and Scandura, T. A. (1987) Toward a psychology of dyadic organizing. In L. L. Cummings and B. M. Staw (eds), *Research in Organizational Behavior* (Vol. 9, pp. 175–208). Greenwich, CT: JAI.

Grant, A. M., and Ashford, S. J. (2008) The dynamics of proactivity at work. *Research in Organizational Behavior*, 28, 3–34.

Grant, A. M., and Parker, S. K. (2009) Redesigning work design theories: The rise of relational and proactive perspectives. *Academy of Management Annals*, 3, 317–375.

Greenberg, J., Roberge, M.-É., Ho, V. T., and Rousseau, D. M. (2004) Fairness in idiosyncratic work arrangements: Justice as an ideal. In J. J. Martocchio (ed.), *Research in Personnel and Human Resources Management* (Vol. 23, pp. 1–34). Greenwich, CT: Elsevier Science/JAI Press.

Hanisch, K. A., and Hulin, C. L. (1990) Job attitudes and organizational withdrawal: An examination of retirement and other voluntary withdrawal behaviors. *Journal of Vocational Behavior*, 37, 60–78.

Hanisch, K. A., and Hulin, C. L. (1991) General attitudes and organizational withdrawal: An evaluation of a causal model. *Journal of Vocational Behavior*, 39, 110–128.

Harrison, R. V. (1978) PE fit and job stress. In C. L. Cooper and R. Payne (eds), *Stress at Work* (pp. 175–205). New York: John Wiley & Sons, Inc.

Heider, F. (1958) *The Psychology of Interpersonal Relations.* New York: John Wiley & Sons, Inc.

Henne, D., and Locke, E. A. (1985) Job dissatisfaction: What are the consequences? *International Journal of Psychology*, 20, 221–240.

Higgins, M. C., and Kram, K. E. (2001) Reconceptualizing mentoring at work: A developmental network perspective. *Academy of Management Review*, 26, 264–288.

Hulin, C. (1991) Adaptation, persistence, and commitment in organizations. In M. D. Dunnette and L. M. Hough (eds), *Handbook of Industrial and Organizational Psychology* (2nd edn, Vol. 2, pp. 445–505). Palo Alto, CA: Consulting Psychologists Press.

Insko, C. A. (1981) Balance theory and phenomenology. In T. M. Ostrom and T. C. Brock (eds), *Cognitive Responses in Persuasion* (pp. 309–338) New York: Lawrence Erlbaum Associates.

James, L. R., and Jones, A. P. (1980) Perceived job characteristics and job satisfaction: An examination of reciprocal causation. *Personnel Psychology*, 33, 97–135.

James, L. R., and Tetrick, L. E. (1986) Confirmatory analytic tests of three causal models relating job perceptions to job satisfaction. *Journal of Applied Psychology*, 71, 77–82.

Jones, G. R. (1986) Socialization tactics, self-efficacy, and newcomers' adjustments to organizations. *Academy of Management Journal*, 29, 262–279.

Judge, T. A., and Cable, D. M. (1997) Applicant personality, organizational culture, and organization attraction. *Personnel Psychology*, 50, 359–394.

Judge, T. A., Erez, A., Bono, J. E., and Thoresen, C. J. (2002) Are measures of self-esteem, neuroticism, locus of control, and generalized self-efficacy indicators of a common core construct? *Journal of Personality and Social Psychology*, 83, 693–710.

Karasek, R. A. (1979) Job demands, job decision latitude, and mental strain: Implications for job redesign. *Administrative Science Quarterly*, 24, 285–308.

Katz, D., and Kahn, R. L. (1966) *The Social Psychology of Organizations*. New York: John Wiley & Sons, Inc.

Kraiger, K., Billings, R. S., and Isen, A. M. (1989) The influence of positive affective states on task perceptions and satisfaction. *Organizational Behavior and Human Decision Processes*, 44, 12–25.

Kristof, A. L. (1996) Person–organization fit: An integrative review of its conceptualizations, measurement, and implications. *Personnel Psychology*, 49, 1–49.

Kristof-Brown, A. L., and Jansen, K. J. (2007) Issues of person–organization fit. In C. Ostroff and T. A. Judge (eds), *Perspectives on Organizational Fit* (pp. 123–153). New York: Lawrence Erlbaum Associates.

Kristof-Brown, A. L., Zimmerman, R. D., and Johnson, E. C. (2005) Consequences of individuals' fit at work: A meta-analysis of person–job, person–organization, person–group, and person–supervisor fit. *Personnel Psychology*, 58, 281–342.

Krueger, J. (1998) On the perception of social consensus. In M. P. Zanna (ed.), *Advances in Experimental Social Psychology* (Vol. 30, pp. 163–240). San Diego, CA: Academic Press.

Larsen, R. J. (2000) Toward a science of mood regulation. *Psychological Inquiry*, 11, 129–141.

Lazarus, R. S., and Folkman, S. (1984) *Stress, Appraisal, and Coping*. New York: Springer.

Lecky, P. (1968) The theory of self-consistency. In C. Gordon and K. J. Gergen (eds), *The Self in Social Interaction* (Vol. 1, pp. 297–298). New York: John Wiley & Sons, Inc.

Lewin, K. (1935) *Dynamic Theory of Personality*. New York: McGraw-Hill.

Lindsley, D. H., Brass, D. J., and Thomas, J. B. (1995) Efficacy-performing spirals: A multilevel perspective. *Academy of Management Review*, 20, 645–678.

Locke, E. A. (1969) What is job satisfaction? *Organizational Behavior and Human Decision Processes*, 4, 309–336.

Locke, E. A. (1970) Job satisfaction and job performance: A theoretical analysis. *Organizational Behavior and Human Performance*, 5, 484–500.

Locke, E. A. (1976) The nature and causes of job satisfaction. In M. Dunnette (ed.), *Handbook of Industrial and Organizational Psychology* (pp. 1297–1350). Chicago: Rand McNally.

Locke, E. A. (1984) Job satisfaction. In M. Gruneberg and T. Wall (eds), *Social Psychology and Organizational Behavior* (pp. 93–117). Chichester: John Wiley & Sons, Ltd.

Marks, G., and Miller, N. (1987) Ten years of research on the false-consensus effect: An empirical and theoretical review. *Psychological Bulletin*, 102, 72–90.

Maslow, A. H. (1968) *Toward a Psychology of Being* (2nd edn). New York: Van Nostrand Reinhold.

Mitchell, T. R., Holtom, B. C., Lee, T. W., Sablynski, C. J., and Erez, M. (2001) Why people stay: Using job embeddedness to predict voluntary turnover. *Academy of Management Journal*, 44, 1102–1121.

Moreland, R. L. (1987) The formation of small groups. In C. Hendrick (ed.), *Group Processes: Review of Personality and Social Psychology* (Vol. 8, pp. 80–110). Newbury Park, CA: Sage.

Morgeson, F. P., and Campion, M. A. (1997) Social and cognitive sources of potential inaccuracy in job analysis. *Journal of Applied Psychology*, 82, 627–655.

Morrison, E. W. (1993a) Longitudinal study of the effects of information seeking on newcomer socialization. *Journal of Applied Psychology*, 78, 173–183.

Morrison, E. W. (1993b) Newcomer information seeking: Exploring types, modes, sources, and outcomes. *Academy of Management Journal*, 36, 557–589.

Morrison, E. W., and Bies, R. J. (1991) Impression management in the feedback-seeking process: A literature review and research agenda. *Academy of Management Review*, 16, 522–541.

Muchinsky, P. M., and Monahan, C. J. (1987) What is PE congruence? Supplementary versus complementary models of fit. *Journal of Vocational Behavior*, 31, 268–277.

Newman, J. E., and Beehr, T. A. (1979) Personal and organizational strategies for handling job stress: A review of research and opinion. *Personnel Psychology*, 32, 1–43.

Nicholson, N. (1984) A theory of work role transitions. *Administrative Science Quarterly*, 29, 172–191.

O'Reilly, C. A., Chatman, J., and Caldwell, D. F. (1991) People and organizational culture: A profile comparison approach to assessing person–organization fit. *Academy of Management Journal*, 34, 487–516.

Organ, D. W. (1975) Effect of pressure and individual neuroticism on emotional responses to task-role ambiguity. *Journal of Applied Psychology*, 60, 397–400.

Ostroff, C., and Schulte, M. (2007) Multiple perspectives of fit in organizations across levels of analysis. In C. Ostroff and T. A. Judge (eds), *Perspectives on Organizational Fit* (pp. 3–69). New York: Lawrence Erlbaum Associates.

Parker, S. K., and Collins, C. G. (2009) Taking stock: Integrating and differentiating multiple proactive behaviors. *Journal of Management*, 36, 633–662.

Perrez, M., and Reicherts, M. (1992) *Stress, Coping and Health*. Seattle, WA: Hogrefe and Huber.

Pervin, L. A. (1981) The relation of situations to behavior. In D. Magnusson (ed.), *Psychological Climate: Theoretical Perspectives and Empirical Research* (pp. 343–360). Hillsdale, NJ: Lawrence Erlbaum Associates.

Pervin, L. A. (1989) Persons, situations, interactions: The history of a controversy and a discussion of theoretical models. *Academy of Management Review*, 14, 350–360.

Phillips, J. M., Hollenbeck, J. R., and Ilgen, D. R. (1996) Prevalence and prediction of positive discrepancy creation: Examining a discrepancy between two self-regulation theories. *Journal of Applied Psychology*, 81, 498–511.

Powers, W. T. (1978) Quantitative analysis of purposive systems: Some spadework at the foundations of scientific psychology. *Psychological Review*, 85, 417–435.

Reichers, A. E. (1987) An interactionist perspective on newcomer socialization rates. *Academy of Management Review*, 12, 278–287.

Robbins, J. M., and Krueger, J. I. (2005) Social projection to ingroups and outgroups: A review and meta-analysis. *Personality and Social Psychology Review*, 9, 32–47.

Rousseau, D. M., Ho, V. T., and Greenberg, J. (2006) I-deals: Idiosyncratic terms in employment relationships. *Academy of Management Review*, 31, 977–994.

Salancik, G. R., and Pfeffer, J. (1978) A social information processing approach to job attitudes and task design. *Administrative Science Quarterly*, 23, 224–253.

Schein, E. H. (1990) Organizational culture. *American Psychologist*, 45, 109–119.

Schwarz, N. (1990) Feelings as information: Informational and motivational functions of affective states. In E. T. Higgins and R. M. Sorrentino (eds), *Handbook on Motivation and Cognition* (Vol. 2, pp. 527–561). New York: Guilford Press.

Schwarz, N., and Clore, G. L. (2003) Mood as information: 20 years later. *Psychological Inquiry*, 14, 296–303.

Sedikides, C. (1992) Mood as a determinant of attentional focus. *Cognition and Emotion*, 6, 129–148.

Sedikides, C. (1995) Central and peripheral self-conceptions are differentially influenced by mood: Tests of the differential sensitivity hypothesis. *Journal of Personality and Social Psychology*, 69, 759–777.

Sedikides, C., and Green, J. D. (2001) Affective influences on the self-concept: Qualifying the mood-congruency principle. In J. P. Forgas (ed.), *Handbook of Affect and Social Cognition* (pp. 145–160). Mahwah, NJ: Lawrence Erlbaum Associates.

Smith, J. E., and Hakel, M. D. (1979) Convergence among data sources, response bias, and reliability and validity of a structured job analysis questionnaire. *Personnel Psychology*, 32, 677–692.

Sprigg, C. A., Jackson, P. R., and Parker, S. K. (2000) Production teamworking: The importance of interdependence and autonomy for employee strain and satisfaction. *Human Relations*, 53, 1519–1543.

Steele, C. M., and Liu, T. J. (1983) Dissonance processes as self-affirmation. *Journal of Personality and Social Psychology*, 45, 5–19.

Taylor, M. S., Fisher, C. D., and Ilgen, D. R. (1984) Individuals' reactions to performance feedback in organizations: A control theory perspective. In K. M. Rowland and G. R. Ferris (eds), *Research in Personnel and Human Resources Management* (Vol. 2, pp. 81–124). Greenwich, CT: JAI Press.

Tesser, A. (2000) On the confluence of self-esteem maintenance mechanisms. *Personality and Social Psychology Review*, 4, 290–299.

Tesser, A., Crepaz, N., Beach, S. R. H., Cornell, D., and Collins, J. C. (2000) Confluence of self-esteem regulation mechanisms: On integrating the self-zoo. *Personality and Social Psychology Bulletin*, 26, 1476–1489.

Van Dyne, L., and LePine, J. A. (1998) Helping and voice extra-role behaviors: Evidence of construct and predictive validity. *Academy of Management Journal*, 41, 108–119.

Van Maanen, J., and Schein, E. H. (1979) Toward a theory of organizational socialization. In B. M. Staw (ed.), *Research in Organizational Behavior* (pp. 209–264). Greenwich, CT: JAI Press Inc.

Webster, D. M., and Kruglanski, A. W. (1994) Individual differences in need for cognitive closure. *Journal of Personality and Social Psychology*, 67, 1049–1062.

Weick, K. E. (1979) *The Social Psychology of Organizing* (2nd edn). Reading, MA: Addison-Wesley.

White, R. W. (1959) Motivation reconsidered: The concept of competence. *Psychological Review*, 66, 297–333.

Wolff, H.-G., and Moser, K. (2009) Effects of networking on career success: A longitudinal study. *Journal of Applied Psychology*, 94, 196–206.

Wrzesniewski, A., and Dutton, J. E. (2001) Crafting a job: Revisioning employees as active crafters of their work. *Academy of Management Review*, 26, 179–201.

Yu, K. Y. T. (2008) Investigating the inter-relationships among different types of PE fit perceptions and job satisfaction. Paper presented at the Annual Meeting of the Academy of Management.

Yu, K. Y. T. (2009) Affective influences in PE fit theory: Exploring the role of affect as both cause and outcome of PE fit. *Journal of Applied Psychology*, 94, 1210–1226.

Yu, K. Y. T., and Cable, D. M. (2009) Recruitment and competitive advantage: A brand equity perspective. In S. W. J. Kozlowski (ed.), *Oxford Handbook of Industrial–Organizational Psychology* (pp. 197–220). New York: Oxford University Press.

Zajonc, R. B. (1980) Feeling and thinking: Preferences need no inferences. *American Psychologist*, 35, 151–175.

3

Dyadic Fit and the Process of Organizational Socialization

John D. Kammeyer-Mueller
Warrington College of Business Administration, University of Florida

Pauline Schilpzand
Army Center of Excellence for the Professional Military Ethic,
US Military Academy at West Point

Alex L. Rubenstein
Warrington College of Business Administration, University of Florida

Person–environment fit matters. Research has repeatedly shown that employees who fit with their jobs, their work groups, and their organizations are more committed and more satisfied (Kristof-Brown *et al.*, 2005). However, despite the demonstrated importance of person–environment fit, there has been a notable absence of research on interpersonal, dyadic fit at work (Ferris *et al.*, 2009). This is a surprising omission, because most people only feel like they really "fit" in a job if they have positive dyadic relationships with their co-workers and supervisor. As such, our understanding of behavior at work is incomplete if we fail to take the role of person-to-person relationships into account. There is also a practical, operational side to understanding dyadic relationships at work, because they facilitate the exchange of information and resources (e.g., Ibarra *et al.*, 2005; Labianca and Brass, 2006; Nebus, 2006). Unfortunately, research on social relationships at work does not yet reflect the rich body of knowledge that has been amassed in other fields (Barry and Crant, 2000). Thus, while we know that interpersonal relationships are important, we currently do not know a great deal about these relationships in organizational contexts.

In this chapter, we outline a model of how person–environment fit develops in the course of social interactions among established organizational members and those who are new to the organization. The focus on the initial period of relationship

Organizational Fit: Key Issues and New Directions, First Edition.
Edited by Amy L. Kristof-Brown and Jon Billsberry.
© 2013 John Wiley & Sons, Ltd. Published 2013 by John Wiley & Sons, Ltd.

development (i.e., organizational socialization) will help to illustrate a number of important processes that occur primarily in the initial acquaintance phase, and unfold as individuals come to know one another better. Our theoretical development will proceed from a relationship science perspective (e.g., Berscheid, 1999; Kelley *et al.*, 1983). This perspective offers insights that have been unexplored in both the person–environment fit and organizational socialization literatures, including an increased understanding of how people come to have close affective bonds with one another, a better set of tools for discussing the processes of social acceptance (and rejection), and a useful typology for differentiating types of relationship. To date, there has been only limited transfer of this material into the organizational behavior literature (for exceptions, see Ferris *et al.*, 2009; Poteat *et al.*, 2009; and Ragins and Dutton, 2007).

Relationships and Fit: Definitions

It is helpful to start our discussion with a clear definition of what is meant by a dyadic relationship, as well as what is meant by fit. These definitions will then be integrated with one another to create a typology of three principal relationship types.

We take our definitions of relationship characteristics from the relationship science literature (Berscheid, 1999; Kelley *et al.*, 1983). A dyadic relationship is a long-range series of interdependent interactions in which two people change one another in some way. Interactions can be based on either emotional exchanges or more tangible exchanges of goods and services. Relationship partners change one another's attitudes, emotions, resources, and behavior. Relationships are personal, meaning that they occur at the dyadic level and are particular to one another as a result of patterns of feelings and cognitions that have developed over the course of repeated interactions.

Person–environment fit occurs when there is a perceived congruence between the attributes of a person and the environment (Cable and Edwards, 2004; Kristof, 1996). In the case of dyadic fit, the "environment" is the other person with whom a fit relationship is being established (Schneider, 1987). The distinction between complementary and supplementary fit is drawn consistently in the fit literature (e.g., Cable and Edwards, 2004; Muchinsky and Monahan, 1987; Piasentin and Chapman, 2007), and is especially useful for our purposes in detailing the relationship development context. Supplementary fit occurs when the person and environment are highly similar to one another, such as when a person's values match very well with the values embodied in the work environment. Complementary fit occurs when the environment is lacking something that the person can supply, and/or the person is lacking something that the environment can supply – such as when two individuals have non-overlapping skill sets that allow them to complete a task that neither would be able to complete independently.

Interpersonal relationships can be differentiated in terms of three distinct dimensions: affective bonds (i.e., communal relationships), instrumentality (i.e., exchange relationships), and animosity (Mills and Clark, 1994; O'Connell, 1984). Relation-ships based on affective bonding suggest a mutual liking and emotional connection between two parties. In a supplementary fit relationship, the parties are well matched because of their inherent similarity. In the case of interpersonal relationships, supple-mentary fit is demonstrated by the degree to which parties are similar to one another, whether in personality, interests, or background. Such similarities have been found to increase liking between parties in the relationship science literature (Fehr, 1996; Gonzales *et al.*, 1983; Woodside and Davenport, 1974), which would be associated with a communal relationship. Complementary fit exists when one of the parties can provide something that the other is missing, such as when one member of the rela-tionship has access to information the other needs to complete a task. Therefore, it is said that one party is instrumental to helping the other party achieve their goals. The result of such complementary fit is an instrumental or exchange-based relationship. Finally, the third form of relationship, animosity, is actually a form of misfit, which occurs when parties are so different from one another on fundamental attributes of importance that they sum to actively dislike or form antagonisms toward each other. This is generally in the form of supplementary misfit.

inter

We note in advance that all relationships contain elements of affective, instru-mental, and animosity factors, so relationships need not be categorized into one of three mutually exclusive categories. It is possible for a relationship to be marked by high levels of affective bonds due to supplemental fit developed across a number of dimensions important for liking, while concurrently to be high in exchange because of complementarities arising from mutual needs on other dimensions that create the conditions for exchange. You might like a new co-worker because he or she is interested in reading the same books that you enjoy, but also find him or her to be instrumental to achieving your work ends because he or she possesses a set of valuable skills that you do not have. It is also possible for a relationship to be high in animosity because the parties have poor supplementary fit on important personality or value dimensions, but for the parties to still have a strong exchange relationship because their personal desires and unique resources complement one another. An example of this last combination of animosity exchange relationships might involve a situation in which you need to interact with a new co-worker because only he or she has access to important organizational resources; however, you may still strongly dislike this person because you believe he or she has very different values and work habits than you.

Contributions of an Interpersonal Socialization Perspective to the Literature on Fit

There are several reasons why exploring dyadic fit can contribute to the general literature on person–environment fit, and particularly why examining dyadic fit from the perspective of organizational newcomers might be especially informative.

Before we outline the processes of relationship development and the consequences of relationship formation, we describe some of the key areas in which a dyadic fit perspective can benefit organizational scholars.

The first benefit of an interpersonal perspective on fit is that it introduces an often overlooked area of analysis – the dyadic fit occurring between two co-workers or team members. Prior work has begun to look at this topic under the rubrics of dyadic personality similarity (Antonioni and Park, 2001), subordinate–supervisor similarity (Schaubroeck and Lam, 2002) and subordinate–supervisor goal congruence (Witt, 1998). This previous work has primarily looked at the relationship between characteristics of the individuals making up the relationship, and has demonstrated that individuals who are more similar to one another have more positive relationships. This is an excellent starting point for investigation, and clearly can be contrasted with the distinct literature on person–group fit.

The fit literature discusses person–group fit as it concerns the compatibility between an individual and their entire work group or team (Judge and Ferris, 1992; Kristof, 1996). Although person–group fit scores have proven meaningful and predictive of various organizational criteria including job satisfaction, organizational commitment, co-worker satisfaction, and group cohesion (see Kristof-Brown *et al.*, 2005), the person–group fit perspective does not consider the idiosyncratic, dyadic relationship that emerges between an employee and each individual co-worker or team member with whom they interact. While the groups and teams literature has revealed the nature of both emergent states and team processes by assessing the shared and similar evaluation of these constructs (Morgeson and Hofmann, 1999), the respective fit perceptions that one person may have for each member in their work group or team can vary considerably. For example, it is quite possible to have a very positive relationship with one colleague in a work group but simultaneously to have an active distain for another member of the same work group. An aggregated person–group fit score would overlook this significant source of variance in work relationships within the group.

A more fine-grained level of fit evaluation, assessed at the dyadic level, may be especially informative because fit with one's *entire* group may not be required to achieve many of the positive benefits reaped by high fit perceptions (Ferris *et al.*, 2009). Indeed, evidence from longitudinal studies suggests that, as compared to the relatively plentiful and shallow relationships of adolescence and early adulthood, mature adults engage in higher levels of relational intimacy and place more importance on a small number of close relationships (Reis *et al.*, 1993). Achieving deep complementary fit with one co-worker, where resources and needs are mutually and reciprocally consummated over a long period of interactions, is probably far more satisfying to employees than sharing many somewhat satisfying, fairly short-term, complementary associations with multiple group members. Similarly, being deeply alike in personality, values, beliefs, or work goals to one co-worker with whom you work intimately is probably more satisfying than being moderately similar to all of the members of a group with whom you work only occasionally.

Furthermore, the negative repercussions of misfit may be catalyzed by a single negative interpersonal tie. Recent research in the teams literature has described the uniquely harmful effects that individually deviant team members can have on other members' motivation and affect (Felps *et al.*, 2006). Having one colleague who is especially dissimilar in values, personality, or work goals may spur turnover intentions or other undesirable outcomes. Despite data suggesting that negative relationships are estimated to average to merely 4 percent of the total number of "important" relationships in organizations (e.g., Gersick *et al.*, 2000; Labianca *et al.*, 1998), research indicates that they have a far greater impact than their prevalence would suggest. Negative information, exchanges, or behaviors are not simply the opposite of their positive counterparts; rather, negative interactions may create a stronger and more memorable impression than positive interactions (Baumeister *et al.*, 2001). Labianca, Brass, and Gray (1998) investigated perceptions of intergroup conflict in the workplace from a network perspective, and concluded that negative workplace ties, while few in number, are especially impactful. They conveyed that "like the 'squeaky wheel,' negative relationships appear to command more attention" (p. 63) and that fostering larger networks of friends did not compensate for the detrimental effects of single negative relationships.

Dyadic Fit and Organizational Socialization

We have discussed evidence suggesting that fit at the dyadic level may be at least as important as person–group fit. In the next section we would like to apply the dyadic fit lens to the organizational socialization process, which we think is one domain that may especially benefit from theory on dyadic fit. Consistent with previous research, we conceptualize the process of organizational socialization as a broader sequence than just an initial period of orientation. Instead, socialization is a process that slowly develops over the first months on a job as workers slowly transition from organizational outsiders to fully integrated insiders (e.g., Wanous, 1992).

Social acceptance is an important component of developing person–environment fit during the newcomer's socialization and adjustment process. Early on, newcomers seek out information about the social norms of their work groups. Learning how to get along with others is one of the most important tasks for establishing themselves in their new jobs. Researchers have also found that individuals who report having more satisfying relationships with their co-workers during the early period of their adjustment to new jobs have higher levels of organizational commitment, even after accounting for other variables related to positive adjustment, such as personality and role clarity (e.g., Kammeyer-Mueller and Wanberg, 2003; Morrison, 1993; Ostroff and Kozlowski, 1992). Yet, comparatively little research has examined the interpersonal processes underlying what contributes to social acceptance. Similarly, research has not studied the obverse of socialization, social rejection, or the factors that detract from social acceptance among organizational newcomers.

Assessing interpersonal fit during socialization can also facilitate investigation of the dynamic nature of dyadic fit perceptions. The notion that social relationships develop over time as a process, rather than occurring as static or discrete states, is supported by socialization researchers in the traditions of symbolic interactionism and social information processing (e.g., Reichers, 1987; Zalesny and Ford, 1990). For example, in the socialization literature the inherent assumption is that a newcomer will assimilate organizational values and adopt organizational goals. In this sense, fit evaluations with the organization and with other organizational members will become stronger as incumbent employees and organizational cultural processes socialize the newcomer (Saks and Ashforth, 1997). Perceptions of fit may be determined by the dispositions of the members of the dyad, but in order to make fit assessments, members of the relationship must become aware of these personality traits as they are shown in behavior over time (Shoda *et al.*, 1994). Conflicts between individuals with poorly fitting personality dispositions manifest as the individuals interact with one another. Helping behaviors and other behavior signaling liking are also likely to increase as people interact and develop more favorable fit perceptions, of either the complementary or the supplementary variety. So, dyadic fit is indeed a process that unfolds, as newcomers are socialized into the organizational environment.

Similarly, the relationship literature is grounded in the idea that relationships are something that people develop with time (Hays, 1984, 1985). Social penetration theory (Altman and Taylor, 1973) describes the gradual evolution of friendship relationships, progressing from superficial interactions in a narrow content domain to deeper interactions spanning broader content domains. As relationships develop and become more intimate, the parties are increasingly able to predict and interpret one another's behavior (Barry and Crant, 2000). Thus, the fit literature, while currently lacking a developmental perspective, may gain from this type of dynamic theory that explains the formation and maintenance of dyadic fit. In the next sections, we outline the antecedents, processes, and outcomes of interpersonal dyadic fit evaluations.

Antecedents of the Development of Dyadic Fit in the Socialization Process

Having laid the groundwork for a dyadic perspective on person–environment fit, we now turn our attention to building a model for research on dyadic fit during organizational socialization. Because so little research has been conducted on dyadic fit in the organizational socialization literature, our review will draw primarily from the relationships science literature. Clearly, this is a prospective model that will need to be tested in the future. A summary of the model is presented in Figure 3.1. The model begins by suggesting that certain personal and environmental conditions tend to foster or inhibit dyadic fit for newcomers. Once these dyadic fit conditions are met, a number of self-reinforcing processes are set into motion that build relationships

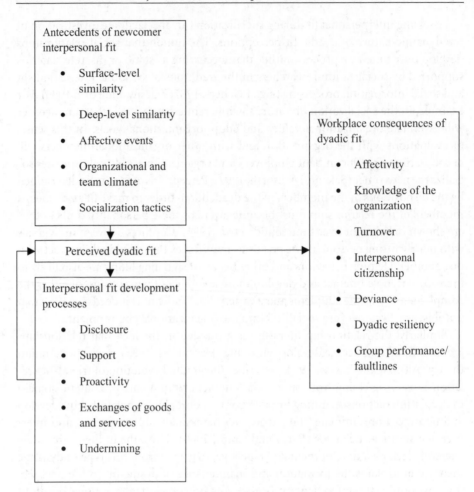

Figure 3.1   A model of dyadic fit and socialization

and increase the strength of ties in a reciprocal fashion. Finally, there are several consequences we expect to result from these processes.

First impressions have a powerful impact on the relationship development process (Snyder *et al.*, 1985), so we begin from this point. First impressions may be influenced by immediately apparent indicators of similarity or difference. Demographic difference variables often associated with impression formation include race, gender, physical attractiveness, and age (e.g., Eagly *et al.*, 1991; Harrison *et al.*, 1998; Harrison *et al.*, 2002). However, other superficially observable similarities, such as a shared interest in music, sports, or literature, political party membership, or membership in the same church, synagogue, or mosque, could also spur individuals to an initial impression that they are similar to someone else. These initial impressions are likely to be important early in relationship development because they are so readily observed, and individuals are motivated to seek out those with whom they fit at any level when they are first trying to make sense of a new situation. On the other hand, newcomers who have few initial similarities with their co-workers may have difficulty establishing a sense of dyadic fit with anyone.

> Proposition 1: First impressions of surface-level similarity enhance dyadic supplementary fit perceptions during the initial period of organizational socialization.

While early impressions are important, these early fit perceptions – grounded in easily notable individual differences – do not wholly explain the development of dyadic fit perceptions. Diversity theory has differentiated the easily recognized differences, or surface-level diversity characteristics, from deep-level diversity characteristics. Deep-level diversity indicators are neither readily observed nor quickly or easily learned. It takes time to observe and assess a person's true personality or values. Instead, deep-level diversity judgments are based in attitudinal (dis)similarity and value (in)congruence. Interestingly, while surface-level characteristics predict the early formation of interpersonal ties, deep-level diversity predicts closeness in the long-term (Harrison *et al.*, 1998; Harrison *et al.*, 2002). With time, newcomers will interact more frequently with their co-workers and get to know these individuals more deeply. The socialized newcomers can learn more accurately what personal goals, values, resources, or skill sets their co-workers hold, and their co-workers will similarly learn about them. This information will probably cause new or amended fit evaluations based on deep-level diversity attributes or based on information that was not easily made sense of during the interpersonal acquaintance phase. Thus, the formation and perceived similarity among these deep-level criteria may also catalyze or amend the process of dyadic fit evaluation.

> Proposition 2: Deep-level similarity enhances dyadic supplementary fit perceptions in the long term of a relationship, especially in the later stages of socialization.

Although similarity in personal characteristics is expected to have an impact on the initial development of fit, there will also be events that occur in the work context that impact perceptions of fit. Affective events theory (Weiss and Cropanzano, 1996) indicates that job attitudes are malleable, and will change in response to events that spur either positive or negative emotions in the workplace. Affective events may similarly alter dyadic fit perceptions at work. Such influential affective incidents may include acts of kindness or insulting gestures that respectively spur "like" or "dislike" emotions and, in turn, can alter fit evaluations. For an individual to eventually make a fit judgment, he or she must first appraise the various cues in these events that have positive or negative signals of fit embedded within them (Beach, 1997; Ehrhart and Ziegert, 2005). These events are similar to those conveyed in the unfolding model (Lee and Mitchell, 1994) outlined in the turnover literature, which has revealed the impact that a "shock" or "a distinguishable event that jars employees toward deliberative judgments about their jobs" (p. 60) can have on turnover intentions and behavior. Notable "shock" events may also sway newcomer fit or misfit evaluations. Without the occurrence of such critical events, the new employee may never have known that the other party felt or thought differently than was expected or that he or she was capable of certain behaviors. These critical events may positively or negatively influence fit perceptions.

> Proposition 3: During the organizational socialization phase, positive affective events will enhance perceptions of dyadic supplementary fit, whereas negative affective events will enhance perceptions of dyadic misfit.

The organizational context may also influence the development of fit among new-comers and incumbent members of its workforce. Organizations that foster climates for cooperation and interdependence may encourage the development of friendships and instrumental cooperative relationships more than organizations with climates espousing norms of competition and independence. Similarly, these influences may also be manifest at the group level; team climates may also be characterized by help-fulness or by independence, which in turn facilitate or dissuade closer interpersonal bonds and fit evaluations. Although we again emphasize that person–group fit and dyadic fit are distinct phenomena, the literature demonstrating the importance of climates (e.g., Dirks, 2000; Tse *et al.*, 2008) on team processes suggests that social relationships can be affected by overarching climates. These increases in fit can come in terms of both better sharing of diverse sources of information and coordination of multiple distinct skills (complementary fit) as well as increases in shared goals (supplementary fit).

> Proposition 4: Organizational and team climates influence newcomers' dyadic fit per-ceptions such that newcomers in climates characterized by cooperation and interde-pendence will have stronger perceptions of both supplementary and complementary dyadic fit.

A final factor that will tend to enhance dyadic fit is the use of socialization tactics that encourage newcomers to interact frequently with established organizational members. In their model of organizational socialization, Van Maanen and Schein (1979) proposed that some organizations structured the socialization process to encourage newcomers to interact with those who were already successfully estab-lished in the organization. Organizations will sometimes deliberately place new recruits in situations that encourage them to actively engage with established or-ganizational members. Activities that enhance these interpersonal opportunities for newcomers include social events, parties, shared work assignments, and job shadowing programs. Chatman (1991) demonstrated that simply spending time with organizational insiders can increase perceptions of fit with the organization. However, because propinquity is one of the greatest correlates of liking (Nahe-mow and Powell, 1975; Segal, 1974), it is expected that higher levels of opportu-nity to interact with others will also increase perceptions of dyadic fit. Moreover, those who interact frequently as part of the socialization process will be better able to assess how to assist one another by learning one another's strengths and weaknesses. This means both supplementary and complementary fit evaluations will be enhanced.

> Proposition 5: Socialization tactics that encourage interaction with established organizational members will enhance supplementary and complementary dyadic fit perceptions.

Dyadic Fit and Interpersonal Processes

Having covered the chronological antecedents of dyadic relationship formation and their relationship with the concept of fit, we now turn our attention to the processes that arise as dyadic relationships develop and mature. These processes can have various effects: they can enhance the positive fit already established in the early acquaintanceship stage of a relationship, they can reduce misfit, or they can even result in a reversal of an initially good or poor relationship. It should be emphasized at this stage that we conceptualize person–environment fit as a dynamic process, so these processes are seen as mechanisms that increase or decrease perceptions of fit differently as relationships progress (Kammeyer-Mueller, 2007). This dynamic conceptualization is crucial for the interpersonal perspective on fit, because the nature of work relationships is progressive and develops in different phases or stages over time (Ferris *et al.*, 2009). It also implies that there will be reciprocal relationships between dyadic processes and fit as shown in Figure 3.1, as initial fit influences the processes that occur, which in turn will influence ongoing perceptions of fit. The five processes we will highlight in this section comprise *disclosure, social support, proactivity, exchanges of goods and services,* and *social undermining.*

Research on interpersonal relationships has repeatedly demonstrated that personal disclosure is the ultimate mechanism for enhancing social bonds between members of a communal relationship (Kelley *et al.*, 1983). Research has shown that self-disclosure is related to interpersonal attraction between individuals (Collins and Miller, 1994), relationship longevity (Hays, 1984), and perceived intimacy in relationships. Thus, an initial perception of supplementary fit is likely to enhance the degree to which individuals will disclose information to one another. At the same time, disclosure behaviors can enhance perceptions of fit. Disclosure is marked by providing others with potentially sensitive or revealing information about oneself, discussing controversial topics, and generally being open in interpersonal communications. Disclosure is such a fundamental part of the process of relationship development that Altman and Taylor (1973) placed it as the central variable in their social penetration theory. Processes of disclosure are an indicator of acceptance as well as a means of increasing the degree of perceived supplementary fit by emphasizing non-observable commonalities. Disclosure facilitates the ability of relationship partners to understand and interpret one another's actions (Barry and Crant, 2000). Further, there is evidence that self-disclosure is an interactive process, with relationship partners being satisfied only when there is mutual revelation of personally relevant information (Laurenceau *et al.*, 1998). We should note that those who exchange resources frequently may not engage in personal disclosure more often. These complementary fit relationships may be "strictly business."

> Proposition 6A: Increases in supplementary dyadic fit during socialization will be accompanied by increases in interpersonal disclosure.

> Proposition 6B: Increases in interpersonal disclosure during socialization will be accompanied by increases in supplementary dyadic fit.

Individuals who build positive relationships will do more than simply disclose information to one another; they will also give one another advice on how to solve problems, validate one another's points of view, and provide positive feedback. These active efforts to foster positive relationships are termed "social support" (Duffy *et al.*, 2002). Social support is different from disclosure in several important ways. Most significantly, social support involves actively working to reduce the level of stressors a fellow co-worker or team member may be experiencing. Meta-analysis shows that social support is an effective means of reducing stress at work (Karasek and Theorell, 1990; Viswesvaran *et al.*, 1999). Most research suggests that individuals are more likely to provide social support to friends and others with whom they share significant similarities (Ensher *et al.*, 2002; Wanberg *et al.*, 2006). Outside of organizational settings, researchers also frequently have examined social support as one of the most crucial benefits of interpersonal relationships (Gleason *et al.*, 2003). These relationship researchers further our understanding of support by demonstrating the dynamics of support in couples over time. This dynamic evidence shows that increases or decreases in social support closely mirror increases or decreases in stress and satisfaction levels for relationship partners. Again, social support is more likely to be a feature of affective relationships than exchange relationships.

> Proposition 7A: Increases in supplementary dyadic fit during socialization will be accompanied by increases in social support.

> Proposition 7B: Increases in social support during socialization will be accompanied by increases in supplementary dyadic fit.

Another category of activity that is likely to increase with greater dyadic fit, and also to enhance dyadic fit, is proactive information seeking. Socialization researchers have recognized that organizational programs to help newcomers fit into an organization and job cannot possibly cover all of the relevant knowledge required by newcomers. As a result, newcomers engage in proactive efforts to fit into their new jobs by seeking information, building relationships, reframing the situation, and independently consulting written organizational policies and procedures (e.g., Ashford and Black, 1996; Morrison, 1993; Ostroff and Kozlowski, 1993). Meta-analysis confirms that newcomer proactivity is among the most significant predictors of positive adjustment (Bauer *et al.*, 2007). However, it has also been noted that this information seeking comes with a price in terms of potential embarrassment, because asking a question is an acknowledgement of ignorance (Ashford and Northcraft, 1992). Individuals who feel like they have a strong dyadic fit with their co-workers will be less self-conscious about asking for information and advice. In addition, when newcomers see that there is a strong complementary relationship between their skills and abilities and the skills and abilities of a co-worker, they will also be more prone to engage in proactivity. As individuals become more proactive and their level of communication with co-workers increases, they will have more opportunities to discover similarities between one another, thereby enhancing supplementary fit. At the same time, those who interact frequently as a result of newcomer proactivity will learn how their abilities, knowledge, and skills can complement one another.

> Proposition 8A: Increases in supplementary and complementary dyadic fit during socialization will be accompanied by increases in newcomer proactivity.

> Proposition 8B: Increases in newcomer proactivity during socialization will be accompanied by increases in supplementary and complementary dyadic fit.

Exchanges of resources and services in instrumental relationships will build up the strength of the relationship over time based on norms of social exchange. Instrumental support is often provided in mentoring relationships. Prior research on leader–member exchange (Graen and Uhl-Bien, 1995) and co-worker exchange (Sherony and Green, 2002) has demonstrated that when individuals are in positive relationships, they will exchange favors with one another. These repeated instances of exchange require trust, which is generally developed over time as parties monitor one another's behavior (Pratt and Dirks, 2007). It should be noted, at the same time, that research suggests that in close relationships marked by communal orientation, relationship partners do not closely track inequalities in exchange (Clark and Mills, 1979). To the extent that relationship partners experience strong interpersonal ties, it is unlikely that formal reciprocity norms will dictate the ongoing status of the relationship. Instead, informal and unmonitored exchanges based on good faith and mutual cooperation will come to dominate. Even if not closely observed, this exchange of resources is the essence of the instrumental, complementary fit relationship.

> Proposition 9: Increases in complementary dyadic fit during socialization will be accompanied by increases in exchanges of resources and services between partners.

Undermining behaviors (Duffy *et al.*, 2002) are active efforts to hinder work-related success and make another person's life difficult, and represent a direct manifestation of dyadic misfit. Undermining is not just the opposite of social support; research in the relationships literature has repeatedly demonstrated that the two sets of behaviors are conceptually and empirically distinct (Finch *et al.*, 1989; Vinokur *et al.*, 1996). While a lack of fit might reduce social support, it probably takes real misfit to generate undermining behavior. Individuals who actively dislike one another are more likely to attempt to engage in direct signals of social disapproval such as rudeness, criticism, belittling, withheld support, reduced effort, or actively hindering others' work efforts (Bies and Tripp, 1996; Tripp and Bies, 1997). Similarly, Pearsson, Andersson, and Porath (2005) suggest that victims of negativity in the form of undermining may attempt to avoid the rude individual or may reduce effort, expended resources, and performance in the workplace. It is therefore clear that undermining resulting from dyadic misfit will be associated with negative outcomes. It also is apparent that when individuals have negative interactions with one another, they will come to see one another in more negative terms, setting in motion a reciprocal process of increasingly negative supplementary fit perceptions.

> Proposition 10A: Supplementary dyadic misfit between partners during the socialization phase will be accompanied by undermining behaviors between partners.

> Proposition 10B: Undermining behaviors between partners during the socialization phase will be accompanied by supplementary dyadic misfit between partners.

These process-oriented variables all highlight a fundamental reality in the development of dyadic fit: it takes time. Individuals neither immediately form close social bonds with others nor are they quick to form strong dislikes. Rather, the initial impressions formed during early acquaintanceship serve as a starting point for the subsequent socialization of individuals into their relationships. On a practical level, this means that researchers will need to examine relationship processes using dynamic data collection and analysis techniques. Weekly or monthly diary surveys of newcomers' experiences and reported fit perceptions provide one obvious mechanism for studying these processes as they unfold. Fortunately, the use of daily diary surveys is a mature topic within the relationship science literature (e.g., Gleason *et al.*, 2003), so researchers can turn to extant literature for guidance in how to conduct such studies in a rigorous manner.

Outcomes of Dyadic Fit in the Socialization Process

The final stage of the model described in Figure 3.1 is a set of expected outcomes of dyadic fit. Some of these outcomes, like retention and citizenship, have been examined previously in the fit literature. Our perspective is somewhat different in that we focus on the uniquely interpersonal nature of dyadic relationships as antecedents of these positive work outcomes. Less research on fit has examined how it can enhance learning over time (i.e., fit predicts not just levels of knowledge, but trajectories of knowledge). Further, to the best of our knowledge, the possibility that misfit will lead to interpersonal deviance has not been previously examined.

One of the most immediate and apparent consequences likely to follow from positive dyadic fit is an increase in one's level of positive affect (i.e., the state-level, situational experience of positive emotional states). The literature linking interpersonal relationships with positive affect is voluminous, and consistently demonstrates that interpersonal relationships are among the most substantial correlates of positive affect yet to be identified (e.g., Demir and Weitekamp, 2007; Diener and Seligman, 2002; Sprecher, 1999). It has been suggested that development of positive interpersonal relationships fulfills a fundamental human need which increases the extent to which individuals are able to experience emotions like happiness or joy. Other research has shown that positive interactions with co-workers involving social support and general helpfulness contribute to job satisfaction (e.g., Baruch-Feldman, Brondolo, Ben-Dayan, and Schwartz, 2002; Organ, 1988). Conversely, negative social relationships lead to a variety of negative emotional states, with poor social interactions ranking as one of the most stressful or negative experiences in most people's lives (e.g., August *et al.*, 2007; Rook, 2003). In fact, it has also been shown that the impact of interpersonal rejection is extremely physiologically similar to the experience of physical pain (Eisenberger *et al.*, 2003). Similarly, negative interactions involving rudeness, undermining, gossiping, or selfishness can impact stress levels and turnover cognitions of employees (e.g., Aquino *et al.*, 1997; Penney and Spector, 2005). Interpersonal misfit may therefore create extremely negative mood states for newcomers, including fear, anxiety, and sadness.

> Proposition 11: Newcomers with more positive supplementary dyadic fit relationships (i.e., communal relationships) will experience more positive affect at work, whereas newcomers with more dyadic misfit will experience more negative affect at work.

Social network development during the socialization process has been explored in some previous research, and knowledge acquisition accompanying an increase in social linkages provides one important outcome of interpersonal relationships at work. Newcomers with more extended friendship networks are more knowledgeable about the organization and are also more committed (Morrison, 2002). Individual mentor–mentee relationships for newcomers also facilitate learning (Ostroff and Kozlowski, 1993). Organizational programs to spread knowledge are not sufficient to give all the details newcomers might need – usually these formal, institutional programs cannot provide the context and nuance required to fully acquaint the newcomer with the complex history of the organization or its deeply embedded values. Conversely, co-workers and supervisors are in a unique position to establish interpersonal relationships that will allow them to frequently exchange information with newcomers as questions arise and new situations that help to illustrate organizational reality occur. As such, informal, dyadic transmission of information is likely one of the most important ways for newcomers to learn about what the organization is "really like."

> Proposition 12: Newcomers with better complementary fit relationships (i.e., exchange relationships) and supplementary fit relationships (i.e., communal relationships) will have more knowledge of the organization.

Retention is also likely to be affected by dyadic fit, because interpersonal relationships are a core component of the construct of job embeddedness (Mitchell *et al.*, 2001). Unlike other perspectives on fit and retention, there is no mediating process through organizational commitment, social exchange, or social identity concepts – the relationship itself and the emotional bond it creates are the direct antecedents of the decision to remain in the job. There is also ample evidence showing that interpersonal conflict is associated with increased turnover intentions, meaning that this form of dyadic misfit process leads to withdrawal and turnover intentions (e.g., Eby and Allen, 2002; Spector and Jex, 1998), as predicted by attraction–selection–attrition theory (Schneider, 1987). Mossholder, Settoon, and Henagan (2005) found that the more central an individual was in their social network, the less likely they were to turn over 5 years later. The unfolding model, which emphasizes the importance of discrete work events on employee turnover decisions, has also shown that employees often make dramatic, rapid decisions to quit on the basis of interpersonal conflicts, rather than making more rational, thought-out choices (Lee *et al.*, 1999). In fact, interpersonal conflicts may yield the most destructive types of turnover for organizational effectiveness, because conflicts lead to abrupt, unplanned turnover.

> Proposition 13: Newcomers with better supplementary dyadic fit relationships (i.e., communal relationships) will be less likely to turn over, whereas those with more misfit (i.e., animosity relationships) will be more likely to turn over.

It has been meta-analytically demonstrated that higher levels of person–organization fit are associated with higher levels of organizational citizenship behavior (Kristof-Brown *et al.*, 2005). In a similar manner, we expect that at the individual level there will also be a relationship between dyadic fit and interpersonal citizenship behavior (see Antonioni and Park, 2001). Dyadic fit and social relationships can lead to more frequent citizenship behavior because interpersonal communal relationships are seldom monetized or direct exchange oriented. The communal nature of these relationships translates to co-workers being more willing to unselfishly provide assistance even in situations in which there are no direct positive personal outcomes attached to behavior. Conversely, when poor relationships between co-workers exist, we expect that citizenship behavior will be especially low. Even the opportunity to initiate citizenship behavior in poor fit relationships will be low because individuals who have relationships marked by high levels of animosity will probably avoid one another.

> Proposition 14: Newcomers with better supplementary dyadic fit relationships (i.e., communal relationships) will engage in more interpersonal citizenship behavior directed toward the other member of the relationship, whereas those with more misfit (i.e., animosity relationships) will engage in less citizenship behavior.

Poor dyadic fit will lead to higher levels of interpersonal deviance. A feeling of generally low fit will probably lead to little more than apathy, but if misfit crosses the line into active animosity, more deliberately harmful actions are likely to result. This should be especially likely if individuals must, perforce, interact with each other in order to fulfill their own job responsibilities, and cannot choose avoidance as a coping mechanism to manage a dysfunctional relationship. Relationship scholars have frequently linked animosity with negative behaviors including aggression, victimization, and isolation (e.g., Card and Hodges, 2007; Parker and Gamm, 2003; Schwartz *et al.*, 2003). We would expect some of these same negative behaviors to surface when there is animosity in the workplace. Relationships that are marked by negative feelings may lead to increased levels of fighting, disrupting work for others, or decisions to withhold information. Prior research in the organizational domain has already demonstrated that high levels of supervisor undermining can lead to higher levels of active counterproductive behaviors (Duffy *et al.*, 2002). Interpersonal conflict is also one of the most substantial predictors of interpersonal aggression in work settings (Herschcovis *et al.*, 2007).

> Proposition 15: Newcomers with supplementary dyadic misfit relationships will engage in (and will be the recipients of) more interpersonal deviance.

High dyadic fit may lead to increased resiliency between the individuals participating in the relationship. Resiliency can be defined as "the capacity to rebound or bounce back from adversity, conflict, or failure" (Luthans, 2002, p. 702). We should expect that the mutual support and positive affect that is fostered over time in the close social bonds with intimate supplementary fit creates a buffer in which individuals can weather, or bounce back from, negative events occurring outside of the relationship (Luthans *et al.*, 2007). The negative feelings associated with challenges or hardships at work, including organizational stressors, job demands, intra-team conflict, or, more proximally, frictions with other co-workers, may be counterbalanced by the positive feelings created in a communal relationship. For example, for a team working on a project in which task and relationship conflict increase to the point of becoming a hindrance (De Dreu and Weingart, 2003), the high dyadic fit between two team members may serve as a "bubble" to shield them from absorbing the strain that would normally accompany such conflict. Thus, a byproduct of these fit relationships would include someone feeling a mutual responsibility for the experiences of their co-worker or team member – an "at least we have each other" mentality.

> Proposition 16: Newcomers with better supplementary dyadic fit relationships (i.e., communal relationships) will be more resilient to negative experiences occurring outside of the dyad.

It is also worth considering the implications of dyadic fit as it relates to group or team outcomes. Despite the positive benefits of resiliency, one negative repercussion of increasing interpersonal supplementary fit during socialization into new work groups may be the creation of faultlines (Lau and Murnighan, 2005) arising from surface- or deep-level differences. Faultlines are hypothetical dividers which give rise to subgroups existing within the larger team (Lau and Murnighan, 2005). Faultlines may be strong or weak depending on the number of demographic or other similarities that the subgroup has in common yet other members outside of the subgroup do not possess. For example, if two members of a five-person team are both young African-American women, and the other three members of the team are middle-aged Caucasian men, a strong faultline is said to exist within the group. As supplementary fit becomes very high (i.e., two team members are similar with respect to a large number of characteristics), these dyads may effectively close themselves off from the rest of the team; consequently, communication flows external to this subgroup may be impeded. Thus, we expect a moderated relationship between dyadic fit and team outcomes: increased supplementary fit between two individuals should lead to smoother interactions, increased satisfaction, and generally positive outcomes; however, if faultlines are created, this relationship will decline and eventually become negative as extreme levels of fit between two co-workers create a barrier in which the relationships with the larger team and broader team outcomes such as cohesion, communication, and performance are negatively impacted.

> Proposition 17: As individuals are socialized into a new work group or team, the association between supplementary dyadic fit (i.e., communal relationships) and group outcomes will be positive, unless fit creates faultlines that obstruct the flow of communication processes among members.

Summary

This chapter has demonstrated just a few of the ways that understanding dyadic fit can inform our understanding of how individuals come to be socialized into a new job. Our research has drawn on concepts from relationship science, person–environment fit, and organizational socialization. First, we developed a typology of three main types of workplace relationships: those based on friendship that arise due to supplementary fit, those based on instrumental exchange that arise due to complementary fit, and those based on animosity that arise due to exceptionally poor overall fit. We argued that surface- and deep-level similarity, positive affective events, a climate for cooperation and high cohesion, and socialization tactics that enhance propinquity all set the stage for increasing newcomer–incumbent dyadic fit. As a result of these initial processes, newcomers who achieve positive dyadic fit will experience higher levels of interpersonal disclosure, social support, higher proactive attempts to fit with the organization, exchanges of resources, and lower undermining. Finally, dyadic fit will result in several operationally important outcomes including positive affect at work, improved information exchange, lower turnover, increased interpersonal citizenship, reduced interpersonal deviance, and increased resiliency, as well as potential team outcomes.

One clear implication of the interpersonal perspective on socialization is the need for new methodological approaches that accurately capture the dynamic and interactive nature of this process (Ferris *et al.*, 2009). Many interpersonal processes and relationships have mostly been investigated from the perspective of one partner in the relationship, as exemplified by leadership research that only looks at the perspective of followers, mentoring research that only examines the perspective of the protégé, or socialization research that only examines the perspective of the newcomer. Research on dyadic fit would be well advised to see how leaders and followers, mentors and protégés, and newcomers and established employees react to one another. As we have noted previously, designs incorporating change over time, including longitudinal approaches or event history analysis (Allison, 1984), will also be needed to investigate the growth of relationships over time.

Another area for research is an examination of exactly who it is that newcomers form important dyadic relationships with. The relationship with the supervisor is likely to be a critical dyadic relationship, but it is also likely to be a relationship that often has a very different set of characteristics relative to relationships with one's peers. It will be interesting to see if newcomers strive to form these more equal dyadic relationships with those in the immediate social environment, or if some workers seek out those who perform quite different types of task but with whom they have much in common. Further, in a large and informal organizational environment in which newcomers may need to proactively socialize themselves, it may be valuable to explore which types of incumbent employee newcomers tend to seek out in terms of their personality dispositions (e.g., highly extroverted or agreeable individuals may quickly capture newcomers' attention) or respective organizational network positions (i.e., network centrality). Subsequently, we will want to assess how these individuals influence the speed and efficacy with which newcomers are socially and instrumentally integrated. In sum, research needs to establish just who these critical others are likely to be.

Although this call for greater attention to dyadic fit is being covered in a book summarizing other fit theories, our development is at least as important for informing future research on organizational socialization. Socialization research has long been concerned with the extent to which newcomers are socially accepted by members of their work group. As we noted in the introduction, though, fitting in with the group as a whole is quite different from fitting in with a specific individual. Future research in the socialization literature should consider variables like supervisor and co-worker support and undermining, and how, over time, these constructs relate to the emergence of fit beliefs.

References

Allison, P. D. (1984) *Event History Analysis: Regression for Longitudinal Event Data, Issues 7–46*. Newbury Park, CA: Sage Publications.

Altman, I., and Taylor, D. (1973) *Social Penetration: The Development of Interpersonal Relationships*. New York: Holt, Rinehart and Winston.

Antonioni, D., and Park, H. (2001) The effects of personality similarity on peer ratings of contextual work behaviors. *Personnel Psychology*, 54, 331–360.

Aquino, K., Griffeth, R. W., Allen, D. G., and Hom, P. W. (1997) Integrating justice constructs into the turnover process: A test of a referent cognitions model, *Academy of Management Journal*, 40, 1208–1227.

Ashford, S. J., and Black, J. S. (1996) Proactivity during organizational entry: Antecedents, tactics, and outcomes. *Journal of Applied Psychology*, 81, 199–214.

Ashford, S. J., and Northcraft, G. B. (1992) Conveying more (or less) than we realize: The role of impression-management in feedback-seeking. *Organizational Behavior and Human Decision Processes*, 53, 310–334.

August, K. J., Rook, K. S., and Newsom, J. T. (2007) The joint effects of life stress and negative social exchanges on emotional distress. *Journal of Gerontology Series B: Psychological Sciences*, 62, S304–S314.

Barry, B., and Crant, J. M. (2000) Dyadic communication relationships in organizations: An attribution/expectancy approach. *Organization Science*, 11, 648–664.

Baruch-Feldman, C., Brondolo, E., Ben-Dayan, D., and Schwartz, J. (2002) Sources of social support and burnout, job satisfaction, and productivity. *Journal of Occupational Health Psychology*, 7, 84–93.

Bauer, T. N., Bodner, T., Erdogan, B., Truxillo, D. M., and Tucker, J. S. (2007) Newcomer adjustment during organizational socialization: A meta-analytic review of antecedents, outcomes, and methods. *Journal of Applied Psychology*, 92 (3), 707–721.

Baumeister, R. F., Bratslavsky, E, Finkenauer, C., and Vohs, K. D. (2001) Bad is stronger than good. *Review of General Psychology*, 5, 323–370.

Beach, L. R. (1997) *The Psychology of Decision Making: People in Organizations*. Thousand Oaks, CA: Sage.

Berscheid, E. (1999) The greening of relationship science. *American Psychologist*, 54, 260–266.

Bies, R. J., and Tripp, T. M. (1996) Beyond distrust: Getting even and the need for revenge. In R. M. Kramer and T. R. Tyler (eds), *Trust in Organizations: Frontiers of Theory and Research* (pp. 246–60). Thousand Oaks, CA: Sage.

Cable, D. M., and Edwards, J. R. (2004) Complementary and supplementary fit: A theoretical and empirical integration. *Journal of Applied Psychology*, 89, 822–834.

Card, N. A., and Hodges, E. V. E. (2007) Victimization within mutually antipathetic peer relationships. *Social Development*, 16, 479–496.

Chatman, J. A. (1991) Matching people and organizations: Selection and socialization in public accounting firms. *Administrative Science Quarterly*, 36 (3), 459–484.

Clark, M. S., and Mills, J. (1979) Interpersonal attraction in exchange and communal relationships. *Journal of Personality and Social Psychology*, 37, 12–24.

Collins, N. L., and Miller, L. C. (1994) Self-disclosure and liking: A meta-analytic review, *Psychological Bulletin*, 116, 457–475.

De Dreu, C. K. W., and Weingart, L. R. (2003) Task versus relationship conflict, team performance, and team member satisfaction: A meta-analysis. *Journal of Applied Psychology*, 88, 741–749.

Demir, M., and Weitekamp, L. A. (2007) I am so happy cause today I found my friend: Friendship and personality as predictors of happiness. *Journal of Happiness Studies*, 8, 181–211.

Diener, E., and Seligman, M. E. P. (2002) Very happy people. *Psychological Science*, 13, 81–84.

Dirks, K. T. (2000) Trust in leadership and team performance: Evidence from NCAA basketball. *Journal of Applied Psychology*, 6, 1004–1012.

Duffy, M. K., Ganster, D. C., and Pagon, M. (2002) Social undermining in the workplace. *Academy of Management Journal*, 45, 331–351.

Eagly, A. H., Ashmore, R. D., Makhijani, M. G., and Longo, L. C. (1991) What is beautiful is good, but . . .: A meta-analytic review of research on the physical attractiveness stereotype. *Psychological Bulletin*, 110, 109–128.

Eby, L. T., and Allen, T. D. (2002) Further investigation of protégés' negative mentoring experiences: Patterns and outcomes, *Group and Organization Management*, 27, 456–479.

Ehrhart, K. H., and Ziegert, J. C. (2005) Why are individuals attracted to organizations? *Journal of Management*, 31, 901–919.

Eisenberger, N. I., Lieberman, M. D., and Williams, K. D. (2003) Does rejection hurt? An fMRI study of social exclusion. *Science*, 302, 290–292.

Ensher, E.A., Grant-Vallone, E. J., and Marelich, W. D. (2002) Effects of perceived attitudinal and demographic similarity on protégés' support and satisfaction gained from their mentoring relationships. *Journal of Applied Social Psychology*, 32, 1407–1430.

Fehr, B. (1996) *Friendship Processes*. Thousand Oaks, CA: Sage.

Felps, W. A., Mitchell, T. R., and Byington, E. K. (2006) How, when and why bad apples spoil the barrel: Negative group members and dysfunctional groups. *Research in Organizational Behavior*, 27, 181–230.

Ferris, G. R., Liden, T. P., Munyon, T. P., Summers, J. K., Basik, K. J., and Buckley, M. R. (2009) Relationships at work: Toward a multidimensional conceptualization of dyadic work relationships. *Journal of Management*, 35, 1379–1403.

Finch, J., Okun, J. A., Barrera, M., Zautra, A., and Reich, J. W. (1989) Positive and negative social ties among older adults: Measurement models and the prediction of psychological distress and well-being. *American Journal of Community Psychology*, 17, 585– 605.

Gersick, C. J. G., Bartunek, J. M., and Dutton, J. E. (2000) Learning from academia: The importance of relationships in professional life. *Academy of Management Journal*, 43, 1026–1044.

Gleason, M. E. J., Iida, M., Bolger, N., and Shrout, P. E. (2003) Daily supportive equity in close relationships. *Personality and Social Psychology Bulletin*, 29, 1036–1045.

Gonzales, M. H, Aronson, E., and Costanzo, M. (1983) Interactional approach to interpersonal attraction. *Journal of Personality and Social Psychology*, 44, 1192–1197.

Graen, G. B., and Uhl-Bien, M. (1995) Relationship-based approach to leadership: Development of leader–member exchange (LMX) theory of leadership over 25 years: Applying a multi-level multi-domain perspective. *Leadership Quarterly*, 6, 219–247.

Harrison, D. A., Price, K. H., and Bell, M. P. (1998) Beyond relational demography: Time and the effects of surface- and deep-level diversity on work group cohesion. *Academy of Management Journal*, 41, 96–107.

Harrison, D. A., Price, K. H., Gavin, J. H., and Florey, A. T. (2002) Time, teams, and task performance: Changing effects of surface- and deep-level diversity on group functioning. *Academy of Management Journal*, 45, 1029–1045.

Hays, R. B. (1984) The development and maintenance of friendship. *Journal of Social and Personal Relationships*, 1, 75–98.

Hays, R. B. (1985) A longitudinal study of friendship development. *Journal of Personality and Social Psychology*, 48, 909–924.

Hershcovis, M. S., Turner, N., Barling, J., Arnold, K. A., Dupré, K. E., Inness, M., *et al.* (2007) Predicting workplace aggression: A meta-analysis. *Journal of Applied Psychology*, 92 (1), 228–238.

Ibarra, H., Kilduff, M., and Tsai, W. (2005) Zooming in and out: Connecting individuals and collectivities at the frontiers of organizational network research. *Organization Science*, 16, 359–371.

Judge, T. A., and Ferris, G. R. (1992) The elusive criterion of fit in human resources staffing decisions. *Human Resource Planning*, 15, 217–231.

Kammeyer-Mueller, J. D. (2007) The dynamics of newcomer adjustment: Dispositions, context, interaction, and fit. In C. Ostroff and T. Judge (eds), *Perspectives on Organizational Fit* (pp. 99–122). Greenwich: CT: Information Age Publishing.

Kammeyer-Mueller, J. D., and Wanberg, C. R. (2003) Unwrapping the organizational entry process: Disentangling multiple antecedents and their pathways to adjustment. *Journal of Applied Psychology*, 88, 779–794.

Karasek, R. A., and Theorell, T. (1990) *Healthy Work: Stress, Productivity, and the Reconstruction of Working Life*. New York: Basic Books.

Kelley, H. H., Berscheid, E., Christensen, A., Harvey, J. H., Huston, T. L., Levinger, G., McClintock, E., Peplau, L. A., and Peterson, D. R. (1983) Analyzing close relationships. In H. H. Kelley, E. Berscheid, A. Christensen, J. H. Harvey, T. L. Huston, G. Levinger, E. McClintock, L. A. Peplau, and D. R. Peterson (eds), *Close Relationships* (pp. 20–67). New York: W. H. Freeman.

Kristof, A. L. (1996) Person–organization fit: An integrative review of its conceptualizations, measurement and implications, *Personnel Psychology*, 49 (1), 1–49.

Kristof-Brown, A. L., Barrick, M. R., and Stevens, C. K. (2005) When opposites attract: A multi-sample demonstration of complementary person–team fit on extraversion. *Journal of Personality*, 73, 935–957.

Kristof-Brown, A. L., Zimmerman, R. D., and Johnson, E. C. (2005) Consequences of individuals' fit at work: A meta-analysis of person–job, person–organization, person–supervisor, and person–group fit. *Personnel Psychology*, 58, 281–342.

Labianca, G., and Brass, D. J. (2006) Exploring the social ledger: Negative relationships and negative asymmetry in social networks in organizations. *Academy of Management Review*, 31, 596–614.

Labianca, G., Brass, D. J., and Gray, B. (1998) Social networks and perceptions of intergroup conflict: The role of negative relationships and third parties. *Academy of Management Journal*, 41 (1), 55–67.

Lau, D. C., and Murnighan, J. K. (2005) Interactions within groups and subgroups: The effects of demographic faultlines. *Academy of Management Journal*, 48, 645–659.

Laurenceau, J., Barrett, L. F., and Pietromonaco, P. R. (1998) Intimacy as an interpersonal process: The importance of self-disclosure, partner disclosure, and perceived partner responsiveness in interpersonal exchanges. *Journal of Personality and Social Psychology*, 74, 1238–1251.

Lee, T. W., and Mitchell, T. R. (1994) An alternative approach: The unfolding model of voluntary employee turnover. *Academy of Management Review*, 19 (1), 51–89.

Lee, T. W., Mitchell, T. R., Holtom, B. C., McDaniel, L. S., and Hill, J. W. (1999) The unfolding model of voluntary turnover: A replication and extension. *Academy of Management Journal*, 42, 450–462.

Luthans, F. (2002) The need for and meaning of positive organizational behavior. *Journal of Organizational Behavior*, 23, 695–706.

Luthans, F., Youssef, C. M., and Avolio, B. J. (2007) *Psychological Capital: Developing the Human Competitive Advantage*. New York: Oxford University Press.

Mills, J., and Clark, M. S. (1994) Communal and exchange relationships: Controversies and research. In R. Erber and R. Gilmour (eds), *Theoretical Frameworks for Personal Relationships* (pp. 29–42). Hillsdale, NJ: Lawrence Erlbaum.

Mitchell, T. R., Holtom, B. C., Lee, T. W., Sablynski, C. J., and Erez, M. (2001) Why people stay: Using job embeddedness to predict voluntary turnover. *Academy of Management Journal*, 44, 1102–1121.

Morgeson, F. P., and Hofmann, D. A. (1999) The structure and function of collective constructs: Implications for multilevel research and theory development, *Academy of Management Review*, 24 (2), 249–265.

Morrison, E. W. (1993) Longitudinal study on the effects of information seeking on newcomer socialization. *Journal of Applied Psychology*, 78, 173–183.

Morrison, E. W. (2002) Newcomers' relationships: The role of social networks during socialization. *Academy of Management Journal*, 45, 1149–1160.

Mossholder, K. W., Settoon, R. P., and Henagan, S. C. (2005) A relational perspective on turnover: Examining structural, attitudinal, and behavioral predictors. *Academy of Management Journal*, 48, 607–618.

Muchinsky, P. M., and Monahan, C. J. (1987) What is person–environment congruence? Supplementary versus complementary models of fit. *Journal of Vocational Behavior*, 31, 268–277.

Nahemow, L., and Powell, L. M. (1975) Similarity and propinquity in friendship formation. *Journal of Personality and Social Psychology*, 32, 205–213.

Nebus, J. (2006) Building collegial information networks: A theory of advice network generation. *Academy of Management Review*, 31, 615–637.

O'Connell, L. (1984) An exploration of exchange in three social relationships: Kinship, friendship, and marketplace. *Journal of Personal and Social Relationships*, 1, 333–345.

Organ, D. W. (1988) *The Good Soldier Syndrome*. Lexington, MA: Lexington Books/DC Heath.

Ostroff, C., and Kozlowski, S. W. (1992) Organizational socialization as a learning process: The role of information acquisition. *Personnel Psychology*, 45, 849–874.

Ostroff, C., and Kozlowski, S. W. (1993) The role of mentoring in the information gathering processes of newcomers during early organizational socialization. *Journal of Vocational Behavior*, 42, 170–183.

Parker, J. G., and Gamm, B. K. (2003) Describing the dark side of preadolescents' peer experiences: Four questions (and data) on preadolescents' enemies. In E. V. E. Hodges and N. A. Card (eds), *Enemies and the Darker Side of Peer Relations: New Directions for Child and Adolescent Development* (Vol. 102, pp. 55–72). San Francisco, CA: Jossey-Bass.

Pearsson, C. M., Andersson, L. M., and Porath, C. L. (2005) Workplace incivility. In S. Fox and P. E. Spector (eds), *Counterproductive Work Behavior: Investigations of Actors and Targets* (pp. 177–200). Washington, DC: American Psychological Association.

Penney, L. M., and Spector, P. E. (2005) Job stress, incivility, and counterproductive work behavior (CWB): The moderating role of negative affectivity, *Journal of Organizational Behavior*, 26, 777–796.

Piasentin, K. A., and Chapman, D. S. (2007) Perceived similarity and complementarity as predictors of subjective person–organization fit. *Journal of Occupational and Organizational Psychology*, 80, 341–354.

Poteat, L. F., Shockley, K. M., and Allen, T. D. (2009) Mentor–protégé commitment fit and relationship satisfaction in academic mentoring. *Journal of Vocational Behavior*, 74, 332–337.

Pratt, M. G., and Dirks, K. T. (2007) Rebuilding trust and restoring positive relationships: A commitment based view of trust. In J. E. Dutton and B. R. Ragins (eds), *Exploring Positive Relationships at Work* (pp. 117–136). Mahwah, NJ: Lawrence Erlbaum.

Ragins, B. R., and Dutton, J. E. (2007) Positive relationships at work: An introduction and invitation. In J. E. Dutton and B. R. Ragins (eds), *Exploring Positive Relationships at Work: Building a Theoretical and Research Foundation* (pp. 1–25). Mahwah, NJ: Lawrence Erlbaum.

Reichers, A. E. (1987) An interactionist perspective on newcomer socialization rates. *Academy of Management Review*, 12, 278–287.

Reis, H. T., Lin, Y., Bennett, E. M., and Nezlek, J. B. (1993) Change and consistency in social participation during early adulthood, *Developmental Psychology*, 29, 633–645.

Rook, K. S. (2003) Exposure and reactivity to negative social exchanges: A preliminary investigation using daily diary data. *Journal of Gerentology Series B: Psychological Science*, 58, 100–111.

Saks, A. M., and Ashforth, B. E. (1997) Organizational socialization: Making sense of the past and present as a prologue for the future. *Journal of Vocational Behavior*, 51, 234–279.

Schaubroeck, J., and Lam, S. S. K. (2002) How similarity to peers and supervisor influences organizational advancement in different cultures. *Academy of Management Journal*, 45, 1120–1136.

Schneider, B. (1987) The people make the place. *Personnel Psychology*, 40, 437–453.

Schwartz, D., Hopmeyer Gorman, A. H., Toblin, R. L., and Abou-ezzedine, T. (2003) Mutual antipathies in the peer group as a moderating factor in the association between community violence exposure and psychosocial maladjustment. In E. V. E. Hodges and N. A. Card (eds), *Enemies and the Darker Side of Peer Relations: New Directions for Child and Adolescent Development* (Vol. 102, pp. 39–54). San Francisco, CA: Jossey-Bass.

Segal, M. W. (1974) Alphabet and attraction: An unobtrusive measure of the effect of propinquity in a field setting. *Journal of Personality and Social Psychology*, 30, 654–657.

Sherony, K. M., and Green, S. G. (2002) Coworker exchange: Relationships between coworkers, leader–member exchange, and work attitudes. *Journal of Applied Psychology*, 87, 542–548.

Shoda, Y., Mischel, W., and Wright, J. C. (1994) Intraindividual stability in the organization and patterning of behavior: Incorporating psychological situations into the idiographic analysis of personality. *Journal of Personality and Social Psychology*, 67, 674–687.

Snyder, M., Berscheid, E., and Glick, P. (1985) Focusing on the exterior and the interior: Two investigations of the initiation of personal relationships. *Journal of Personality and Social Psychology*, 48, 1427–1439.

Spector, P. E., and Jex, S. M. (1998) Development of four self-report measures of job stressors and strain: Interpersonal Conflict at Work Scale, Organizational Constraints Scale, Quantitative Workload Inventory, and Physical Symptoms Inventory. *Journal of Occupational Health Psychology*, 3, 356–367.

Sprecher, S. (1999) "I love you more today than yesterday": Romantic partners' perceptions of changes in love and related affect over time. *Journal of Personality and Social Psychology*, 76, 46–53.

Tripp, T. M., and Bies, R. J. (1997) What's good about revenge? The avenger's perspective. In R. J. Lewicki, R. J. Bies, and B.H. Sheppard (eds), *Research on Negotiation in Organizations* (Vol. 6, pp. 145–160). Greenwich, CT: JAI Press.

Tse, H. H. M., Dasborough, M. T., and Ashkanasy, N. M. (2008) A multi-level analysis of team climate and interpersonal exchange relationships at work. *Leadership Quarterly*, 19, 195–211.

Van Maanen, J., and Schein, E. H. (1979) Toward a theory of organizational socialization. In B. M. Staw (ed.), *Research in Organizational Behavior* (Vol. 1, pp. 209–264). Greenwich, CT: JAI Press.

Vinokur, A. D., Price, R., and Caplan, R. (1996) Hard times and hurtful partners: How financial strain affects depression and relationship satisfaction of unemployed persons and their spouses. *Journal of Personality and Social Psychology*, 71, 166–179.

Viswesvaran, C., Sanchez, J. I., and Fisher, J. (1999) The role of social support in the process of work stress: A meta-analysis. *Journal of Vocational Behavior*, 54, 314–334.

Wanberg, C. R., Kammeyer-Mueller, J., and Marchese, M. (2006) Mentor and protégé predictors and outcomes of mentoring in a formal mentoring program. *Journal of Vocational Behavior*, 69, 410–423.

Wanous, J. P. (1992) *Organizational Entry: Recruitment, Selection, Orientation, and Socialization of Newcomers*. Reading, MA: Addison-Wesley.

Weiss, H. M., and Cropanzano, R. (1996) Affective events theory: A theoretical discussion of the structure, causes and consequences of affective experiences at work. In B. M. Staw and L. L. Cummings (eds), *Research in Organization Behavior: An Annual Series of Analytical Essays and Critical Reviews* (Vol. 18, pp. 1–74). Greenwich, CT: JAI Press.

Witt, L. A. (1998) Enhancing organizational goal congruence: A solution to organizational politics. *Journal of Applied Psychology*, 83, 666–674.

Woodside, A. G., and Davenport, J. W. (1974) Effects of salesman similarity and expertise on consumer purchasing behavior. *Journal of Marketing Research*, 11, 198–202.

Zalesny, M. D., and Ford, J. K. (1990) Extending the social information processing perspective: New links to attitudes, behaviors, and perceptions. *Organizational Behavior and Human Decision Processes*, 47, 205–246.

4

A Self-Regulation Approach to Person–Environment Fit

Russell E. Johnson
Department of Management, Michigan State University

Meng U. Taing
Department of Psychology, University of South Florida

Chu-Hsiang Chang
Department of Psychology, Michigan State University

Cristina K. Kawamoto
Department of Psychology, University of South Florida

Person–environment (PE) fit refers to the compatibility between ideal aspects and experienced aspects of people's external environment (Edwards, 1991; Kristof, 1996).[1] Typically, when fit exists, employees report more favorable attitudes, experience greater well-being, and perform more effectively (Hoffman and Woehr, 2006; Kristof-Brown *et al.*, 2005; Verquer, Beehr, and Wagner, 2003). Much of the attention in the PE fit literature has revolved around how fit is conceptualized (e.g., supplementary versus complementary fit) and measured (e.g., direct versus indirect measures; Billsberry *et al.*, 2005; Edwards *et al.*, 2006; Muchinsky and Monahan, 1987). Although this research has advanced our understanding of the phenomenon of PE fit, additional theory is needed to better understand why the extent to which workers fit with their environment predicts their attitudes, behavior, and well-being. Employees are motivated to attain a sufficient level of fit and they regulate their cognition and behavior in order to do so (Latham and Pinder, 2005). Despite this motivation to attain fit, there have been relatively few attempts to integrate the concept of PE fit with contemporary theories of self-regulation (for exceptions, see Edwards, 1992, and French *et al.*, 1982). This lack of integration is unfortunate because

Organizational Fit: Key Issues and New Directions, First Edition.
Edited by Amy L. Kristof-Brown and Jon Billsberry.
© 2013 John Wiley & Sons, Ltd. Published 2013 by John Wiley & Sons, Ltd.

understanding how PE fit "fits" within the broader context of employee self-regulation helps bridge current gaps in PE fit theory as well as identify promising directions for future research. In this chapter we draw attention to the parallels between theories of self-regulation and PE fit. It is our belief that self-regulation theories, which explain why discrepancies between desired conditions and experienced conditions influence affect, cognition, and behavior (Austin and Vancouver, 1996; Bandura, 1986; Carver and Scheier, 1998; Johnson, Chang, and Lord, 2006), can be leveraged to advance PE fit theory.

Theories of self-regulation, which at their core involve goal-related processes, are a leading paradigm for understanding employee behavior (Latham and Pinder, 2005; Lord *et al.*, 2010). According to these theories, people are motivated to reduce discrepancies between ideal or goal conditions and experienced conditions (Miller *et al.*, 1960; Newell *et al.*, 1958). In fact, dedicated neurological structures in humans have evolved for the purpose of comparing incoming information from the environment with ideal or expected mental representations in memory (Gehring *et al.*, 1993; Stuss, 1991). For example, the hippocampus, a part of the limbic system located in the medial frontal lobe, operates as a comparator that monitors for discrepancies between incoming sensory information and information stored in memory (Vinogradova, 1975). The septo-hippocampal circuit is activated when a discrepancy is detected, which then directs people's attention toward the source of the discrepancy and elicits avoidance-oriented motivations aimed at resolving the discrepancy. In cases where discrepancies exist, such as when employees desire high levels of job autonomy yet perceive very little autonomy, people are motivated to take corrective action in order to reduce these differences. The motivational force elicited by a discrepancy is channeled into changing the experienced condition (e.g., demanding more autonomy from one's supervisor or pursuing a more autonomous job elsewhere) or changing the ideal condition (e.g., reducing the value placed on job autonomy) in an attempt to reduce the discrepancy. Ideal–experienced discrepancies also influence affect and attitudes (Bandura, 1986; Carver and Scheier, 1998). For example, job satisfaction depends in part on what employees need or value and what their job actually provides them, such that smaller ideal–experienced discrepancies produce higher job satisfaction (Hackman and Oldham, 1976; Locke, 1976).

Our central thesis is that PE fit can be conceptualized as a discrepancy between people's ideal conditions, which are derived from their own needs and values, and experienced conditions, which are based on perceptions of their environment. Take, for example, a situation where job applicants decide whether or not to apply to a particular company based on person–organization ethical fit (see Coldwell *et al.*, 2008). In this example, applicants compare their ideal standards for ethical behavior to their experienced levels of the company's corporate responsibility in order to judge the extent to which fit exists between the two. Other instances of PE fit can be similarly framed as ideal–experienced discrepancies (see Edwards, 1992; French *et al.*, 1982). In the sections below we first provide an overview of the goal-based process of self-regulation and then specify how this process can be applied to PE fit. Given what we know about human self-regulation, the remainder of this chapter is devoted to discussing three key implications of self-regulation theory for PE fit theory. These implications concern the hierarchical organization of different bases of PE fit, changes in PE fit over time, and motivation-based individual differences that may moderate the effects of PE fit on its outcomes.

Theories of Self-Regulation

Self-regulation refers to the motivation-based processes that underlie goal-directed behavior (Carver and Scheier, 1998; Kanfer, 1990; Lord et al., 2010). Central to all theories of self-regulation is the important role played by goals (i.e., internal representations of desired conditions; Austin and Vancouver, 1996), which give meaning to people's behavior and guide the allocation of their time and effort (Bandura, 1986; Carver and Scheier, 1998; Locke and Latham, 1990). The process begins with deliberating over what goals to pursue, followed by planning and taking action once goals are established, and then evaluating progress towards those goals. This may require that people revise their plans, actions, or goals when discrepancies exist between ideal and experienced conditions (Austin and Vancouver, 1996; Bandura, 2001; Gollwitzer, 1990). Most relevant to PE fit theory is the goal-striving portion of this process, during which people compare ideal and experienced conditions and modify behavior and/or cognition when the two are discrepant (French et al., 1982).

The goal-striving process can be explained as a negative feedback loop comprising five elements: an input function, a standard, a comparator, an output function, and a disturbance (Carver and Scheier, 1998; Klein, 1989; Lord et al., 2010; Vancouver, 2005). The *input function* senses information from the external environment and brings it into the feedback loop. The *standard* (or goal) represents an ideal condition that is actively sustained by the system. The *comparator* engages in self-evaluative activities that assess the sensed environment (from the input function) vis-à-vis the standard to determine whether a discrepancy exists between them. When there is little or no difference, no action is taken to alter the input or standard. However, when a discrepancy is detected, the *output function* engages in corrective self-reactions in order to bring the input in line with the standard. The motivation to act derives from the presence of discrepancies between ideal and experienced states. Discrepancies are reduced using one of two tactics. The output function may target the external environment in order to alter the perceived input, or it may alter the ideal standard. For example, when perceived performance levels fall below the standard in achievement domains, people typically respond by increasing their effort in an attempt to change the input (i.e., to increase their performance; Kernan and Lord, 1990). If discrepancies remain stable despite increased efforts, people may eventually opt to reduce the standard instead (i.e., set easier achievement goals; Donovan and Williams, 2003). It is important to note

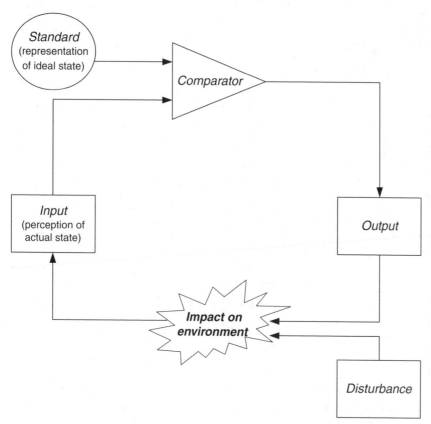

Figure 4.1 Negative feedback loop

that inputs (e.g., performance levels) are affected not only by the output functions (e.g., changes in effort) but also by external influences that exist outside the feedback system (e.g., equipment failure, assistance from other people). The *disturbance* represents these external influences. A negative feedback loop is illustrated in Figure 4.1.

Self-regulation theories also propose that standards and their respective feedback loops are organized hierarchically (Austin and Vancouver, 1996; Carver and Scheier, 1998; Cropanzano *et al.*, 1993; Johnson *et al.*, 2006; Lord and Levy, 1994; Powers, 1973). At the top of the hierarchy are long-term, abstract standards that are central to people's self-concepts. Examples of these standards include basic values (e.g., benevolence and achievement; see Schwartz, 1992) and "be" goals (e.g., the desire to be a good person or a successful person). In contrast, the standards at lower levels in the hierarchy are short-term ones that reference specific behaviors or tasks. Examples of these standards include personal projects and "do" goals (e.g., the desire to give money to charity or be promoted at work). Although standards exist at different levels, they are interrelated because the output of a high-level

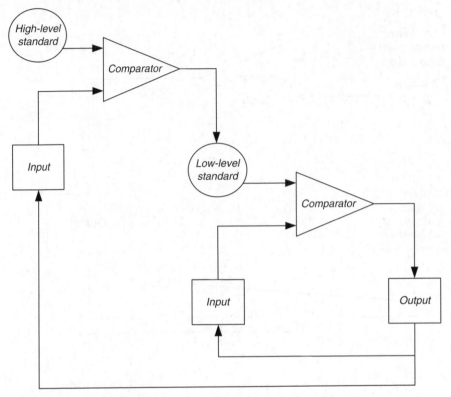

Figure 4.2   Hierarchical organization of two negative feedback loops

feedback loop sets the standards in the feedback loops below it. For example, when discrepancies are detected for high-level "be" goals (e.g., being a successful employee), "do" goals aimed at resolving these discrepancies are established at lower levels (e.g., finishing a work project or exceeding a sales quota). When the standards at lower levels are met, this information then serves as input at higher levels. Striving for lower-level standards is therefore the means by which higher-level standards are attained, and reaching lower-level standards helps reduce ideal–experienced discrepancies at higher levels (Lord and Levy, 1994). Depicted in Figure 4.2 is a hierarchy consisting of two feedback loops. Having reviewed how ideal–experienced discrepancies function within a system of interconnected negative feedback loops, we now describe how this framework can be applied to PE fit theory.

Viewing PE Fit within a Self-Regulation Framework

How is the process of self-regulation relevant to the phenomenon of PE fit? In essence, PE fit concerns discrepancies between ideal conditions and experienced conditions (Edwards, 1992; French *et al.*, 1982). Ideal standards that are used to evaluate the environment include people's needs, values, personality traits, and task-based goals, knowledge, and skills (e.g., Antonioni and Park, 2001; Bretz and Judge, 1994; Kristof-Brown and Stevens, 2001). These ideal conditions are compared to targets in the perceived environment, including vocations, work organizations, groups within organizations (e.g., teams), specific people (e.g., supervisors), and job tasks and characteristics (e.g., Chatman, 1991; Engle and Lord, 1997; Ferris *et al.*, 1985). Self-regulation and PE fit are inexorably intertwined because ideal–experienced discrepancies are at the heart of both self-regulation theories and PE fit theories. Before continuing, it is important to note that we view PE fit as a continuous variable (i.e., employees vary in the extent to which they fit with their environment) rather than a categorical variable (i.e., employees either fit or misfit with their environment). This perspective is consistent with our discussion in this chapter of the size of ideal–experienced discrepancies and the rate at which discrepancies shrink or grow. In the case of PE fit, the ideal standards used to judge the environment often represent optima, meaning that both negative discrepancies (i.e., experiencing less than desired) and positive discrepancies (i.e., experiencing more than desired) are detrimental (Edwards, 1992). In these cases, only when there are few or no discrepancies do people tend to react in favorable ways.[2] However, when discrepancies between ideal conditions and experienced conditions are detected, it disrupts the system (e.g., elicits negative affect) and motivates people to alter their behavior or change their ideals. For example, people often increase their effort or adopt new behavioral strategies when faced with ideal–experienced discrepancies (Campion and Lord, 1982; Chang *et al.*, 2010). These actions are taken in order to increase the alignment of the perceived environment with people's ideal standards, thereby reducing the discrepancy. People may also revise their ideal standards in order to reduce discrepancies, especially when altering effort and behavioral strategies proves ineffective (Donovan and Williams, 2003).

To illustrate how the process of monitoring and responding to discrepancies unfolds, we return to the example of a job applicant deciding whether or not to apply to a company based on person–organization ethical fit (Coldwell *et al.*, 2008). Using information gleaned from various sources (e.g., newspapers, trade magazines, current and former employees, the internet), the applicant forms a perception of the company's corporate responsibility. This perception, which represents the input, is evaluated vis-à-vis his or her personal standard for ethical behavior. This comparison results in a judgment of the extent to which alignment exists between the ideal and perceived conditions. If there is little or no ideal–experienced discrepancy, then the applicant is expected to show favorable affect and attitudes towards the company and maintain his or her current course of action (i.e., applying to the company). In cases where a sufficiently large discrepancy is detected, negative affect is elicited which halts self-regulation and captures the applicant's attention (Carver and Scheier, 1998). The applicant may respond by changing the input (e.g., seeking additional information about the company in question or considering a different company altogether) or by changing the standard (e.g., altering the level or importance of his or her ideals concerning ethical behavior; French, Caplan, and Harrison, 1982).

Regardless of what action is taken, well-being is often impacted in a negative manner when discrepancies are encountered (cf. Edwards and Shipp, 2007). The final piece in the feedback loop is the disturbance, which in this case represents environmental influences that constrain the company's corporate responsibility (e.g., legislation or pressure owing to cultural norms and client demands). These influences can either exacerbate or attenuate ideal–experienced discrepancies.

We have described a single feedback loop that is dedicated to regulating the fit between an applicant's ideal standard for ethical behavior and his or her perception of a company's ethical culture. However, the process of self-regulation is more complex because, as noted earlier, there are multiple feedback loops and they are organized hierarchically. For the purposes of this chapter, we will discuss a hierarchical structure comprised of three levels. At the highest level is the overall fit between the person and the environment, which is an amalgamation of all possible foci (e.g., person–vocation, person–organization, person–group, person–supervisor, person–job fit) and dimensions (e.g., values, goals, personality, and skills; see Jansen and Kristof-Brown, 2006). In line with the assumptions of goal hierarchies, the standard at this highest level (i.e., the person as a complete entity) is the most abstract (Powers, 1973). Moving down a level, the standards in the middle layer are needs, values, and personality traits. While a hierarchical ordering may exist among needs, values, and traits (see Cropanzano *et al.*, 1993; Edwards, 1992), we consider them together as a set because they are all person-level qualities. Finally, the standards at the lowest level in the hierarchy are concrete task-level characteristics. Examples include task-specific knowledge, skills, abilities, and goals. As per the hierarchical structure, information about ideal–experienced discrepancies at lower levels serves as input for higher levels. This hierarchical organization of PE fit is illustrated in Figure 4.3.

> Proposition 1: Person–environment discrepancies are arranged hierarchically, such that the overall fit of the person exists at the top of the hierarchy, fit based on enduring person-level characteristics (e.g., needs, values, and traits) exists at the middle of the hierarchy, and fit based on task-level characteristics (e.g., task knowledge, skills, abilities, and task-focused goals) exists at the bottom of the hierarchy.

Using a self-regulation approach, a key variable for distinguishing between different forms of PE fit is the dimension or basis of fit (e.g., fit based on higher-level ideals such as needs and values, versus lower-level ones such as task-level knowledge and goals). As shown in Figure 4.3, the bases of fit are arranged hierarchically, consistent with self-regulation theorists' treatment of goal hierarchies (e.g., Carver and Scheier, 1998; Powers, 1973). At the top of the hierarchy is global or entity-level PE fit, which is similar to Jansen and Kristof-Brown's (2006) higher-order construct of multidimensional PE fit. Moving one level down, relatively enduring person-level characteristics like needs, values, and traits comprise the basis of fit. The ideal standards at this intermediate level are central to one's sense of self and they guide people's cognition

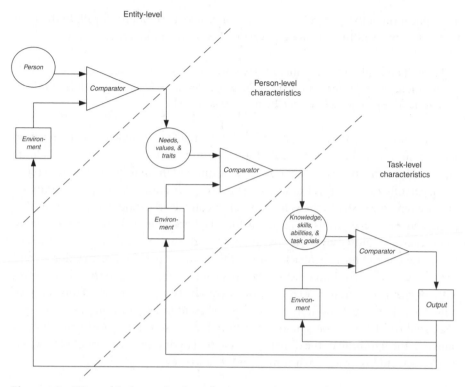

Figure 4.3 Hierarchical organization of person–environment fit

and behavior (Lord and Brown, 2004). At the bottom of the hierarchy are task-level characteristics that correspond to specific activities and situations. The standards at this level are the least abstract and the most short-lived compared to standards at higher levels (Johnson *et al.*, 2006).

Consistent with this hierarchical structure, the feedback loops that regulate ideal standards at the top of the hierarchy (e.g., the need for belonging) set the task-level standards that emerge at lower levels (e.g., consensus on a team-based project). Thus, task-level standards are important insofar as they service higher person-level standards. However, there usually exist multiple means for achieving a person-level standard, which lessens the value or importance of any one task-level standard (Carver and Scheier, 1998). That is, when the achievement of a task-level standard (e.g., retrieving a journal article via the internet) is obstructed, an alternative task-level standard (e.g., photocopying the article at the library) can be substituted in its place with little or no negative consequences for the employee (e.g., experiencing anxiety and low self-efficacy). Furthermore, task-level standards are not central to people's self-concept (Lord and Brown, 2004), which means that reactions to (un)successful self-regulation of task-level ideal–experienced discrepancies are weaker than reactions to person-level discrepancies (Carver and Scheier, 1998; Klein, 1989).[3] Thus, an implication of the hierarchical organization of ideal standards for PE fit theory is that not all bases of fit will have equivalent effects on employee reactions.

Proposition 2: PE fit at the entity level will have stronger effects on employee affect, cognition, and behavior than PE fit at the person level. PE fit at the person level will, in turn, have stronger effects than PE fit at the task level.

This is not to say, however, that the foci or target of fit (e.g., fit with an organization versus a supervisor) is irrelevant. Instead, the different foci correspond to separate hierarchal systems of feedback loops. That is, one system may be dedicated to regulating person–vocation fit, another for person–organization fit, and so on. Although they are separate systems, the systems are interconnected owing to the spillover that exists between perceptions of different foci. For example, employee appraisals of companies are colored by their appraisals of work supervisors (Gerstner and Day, 1997). Two hierarchical feedback systems that regulate person–organization fit and person–supervisor fit simultaneously are depicted in Figure 4.4. Vertical lines represent linkages across different levels of the hierarchy (e.g., reciprocal relationships of value fit with goal fit) and horizontal lines represent linkages within the same level (e.g., spillover between person–organization and person–supervisor value fit). As shown in the figure, all of the dimensions and foci of fit influence overall fit between the person and his or her environment at the entity level.

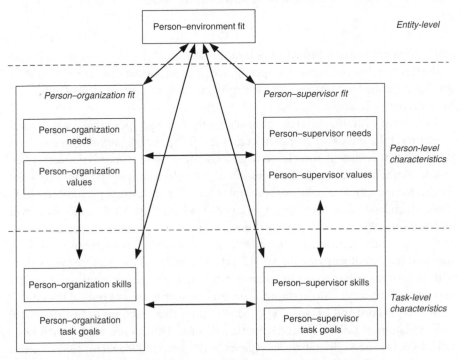

Figure 4.4   Hierarchical organization of multiple person–environment fits

In this section we proposed that a self-regulation framework can be success-fully applied to the phenomenon of PE fit. Although PE fit has been previously portrayed as an ideal–experienced discrepancy within a negative feedback loop (e.g., Edwards, 1992; French *et al.*, 1982), the implications of this insight have not been fully developed. Drawing from recent advances in self-regulation theory (e.g., Johnson *et al.*, 2006; Lord *et al.*, 2010; Vancouver, 2005, 2008), we expound on several novel implications in the remainder of this chapter.

Regulating Person–Environment Fit over Time

Theories of self-regulation describe how people work towards reducing discrepan-cies between ideal and experienced conditions, which is an iterative process that unfolds over time (Bandura, 1986; Carver and Scheier, 1998; Johnson *et al.*, 2006; Mitchell and Beach, 1990). Consistent with this idea, research on PE fit has be-gun to examine whether the magnitude of changes in fit predict job satisfaction, absenteeism, and turnover intentions (e.g., Caldwell *et al.*, 2004; Caplan, Tripathi and Naidu, 1985; Chatman, 1991; DeRue and Morgeson, 2007; Jansen and Kristof-Brown, 2006; Roberts and Robins, 2004; Schmitt *et al.*, 2008). PE fit researchers have also investigated PE fit at distinct points in time (i.e., past, present, and future fit) and the ability of these different fits to predict employee outcomes (Caplan, 1987; Caplan *et al.*, 1985). These studies, however, do not speak directly to the issue of the rate of change in ideal–experienced discrepancies and whether such change is important to consider. As we explain below, adopting a longitudinal per-spective within a self-regulation framework offers insight into the phenomenon of PE fit.

When a dynamic perspective of self-regulation is adopted, not only is discrepancy information important but so too is velocity information. Velocity information refers to the direction and rate of change in the size of discrepancies over time whereas discrepancy information refers simply to the current size of discrepancies (Carver and Scheier, 1998). Note that the direction of change can be positive or negative. That is, ideal–experienced discrepancies may be shrinking (i.e., positive velocity) or growing (i.e., negative velocity). Although the direction of velocity matters (i.e., positive and negative velocities produce favorable and unfavorable responses, respectively), differences in the rate of velocity (i.e., fast versus slow velocity) also explain variance in people's reactions to self-regulation activities (e.g., Lawrence *et al.*, 2002). Both positive and negative velocities also predict reactions to ideal–experienced discrepancies incremental to the size of those discrepancies, as we discuss next.[4]

While our discussion of discrepancies has thus far treated them as static, the direction and rate of change in ideal–experienced discrepancies are key elements in the self-regulation process that ought to be considered in tandem with the size of discrepancies (e.g., Chang *et al.*, 2010; Donovan and Williams, 2003; Ilies and Judge, 2005; Lawrence *et al.*, 2002; Schmidt and DeShon, 2007; Schmidt *et al.*, 2009). In the case of PE fit, for example, researchers typically examine the size of the difference between ideals and experiences (which we label "PE discrepancy") rather than the direction and rate at which PE discrepancies are changing over time (which we label "PE velocity"). As has been demonstrated with ideal–experienced discrepancies and goal–performance discrepancies outside the PE literature, the direction and rate of change in discrepancies (i.e., velocity) impact attitudes, affect, and behavior (e.g., Chang et al., 2010; Lawrence et al., 2002). In fact, Carver and Scheier (1998) proposed that velocity information has a stronger impact on affective reactions compared to discrepancy information. That is, people's emotional responses to ideal–experienced discrepancies depend more on the rate at which discrepancies are changing than on the current size of discrepancies. Lawrence et al. (2002) supported this proposition by showing that participants who began with large goal–performance discrepancies but experienced fast positive velocities (i.e., discrepancies decreased quickly) reported more positive moods than participants who began with small goal–performance discrepancies but experienced slow positive velocities. Interestingly, participants who began with favorable (i.e., small) goal–performance discrepancies reported strong negative moods if they experienced negative velocity (i.e., discrepancies became larger). Overall, moods were most positive for participants with fast positive velocities, despite the fact that their average performance across the multi-trial task was worse than participants who experienced slow positive velocities and participants who experienced negative velocities.

Successful self-regulation depends on both discrepancy and velocity information. Take, for example, newly-hired employees who are beginning on-the-job training. At first, there is likely to be a large discrepancy between trainees' current skill levels and the skill levels required to perform the job successfully. Initial discrepancies in learning contexts can often be quite large – enough to provoke acute frustration and anxiety. Why is it, then, that new hires persevere with training despite potentially daunting ideal–experienced discrepancies? The answer to this question lies with their velocity. While initial discrepancies may be large, often the rate at which discrepancies are shrinking (i.e., velocity) is fast, which reduces the likelihood that trainees will experience negative emotions and withdraw. Thus, fast velocities can compensate for undesirably large discrepancies (Chang et al., 2010).

The idea that velocity impacts people's affect, cognition, and behavior has received empirical support. For example, in one of the first studies of velocity, Hsee and Abelson (1991) found that the rate of change in ideal–experienced discrepancies (i.e., velocity) was positively related to people's satisfaction across a variety of life domains such as work and school. For instance, people preferred a salary that increased from low to high (i.e., a positive velocity) versus a steady high salary. Conversely, people preferred a steady low salary versus a salary that decreased from high to low (i.e., a negative velocity). These findings provided initial evidence that people rely on velocity information. Building on this initial evidence, Lawrence, Carver, and Scheier (2002) found that the moods of participants while performing a social judgment task were influenced by changes in ideal–experienced task performance levels. Although the size of discrepancies was the same for all participants at the end of the task, those who experienced positive velocities (i.e., shrinking ideal–experienced discrepancies) reported positive moods and those who experienced negative velocities (i.e., growing ideal–experienced discrepancies) reported negative moods. Interestingly, the participants with negative velocities reported negative moods despite having the smallest ideal–experienced discrepancies on average across multiple trials. This finding suggests it is velocity, rather than size, that shapes people's emotional responses to ideal–experienced discrepancies. More recently, Chang, Johnson, and Lord (2010) examined the impact of velocity on a broader range of outcomes. In Study 1 the authors examined discrepancies and velocities in ideal and experienced job characteristics involving rewards, interpersonal interactions, and challenges. In line with previous findings, the authors found that the rate of change in ideal–experienced job characteristics predicted employee job satisfaction. In Study 2 the authors examined discrepancies between goal levels and experienced performance levels on a multi-trial achievement task. Results revealed that the rate of change in goal–performance discrepancies predicted people's satisfaction with the task and their success expectancies. When velocities were fast, people experienced positive emotions and were confident that they would reach their performance goals. Chang, Johnson, and Lord (2010) also observed significant discrepancy by velocity interactions, such that large discrepancies had minimal impact on task satisfaction, success expectancies, and goal commitment so long as velocity was fast rather than slow. Only when large discrepancies were paired with slow velocities did people respond in unfavorable ways. Taken together, the findings of Hsee and Abelson (1991), Lawrence, Carver, and Scheier (2002), and Chang, Johnson, and Lord (2010) clearly indicate that velocity, or the rate of change in ideal–experienced discrepancies, is important.

What are the implications of velocity for PE fit theory? One obvious implication is that researchers ought to measure discrepancies between ideal standards and the experienced environment across time and examine the consequences of the rate of change in PE discrepancies (i.e., PE velocity) in addition to the size of PE discrepancies. Based on the findings of the aforementioned studies, we suspect that PE velocity will enhance the prediction of outcomes common to the fit literature, including attitudes like job satisfaction and commitment and behaviors like task and contextual performance. Thus, job satisfaction may not only depend on the current fit between employees' skills and the demands of their jobs, but also on the velocity of changes in demands–abilities fit. Specifically, employees who perceive that discrepancies between their skills and job demands are shrinking will report greater satisfaction than those who perceive that discrepancies are static or becoming larger. The idea that velocity information is important for PE fit is captured by our second proposition:

> Proposition 3: PE velocities (i.e., rate of change in PE discrepancies) predict employee affect, cognition, and behavior incremental to PE discrepancies.

As mentioned earlier, it has been suggested that unique ties exist between velocity and emotional responses (Carver and Scheier, 1998). If this is true, and initial empirical findings suggest that it is (Lawrence *et al.*, 2002), then PE velocity may account for a larger proportion of variance in affect-based outcomes like employee satisfaction and mood compared to PE discrepancies. In addition to affect-based outcomes, velocity is also critical for predicting withdrawal behaviors (e.g., absenteeism and quitting) because velocity information plays a central role in the assessment of success expectancies and deciding whether or not to disengage (Carver and Scheier, 1998; Chang *et al.*, 2010). People rely on velocity information to judge the likelihood that ideal–experienced discrepancies will be resolved eventually, and if the likelihood is believed to be small, then people either revise their ideals downward (e.g., Chang *et al.*, 2009; Donovan and Williams, 2003) or disengage completely from the situation (e.g., Duval *et al.*, 1992; Wrosch *et al.*, 2007). This implies that if employees perceive their PE discrepancies to be static (or worse, if they perceive them to be growing), then employees may begin to withdraw from their organization. Lee and Mitchell (1994) suggested that turnover is often precipitated by "shocks," which are jarring events that initiate psychological analyses involved in quitting a job. Abrupt changes in the size of PE discrepancies, which are captured by PE velocity, may serve as shocks that precede reassessments of organizational membership which trigger turnover. The role of PE velocity in predicting employee withdrawal is important given that PE fit is believed to be a key determinant of whether or not employees stay with their company. Researchers may discover that the effects of PE fit on employee turnover are underestimated when velocity information is not taken into account. All told, PE velocities may prove to be a stronger predictor than PE discrepancies for outcomes involving affect and withdrawal.

> Proposition 4: PE velocities account for a larger proportion of variance in affect- and withdrawal-related outcomes compared to PE discrepancies.

In addition to independent effects of PE discrepancies and velocities, there is the possibility that PE discrepancies and velocities have interactive effects on employee affect, cognition, and behavior. This possibility derives from the findings of Chang *et al.* (2010), who observed significant discrepancy by velocity interactions. The nature of these interactions was such that large ideal–experienced discrepancies were not damaging to people's satisfaction, commitment, and success expectancies so long as velocity was fast rather than slow. Perhaps a similar pattern may occur in the case of PE fit, such that employees will tolerate large ideal–experienced discrepancies if they believe that the discrepancies are shrinking at an acceptable pace. For example, when entering an organization, new hires may experience large discrepancies between their existing self-concepts and values vis-à-vis their new self-concepts and values as organizational members (Swann *et al.*, 2009). These discrepancies can initially be quite frustrating as employees begin to navigate the social context at work. Despite the large ideal–experienced discrepancies, most employees persevere and remain with their new employer. The reason for this, we believe, is favorable PE

velocity. That is, so long as employees experience sufficient velocity towards recon-
ciling discrepancies, then they will circumvent the negative affect and withdrawal
cognitions that would otherwise occur (Swann *et al.*, 2009). It is therefore important
to consider PE discrepancies and velocities in combination.

> Proposition 5: PE discrepancies and PE velocities interact, such that large discrepancies
> have weaker detrimental effects on employee affect, cognition, and behavior when
> velocities are fast versus slow.

We have argued that self-regulation theories shed light on how PE discrepancies
function over time, and why PE velocity is expected to impact employee outcomes.
However, consideration of velocities has ramifications for the measurement of fit.
Specifically, examining velocity creates the need for longitudinal studies where
data pertaining to PE discrepancies are collected at multiple points in time. A
minimum of two time points is needed to create an objective index of the rate of
change in PE discrepancies (see Chang *et al.*, 2009). Multiple indices of velocity
can be created when data pertaining to PE discrepancy are collected at three or
more time periods.[5] Alternatively, rather than calculating the difference between
two PE discrepancy scores, employees' perceived velocity can instead be measured
directly at one point in time (see Chang *et al.*, 2010). Measures of perceived PE
velocity resemble what Edwards *et al.* (2006) label molar and molecular measures
of fit. Importantly, different approaches for assessing PE discrepancies (e.g.,
measuring perceived person–environment discrepancies versus calculating the
difference between separate measures of the person and environment) do not
appear to be interchangeable (Edwards *et al.*, 2006). Thus, research that teases
apart the similarities and differences between various measures of PE velocity
is needed.

In addition to measurement issues, another issue is the relevance of velocity at
high levels in the PE fit hierarchy. That is, does it make sense to examine velocity
when the bases of fit at high levels are seemingly enduring qualities like needs, values,
and traits? We believe that the answer to this question is "yes" for a few reasons.
First, although the structure of basic needs, values, and traits is stable, people's
levels on these universal qualities can change over time or across domains (e.g.,
Lord and Brown, 2004; Maslow, 1943; Roberts *et al.*, 2006; Schwartz, 1992). Thus,
while the probability of change is higher for low-level, task-based knowledge, skills,
abilities, and goals, changes in high-level ideals are also possible. Second, even in
cases where high-level ideals are stable, perceptions of the environment may change
due to, for example, organizational restructuring or leader succession, which may
produce change in PE discrepancies (in other words, produce PE velocity). Third,
given the hierarchical organization of feedback loops (Powers, 1973), it has been
proposed that discrepancy information in low-level feedback loops accumulates
over time and is then communicated to feedback loops at higher levels in the
form of velocity information (Johnson *et al.*, 2006). For example, changes in ideal–
experienced sales discrepancies that occur over time at the task level become input

that is compared to achievement needs at the person level. In fact, Johnson, Chang, and Lord (2006) argued that velocity information (i.e., changes in discrepancies over time) and acceleration information (i.e., changes in velocity over time) are the primary means through which information is communicated upward in feedback hierarchies because the regulation of lower-level discrepancies operates at speeds that are too fast to be detected at higher levels. In sum, regardless of the level of PE fit (i.e., entity-level versus person-level characteristics versus task-level characteristics), velocity information is valuable.

> Proposition 6: Velocity information at all three levels in the fit hierarchy (i.e., entity level, person level, and task level) predict employee affect, cognition, and behavior.

Individual Differences that Impact PE Fit

Thus far we have argued that the nature of PE fit may differ depending on the basis of fit (i.e., entity versus person versus task) and the type of fit information (i.e., discrepancies versus velocities). In this section we highlight some individual difference variables that may influence the importance people place on these different bases and information, thereby moderating relationships of PE fit with its outcomes. To date, researchers have examined personality variables, such as extraversion, openness to experience, and conscientiousness (Piasentin and Chapman, 2006; Shantz, 2003), that moderate relationships of PE fit with its outcomes. Other researchers have looked at primary needs like the needs for affiliation and achievement (Piasentin and Chapman, 2006; Turban et al., 2001). Using a self-regulation framework, we identify additional variables that potentially moderate relationships between fit and its outcomes. Although these variables have not yet been incorporated into the PE fit literature, they are relevant because they alter (a) people's sensitivities to ideal–experienced discrepancies, (b) the relative importance of high-level versus low-level ideals, or (c) the relative importance of PE discrepancies versus PE velocities.

Some individual differences increase people's sensitivities to ideal–experienced discrepancies, thereby increasing the effects of those discrepancies on affect, cognition, and behavior. One such variable is self-consciousness, which refers to the propensity to focus attention on the self (Fenigstein et al., 1975). Note that we do not refer to self-consciousness in the sense that individuals fear embarrassment, as the term is colloquially used. Instead self-consciousness simply implies the tendency for people to be aware of themselves in relation to their surroundings. Self-consciousness and its state-level counterpart, self-focus, cause people to pay greater attention to ideal standards and to regulate more tightly around them (Carver and Scheier, 1998). For example, Scheier and Carver (1983) found that both dispositional self-consciousness and situation-induced self-focus were associated with higher levels of feedback seeking in an assigned task. Compared to participants low in self-focus, high self-focused participants checked more often to verify that they were performing the task correctly. Similarly, Carver (1975) found that self-focus increased the extent to which people's behavior conformed to personally held attitudes. These findings demonstrate that when self-focus is high, people pay more attention to whether or not experienced conditions are consistent with ideal conditions.

The discussion above suggests that high self-consciousness increases the salience of the extent that fit exists between one's ideal standards and perceptions of the environment. This increased salience is likely to accentuate the consequences of PE discrepancies and velocities. Consistent with this notion, when people perceive that they can meet the demands of the situation, they are more likely to persist on a task when self-focus is high versus low (Carver *et al.*, 1979). Such findings may also apply to other situations that involve ideal–experienced discrepancies. For example, self-conscious individuals who perceive discrepancies between ideal and experienced levels of job autonomy may be more likely to turnover than their less self-conscious counterparts who perceive similar circumstances. Thus, people who are more self-aware are more likely to take action to eliminate ideal–experienced discrepancies (Resick *et al.*, 2007; Singh and Greenhaus, 2004). This leads us to our seventh proposition:

> Proposition 7: Self-consciousness and self-focus moderate the effects of PE discrepancies and velocities on employee affect, cognition, and behavior, such that effects are stronger when self-focus or self-consciousness is high versus low.

As illustrated in Figure 4.3 and Figure 4.4, the different types of PE fit exist at different levels in the feedback hierarchy. Furthermore, PE fit at higher levels is viewed as more important to employees than fit at lower levels, and thus, the former should have stronger effects on employee affect, cognition, and behavior. However, the extent to which these differences in effects hold true depends on people's action identification, or the level of abstraction that they typically associate with their behaviors (Vallacher and Wegner, 1985). Those who identify actions at lower levels tend to think of their behaviors in more concrete terms, whereas those who identify actions at higher levels tend to think of their behaviors more abstractly. Consider two people who are both writing a research paper. Although they are engaged in the same behavior, a person with low action identification is focused on task-level facets like using proper sentence structure and presenting coherent arguments, while a person with high action identification is focused on more abstract goals like publishing the paper in a respectable journal and earning tenure. Although this difference may seem trivial, the level of action identification has important implications for people's goal-based motivations, as we explain next.

According to Vallacher and Wegner (1989), those who identify actions at low levels focus on task-level details and are especially receptive to task-based feedback, whereas those who identify actions at higher levels focus on the meaning and instrumentalities of their actions. The source of motivation for this latter group derives from moving closer to high-level, self-based goals. Because people focus attention at different levels of abstraction, it is likely that the salience of particular types of PE fit differs across people. For example, imagine a situation where an employee possesses the requisite skills to meet the demands of his or her job, thereby enabling the job to meet the employee's need to feel competent. If the employee identifies actions at low levels, then he or she will pay particular attention to fit based on task-level characteristics (e.g., knowledge, skills, abilities, and task goals). However, if the employee identifies actions at higher levels, then he or she will be sensitive to fit based on person-level characteristics (e.g., needs, values, and traits). Because of these differences in salience, the relative importance of PE fit at different levels and the effects that fit has on outcomes depends on individual differences in action identification.

> Proposition 8: When PE fit is based on high-level standards (e.g., needs, values, and traits), action identification moderates the effects of PE fit on employee affect, cognition, and behavior, such that effects are stronger when action identification is high versus low.

> Proposition 9: When PE fit is based on low-level standards (e.g., task-based knowledge, skills, abilities, and goals), action identification moderates the effects of PE fit on employee affect, cognition, and behavior, such that effects are stronger when action identification is low versus high.

Lastly, individual differences may also impact the relative importance of PE discrepancies and velocities in predicting outcomes. One variable that displays such effects is temporal orientation, which refers to chronic tendencies to focus on the past, present, or future (Holman and Silver, 1998). Those with a strong present orientation have been found to react more strongly to immediate outcomes (Alberts and Dunton, 2008) and to prefer immediate gratifications over delayed ones (Lasane and Jones, 2000). This suggests that present-oriented individuals place greater weight on PE discrepancies, which reflect differences between perceived and ideal states at the current moment in time, rather than considering the long-term implications of PE velocities. In support of this idea, Chang, Johnson, and Rosen (2009) found that goal–performance discrepancies had stronger effects on goal revision when people reported strong versus weak present orientation. That is, people with strong present orientations were more reactive to the existence of goal–performance discrepancies and sought to reduce these discrepancies by changing their goals.

In contrast to present orientation, individuals who possess a strong future orientation tend to be more aware of the long-term effects of their actions (Alberts and Dunton, 2008). They have also been shown to be more effective at forecasting progress toward distal goals (Pezzo et al., 2006) and to persist longer in the face of adversity (Brown and Jones, 2004). This suggests that future-oriented individuals may be more in tune with PE velocity, which provides information concerning improvement or deterioration in ideal–experienced discrepancies over the long run. Consistent with this suggestion, Chang and Johnson (2006) found that velocity was more important in predicting job satisfaction among those with strong future orientations. Interestingly, Shipp (2006) examined whether temporal orientation moderated relationships of PE fit with its outcomes, but found little support. However, as proposed in this chapter, we believe that temporal orientation has relevance for specific types of PE fit information (i.e., discrepancies and velocities) rather than PE fit in general. Our final two propositions, which pertain to temporal orientation, are as follows:

> Proposition 10: Present orientation moderates the effects of PE discrepancies on employee affect, cognition and behavior, such that effects are stronger when present orientation is high versus low.

> Proposition 11: Future orientation moderates the effects of PE velocities on employee affect, cognition, and behavior, such that effects are stronger when future orientation is high versus low.

While previous research clearly shows that PE fit is a phenomenon with far-reaching implications (Hoffman and Woehr, 2006; Kristof-Brown *et al.*, 2005; Verquer *et al.*, 2003), an important next step for future research is to specify the boundary conditions of PE fit effects. Applying a self-regulation framework to PE fit is useful in this regard because doing so highlights different means through which individual differences may moderate relationships between fit and employee affect, cognition, and behavior. For example, some variables moderate the overall effects of PE fit (e.g., self-awareness) on its outcomes, while other variables moderate the relative importance of fit at different levels in the feedback hierarchy (e.g., action identification) or the relative importance of PE discrepancies and velocities (e.g., temporal orientation). Future research that explores these possible moderator effects and that identifies additional moderator variables would provide worthwhile contributions to the PE fit literature.

Limitations

Prior to our concluding remarks we briefly mention three limitations with our conceptualization of PE fit within a self-regulation framework. First, our framework does not distinguish between PE discrepancies owing to oversupply versus undersupply. Although both represent a misalignment between the person and the environment, oversupply and undersupply may have different implications for employee outcomes such as job satisfaction and strain reactions (e.g., Edwards and Shipp, 2007; Irving and Montes, 2009; Lambert *et al.*, 2003; Warr, 1990). Our focus in this chapter was discussing the process through which PE discrepancies are regulated rather than the unique effects of different types of discrepancy.

Second, our model examines fit from the perspective of employees rather than organizations, yet the latter perspective is also important. For example, demands–abilities fit is conceptualized as the organization's assessment of whether or not employees' attributes complement and therefore satisfy situational demands and deficiencies (e.g., Kristof, 1996). However, because our framework captures self-regulatory processes in individuals, it is less informative for understanding how fit unfolds from the standpoint of social collectives like work teams and organizations.

Third, our framework considers psychological attributes, rather than physical ones, as the bases for evaluating fit. Research on relational demography has suggested that demographic differences, such as race, gender, and age, have implications for the extent to which employees fit with their groups and supervisors (e.g., Jackson *et al.*, 1991; Pelled and Xin, 2000). However, psychological characteristics like needs, values, and traits are critical mechanisms that may underlie fit based on demographic variables (e.g., automatic trait inferences are made about people based on their physical attributes; Banaji *et al.*, 1993). Thus, when appraising fit based on demographic variables, the basis of fit may involve implicit beliefs that certain needs, values, skills, etc., covary with particular physical characteristics (e.g., the belief that relatedness and achievement needs vary across males and females). If so, then a self-regulatory framework based on psychological characteristics may also be useful for understanding fit based on demographic characteristics.

Conclusion

This chapter has explored how a self-regulation framework might inform our understanding of PE fit. We conceptualized PE fit as discrepancies between ideal standards and perceptions of the environment that are regulated within negative feedback loops. These feedback loops are organized hierarchically based on the level of abstraction and self-relevance of personal standards, such that overall or entity-level PE fit is regulated in higher-order loops, person-based characteristics (e.g., needs and values) are regulated in intermediate loops, and task-based characteristics (e.g., knowledge and skills) are regulated in lower-level loops. Integrating theories of PE fit and self-regulation led to three major insights. First, doing so highlighted the impact of changes in PE discrepancies over time – that is, PE velocities – on employee outcomes. The importance of PE velocity derives not only from its proposed incremental predictive validity above and beyond PE discrepancy, but also from its ability to attenuate the detrimental effects of large ideal–experienced discrepancies, which may be unavoidable in some situations (e.g., learning contexts). Next, we discussed how different bases of PE fit can be conceptualized as representing different levels within a feedback hierarchy of fit. Fit based on person-level characteristics like values and needs is regulated within higher levels of the feedback loop, whereas fit based on task-level characteristics like knowledge and skills operates at lower levels. This insight is valuable because people place greater importance on ideal–experienced discrepancies that exist at higher levels. Thus, we would expect that fit based on needs and values will have stronger effects on employee well-being and performance compared to fit based on task knowledge and skills. Lastly, we introduced some motivation-based individual difference variables that are expected to moderate the effects of PE fit on employee affect, cognition, and behavior. Depending on the variable, they may moderate the overall effects of PE fit on outcomes (self-consciousness and self-focus), the relative effects of person-level fit versus task-level fit on outcomes (action identification), or the relative effects of PE discrepancies versus velocities on outcomes (temporal orientation). To date, these individual difference variables have received little attention from PE fit scholars, despite their potential relevance. These and other insights are possible when PE fit is viewed through the lens of a self-regulation framework, which can guide future research in this area.

Notes

1. The authors are grateful to Jeff Edwards for his comments on an earlier version of this manuscript.
2. Ideal conditions do not, however, always represent optima (see Edwards and Shipp, 2007). There can be situations where people's experience of oversupply or undersupply relative to their ideal conditions is not detrimental (e.g., an environment that oversupplies a person's psychological needs, such as competence or autonomy; Deci and Ryan, 1985). Thus, the assumption that misfits due to oversupply and undersupply are equivalent does not hold in every case.
3. The value or importance of standards at the same level may also vary. Take, for example, the task-level goal of coordinating the activities of subordinates while serving as a project leader. This task-level goal is unique in that it represents a means for accomplishing two higher-level standards: satisfying one's needs for power and for relatedness. This task-level goal therefore has more value than other task-level goals that only satisfy one higher-level standard.
4. Unless otherwise noted, our use of the term "velocity" in the text refers to instances of positive velocity (i.e., ideal–experienced discrepancies are shrinking).
5. While we have limited our focus in this chapter to changes in PE discrepancies over time, it is also possible (and may prove meaningful) to examine changes in PE velocities over time. Whereas velocity is the first derivative of distance over time, acceleration is the second derivative of distance over time. That is, the rate at which PE discrepancies change over time may also change (i.e., speed up or slow down). Take, for example, a situation where new hires quickly learn to perform the easier tasks of a new position, resulting in fast velocity. However, these employees will experience negative acceleration as their rate of learning slows down once they are assigned more difficult tasks. Thus, PE acceleration, which requires a minimum of three time periods in order to calculate an objective index, may also predict employee affect, attitudes, and behavior.

References

Alberts, J., and Dunton, G. F. (2008) The role of temporal orientation in reactive and proactive illness management. *Psychology and Health*, 23, 175–179.

Antonioni, D., and Park, H. (2001) The effects of personality similarity on peer ratings of contextual work behaviors. *Personnel Psychology*, 54, 331–360.

Austin, J. T., and Vancouver, J. B. (1996) Goal constructs in psychology: Structure, process, and content. *Psychological Bulletin*, 120, 338–375.

Banaji, M. R., Harden, C. D., and Rothman, A. J. (1993) Implicit stereotyping in person judgment. *Journal of Personality and Social Psychology*, 65, 136–141.

Bandura, A. (1986) *Social Foundations of Thought and Action: A Social Cognitive Theory.* Englewood Cliffs, NJ: Prentice Hall.

Bandura, A. (2001) Social cognitive theory: An agentic perspective. *Annual Review of Psychology*, 52, 1–26.

Billsberry, J., Ambrosini, V., Moss-Jones, J., and Marsh, P. J. G. (2005) Some suggestions for mapping organizational members' sense of fit. *Journal of Business and Psychology*, 19, 555–570.

Bretz, R. D., and Judge, T. A. (1994) Person–organization fit and the theory of work adjustment: Implications for satisfaction, tenure, and career success. *Journal of Vocational Behavior*, 44, 32–54.

Brown, W. T., and Jones, J. M. (2004) The substance of things hoped for: A study of the future orientation, minority status perceptions, academic engagement, and academic performance of black high school students. *Journal of Black Psychology*, 34, 248–273.

Caldwell, S. D., Herold, D. M., and Fedor, D. B. (2004) Toward an understanding of the relationships among organizational change, individual differences, and changes in person–environment fit: A cross-level study. *Journal of Applied Psychology*, 89, 868–882.

Campion, M. A., and Lord, R. G. (1982) A control systems conceptualization of the goal setting and changing process. *Organizational Behavior and Human Performance*, 30, 265–287.

Caplan, R. D. (1987) Person–environment fit theory and organizations: Commensurate dimensions, time perspectives, and mechanisms. *Journal of Vocational Behavior*, 31, 248–267.

Caplan, R. D., Tripathi, R. C., and Naidu, R. K. (1985) Subjective past, present, and future fit: Effects on anxiety, depression, and other indicators of well-being. *Journal of Personality and Social Psychology*, 48, 180–197.

Carver, C. S. (1975) Physical aggression as a function of objective self awareness and attitudes toward punishment. *Journal of Experimental Social Psychology*, 11, 510–519.

Carver, C. S., and Scheier, M. F. (1998) *On the Self-Regulation of Behavior*. Cambridge, UK: Cambridge University Press.

Carver, C. S., Blaney, P. H., and Scheier, M. F. (1979) Reassertion and giving up: The interactive role of self-directed attention and outcome expectancy. *Journal of Personality and Social Psychology*, 37, 1859–1870.

Chang, C.-H., and Johnson, R. E. (2006) Discrepancy, velocity, and job satisfaction: Temporal orientation as a moderator. Paper presented at the 21st Annual Conference of the Society for Industrial and Organizational Psychology, Dallas, TX.

Chang, C.-H., Johnson, R. E., and Lord, R. G. (2010) Moving beyond discrepancies: The importance of velocity as a predictor of satisfaction and motivation. *Human Performance*, 23, 58–80.

Chang, C.-H., Johnson, R. E., and Rosen, C. C. (2009) Discrepancy, velocity, and goal revision: Temporal orientation as a moderator. Paper presented at the 24th Annual Society for Industrial and Organizational Psychology Conference, April, New Orleans, LA.

Chatman, J. A. (1991) Matching people and organizations: Selection and socialization in public accounting firms. *Administrative Science Quarterly*, 36, 459–484.

Coldwell, D. A., Billsberry, J., van Meurs, N., and Marsh, P. J. G. (2008) The effects of person–organization ethical fit on employee attraction and retention: Towards a testable explanatory model. *Journal of Business Ethics*, 78, 611–622.

Cropanzano, R., James, K., and Citera, M. A. (1993) A goal hierarchy model of personality, motivation, and leadership. In L. L. Cummings and B. M. Staw (eds), *Research in Organizational Behavior* (Vol. 15, pp. 267–322). Greenwich, CT: JAI Press.

Deci, E. L., and Ryan, R. M. (1985) *Intrinsic Motivation and Self-Determination in Human Behavior*. New York: Plenum Press.

DeRue, D. S., and Morgeson, F. P. (2007) Stability and change in person–team and person–role fit over time: The effects of growth satisfaction, performance, and general self-efficacy. *Journal of Applied Psychology*, 92, 1242–1253.

Donovan, J. J., and Williams, K. J. (2003) Missing the mark: Effects of time and causal attributions on goal revision in response to goal–performance discrepancies. *Journal of Applied Psychology*, 88, 379–390.

Duval, T. S., Duval, V. H., and Mulilis, J.-P. (1992) Effects of self-focus, discrepancy between self and standard, and outcome expectancy favorability on the tendency to match self to standard or to withdraw. *Journal of Personality and Social Psychology*, 62, 340–348.

Edwards, J. R. (1991) Person–job fit: A conceptual integration, literature review, and methodological critique. In C. L. Cooper and I. T. Robertson (eds), *International Review of Industrial and Organizational Psychology* (Vol. 6, pp. 283–357). New York: John Wiley & Sons, Inc.

Edwards, J. R. (1992) A cybernetic theory of stress, coping, and well-being in organizations. *Academy of Management Review*, 17, 238–274.

Edwards, J. R., and Shipp, A. J. (2007) The relationship between person–environment fit and outcomes: An integrative theoretical framework. In C. Ostroff and T. A. Judge (eds), *Perspectives on Organizational Fit* (pp. 209–258). San Francisco: Jossey-Bass.

Edwards, J. R., Cable, D. M., Williamson, I. O., Lambert, L. S., and Shipp, A. J. (2006) The phenomenology of fit: Linking the person and environment to the subjective experience of person–environment fit. *Journal of Applied Psychology*, 91, 802–827.

Engle, E. M., and Lord, R. G. (1997) Implicit theories, self-schemas, and leader–member exchange. *Academy of Management Journal*, 40, 988–1010.

Fenigstein, A., Scheier, M. F., and Buss, A. H. (1975) Public and private self-consciousness: Assessment and theory. *Journal of Consulting and Clinical Psychology*, 43, 522–527.

Ferris, G. R., Youngblood, S. A., and Yates, V. L. (1985) Personality, training performance, and withdrawal: A test of the Person–Group Fit Hypothesis for organizational newcomers. *Journal of Vocational Behavior*, 27, 377–388.

French, J. R. P., Jr, Caplan, R. D., and Harrison, R. V. (1982) *The Mechanisms of Job Stress and Strain*. London: John Wiley & Sons, Ltd.

Gehring, W. J., Goss, B., Coles, M. G. H., Meyer, D. E., and Donchin, E. (1993) A neural system for error detection and compensation. *Psychological Science*, 4, 385–390.

Gerstner, C. R. and Day, D. V. (1997) Meta-analytic review of leader–member exchange theory: Correlates and construct issues. *Journal of Applied Psychology*, 82, 827–844.

Gollwitzer, P. M. (1990) Action phases and mind-sets. In E. T. Higgins and R. M. Sorrentino (eds), *The Handbook of Motivation and Cognition: Foundations of Social Behavior* (Vol. 2, pp. 53–92). New York: Guilford Press.

Hackman, J. R., and Oldham, G. R. (1976) Motivation through the design of work: Test of a theory. *Organizational Behavior and Human Performance*, 16, 250–279.

Hoffman, B. J., and Woehr, D. J. (2006) A quantitative review of the relationship between person–organization fit and behavioral outcomes. *Journal of Vocational Behavior*, 68, 389–399.

Holman, E. A., and Silver, R. C. (1998) Getting "stuck" in the past: Temporal orientation and coping with trauma. *Journal of Personality and Social Psychology*, 74, 1146–1163.

Hsee, C. K., and Abelson, R. P. (1991) Velocity relation: Satisfaction as a function of the first derivative of outcome over time. *Journal of Personality and Social Psychology*, 60, 341–347.

Ilies, R., and Judge, T. A. (2005) Goal regulation across time: The effects of feedback and affect. *Journal of Applied Psychology*, 90, 453–467.

Irving, P. G., and Montes, S. D. (2009) Met expectations: The effects of expected and delivered inducements on employee satisfaction. *Journal of Occupational and Organizational Psychology*, 82, 431–451.

Jackson, S., Brett, S., Sessa, V., Cooper, D., Julin, J., and Peyronnin, K. (1991) Some differences make a difference: Individual dissimilarity and group heterogeneity as correlates of recruitment, promotions, and turnover. *Journal of Applied Psychology*, 76, 675–689.

Jansen, K. J., and Kristof-Brown, A. (2006) Toward a multidimensional theory of person–environment fit. *Journal of Managerial Issues*, 18, 193–212.

Johnson, R. E., Chang, C.-H., and Lord, R. G. (2006) Moving from cognition to behavior: What the research says. *Psychological Bulletin*, 132, 381–415.

Kanfer, R. (1990) Motivation theory and industrial/organizational psychology. In M. D. Dunnette and L. Hough (eds), *Handbook of Industrial and Organizational Psychology. Vol. 1. Theory in Industrial and Organizational Psychology* (pp. 75–170). Palo Alto, CA: Consulting Psychologists Press.

Kernan, M. C., and Lord, R. G. (1990) Effects of valence, expectancies, and goal–performance discrepancies in single and multiple goal environments. *Journal of Applied Psychology*, 75, 194–203.

Klein, H. J. (1989) An integrated control theory model of work motivation. *Academy of Management Review*, 14, 150–172.

Kristof, A. L. (1996) Person–organization fit: An integrative review of its conceptualizations, measurement, and implications. *Personnel Psychology*, 49, 1–49.

Kristof-Brown, A. L., and Stevens, C. K. (2001) Goal congruence in project teams: Does the fit between members' personal mastery and performance goals matter? *Journal of Applied Psychology*, 86, 1083–1095.

Kristof-Brown, A. L., Zimmerman, R. D., and Johnson, E. C. (2005) Consequences of individuals' fit at work: A meta-analysis of person–job, person–organization, person–group, and person–supervisor fit. *Personnel Psychology*, 58, 281–342.

Lambert, L. S., Edwards, J. R., and Cable, D. M. (2003) Breach and fulfillment of the psychological contract: A comparison of traditional and expanded views. *Personnel Psychology*, 56, 895–934.

Lasane, T. P., and Jones, J. M. (2000) When socially induced temporal myopia interferes with academic goal-setting. *Journal of Social Behavior and Personality*, 15, 75–86.

Latham, G. P., and Pinder, C. C. (2005) Work motivation theory and research at the dawn of the twenty-first century. *Annual Review of Psychology*, 56, 485–516.

Lawrence, J. W., Carver, C. S., and Scheier, M. F. (2002) Velocity toward goal attainment in immediate experience as a determinant of affect. *Journal of Applied Social Psychology*, 32, 788–802.

Lee, T. W., and Mitchell, T. R. (1994) An alternative approach: The unfolding model of voluntary employee turnover. *Academy of Management Review*, 19, 51–89.

Locke, E. A. (1976) The nature and causes of job satisfaction. In M. D. Dunnette (ed.), *Handbook of Industrial and Organizational Psychology* (pp. 1297–1349). Chicago: Rand McNally.

Locke, E. A., and Latham, G. P. (1990) *A Theory of Goal Setting and Task Performance.* Englewood Cliffs, NJ: Prentice Hall.

Lord, R. G., and Brown, D. J. (2004) *Leadership Processes and Follower Self-Identity.* Mahwah, NJ: Lawrence Erlbaum.

Lord, R. G., and Levy, P. E. (1994) Moving from cognition to action: A control theory perspective. *Applied Psychology: An International Review, 43,* 335–367.

Lord, R. G., Diefendorff, J. M., Schmidt, A. M., and Hall, R. J. (2010) Self-regulation at work. *Annual Review of Psychology, 61,* 543–568.

Maslow, A. (1943) A theory of human motivation. *Psychological Review, 50,* 370–396.

Miller, G. A., Galanter, E. H., and Pribram, K. H. (1960) *Plans and the Structure of Behavior.* New York: Holt, Rinehart, & Winston.

Mitchell, T. R., and Beach, L. R. (1990) "... Do I love thee? Let me count... " Toward an understanding of intuitive and automatic decision making. *Organizational Behavior and Human Decision Processes, 47,* 1–20.

Muchinsky, P. M., and Monahan, C. J. (1987) What is person–environment congruence? Supplementary versus complementary models of fit. *Journal of Vocational Behavior, 31,* 268–277.

Newell, A., Shaw, J. C., and Simon, H. A. (1958) Elements of a theory of human problem solving. *Psychological Review, 65,* 151–166.

Pelled, L. H., and Xin, K. R. (2000) Relational demography and relationship quality in two cultures. *Organizational Studies, 21,* 1077–1094.

Pezzo, M. V., Litman, J. A., and Pezzo, S. P. (2006) On the distinction between yuppies and hippies: Individual differences in prediction biases for planning future tasks. *Personality and Individual Differences, 41,* 1359–1371.

Piasentin, K. A., and Chapman, D. S. (2006) Subjective person–organization fit: Bridging the gap between conceptualization and measurement. *Journal of Vocational Behavior, 69,* 202–221.

Powers, W. T. (1973) *Behavior: The Control of Perception.* Chicago: Aldine.

Resick, C. J., Baltes, B. B., and Shantz, C. W. (2007) Person–organization fit and work-related attitudes and decisions: Examining interactive effects with job fit and conscientiousness. *Journal of Applied Psychology. 92,* 1446–1455.

Roberts, B. W., and Robins, R. W. (2004) Person–environment fit and its implications for personality development: A longitudinal study. *Journal of Personality, 72,* 91–110.

Roberts, B. W., Walton, K., and Viechtbauer, W. (2006) Patterns of mean-level change in personality traits across the life course: A meta-analysis of longitudinal studies. *Psychological Bulletin, 132,* 1–25.

Scheier, M. F., and Carver, C. S. (1983) Self-directed attention and the comparison of self with standards. *Journal of Experimental Social Psychology, 19,* 205–222.

Schmidt, A. M., and DeShon, R. P. (2007) What to do? The effects of discrepancies, incentives, and time on dynamic goal prioritization. *Journal of Applied Psychology, 92,* 928–941.

Schmidt, A. M., Dolis, C. M., and Tolli, A. P. (2009) A matter of time: Individual differences, contextual dynamics, and goal progress effects on multiple-goal self-regulation. *Journal of Applied Psychology, 94,* 692–709.

Schmitt, N., Oswald, F. L., Freide, A., Imus., A., and Merritt, S. (2008) Perceived fit with an academic environment: Attitudinal and behavioral outcomes. *Journal of Vocational Behavior, 72,* 317–335.

Schwartz, S. H. (1992) Universals in the content and structure of values: Theoretical advances and empirical tests in 20 countries. In M. Zanna (ed.), *Advances in Experimental Social Psychology* (Vol. 25, pp. 1–65). San Diego, CA: Academic Press.

Shantz, C. A. (2003) Person–organization fit: Individual differences, socialization, and outcomes. *Dissertation Abstracts International: Section B: The Sciences and Engineering*, 64 (3-B), 1536.

Shipp, A. J. (2006) The moving window of fit: Extending person–environment fit research with time. Unpublished doctoral dissertation, University of North Carolina at Chapel Hill.

Singh, R., and Greenhaus, J. H. (2004) The relation between career decision-making strategies and person–job fit: A study of job changers. *Journal of Vocational Behavior*, 64, 198–221.

Stuss, D. T. (1991) Self, awareness, and the frontal lobes: A neuropsychological perspective. In J. Strauss and G. R. Goethals (eds), *The Self: Interdisciplinary Approaches* (pp. 255–278). New York: Springer.

Swann, W. B., Jr, Johnson, R. E., and Bosson, J. K. (2009) Identity negotiation at work. In B. M. Staw and A. P. Brief (eds), *Research in Organizational Behavior* (Vol. 29, pp. 81–109). Oxford: Elsevier.

Turban, D. B., Lau, C., Ngo, H., Chow, I. H., and Si, S. X. (2001) Organizational attractiveness of firms in the People's Republic of China: A person–organization fit perspective. *Journal of Applied Psychology*, 86, 194–206.

Vallacher, R. R., and Wegner, D. M. (1985) *A Theory of Action Identification*. Hillsdale, NJ: Lawrence Erlbaum.

Vallacher, R. R., and Wegner, D. M. (1989) Levels of personal agency: Individual variation in action identification. *Journal of Personality and Social Psychology*, 57, 660–671.

Vancouver, J. B. (2005) The depth of history and explanation as benefit and bane for psychological control theories. *Journal of Applied Psychology*, 90, 38–52.

Vancouver, J. B. (2008) Integrating self-regulation theories of work motivation into a dynamic process theory. *Human Resource Management Review*, 18, 1–18.

Verquer, M. L., Beehr, T. A., and Wagner, S. H. (2003) A meta-analysis of relations between person–organization fit and work attitudes. *Journal of Vocational Behavior*, 63, 473–489.

Vinogradova, O. S. (1975) Functional organization of the limbic system in the process of registration of information: Facts and hypotheses. In R. L. Isaacson and K. H. Pribram (eds), *The Hippocampus: 2. Neurophysiology and Behavior* (pp. 1–70). New York: Plenum Press.

Warr, P. (1990) Decision latitude, job demands, and employee well-being. *Work and Stress*, 4, 285–294.

Wrosch, C., Miller, G. E., and Scheier, M. F. (2007) Giving up on unattainable goals: Benefits for health? *Personality and Social Psychology Bulletin*, 33, 251–265.

5

Person–Organization Fit, Organizational Citizenship, and Social-Cognitive Motivational Mechanisms

Christian J. Resick
Drexel University

Tomas R. Giberson
Oakland University

Marcus W. Dickson
Wayne State University

Kevin T. Wynne
Wayne State University

Linda M. Bajdo
Macomb Community College

Person–organization (PO) fit provides an integrative mechanism for examining the linkages between people and the organizations for which they work (Chatman, 1989; Kristof, 1996). Previous research has demonstrated that PO fit is associated with a wide range of positive outcomes for both employees and employers (see Kristof-Brown *et al.*, 2005). Citizenship performance (e.g., Cable and DeRue, 2002; Lauver and Kristof-Brown, 2001) and motivation are two important outcomes (Bretz and Judge, 1994; Mitchell, 1997). More specifically, people who perceive a strong sense of fit with their employing organization tend to be good organizational citizens (see Kristof-Brown *et al.*, 2005) by regularly engaging in discretionary behaviors that benefit both co-workers and the firm as a whole (Borman and Motowidlo, 1993).

Organizational Fit: Key Issues and New Directions, First Edition.
Edited by Amy L. Kristof-Brown and Jon Billsberry.
© 2013 John Wiley & Sons, Ltd. Published 2013 by John Wiley & Sons, Ltd.

Moreover, because of the discretionary nature of citizenship performance, Kristof-Brown and Guay (2011) posited that PO fit brings about a motivation to support the overall success of an organization, not just to perform a job well. As such, motivational forces are likely to serve as an important mediating mechanism linking PO fit to citizenship performance. To date, however, there has been little consideration of the psychological mechanisms that provide the underlying motivation that links PO fit and organizational citizenship.

The purpose of this chapter is to present a theoretical model examining the social-cognitive psychological processes that are triggered by a person's conscious perception of fit with an organization, and which then motivate that person to be a good organizational citizen. We begin by discussing the link between PO fit and citizenship performance. Next, we draw upon Mischel and Shoda's (1995) cognitive-affective personality system (CAPS) theory to identify the psychological mechanisms linking PO fit perceptions to organizational citizenship. We discuss the formation of fit-related schema and examine how an encoding process of matching organizational features to the content of fit-related schema results in the conscious determination of the degree of fit with an organization. This determination, in turn, activates a series of cognitive and affective reactions (or mediating units), which together provide the motivational drive to engage in citizenship performance behaviors. Finally, recognizing that the model of processes unfolds in a dynamic manner, we discuss the role of self-regulation processes in the on going activation of the cognitive and affective mediating units, and refinement of fit perceptions and fit-related schema. We present 10 propositions to guide future research, and conclude with a discussion of the theoretical implications of the proposed model. As a point of clarification, in this chapter we limit our discussion to perceptions of strong versus weak PO fit, as opposed to perceptions of PO fit versus misfit.

Organizational Fit and Citizenship

PO fit and performance

Findings from several comprehensive meta-analyses indicate that people who perceive themselves to be a good fit with the organization they work for tend to have more positive attitudes and form stronger intentions to remain with the organization than people who perceive that they fit the organization less well (see Hoffman and Woehr, 2006; Kristof-Brown *et al.*, 2005; Verquer *et al.*, 2003). Interestingly, the link between PO fit and task or overall job performance is "quite small to nonexistent" (Kristof-Brown and Guay, 2011, p. 33) as the estimated effect size across studies is near zero ($\rho = 0.07$; see Kristof-Brown *et al.*, 2005). However, when the focus shifts to citizenship performance or behaviors, the estimated effects are substantially larger ($\rho = 0.27$; see Kristof-Brown *et al.*, 2005).

Prior studies indicate that PO fit tends to be more strongly related to organization-focused outcomes than job-focused outcomes (Cable and DeRue, 2002; Greguras and Diefendorff, 2009). As citizenship is targeted at the benefit of an organization and its members, it is an important performance-related outcome of PO fit. In addition, citizenship is a discretionary form of performance: employees must decide whether or not to engage in acts of citizenship (Borman and Motowidlo, 1993). Motivation is therefore a key driver of citizenship-oriented behaviors, and PO fit is a trigger of those motivational forces (Kristof-Brown and Guay, 2011).

Citizenship performance

In an effort to integrate various perspectives on citizenship behaviors and contextual performance, Coleman and Borman (2000) identified 27 behaviors encompassing the domain of prosocial work behaviors. Using multidimensional scaling and cluster analysis techniques, they grouped these behaviors into three dimensions: interpersonal-focused citizenship, organizational-focused citizenship, and job/task conscientiousness. Following the suggestions of Organ (1997), Coleman and Borman (2000) referred to the overall set of dimensions as citizenship performance, representing discretionary behaviors that shape "the organizational, social, and psychological context that serves as the critical catalyst for task activities and processes" (Borman and Motowidlo, 1993, p. 71). Throughout this chapter, we use the term *citizenship performance* to refer to the domain of discretionary, prosocial work performance.

Interpersonal-focused citizenship involves behaviors that directly benefit other organization members such as helping, cooperation, and courtesy. Organization-focused citizenship involves behaviors that benefit the overall organization, including supporting organizational initiatives, following procedures, and loyalty. Job/task conscientiousness citizenship involves behaviors that benefit the job or task, including initiative, extra effort, or dedication (Coleman and Borman, 2000).

As noted previously, perceptions of PO fit have been found to be positively related to citizenship across studies (Hoffman and Woehr, 2006; Kristof-Brown *et al.*, 2005). However, to date, there has been little attention devoted to understanding how and why PO fit is linked to organizational citizenship. We draw on Mischel and Shoda's (1995) CAPS theory to examine how PO fit perceptions trigger a series of cognitive-affective motivational mechanisms within the context of a particular organization, which then generate citizenship performance.

An Integrative Social-Cognitive Model

CAPS

According to Mischel and Shoda's (1995) CAPS theory – a social-cognitive theory of personality – individuals have stable overall behavioral dispositions and tendencies, as well as "stable patterns of behavioral variability across situations" (p. 246). In general, CAPS theory is based on "if ... then" logic; *if* a person recognizes environmental features that have personal relevance, *then* a set of cognitive and affective reactions are activated which then generate patterns of behavior. The environmental features that are important, and ways in which they are relevant, differ from person to person, based on factors such as preferences, experiences, etc.

According to Mischel and Shoda (1995), the first stage of the CAPS model is an encoding process. Here, individuals recognize situational features, and match these features to existing cognitive categories about situations, events, people, and the self. Once situational features are encoded, a series of cognitive and affective reactions (or mediating units) occur, including *expectancies and beliefs, affect, goals and values,* and *competencies and self-regulatory plans. Expectancies and beliefs* refer to beliefs about the situation and outcomes of behavior in that particular situation. *Affect* refers to the emotions and moods that occur as a reaction to the situation. *Goals and values* represent the desired outcomes that people pursue. *Competencies and self-regulatory plans* involve strategies, potential behaviors, and scripts that people form to organize their behavior. The activation of the set of cognitive and affective reactions, and the interrelationships among these reactions, form a processing disposition, which is the second stage of the CAPS model. The processing disposition is a mediating mechanism that links the encoding of situational features to patterns of behavior in that situation. Thus, the activation of the cognitive and affective mediating units explains why a person engages in similar patterns of behavior in environments that have similar psychosocial features and acts differently in environments that have different psychosocial features. Again, the personal relevance of those psychosocial features differs from person to person.

Mischel and Shoda's (1995) CAPS theory provides an integrative framework for understanding the motivational mechanisms linking PO fit to citizenship performance. The process begins with an encoding process that involves an individual matching psychosocial features of the organization to fit-related schema and making a conscious determination of the degree of fit with that organization. This determination then activates four cognitive-affective processes, including the incorporation of organizational membership into one's social identity, the experience of positive affective states, the formation of goal strivings aimed at organizational success, and the shaping of expectations of how personal effort will contribute to organizational success. These processes provide the underlying motivation to engage in citizenship performance. We then use self-regulation processes, which are a core element of both cognitive motivation (Bandura, 1991; Kanfer, 1990) and CAPS theory (Mischel and Schoda, 1995), to examine how these processes unfold over time. We argue that self-regulation processes create a series of feedback loops; self-reactions to the feedback alter the intensity of cognitive and affective reactions, the strength of fit perceptions, and the content of fit-related schema over time. The process is summarized graphically in Figure 5.1.

Fit-related schema and encoding processes

CAPS theory argues that people match features of the environment to existing categories that they have stored cognitively (Mischel and Shoda, 1995). These cognitive

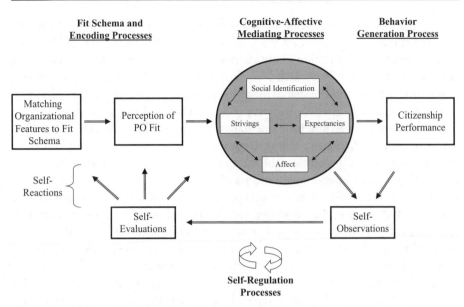

Figure 5.1 Proposed model of the cognitive and affective motivational processes linking PO fit to citizenship performance

categories equate to schemas, which are cognitive knowledge structures (Fiske and Taylor, 1991; Rumelhart and Ortony, 1977). Schemas contain a set of attributes that people use to recognize objects, events, and ideas (Kraiger and Wenzel, 1997), make predictions about unknown attributes, and process new information that relates to the central aspects of the schema (Norman *et al.*, 1976). These knowledge structures are stored in long-term memory, and people use them to make sense of and interact with the world around them (Rumelhart, 1984). Two assumptions about schemas are particularly important for understanding the formation of fit perceptions. First, schemas contain general knowledge rather than time-bound episodes. Second, schemas are activated when a person comes in contact with relevant information (see Smith, 1998). We propose that people develop a schema containing attributes of organizational environments that are a good fit, and use this schema to determine their degree of fit with an organization.

CAPS theory also argues that people attend to the elements in their psychosocial environment that are personally relevant (Mischel and Shoda, 1995). Regarding the elements of fit-related schemas, prior research has identified a number of environmental features that people take into account when assessing fit with an organization, including cultural values, climates, structural characteristics, goals, ethics, demands, and the personality and values of other organizational members (e.g., Ambrose *et al.*, 2007; Brigham *et al.*, 2007; Cable and Edwards, 2004; Cable and Judge, 1996; Coldwell *et al.*, 2008; Edwards and Cable, 2009; Gregarus and Diefendorff, 2009; Herrback and Mignonac, 2007; Judge and Cable, 1997; O'Reilly *et al.*, 1991; Ostroff and Rothausen, 1997; Resick *et al.*, 2007; Van Vianen, 2000; Vancouver and Schmitt, 1991).

Organizational environments are frequently characterized in terms of their culture and climates (see Ashkanasy *et al.*, 2000; Reichers and Schneider, 1990). Congruence with an organization's culture, particularly its shared values, has been a common focus in PO fit research (see Kristof-Brown and Guay, 2011). Organizational culture represents the shared meaning behind organizational events (Rentsch, 1990) that manifests itself in artifacts (e.g., structures, work processes, physical features), shared values, and fundamental assumptions that guide collective behavior (Rousseau, 1990; Schein, 2003). Organizational climate is a similar construct that refers to shared perceptions of the practices, expectations, and policies that characterize a work environment and provide a frame of reference for determining appropriate behavior (James and James, 1989; Schneider, 1975; Schneider and Reichers, 1983). In addition to shared values, cultural artifacts and organizational climates provide evidence of the psychosocial features of an organization that supply the psychological needs for some employees. At the same time, distinct organizational environments and modal personality characteristics emerge from the personality and values of people who are attracted to, selected by, and remain with an organization (Schneider, 1987; Schneider *et al.*, 1998). A person's sense of organizational compatibility is enhanced when "the things that are most important to that employee are also important to other employees" (Cable and Edwards, 2004, p. 823). Finally, organizational goals (e.g., Vancouver and Schmitt, 1991), demands (e.g., Brigham *et al.*, 2007), and ethical expectations (e.g., Ambrose, Arnaud, and Schminke, 2007) are also important organizational features used in the evaluation of organizational fit.

Some individuals may have a strong preference to work in organizations with structural characteristics or work arrangements that supply psychological needs such as performance-based reward programs. Others may seek out organizations with one or more specific cultural values such as competitive excellence, teamwork, or innovation. Still others may take a holistic approach that takes into consideration their interactions with other members, their perceptions of the firm's culture and climate, and the extent to which structural or work characteristics supply psychological needs. As such, we expect that the types of information people take into account when determining their compatibility with a firm vary considerably from person to person, and thus we present the following proposition.

Proposition 1: People develop fit schemas containing unique psychosocial features of organizational environments for which they are compatible.

Mischel and Shoda's (1995) CAPS theory proposes that the recognition of important situational features begins an encoding process in which environmental features are matched to existing categories. People find relevant cues about an organization's environment through the characteristics of other members (micro level), the values, perceptions, and norms shared among members (meso level), and the organization's goals, structures, systems, and practices (macro level). These cues provide information about the prevalence of desired and disliked organizational features. When a person recognizes the personally relevant organizational features, an encoding process is initiated in which the more and less desired organizational features are matched to the contents of fit-related schema. As a result, a person makes a conscious determination of the extent to which he or she fits the organization. This assessment represents a "molar" perception of PO fit, which is based on an individual's overall assessment of compatibility with the organization (Edwards *et al.*, 2006). Molar perceptions of fit are thought to be a cognitively accessible filter through which the objective fit between a person's characteristics and an organization's characteristics is translated into personal attitudes, decisions, and actions (Cable and DeRue, 2002; Edwards *et al.*, 2006; Judge and Cable, 1997; Kristof-Brown *et al.*, 2005).

In addition, this determination of fit may happen actively or passively. Some individuals may actively seek out information about the features that are most critical for determining fit with that organization, particularly when considering applying for a position, when accepting an offer, or having just entered the firm. Other individuals in these same situations may take a more passive, reflective approach that involves reflecting upon events that occur or experiences with people they encounter and making a determination about the issues that are most important to them. Therefore, we propose that molar PO fit perceptions are formed by actively or reflectively matching features of the organization's psychosocial environment to fit-related schema and present the following proposition.

Proposition 2: Recognition of relevant organizational features activates a fit-related schema that results in the conscious determination of the degree of PO fit.

Schemas are reflective of a learning process and develop as a result of life experiences (Poole *et al.*, 1990). By experiencing different degrees of fit over time, we expect that the contents of fit-related schemas are continuously refined. New graduates enter the workforce with little understanding of organizational life, which subsequently limits their ability to make informed employment decisions based on organizational environments (Billsberry, 2007). When people first begin their working career, they are joining organizations based upon a more rudimentary understanding of the type of firm they want to work for. This may be based on an organization being listed among Fortune's *100 Best Companies to Work For* (e.g., Colvin, 2006) or opinions that people tend to form about the qualities of well-known companies (e.g., Brooks *et al.*, 2003). These generally superficial forms of company information may contribute to the formation of unrealistic expectations for less experienced workers. For example, new graduates also have a tendency to enter into their first jobs with unrealistic expectations about the firms for which they work (e.g., Arnold, 1985; Mabey, 1986; Nicholson and Arnold, 1991). Then, as people gain experience working for one or more organizations, they begin to develop a more nuanced understanding of the types of organizational features that are personally important. As a result, people are able to refine the contents of fit-related schemas. In turn, experienced individuals should be able to recognize features of an organization's psychosocial environment that are personally relevant more quickly than less experienced individuals, and they should also make more accurate judgments of the degree of fit with a particular organization. Therefore, we present the following proposition.

> Proposition 3: Work experience is positively related to the complexity of the content of fit schemas; experienced workers are more able to quickly and accurately determine their degree of fit with an organization than are less experienced workers.

Cognitive-affective mediating processes

According to CAPS theory, the encoding process activates a set of interrelated cognitive-affective mediating mechanisms that ultimately generate behavior (Mischel and Shoda, 1995). Drawing upon CAPS theory and findings from prior PO fit research (see Kristof-Brown, Zimmerman, and Johnson's 2005 meta-analysis), we point to four cognitive and affective mechanisms that provide the motivational force mediating the relationship between PO fit perceptions and citizenship performance. These mechanisms are: (a) social identification, (b) positive affective states, (c) goal strivings, and (d) expectancies. We now examine each mechanism further.

Social identification. Through social identification, people integrate their membership of various social groups (e.g., ethnic groups, religious organizations, work organizations, etc.) into their self-concept and define themselves in terms of membership in these groups (Banaji and Prentice, 1994; Tajfel and Turner, 1985; Turner and Haslam, 2001). This identification increases group commitment (O'Reilly, 1989), engenders a sense of belonging, and elicits motivation to work toward the group's interests (van Knippenberg, 2000).

Organizational identification is a form of social identification in which people define themselves in terms of their membership in a particular organization (Ashforth and Mael, 1989; Mael and Ashforth, 1992; Mael and Tetrick, 1992; Pratt, 1998). Ashforth and Mael (1989) have argued that two factors facilitate the formation of organizational identification. First, people more easily identify with organizations that have distinct values and normative practices. Second, people are more likely to identify with organizations when they like their co-workers and work with similar types of people. Organizational identification, in turn, influences the ways in which a person interacts with other members of the organization (Turner and Haslam, 2001).

Social identification emerges from the cognitive links that people form between personal and group identities; these links are thought to form through social comparison and self-categorization processes (Hogg and Abrams, 1988). In terms of social comparison processes, people accentuate the positive characteristics of the social groups they belong to and use these characteristics to amplify between-group differences (e.g., Abrams and Hogg, 1990; Wood, 1989). People then engage in self-categorization processes through which they come to emphasize membership in social groups, particularly those that are distinctive and prestigious (Hogg and

Abrams, 1988). Recently, researchers have begun to examine the dynamic nature of social identification processes. For example, Ashforth, Harrison, and Corley (2008) argued that organizational identification evolves through a dynamic "interplay between individuals and organizations" (p. 340); individuals engage in sense-making activities while organizations engage in sense-giving activities. These activities engender the social comparisons and self-categorizations that promote and encourage organizational identification.

Perceptions of organizational fit have been found to be strongly related to organizational identification (e.g., Cable and DeRue, 2002). People who perceive high levels of compatibility with an organization for which they work define themselves in terms of their membership in those organizations (Saks and Ashforth, 1997). As such, organizational membership becomes a salient aspect of the working self-concept. Identity salience is important in the context of the proposed model as more salient identities within the self-concept have a greater motivational impact than less salient identities (Shamir, 1990; van Knippenberg, 2000). When organizational identification is high and organizational membership is salient, people perceive that their fate is intertwined with the group's fate (Ashforth and Mael, 1989), and they personally experience the successes and failures of the group (Foote, 1951; Tolman, 1943). Acts of organizational citizenship help the organization to operate successfully, and by doing so are self-enhancing for individuals who have a high level of organizational identification. As such, we propose that organizational identification is one cognitive mechanism through which perceived PO fit is linked to citizenship performance, and we present the following proposition.

> Proposition 4: The degree of perceived fit with an organization is positively related to social identification with the organization and the integration of organizational membership into the working self-concept, such that being an employee of the organization is a salient and important aspect of one's self identity.

Affect. Positive affect refers to "pleasant feelings induced by commonplace events or circumstances" (Isen and Baron, 1991, p. 1). In adults, affective states are brought about by perceptions of environmental characteristics and events (Lazarus, 1982). The workplace provides one set of environmental factors that has a powerful impact on employee affective states (George, 1991; Spector and Fox, 2002). Moods and emotions are two forms of affective reactions. Emotions are short-lived, intense, and stem from a specific incident (e.g., Frijda, 1993; Simon, 1982; Zajonc, 1998). Moods, on the other hand, are longer-lasting affective experiences that influence thought processes and behaviors, but are not associated with any particular event (Brief and Weiss, 2002; Clark and Isen, 1982; George and Brief, 1992). In turn, moods and emotions induced by the workplace are key drivers of work-related beliefs, attitudes, discretionary behaviors, and performance (e.g., Beal *et al.*, 2005; Forgas and George, 2001; Weiss and Cropanzano, 1996).

According to CAPS theory (Mischel and Shoda, 1995), people experience positive moods and emotions when they view a particular situation favorably, and these positive affective states contribute to the motivation to engage in certain patterns of behavior. According to person–environment (PE) fit theory, the optimal congruence between people and their environment leads to positive experiences (Dawis, 1992; Dawis and Lofquist, 1984). Based on the consistent finding that PO fit is related to positive work-related attitudes such as satisfaction and commitment (see Kristof-Brown *et al.*, 2005; Verquer *et al.*, 2003), we expect that PO fit perceptions induce positive affective experiences. As moods are more general affective reactions than emotions, we expect that the encoding process and determination of the degree of PO fit induce generally positive moods. In turn, specific events that reinforce perceptions of the environment or provide new cues regarding the organization's environment should induce emotional reactions. For example, a person who has a performance orientation, who values the spirit of competition, and who works for an organization that rewards people for their performance is likely to perceive a sense of compatibility with the organization. We expect that person to experience generally positive moods during the workday. Later, if that same person comes to learn that the organization is a true meritocracy that uses a detailed performance management system to link rewards with performance, he or she receives reinforcing information. As a result, the employee should experience a happy or positive emotional reaction to the information. In contrast, if that same person comes to learn that the organization actually encourages little differentiation in performance ratings or pay, he or she receives incongruent information. As a result, the employee is likely to react with emotional reactions such as disappointment or irritation.

A substantial amount of literature indicates that positive affect is associated with prosocial behaviors such as cooperation, helping, and negotiation (see Isen and Baron, 1991). In organizational settings, positive affective states may lead to favorable opinions about the firm, co-workers, supervisors, or customers, which then results in increased levels of citizenship performance (Dalal, 2005; George, 1991; Spector and Fox, 2002). Engaging in helping behavior is also self-reinforcing, such that it enables a person to maintain a positive affective condition (Clark and Isen, 1982; Isen *et al.*, 1978). When people form a strong sense of fit with their organization and subsequently experience positive feelings, they are likely to engage in behaviors that help to maintain the positive state and that serve to protect or benefit the organization (George and Brief, 1992). We therefore propose that positive mood and emotions brought on by PO fit perceptions contribute to the motivation to engage in citizenship performance behaviors and present the following proposition.

Proposition 5: The degree of perceived fit with an organization is positively related to the frequency and duration of positive affective states concerning the organization and employment with the company.

Goal strivings. Intentions are a proximal indicator of behavior (Ajzen, 1985; Klein, 1991) and encompass "both the *objective* (or goal) one is striving for and the *action plan* one intends to use to reach that objective" (Tubbs and Ekeberg, 1991, p. 181).

Intentions are reflected in the things that people strive for, and these goal strivings represent the cognitive motivation to act (Barrick *et al.*, 2002). Hogan and Shelton (1998) noted that people have two basic goals they strive to attain, "getting along" and "getting ahead" (p. 130). Barrick, Stewart, and Piotrowski (2002) built on this distinction and defined three types of motivational striving important in work settings: *communion striving, status striving,* and *accomplishment striving.* Each form of striving is believed to motivate behavior congruent with that striving.

Both communion striving and status striving are broad intentions focusing on social interactions (Bakan, 1966; Hogan, 1996; Hogan and Shelton, 1998; Wiggins and Trapnell, 1996). Communion striving involves intentions to affiliate and get along well with others at work, such as striving to include co-workers in key decisions. Status striving involves intentions to obtain positions of prominence in the organization's status hierarchy, as well as seeking to gain recognition within the organization. Accomplishment striving focuses on work-related goals, such as completing projects and devoting effort to assignments.

Mischel and Shoda's (1995) CAPS theory argues that the recognition of psychosocial organizational features also triggers behavioral intentions, scripts, and strategies for organizing actions and internal states. When people experience a strong sense of fit with their employing organization, they are likely to place a high value on both their personal success within the firm and the overall success of the firm. As a result, we expect that they will strive to: (a) achieve success in their respective roles, (b) actively contribute toward the achievement of the organization's strategic goals, (c) gain visibility and positions of higher prominence, and (d) get along well with co-workers. For example, people who fit their organizations are likely to cooperate with others and volunteer to help co-workers, as these actions help to build cohesion and enhance the work environment. Likewise, people who have a strong sense of organizational fit will want to maintain employment and strive to gain positions of higher status and visibility. In addition, the overall success of the organization is likely to be important and self-enhancing, and people will strive to contribute to the organization's success, either by performing acts that benefit the organization or by striving to do a good job. Therefore, we propose the following proposition.

> Proposition 6: The degree of perceived fit with an organization is positively related to the formation of: (a) communion strivings, (b) status strivings, and (c) achievement strivings.

Expectancies. Expectancies are a central component of Mischel and Shoda's (1995) CAPS theory and Vroom's (1964) expectancy motivation theory. According to expectancy theory, people are motivated to put forth effort if they believe that: (a) their efforts will lead to higher performance (expectancies), (b) higher performance will be instrumental in gaining important outcomes (instrumental), and (c) those outcomes are highly valued (valence). CAPS theory focuses specifically on the expectancy component, which addresses the perceived probability that personal efforts will lead to a performance outcome. Across studies, expectancy has been found to be related to motivational effort and intentions, along with supervisor ratings of performance (see Van Eerde and Thierry, 1996).

Mischel and Shoda (1995) argued that the recognition of situational features triggers expectations and beliefs about the situation and outcomes of behavior. Extending their theory to the organizational fit arena, for people who have a strong sense of organizational fit, the success of the organization is personally important as it enables the company to sustain a competitive market position, provides resources that enhance the work environment, and lessens the potential for downsizing initiatives. In addition, PO fit is negatively related to turnover intentions (see Hoffman and Woehr, 2006; Kristof-Brown *et al.*, 2005), which indicates a desire to maintain employment with that organization. As a result, people may form expectations that their efforts will contribute to being viewed as a valued member of the firm, and help to protect their employment. As such, we expect that people who have a strong sense of fit with an organization engage in citizenship performance, in part because they expect their efforts to contribute to the overall success of the organization and their ability to maintain their employment with that firm. For example, people who have a strong sense of PO fit are more likely to stay late to meet a project deadline, assist a colleague in meeting a deadline, or volunteer to serve on an orientation committee than someone who perceives a weaker level of fit with the organization because they expect their efforts to help the organization to be successful. Therefore, expectancies provide another cognitive mechanism linking PO fit perceptions to citizenship, and we offer the following proposition.

> Proposition 7: The degree of perceived fit with an organization is positively related to expectations that personal efforts will: (a) help the organization to be successful and (b) enhance the work environment.

Behavior generation process

Mischel and Shoda (1995) also argued that each of the four cognitive and affective units are connected through a stable network of relationships. As such, the units work together and influence one another. For example, positive moods and emotions tend to influence the behaviors people choose to adopt (George and Brief, 1996), expectancy motivation (Erez and Isen, 2002), and how people make judgments and think about their settings (Forgas and George, 2001; Isen and Baron, 1991). Likewise, because the success of the organization is self-enhancing to people who identify with the organization (Turner and Haslam, 2001), they are likely to form strivings and behaviors aimed at helping the organization succeed and expectations that personal efforts are an important contributor to organizational success.

CAPS theory goes on to propose that the four cognitive and affective mechanisms, and the network of interrelationships among them, create a processing disposition

(Mischel and Shoda, 1995). This processing disposition generates patterns of behavior in that situation. More specifically, the activation of one or more cognitive or affective units in response to features of a situation activates the remaining units through the network of interrelations that forms. This network of activated mechanisms is a processing disposition that provides an arousal for behavior generation and direction for that behavior.

Turning to the proposed model, we expect that the four cognitive and affective mechanisms combine through a network of interrelationships to form a processing disposition that channels effort toward citizenship performance. More specifically, the conscious determination of PO fit triggers positive reactions in each of the cognitive and affective mechanisms, and each activated mechanism contributes to the desire to be a good organizational citizen. In addition, organizational identification, positive affective reactions, expecting efforts to enhance the firm, and developing organization-enhancing goal strivings also form a network of interrelationships that activate and intensify the reactions among the units. This network of interrelationships, or processing disposition, creates an upward spiraling effect that provides a motivational basis for engaging in citizenship performance behaviors. Once activated, the processing disposition creates an arousal and directs efforts toward interpersonal-, organizational-, and job-focused citizenship, and increases the intensity and persistence of those efforts. Individuals who fit an organization well have little to lose and much to gain by helping the organization and co-workers to succeed because of the set of cognitive and affective reactions. In contrast, people who form a weak sense of fit with an organization experience more neutral, or perhaps even negative, cognitions and affective states. These experiences likely deter people from engaging in work outside of their specific role or area of responsibility and may cause people to view acts of citizenship as detracting from personal success. Therefore, we propose the following proposition.

> Proposition 8: People who perceive that they fit an organization well form a processing disposition that involves the activation of each of the four cognitive-affective units and a series of interrelationships among them, which in turn lead to the engagement in citizenship performance.

We also expect that the degree of perceived organizational fit directly influences the magnitude of the relationships with each of the cognitive and affective mechanisms. People with a strong sense of organizational fit are likely to incorporate organizational membership as a salient aspect of their self-concept and consistently experience positive moods in the workplace. At the same time, they are also likely to form clear motivational strivings that focus on organizational achievement, and hold steadfast expectations that their efforts contribute to organizational success. The strength of fit perceptions and the strength of the relationships with each of the cognitive and affective units should then spill over and influence the magnitude of the pattern of interrelationships among the cognitive and affective mediating units. Strong relationships between PO fit and any one of the four cognitive-affective reactions are likely to enhance the remaining reactions and thus intensify the processing disposition. That is, we propose that the degree of perceived fit is related to the magnitude of: (a) the relationships between fit perceptions and each cognitive or affective reaction, and (b) the interrelationships among the cognitive and affective reactions. The magnitude of these relationships and interrelationships represents the strength of the processing disposition; stronger processing dispositions lead to higher levels of citizenship performance.

> Proposition 9: The degree of perceived fit with an organization is positively related to the magnitude of the interrelations: (a) between perceived PO fit and each of the cognitive-affective units, and (b) among the cognitive-affective units. The magnitude of the interrelations is positively related to citizenship performance.

Self-regulation processes

People exercise control over their actions by making self-relevant evaluations and regulating the allocation of effort and attention to various goals and intentions (Kanfer and Ackerman, 1989; Lord and Hanges, 1987). Self-regulation operates through three psychological sub-functions, comprising self-observation, self-evaluation, and self-reaction (Bandura, 1982; 1991; Kanfer, 1970). In the self-observation sub-function, individuals gather information about their own behaviors that are relevant for attaining specific goals of interest (Bandura, 1982; 1986). These observations provide the diagnostic information that is used in the self-evaluation sub-function to judge progress by comparing behaviors or results to various standards (Bandura, 1991; Kanfer, 1990). Self-evaluation also involves an evaluation of the importance of these actions, as people are not likely to devote attention to activities they care little about (Bandura, 1991; Kanfer, 1990). Then, during the self-reaction sub-function, people respond to their evaluations by adjusting: (a) their goal-directed behavior, (b) the goals they are striving for, and (c) their beliefs about goals and their ability to achieve them (Bandura, 1991; Kanfer, 1990). These reactions typically lead to some level of satisfaction or dissatisfaction with performance or with the self (Kanfer and Ackerman, 1989). As such, self-regulation is a dynamic process through which people adjust their actions and beliefs in pursuit of desired goals (Bandura, 1991; Kanfer, 1990).

   Mischel and Shoda's (1995) CAPS theory indicates that self-regulation is important for organizing the competencies, plans, and strategies that generate patterns of social behavior, and thus it includes self-regulation processes as another cognitive-affective mediating unit. However, because of its dynamic nature, we use self-regulation to explain how these processes evolve over time. In what follows we examine how self-regulation processes create a series of feedback loops through which people adjust the intensity of their cognitive and affective reactions, and through which they refine their perceptions of organizational fit and the contents of their fit-related schemas.

Through self-regulation processes, people who perceive a strong sense of fit with an organization control the allocation of their attention and efforts toward the goal of building a successful organization and work environment. The process begins with people making self-observations of their citizenship, including how they support co-workers and the activities of the organization in general. People also make observations of the overall importance of their employing organization and role within the organization, the goals they strive for, the moods and emotions they experience at work, and whether they expect their efforts to generate success. These observations may be the result of self-awareness and internal interpretations of behavior. The observations may also stem from reflecting upon feedback from external sources such as supervisors and colleagues. Ultimately, self-observations provide important diagnostic information used to make self-evaluations of the extent to which behaviors, beliefs, and affective states exceed, match, or fall short of standards. People then react to these judgments by adjusting: (a) the intensity of cognitive and affective reactions, (b) perceptions of fit with the organization, and (c) the content of fit-related schema.

People are thought to experience some degree of satisfaction or dissatisfaction in reaction to evaluations of their progress, and, in turn, they adjust the intensity of their efforts (Bandura, 1991; Kanfer and Ackerman, 1989). Favorable evaluations of citizenship performance or progress toward important goals should lead to positive emotional reactions, such as happiness and a sense of satisfaction, while unfavorable judgments should produce less positive emotional reactions, such as disappointment or frustration. When judgments indicate that standards have not been met, mild affective reactions lead to more intense efforts whereas stronger affective reactions lead to the adjustment of standards and beliefs (Bandura, 1991), in this case about citizenship and the organization. Self-evaluations should also influence goal strivings and expectancies. Favorable judgments should result in maintaining current goal striving levels – or even intensifying strivings – and therefore reinforce expectations that personal efforts are an important contributor to organizational success. Less favorable judgments may result in adjusting expectations or goal strivings downwards to be congruent with beliefs about the organization and its capabilities. Judgments should also impact the distinctiveness of the organization and the salience of membership in the working self-concept.

The next set of self-reactions focus on clarifying perceptions of organizational fit and refining personal fit-related schemas. People develop and refine their assessments of fit with an organization over multiple pre- and post-hire experiences (Dickson *et al.*, 2008). These experiences are an important guide to organizing self-relevant information, and the importance people attach to a particular situation is influenced by how they feel in that situation (Greenwald and Pratkanis, 1984). For example, people who see themselves in a good mood at work and make a favorable judgment about the organization are likely to determine that the organization is a good match for their personal preferences or values. In contrast, people who form a more negative or neutral judgment about the organization are less likely to determine that they are a good fit with the organization. Thus, self-regulation processes help people to refine their perceptions of compatibility with the organization. In addition, once feedback is internalized, it is interpreted in the context of current schemas (DeNisi et al., 1984) and enables people to refine personally relevant schemas (London, 1995). Through reflections upon cognitive and affective reactions, acts of citizenship, and the outcomes of citizenship performance, people refine schemas containing the general and specific characteristics of compatible organizations. Therefore, we propose that self-regulation processes provide insights into the dynamic nature of the motivational processes linking PO fit and citizenship performance.

> Proposition 10: Through self-regulatory processes, individuals engage in self-observations and self-evaluations of their citizenship performance and cognitive and affective reactions. These evaluations lead to self-reactions that include adjustments to: (a) fit-related schema content, (b) the strength of PO fit perceptions, (c) social identification assessments, (d) affective states, (e) goal strivings, and (f) expectancies.

Discussion

At the conclusion of their comprehensive meta-analysis of the PE fit literature, Kristof-Brown, Zimmerman, and Johnson (2005) concluded that consistent patterns of relationships between fit and job-related attitudes, decisions, and behaviors provide "conclusive evidence that fit matters" (p. 325). In this chapter we have focused on one behavior-related outcome with the goal of explaining *how* and *why* PO fit matters relative to organizational citizenship. Good theory in the organizational sciences needs to provide explanation (Campbell, 1990), as well as meaning and direction for future research (Klein and Zedeck, 2004). To this aim, we formulated a theoretical model of the psychological mechanisms that link PO fit to citizenship, and we presented a series of propositions to guide future research. Aside from the formal propositions, the model also raises a number of broad issues for consideration in the organizational fit literature.

Theoretical issues for consideration

In this chapter, we view the perception of fit and the activation of the cognitive and affective mediating mechanisms as operating at a conscious level. However, the extent to which the encoding, mediating, and self-regulation processes operate at a conscious level versus an unconscious level is an issue that warrants greater theoretical and empirical examination. Goal-setting research provides some indication that motivational processes unfold on both a conscious and an unconscious level. For example, Stajkovic, Locke, and Blair (2006) found that goals have a stronger relationship with performance when the goal is conscious versus unconscious. However, they also found that subconscious goals interacted with conscious goals to enhance their effects on performance, suggesting that some mechanisms may unfold at an unconscious level. When people determine that the organization they work for is a good fit, they may consciously form communion, status, and accomplishment strivings that focus on helping the company and colleagues succeed. In contrast, people may experience positive moods and emotions when they have a strong sense of PO fit without being consciously aware of the reasons. Future research should examine which processes are more (or less) likely to unfold consciously as opposed to unconsciously. Similarly, some individuals are attuned to their environments and are generally more self-aware than others. As a result, individual differences may impact the extent to which these processes unfold consciously versus unconsciously. These are questions that present fruitful avenues for future research.

PO fit is a positive psychological experience and this chapter examines the motivational consequences of strong organizational fit. However, there have been few attempts to determine the extent to which organizational fit and organizational misfit are distinct psychological experiences. In relation to the proposed conceptual model, this raises two important questions: (a) what work-related behaviors are people who experience misfit motivated to engage in? and (b) what are the social-cognitive psychological processes that trigger these behaviors? Just because a person does not experience a sense of fit with an organization does not necessarily mean that the person experiences a sense of misfit. Different psychological processes are likely to be activated when a person makes a determination that "my organization cares about things that I don't care about" (perception of weak fit) and "my organization and I care about the same things, but we have opposing viewpoints" (perception of misfit; J. Billsberry, personal communication, June 28, 2010). Perhaps people react to misfit by disengaging from their job and organization and by focusing more intently on job-seeking behaviors. Alternatively, prior research has found that people who experience some forms of misfit are motivated to over-perform to protect their employment (Shallenberger, 1994). People who experience misfit and also have few alternative employment options may be motivated to engage in exceptional levels of task performance to protect their employment (J. Billsberry, personal communication, June 28, 2010). Others may experience extreme emotional reactions and become motivated to engage in deviant behaviors to ease the tensions they experience. Research is needed to determine if perceptions of organizational misfit activate a different series of cognitive-affective motivational mechanisms leading to a different set of behaviors, or if perceptions of PO misfit activate the same types of motivational mechanisms but with different reactions motivating different behaviors.

In this chapter, we have focused on the role of PO fit and cognitive and affective reactions to fit as motivational drivers of citizenship performance. At the same time, personality traits, particularly conscientiousness and agreeableness, have been found to be important internal indicators of both individual- and organizational-focused citizenship across a range of conditions and after controlling for relevant variables (e.g., Borman *et al.*, 2001; Dalal, 2005; Illies *et al.*, 2009; LePine *et al.*, 2002; Organ and Ryan, 1995). As personality traits have been linked with preferences for organizational culture values (Judge and Cable, 1997), agreeableness and conscientiousness traits may also be important indicators of organizational preferences. Agreeableness has been linked with communion striving (Barrick *et al.*, 2002) and preferences for supportive and team-oriented cultures (Judge and Cable, 1997). Perhaps agreeable individuals naturally seek out cooperative cultures where citizenship is outwardly encouraged. In these organizations, high agreeableness individuals are likely to experience positive moods and reactions, form communion strivings, naturally identify with their employer, and be highly motivated to engage in citizenship performance. Likewise conscientious individuals are dependable and driven (see Digman, 1989; Roberts *et al.*, 2005), tend to form accomplishment strivings (Barrick *et al.*, 2002), and prefer cultures that are detail oriented and outcome oriented. As a result, they may seek out organizations with similarly conscientious members who strive to work for a successful organization and expect their efforts to generate success. Highly conscientious individuals tend to place greater emphasis on PO fit perceptions than less conscientious individuals in their employment intentions and decisions (Resick *et al.*, 2007). As a result, the cognitive and affective mediating units may play a stronger mediating role in high versus low conscientious individuals.

Conclusion

Employees who are good organizational citizens help organizations to operate successfully. For example, unit-level citizenship has been linked with employee retention, cost containment, and enhanced productivity, efficiency, and profitability (see Podsakoff *et al.*, 2009). The reasons why people engage in organizational citizenship are numerous (see Ilies *et al.*, 2009; LePine *et al.*, 2002; Venkataramani and Dalal, 2007). In this chapter, our intent was not to provide a comprehensive discussion of the origins and antecedents of organizational citizenship. Rather, our intent was to focus specifically on the organizational fit–organizational citizenship linkage and outline the motivation-related processes that explain this relationship. Because PO fit arises from the unique interactions between people and the organizations in which they work, fit perceptions provide important insights into the motivational mechanisms that explain why people behave as they do at work.

References

Abrams, D., and Hogg, M. A. (1990) Social identification, self-categorization and social influence. In W. Stroebe and M. R. C. Hewstone (eds), *European Review of Social Psychology* (Vol. 1). Chichester: Wiley.

Ajzen, I. (1985) From intentions to actions: A theory of planned behavior. In J. Kuhl and J. Beckman (eds), *Action Control: From Cognition to Behavior* (pp. 11–39). Berlin: Springer.

Ambrose, M. L., Arnaud, A., and Schminke, M. (2007) Individual moral development and ethical climate: The influence of person–organization fit on job attitudes. *Journal of Business Ethics*, 77, 323–333.

Arnold, J. (1985) Tales of the unexpected: Surprises experienced by graduates in the early months of employment. *British Journal of Guidance and Counseling*, 13, 308–319.

Ashforth, B. E., and Mael, F. (1989) Social identity theory and the organization. *Academy of Management Review*, 14, 20–39.

Ashforth, B. E., Harrison, S. H., and Corley, K. G. (2008) Identification in organizations: An examination of four fundamental questions. *Journal of Management*, 34 (3), 325–374.

Ashkanasy, N. M., Wilderom, C. P. M., and Peterson, M. F. (2000) Introduction. In N. M. Ashkanasy, C. P. M. Wilderom, and M. F. Peterson (eds), *Handbook of Organizational Culture and Climate* (pp. 1–18). Thousand Oaks, CA: Sage.

Bakan, D. (1966) *The Duality of Human Existence: Isolation and Communion in Western Man.* Boston, MA: Beacon Press.

Banaji, M. R., and Prentice, D. A. (1994) The self in contexts. *Annual Review of Psychology*, 45, 297–332.

Bandura, A. (1982) The self and mechanisms of agency. In J. Suls (ed.), *Psychological Perspectives on the Self* (Vol. 1, pp. 3–39). Hillsdale, NJ: Lawrence Erlbaum.

Bandura, A. (1986) *Social Foundations of Thought and Action: A Social Cognitive Theory.* Englewood Cliffs, NJ: Prentice Hall.

Bandura, A. (1991) Social cognition theory on self-regulation. *Organizational Behavior and Human Decision Processes*, 50, 248–287.

Barrick, M. R., Stewart, G. L., and Piotrowski, M. (2002) Personality and job performance: Test of the mediating effects of motivation among sales representative. *Journal of Applied Psychology*, 87, 43–51.

Beal, D. J., Weiss, H. M., Barros, E., and MacDermid, S. M. (2005) An episodic process model of affective influences on performance. *Journal of Applied Psychology*, 90, 1054–1068.

Billsberry, J. (2007) Attracting for values: An empirical study of ASA's attraction proposition. *Journal of Managerial Psychology*, 22, 132–149.

Borman, W. C., and Motowidlo, S. J. (1993) Expanding the criterion domain to include elements of contextual performance. In N. Schmidt and W. C. Borman (eds), *Personnel Selection in Organizations* (pp. 71–98). San Francisco: Jossey-Bass.

Borman, W. C., Penner, L. A., Allen, T. A., and Motowidlo, S. J. (2001) Personality predictors of citizenship performance. *International Journal of Selection and Assessment*, 9, 52–69.

Bretz, R. D., and Judge, T. A. (1994) Person–organization fit and the theory of work adjustment: Implications for satisfaction, tenure, and career success. *Journal of Vocational Behavior*, 44, 32–54.

Brief, A. P., and Weiss, H. M. (2002) Organizational behavior: Affect in the workplace. *Annual Review of Psychology*, 53, 279–307.

Brigham, K. H., De Castro, J. O., and Shepherd, D. A. (2007) A person–organization fit model of owner-managers' cognitive style and organizational demands. *Entrepreneurship Theory and Practice*, 31, 29–51.

Brooks, M. E., Highhouse, S., Russell, S. S., and Mohr, D. C. (2003) Familiarity, ambivalence, and firm reputation: Is corporate fame a double-edged sword? *Journal of Applied Psychology*, 88 (5), 904–914.

Cable, D. M., and DeRue, D. S. (2002) The convergent and discriminant validity of subjective fit perceptions. *Journal of Applied Psychology*, 87, 875–884.

Cable, D. M., and Edwards, J.R. (2004) Complementary and supplementary fit: A theoretical and empirical integration. *Journal of Applied Psychology*, 89, 822–834.

Cable, D. M., and Judge, T. A. (1996) Person–organization fit, job choice decisions, and organizational entry. *Organizational Behavior and Human Decision Processes*, 67, 294–311.

Campbell, J. P. (1990) The role of theory in industrial and organizational psychology. In M. D. Dunnette and L. M. Hough (eds), *Handbook of Industrial and Organizational Psychology* (2nd edn, Vol. 1). Palo Alto, CA: Consulting Psychologists Press.

Chatman, J. A. (1989) Improving interactional organizational research: A model of person–organization fit. *Academy of Management Review*, 14, 333–349.

Clark, M. S., and Isen, A. M. (1982) Toward understanding the relationship between feeling states and social behavior. In A. Hastrof and A. M. Isen (eds), *Cognitive Social Psychology* (pp. 73–108). New York: Elsevier.

Coldwell, D. A., Billsberry, J., van Meurs, N., and Marsh, P. J. G. (2008) The effects of person–organization fit on employee attraction and retention: Towards a testable explanatory model. *Journal of Business Ethics*, 78, 611–622.

Coleman, V. I., and Borman, W. C. (2000) Investigating the underlying structure of the citizenship performance domain. *Human Resource Management Review*, 10, 25–44.

Colvin, G. (2006) The 100 best companies to work for 2006. *Fortune*, January 23, 71–74.

Dalal, R. S. (2005) A meta-analysis of the relationship between organizational citizenship behavior and counterproductive behavior. *Journal of Applied Psychology*, 90, 1241–1255.

Dawis, R. V. (1992) Person–environment fit and job satisfaction. In C. J. Cranny, P. C. Smith, and E. F. Stone (eds), *Job Satisfaction: How People Feel about Their Jobs and How It Affects Their Performance* (pp. 69–88). New York: Lexington Books.

Dawis, R. V., and Lofquist, L. H. (1984) *A Psychological Theory of Work Adjustment*. Minneapolis, MN: University of Minnesota Press.

DeNisi, A. S., Cafferty, T. P., and Meglino, B. M. (1984) A cognitive view of the performance appraisal process: A model and research propositions. *Organizational Behavior and Human Performance*, 33, 360–396.

Dickson, M. W., Resick, C. J., and Goldstein, H. W. (2008) Seeking explanations in people not in the results of their behavior: Twenty-plus years of the Attraction-Selection-Attrition Model. In D. B. Smith (ed.), *The People Make the Place: Dynamic Linkages between Individuals and Organizations* (pp. 5–36). New York: Taylor and Francis Group/Lawrence Erlbaum Associates.

Digman, J. M. (1989) Five robust trait dimensions: Development, stability, and utility. *Journal of Personality*, 57, 195–214.

Edwards, J. E., Cable, D. M., Williamson, I. O., Lambert, L. S., and Shipp, A. J. (2006) The phenomenology of fit: Linking the person and environment to the subjective experience of person–environment fit. *Journal of Applied Psychology*, 91 (4), 802–827.

Edwards, J. R., and Cable, D. M. (2009) The value of value congruence. *Journal of Applied Psychology*, 94, 654–677.

Erez, A., and Isen, A. M. (2002) The influence of positive affect on the components of expectancy motivation. *Journal of Applied Psychology*, 87, 1055–1067.

Fiske, S. T., and Taylor, S. E. (1991) *Social Cognition* (2nd edn). New York: McGraw-Hill.

Foote, N. N. (1951) Identification as a basis for a theory of motivation. *American Sociological Review*, 16, 14–21.

Forgas, J. P., and George, G. M. (2001) Affective influences on judgment and behavior in organizations: An information processing perspective. *Organizational Behavior and Human Decision Processing*, 86, 3–34.

Frijda, N. H. (1993) The place of appraisal in emotion. *Cognition and Emotion*, 7, 357–387.

George, J. M. (1991) State or trait: Effects of positive mood on prosocial behaviors at work. *Journal of Applied Psychology*, 76, 299–307.

George, J. M., and Brief, A. P. (1992) Feeling good – doing good. A conceptual analysis of the mood at work–organizational spontaneity relationship. *Psychological Bulletin*, 112, 310–329.

George, J. M., and Brief, A. P. (1996) Motivational agendas in the workplace: The effects of feelings on focus of attention and work motivation. In B. M. Staw and L. L. Cummings (eds), *Research in Organizational Behavior: An Annual Series of Analytical Essays and Critical Reviews* (pp. 75–109). Greenwich, CT: JAI Press.

Greenwald, A. G., and Pratkanis, A. R. (1984) The self. In R. S. Wyer and T. K. Srull (eds), *Handbook of Social Cognition* (pp. 129–178). Hillsdale, NJ: Lawrence Erlbaum.

Greguras, G. J., and Diefendorff, J. M. (2009) Different fits satisfy different needs: Linking person–environment fit to employee commitment and performance using self-determination theory. *Journal of Applied Psychology*, 94, 465–477.

Herrback, O., and Mignonac, K. (2007) Is ethical P–O fit really related to individual outcomes? A study of management-level employees. *Business and Society*, 46, 304–330.

Hoffman, B. J., and Woehr, D. J. (2006) A quantitative review of the relationship between person–organization fit and behavioral outcomes. *Journal of Vocational Behavior*, 68, 389–399.

Hogan, R. (1996) A socioanalytic perspective on the five-factor model. In J. S. Wiggins (ed.), *The Five-Factor Model of Personality* (pp. 163–179). New York: Guilford Press.

Hogan, R., and Shelton, D. (1998) A socioanalytic perspective on job performance. *Human Performance*, 11, 129–144.

Hogg, M. A., and Abrams, D. (1988) *Social Identification: A Social Psychology of Intergroup Relations and Group Processes.* London: Routledge.

Ilies, R., Fulmer, I. S., Spitzmuller, M., and Johnson, M. D. (2009) Personality and citizenship behavior: The mediating role of job satisfaction. *Journal of Applied Psychology*, 94 (4), 945–959.

Isen, A. M., and Baron, R. A. (1991) Positive affect as a factor in organizational behavior. In L. L. Cummings and B. M. Staw (eds), *Research in Organizational Behavior* (Vol. 13, pp. 1–53), Greenwich, CT: JAI Press.

Isen, A. M., Shalker, T. E., Clark, M., and Karp, L. (1978) Affect, accessibility of material in memory, and behavior: A cognitive loop? *Journal of Personality and Social Psychology*, 36, 1–12.

James, L. A., and James, L. R. (1989) Integrating work environment perspectives: Explorations into the measurement of meaning. *Journal of Applied Psychology*, 74, 739–751.

Judge, T. A., and Cable, D. M. (1997) Applicant personality, organizational culture, and organizational attraction. *Personnel Psychology*, 50, 359–393.

Kanfer, F. (1970) Self-regulation: Research, issues and speculations. In C. Neuringer and K. L. Michael (eds), *Behavior Modification in Clinical Psychology* (pp. 178–220). New York: Appleton-Century-Crofts.

Kanfer, R. (1990) Motivation theory and industrial and organizational psychology. In M. Dunnette and L. M. Hough (eds), *Handbook of Industrial and Organizational Psychology* (2nd edn, Vol. 1, pp. 75–170). Palo Alto, CA: Consulting Psychologists Press.

Kanfer, R., and Ackerman, P. L. (1989) Motivation and cognitive abilities: An integrative/ aptitude-treatment interaction approach to skill acquisition [Monograph]. *Journal of Applied Psychology*, 74, 657–690.

Klein, H. J. (1991) Further evidence on the relationship between goal setting and expectancy theories. *Organizational Behavior and Human Decision Processes*, 49, 230–705.

Klein, K. J., and Zedeck, S. (2004) Theory in applied psychology: Lessons (re)learned. *Journal of Applied Psychology*, 89 (6), 931–933.

Kraiger, K., and Wenzel, L. H. (1997) Conceptual developments and empirical evaluations of measures of shared mental models as indicators of team effectiveness. In E. Salas, M. T. Brannick, and C. Prince (eds), *Team Performance Assessment and Measurement: Theory, Methods, and Applications*. Mahwah, NJ: Lawrence Erlbaum.

Kristof, A. L. (1996) Person–environment fit: An integrative review of its conceptualizations, measurement, and implications. *Personnel Psychology*, 49 (1), 1–49.

Kristof-Brown, A. L., and Guay, R. P. (2011) Person–environment fit. In S. Zedeck (ed.), *APA Handbook of Industrial and Organizational Psychology* (pp. 3–50). Washington, DC: American Psychological Association.

Kristof-Brown, A. L., Zimmerman, R. D., and Johnson, E. C. (2005) Consequences of individuals' fit at work: A meta-analysis of person–job, person–organization, person–group, and person–supervisor fit. *Personnel Psychology*, 58 (2), 281–342.

Lauver, K. J., and Kristof-Brown, A. (2001) Distinguishing between employees' perceptions of person–job and person–organization fit. *Journal of Vocational Behavior*, 59, 454–470.

Lazarus, R. S. (1982) Thoughts on the relationship between emotion and cognition. *American Psychologist*, 37, 1019–1024.

LePine, J. A., Erez, A., and Johnson, D. E. (2002) The nature and dimensionality of organizational citizenship behavior: A critical review and meta-analysis. *Journal of Applied Psychology*, 87, 52–65.

London, M. (1995) *Self and Interpersonal Insight: How People Gain Understanding of Themselves and Others in Organizations*. New York: Oxford University Press.

Lord, R. G., and Hanges, P. J. (1987) A control system model of organizational motivation: Theoretical development and applied implications. *Behavioral Science*, 32, 161–178.

Mabey, C. (1986) *Graduates into Industry*. Aldershot, Hampshire: Gower.

Mael, F., and Ashforth, B. E. (1992) Alumni and their alma mater: A partial test of the reformulated model of organizational identification. *Journal of Organizational Behavior*, 13, 103–123.

Mael, F., and Tetrick, L. E. (1992) Identifying organizational identification. *Educational and Psychological Measurement*, 52, 813–824.

Mischel, W., and Shoda, Y. (1995) A cognitive-affective system theory of personality: Reconceptualizing situations, dispositions, dynamics, and invariance in personality structure. *Psychological Review*, 102, 246–268.

Mitchell, T. R. (1997) Matching motivational strategies with organizational contexts. In L. L. Cummings and B. M. Staw (eds), *Research in Organizational Behavior* (Vol. 19, pp. 57–149), Greenwich, CT: JAI Press.

Nicholson, N., and Arnold, J. (1991) From expectation to experience: Graduates entering a large corporation. *Journal of Organizational Behavior*, 12, 413–429.

Norman, D. A., Gentner, S. and Stevens, A. L. (1976) Comments on learning schemata and memory representation. In D. Klahr (ed.), *Cognition and Instruction.* Hillsdale, NJ: Lawrence Erlbaum Associates.

O'Reilly, C. (1989) Corporations, culture, and commitment: Motivation and social control in organizations. *California Management Review,* Summer, 9–25.

O'Reilly, C. A., Chatman, J., and Caldwell, D. F. (1991) People and organizational culture: A profile comparison approach to assessing person–organization fit. *Academy of Management Journal,* 34, 487–516.

Organ, D. W. (1997) Organizational citizenship behavior: It's construct clean-up time. *Human Performance,* 10, 85–97.

Organ, D. W., and Ryan, K. (1995) A meta-analytic review of attitudinal and dispositional predictors of organizational citizenship behavior. *Personnel Psychology,* 48, 775–802.

Ostroff, C., and Rothausen, T. J. (1997) The moderating effect of tenure in person–environment fit: A field study in educational organizations. *Journal of Occupational and Organizational Psychology,* 70, 173–188.

Podsakoff, N. P., Whiting, S. W., Podsakoff, P. M., and Blume, B. D. (2009) Individual- and organizational-level consequences of organizational citizenship behaviors: A meta-analysis. *Journal of Applied Psychology,* 94, 122–141.

Poole, P. P., Gray, B., and Gioia, D. A. (1990) Organizational script development through interactive accommodation. *Group and Organization Studies,* 15 (2), 212–232.

Pratt, M. G. (1998) To be or not to be: Central questions in organizational identification. In D. A. Whetten and P. C. Godfrey (eds), *Identity in Organizations* (pp. 171–208). Thousand Oaks, CA: Sage.

Reichers, A. E., and Schneider, B. (1990) Climate and culture: An evolution of constructs. In B. Schneider (ed.), *Organizational Climate and Culture* (pp. 5–39). San Francisco: Jossey-Bass.

Rentsch, J. R. (1990) Climate and culture: Interaction and qualitative differences in organizational meaning. *Journal of Applied Psychology,* 75, 668–681.

Resick, C. J., Baltes, B. B., and Shantz, C. A.W. (2007) Person–organization fit and work-related attitudes and decisions: Examining interactive effects with job fit and conscientiousness. *Journal of Applied Psychology,* 92, 1446–1455.

Roberts, B. R., Chernyshenko, O. S., Stark, S., and Goldberg, L. R. (2005) The structure of conscientiousness: An empirical investigation based on seven major personality questionnaires. *Personnel Psychology,* 58 (1), 103–139.

Rousseau, D. M. (1990) Assessing organizational culture: The case for multiple methods. In B. Schneider (ed.). *Organizational Climate and Culture* (pp. 153–192). San Francisco: Jossey-Bass.

Rumelhart, D. E. (1984) Schemata and the cognitive system. *Handbook of Social Cognition,* 1, 161–187.

Rumelhart, D. E., and Ortony, A. (1977) The representation of knowledge in memory. In R. C. Anderson, R. J. Spiro, and W. E. Montague (eds), *Schooling and the Acquisition of Knowledge* (pp. 99–136). Hillsdale, NJ: Lawrence Erlbaum.

Saks, A. M., and Ashforth, B. E. (1997) A longitudinal investigation of the relationships between job information sources, applicant perceptions of fit, and work outcomes. *Personnel Psychology,* 50, 395–426.

Schein, E. H. (2003) Five traps for consulting psychologists: Or, how I learned to take culture seriously. *Consulting Psychology Journal: Practice and Research,* 55, 75–83.

Schneider, B. (1975) Organizational climates: An essay. *Personnel Psychology*, 28, 447–479.

Schneider, B. (1987) The people make the place. *Personnel Psychology*, 40, 437–453.

Schneider, B., and Reichers, A. E. (1983) On the etiology of climates. *Personnel Psychology*, 36, 19–39.

Schneider, B., Smith, D. B., Taylor, S., and Fleenor, J. (1998) Personality and organizations: A test of the homogeneity of personality hypothesis. *Journal of Applied Psychology*, 83, 462–470.

Shallenberger, D. (1994) Professional and openly gay: A narrative study of the experience. *Journal of Managerial Inquiry*, 3, 119–142.

Shamir, B. (1990) Calculations, values, and identities: The sources of collectivistic work motivation. *Human Relations*, 43, 313–332.

Simon, H. A. (1982) Comments. In M. S. Clark and S. T. Fiske (eds), *Affect and Cognition: The Seventeenth Annual Carnegie Symposium on Cognition* (pp. 333–342). Hillsdale, NJ: Lawrence Erlbaum.

Smith, E. R. (1998) Mental representation and memory. In D. T. Gilbert, S. T. Fiske, and G. Lindzey (eds), *The Handbook of Social Psychology* (4th edn, Vol. 1, pp. 391–445). New York: McGraw-Hill.

Spector, P. E., and Fox, S. (2002) An emotion-centered model of voluntary work behavior: Some parallels between counterproductive work behavior and organizational citizenship behavior. *Human Resource Management Review*, 12, 269–292.

Stajkovic, A. D., Locke, E. A., and Blair, E. S. (2006) A first examination of the relationships between primed subconscious goals, assigned conscious goals, and task performance. *Journal of Applied Psychology*, 91 (5), 1172–1180.

Tajfel, H., and Turner, J. C. (1985) The social identity theory of intergroup behavior. In S. Worchel and W. G. Austin (eds), *Psychology of Intergroup Relations* (2nd edn, pp. 7–24). Chicago, IL: Nelson-Hall.

Tolman, E. C. (1943) Identification and the post-war world. *Journal of Abnormal and Social Psychology*, 38, 141–148.

Tubbs, M. E., and Ekeberg, S. E. (1991) The role of intentions in work motivation: Implications for goal-setting theory and research. *Academy of Management Review*, 16, 180–199.

Turner, J. C., and Haslam, S. A. (2001) Social identity, organizations, and leadership. In M. R. Turner (ed.), *Groups at Work: Theory and Research* (pp. 25–65). Mahweh, NJ: Lawrence Erlbaum.

Van Eerde, W., and Thierry, H. (1996) Vroom's expectancy models and work-related criteria: A meta-analysis. *Journal of Applied Psychology*, 81, 575–586.

Van Knippenberg, D. (2000) Work motivation and performance: A social identify perspective. *Applied Psychology: An International Review*, 49, 357–371.

Van Vianen, A. E. M. (2000) Person–organization fit: The match between newcomers' and recruiters' preferences for organizational cultures. *Personnel Psychology*, 53, 113–149.

Vancouver, J. B., and Schmitt, N. W. (1991) An exploratory examination of person–organization fit: Organizational goal congruence. *Personnel Psychology*, 44, 333–352.

Venkataramani, V., and Dalal, R.S. (2007) Who helps and harms whom? Relational antecedents of interpersonal helping and harming in organizations. *Journal of Applied Psychology*, 92 (4), 952–966.

Verquer, M. L., Beehr, T. A., and Wagner, S. H. (2003) A meta-analysis of relations between person–organization fit and work attitudes. *Journal of Vocational Behavior*, 63, 473–489.

Vroom, V. H. (1964) *Work and Motivation*. New York: Wiley.

Weiss, H. M., and Cropanzano, R. (1996) Affective events theory: A theoretical discussion of the structure, causes and consequences of affective experiences at work. In L. L. Cummings and B. M. Staw (eds), *Research in Organizational Behavior* (Vol. 18, pp. 1–74). Greenwich, CT: JAI Press.

Wiggins, J. S., and Trapnell, P. D. (1996) A dyadic-interactional perspective on the five-factor model. In J. S. Wiggins (ed.), *The Five-Factor Model of Personality* (pp. 88–162). New York: Guilford Press.

Wood, J. V. (1989) Theory and research concerning social comparisons of personal attributes. *Psychological Bulletin*, 106, 231–248.

Zajonc, R. B. (1998) Emotions. In D. T. Gilbert, S. T. Fiske, and G. Lindzey (eds), *Handbook of Social Psychology* (pp. 591–632). Boston: McGraw-Hill.

6

Mapping Fit: Maximizing Idiographic and Nomothetic Benefits

Jon Billsberry
Deakin University

Danielle L. Talbot
Coventry University

Véronique Ambrosini
Monash University

Introduction

Recently there has been some concern about the conceptual clarity of person–organization fit (e.g., Harrison, 2007). While noting that the construct has solid roots in person–environment (PE) psychology, Harrison (2007) notes that it has been studied in so many forms that it seems to defy definition, saying:

> As an outsider peering through the store window ... on fit theory and research, I get the sense that if fit doesn't encompass the entirety of creation, it comes awfully close. The merchandise racks have titles for *micro, meso, macro,* and *multilevel* conceptualizations. There is *direct* and *indirect* assessment of *perceived* and *actual* fit. Fit comes in *supplementary* or *complementary* flavors ... In one display corner there is a tool for fit by profile comparison, and in another there is fit by response-surface methodology. A case by the checkout stand holds a box of gooey *fit clusters*. Fit can be *similarity, congruence, alignment, agreement, composition, configuration, matching,* and *interactionist*. There are *needs-supplies* barrels of fit fruit and *demands-abilities* bins of fit grain. On one shelf, there is PJ fit. Another holds PG fit. Across the way, there are barcodes for PO, PV, PP, PS, SV, NS, and SS fit. I'm lost in the supermarket of fit research, and I haven't yet stepped inside! (Harrison, 2007, p. 389)

Organizational Fit: Key Issues and New Directions, First Edition.
Edited by Amy L. Kristof-Brown and Jon Billsberry.
© 2013 John Wiley & Sons, Ltd. Published 2013 by John Wiley & Sons, Ltd.

When we walked past the PE fit shop front over a decade ago, our attention was caught by two things in the window: first, the idea that applicants look for organizations where they believe they will fit in, and conversely, that selectors also want to recruit new staff who will fit in; and second, the notion of misfit, its theoretical link to organizational exit, and the notable absence of discussion about this concept. Both fit and misfit resonated with us because of the impact they have on people's lives and organizational functioning.

As researchers who have worked in this fit supermarket for over a decade, our own thoughts about the domain are aligned with Harrison's views. We are keen to understand fit as a psychological construct that seems to play an important role in the key decisions of organizational entrance and exit, only to find that much that surrounds us is oddly tangential to fit as a psychological construct. Much of the research conducted to date takes one of three different routes. One common theme is the examination of one element of the fit between employee and employer. For example, there is work looking at value congruence (e.g., Chatman, 1991; Ravlin and Meglino, 1989), the homogeneity of personalities in an organization (e.g., Schneider *et al.*, 1998), or the alignment of motivational needs and organizational pay systems (e.g., Turban and Keon, 1993). These have all helped us understand the "similarity leads to attraction" proposition, but they do not address the psychological constructs of fit and misfit directly. The second route that organizational fit research has taken is a methodological one. In particular, studies such as Cable and Edwards (2004) have explored the nature of interactions and relationships between individual and environmental factors and different types of fit. The third route is studies of perceived fit which directly address fit (and misfit) as a psychological construct. Unfortunately, though, most of this research has been done using all-encompassing direct methods (e.g., "How well do you fit this organization?"). As a result, we know something about the construct of fit as an antecedent of other psychological constructs and something about its antecedents (see Kristof-Brown, Zimmerman, and Johnson (2005) for a review), but all of this relates to perceived fit as an overarching, undeconstructed phenomenon. What is lacking is an understanding of how people experience organizational fit and misfit, and the effects that the experience has on both the individual and the organization.

Harrison's metaphor is helpful in making sense of the apparent confusion in the fit supermarket window. We argue that this confusion exists because we have conducted fit research without first establishing what the psychological construct of fit actually is. We have built methodologies and techniques to explore interactions. We have sampled elements of fit and explored those. And we have taken overall fit perceptions and looked at their antecedents and consequences. But we have done all of this without first understanding what constitutes people's sense of fit or misfit. Until we do that, we shall never know what is fit and what it is not. In short, we have forgotten to do the initial exploratory work to understand what constitutes employees' sense of fit. This requires research that explores how employees experience and perceive both fit and misfit. We need to find out what this thing called fit (and misfit) is and what it is not.

In this chapter we look at how organizational fit researchers might conduct exploratory research into the construct. We begin by discussing nomothetic and idiographic research and call for a separation of data gathering and data analysis stages to help us understand the richness of the construct whilst retaining the ability to draw testable propositions about its general characteristics. In particular, we will examine Chatman's (1989) discussion of nomothetic and idiographic techniques in organizational fit research and critically assess the contribution of the Organizational Culture Profile (OCP: O'Reilly *et al.*, 1991), which has been advocated as a technique that simultaneously employs nomothetic and idiographic approaches. An analysis of this technique provides insights about the combination of idiographic and nomothetic approaches that help us build a heuristic model showing the nature of theory generation work in organizational fit. Following this, we will look at cognitive mapping, which is considered one of the most effective ways of revealing complex perceptions. We will explain how the technique can be used to gain in-depth understanding of people's sense of fit. The final section will explore how causal maps, probably the most useful form of cognitive maps, can help researchers bridge the nomothetic–idiographic research gap (Larsson, 1993; Larsson and Finkelstein, 1999). Bridging this gap means that in analyzing multiple causal maps the researcher can combine rich, detailed data with large sample breadth and hence maximize the benefits of both idiographic and nomothetic research methods. In doing this, our goal is to present a practical way forward that can be deployed by researchers to help us reveal how people construct their fit and misfit perceptions.

Nomothetic and Idiographic Research

Most studies conducted in organizational fit have had a nomothetic design in that they aim to "yield explanations and predictions that are true for 'most of the people most of the time'" (Krahé, 1992, p. 129). Although this does not necessarily mean that researchers have avoided looking at the structure and nature of fit, it has led to observation simplification to make comparison possible: that is, measures are simplified and tightly constructed around main effects rather than broadly constructed to explore differences. The alternative idiographic approach, which employs "methodologies designed to capture the uniqueness of the individual person" (Krahé, 1992, p. 8), provides techniques for understanding the complexity of people. In doing so, they embrace exploratory research that can establish how people conceptualize thoughts, feelings, and aspirations. Although there have been many years of fit research, it is not too late to study the construct with idiographic techniques that seek to establish the richness of individuals' perceptions. Indeed, by taking such an approach, we shall be better equipped to resolve definitional and conceptualization ambiguities.

The idiographic approach is commonly associated with qualitative techniques, as these allow for the exploration of an individual's thoughts with minimal direction from researchers, which aligns well with the exploratory research that we believe is necessary in fit and misfit research. Edmondson and McManus (2007) argue that when theory is nascent with many open-ended questions needing to be answered, qualitative research methods are recommended; it is only when the theory is more mature that quantitative methods should be used to test hypotheses. In many senses, organizational fit theory is still nascent; hence, it is appropriate to conduct exploratory idiographic studies. However, there is a major difficulty in using idiographic research: how do we generalize from in-depth studies of the individual? Although idiographic research faces the challenge of moving beyond the individual case, we believe that it is possible to draw conclusions for more generalized study of the subject. As Krahé notes, "it is perfectly possible to employ idiographic or individual-centered methods to test nomothetic, that is, general hypotheses" (Krahé, 1992, p. 131).

A nomothetic approach is generally understood to be one where research seeks to identify what is true or generalizable for groups or populations (Grice *et al.*, 2006; Luthans and Davis, 1982). In nomothetic research, the goal is to identify general laws, to find what holds true not just for the individual, but for people in general. In contrast, an idiographic approach focuses on the individual. It is important to note that in the study of psychology and in the management field in general, the term *nomothetic* "has become equated with aggregate measures of data collection and analysis" whereas *idiographic* "has come to describe research strategies that place considerably more emphasis on the individual" (Grice *et al.*, 2006, p. 1191). As a corollary, the nomothetic method "emphasizes quantitative analysis of a few variables across large samples" (Larsson, 1993, p. 1515) and the idiographic case study method "focuses primarily on the qualitative, multi aspect, in-depth study of one or a few cases" (Larsson, 1993, p. 1515).

Combining approaches

Although these are fundamentally different approaches to research, in a seminal paper in the organizational fit domain, Chatman (1989) argues that an idiographic approach is important because "a given trait may or may not be relevant for the person in question", but that a nomothetic approach is also needed because "we also should compare people either to one another or to themselves over time, and these comparisons require nomothetic methods" (Chatman, 1989, p. 336). She argues that it is possible to combine both approaches in the same technique and argues that a Q-sort procedure such as the Organizational Culture Profile (OCP; O'Reilly *et al.*, 1991) can perform this function. An analysis of the compromises required to create an instrument that simultaneously addresses idiographic and nomothetic research designs is very revealing and provides the rationale for a different approach to combining idiographic and nomothetic research designs.

The OCP is a 54-item card sort. Each card contains a "value statement." These 54 values were identified by an exhaustive analysis of the organizational culture literature and were initially filtered for equivalent relevance to people and organizations and for ease of comprehension. Then they were filtered again for generality, discriminability, non-redundancy, and readability. Participants are asked to sort the 54 cards in response to the question, "How important is it for this characteristic to be a part of the organization you work for?" (O'Reilly *et al.*, 1991, p. 496), with the cards placed into a forced 2-4-6-9-12-9-6-4-2 distribution ranging from "most desirable" to "most undesirable." Then, if an objective fit approach is taken as outlined in O'Reilly, Chatman, and Caldwell (1991), other people sort the values in response to the prompt "Please sort the 54 values into a row of nine categories, placing at one end of the row those cards that you consider to be the most characteristic aspects of the culture of your organization, and at the other end those cards that you believe to be the least characteristic" (O'Reilly *et al.*, 1991, p. 495), using the same response distribution. If a subjective fit approach is adopted, the person sorting the cards to capture their values will then do it again for the organization's values. Correlation analysis is used to determine each person's level of PO fit.

The OCP has limitations with regard to its use for idiographic purposes. The predetermined values mean that the idiographic richness is restricted within the boundaries of the values presented to participants. Further, the forced distribution assumes equal "distance" between each value, which is a convenience for their subsequent nomothetic analysis. While the OCP provides a rich picture of individuals' values, it only provides an understanding of individuals within the constraints of the predetermined values. A truly idiographic approach would require the separate elicitation of the values of each individual in the study so that the "true" picture of each individual's values can be revealed. However, such a fully idiographic approach hampers research because each participant's values will differ, making it difficult, but not impossible, as we will show later, to find generalizable conclusions.

Ironically, although the OCP has nomothetic properties limiting its idiographic suitability, some of its design features making it suitable for idiographic research limit its suitability for nomothetic research too. The first of these compromises is the inclusion of 54 different values. Researchers wanting to use the OCP in nomothetic research designs have argued that this is too many; although this number of values might give some idiographic richness, it contains values that are too similar or of trivial importance (Billsberry, 2007; Cable and Judge, 1997; Sarros *et al.*, 2005). These authors made another change to the original OCP by abandoning the card sort and opting for a simpler questionnaire design to avoid the logistical nightmare associated with the circulation and retrieval of the card sets when the researcher is not face-to-face with respondents. Unfortunately though, a verbal protocol analysis has shown that this adaptation (a sorting of 40 items on a sheet of paper) does not replicate the sorting of cards (Barber and Wesson, 1998). Billsberry (2007) and Sarros *et al.* (2005) moved further away from the original design by abandoning the ipsative design of the OCP measure which allows respondents to report the comparative importance of the values, in favor of a Likert-scaled design that captures absolute scores for each of the values. They did this in response to the study by Barber and Wesson (1998) which showed that Likert-designed questionnaires performed similarly to the original OCP.

The purpose of this critique of the OCP is not to disparage the tool or discourage researchers from using it; quite the opposite. The OCP has been, and continues to be, one of the most valuable tools we have for assessing PO fit. O'Reilly, Chatman, and

Caldwell (1991, p. 481) themselves note the limitations of the tool: "the application of a Q-sort technique appears to be a useful way to obtain *semi*-idiographic assessments of fit" [emphasis added]. Instead, the purpose of this analysis is to highlight the problems of combining idiographic and nomothetic approaches in a single intervention. These are fundamentally different approaches and major compromises have to be made to combine both, meaning that the outcome is neither truly idiographic nor truly nomothetic. As noted by O'Reilly, Chatman, and Caldwell (1991, p. 480), "the difficulty, however, with an idiographic approach is that it isn't clear what to do once a rating has been made. What is then needed is to be able to compare individuals even though descriptors may be differentially relevant to them."

A heuristic model

As the above discussion shows, one of the big problems with combining idiographic and nomothetic approaches is that it compromises data gathering so that the emerging data are suitable for analysis. The problem arises because two processes are being collapsed together in a single process, rather than allowing the two phases to be considered, and approached, separately and differently. It is only when these two phases are separated that a research study can simultaneously be idiographic and nomothetic. As we shall show, separating these two processes produces some radically different and useful research designs (see Figure 6.1).

Figure 6.1 contains a heuristic 2 × 2 model showing the four different research designs that emerge when the processes of data gathering and data analysis are separated out. In the following paragraphs we briefly explain the contents of the four boxes, starting in the bottom left-hand corner and working clockwise around the grid. Later in the chapter we look at the individual process of idiographic and nomothetic data gathering and data analysis, so our purpose here is simply to outline the nature of the research design in each box.

Box 1: Idiographic data gathering/idiographic data analysis. This box contains idiographic research in its purest form with the intention being to understand the richness of the individual. In organizational behavior research, this might be to understand the nature of someone's fit to an organization, or to explore the causes of their actions, or to help the person better understand themselves, such as in a counseling situation. A pure idiographic approach might also be used to understand a particular location such as a team or an organization, or even a specific event (Tsoukas, 1989). The point is that the purpose of this type of research is to understand an individual person, place, or event, but not to generalize further to a larger population. Even if multiple people, places, or events are studied, the analysis is specific to each individual.

Box 2: Nomothetic data gathering/idiographic data analysis. Box 2 contains an approach that is rarely used in academic research, but that is often the province

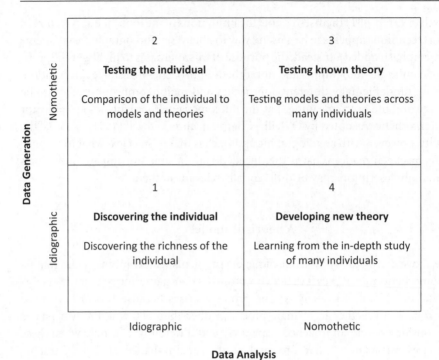

Figure 6.1   A heuristic model for data generation and analysis

of people using academic research for managerial purposes. Here, researchers use nomothetic tools to gather information about people, but use the data for personal insight. A classic example would be the use of personality questionnaires during recruitment and selection (or staff development). In this situation, the individual is compared to norms or other predetermined criteria, and similarities and differences have meaning about, or for, the individual.

Box 3: Nomothetic data gathering/nomothetic data analysis. This box needs little explanation as it captures the mainstream of management research where theories and conjectures are tested to provide generalizable conclusions. For example, Schneider, Smith, Taylor, and Fleenor (1998) used a nomothetic data-gathering device, a personality blank called the Myers–Briggs Type Indicator (MBTI), to test the proposition that organizations are homogeneous with regard to their managers' personalities. Their data supported this proposition and they were able to draw the generalizable conclusion "that organizations are relatively homogeneous with regard to the personality characteristics of their managers" (Schneider *et al.*, 1998, p. 467).

Box 4: Idiographic data gathering/nomothetic data analysis. This box reflects the desire to capture the richness of individuals while still being able to draw generalizable conclusions. When the two research phases are separated out, the researcher can gather rich idiographic data from multiple respondents and seek similarities and differences across the set. For example, if a number of people were asked to describe their fit to their employers in their own terms, the researcher may find that everyone who was positive about their employment talked about their jobs while everyone who was negative talked about their supervisors. Such insight would generate conjectures that could be tested in further studies. This combination of idiographic and nomothetic methods should not be confused with grounded theory (Glaser and Strauss, 1967) because although the data-gathering approach is free from extant theory, the data analysis element may use past findings, theories, and other cues to search for patterns in the data, which would not be the case with grounded theory.

Mapping Fit

As stated in the introduction, in the remainder of this chapter we focus on one specific research method: cognitive mapping. Cognitive maps are used to capture individuals' mental representation of a situation or phenomenon, such as employees' perceptions of their organizational fit. Scholars have argued that cognitive maps have the potential to be used both idiographically and nomothetically (Clarkson and Hodgkinson, 2005). In other words, they can be used to help researchers bridge the nomothetic–idiographic research gap (Larsson, 1993; Larsson and Finkelstein, 1999). In the remainder of this chapter we want to illustrate how this might operate with organizational fit and cognitive maps. We shall begin this section by briefly describing the various forms of cognitive maps and then show how they can be used for idiographic and nomothetic data generation. Then we shall show how both types of map can be analyzed both nomothetically and idiographically. In effect, we illustrate our 2 × 2 model and show that the separation of the data gathering and data analysis phases is feasible when cognitive maps are used for data generation. Although we consider all four quadrants, it is the fourth quadrant, idiographic data generation and nomothetic analysis, that is possibly the most interesting in the study of organizational fit as it seems to afford us the best opportunity to generate new insights about the construct.

Different forms of cognitive maps

Cognitive maps are visual representations. They are ways of representing individuals' views of reality (Eden *et al.*, 1981) and "are intended to relate to the way in which a person 'makes sense of' and explains the world around him" (Eden, 1990, p. 37). They represent an individual's personal knowledge of their own experience (Weick and Bougon, 1986). Constructing cognitive maps allows the individual to surface and explore "his own belief and value system in relation to particular issues" (Eden *et al.*, 1981, p. 41).

There are different types of cognitive map (see Huff (1990) or Huff and Jenkins (2002) for a full account); two of them are ways of analyzing datasets and there are a further three types of map geared towards generating data. The first data analysis method of cognitive mapping is used by researchers to analyze material that has already been generated or sourced. Commonly, they are used to assess attention, association, and the importance of concepts. The focus is on content or word analysis. For instance, the researcher might be interested in how often a concept is mentioned in interviews or any other materials (e.g., annual reports), or how the concept changes. Mapping can be used to locate and chart the pattern of occurrences in the dataset. This approach allows for quantitative comparison and these sorts of maps often look like histograms. A second type of map is also used to analyze data such as interview transcripts, speeches, documents, and other records. It is used to highlight the structure of the argument and the way that conclusions are justified. In this way, it is akin to critical thinking analysis (e.g., Hughes *et al.*, 2010; van den Brink-Budgen, 2000).

The first of the data generation type of cognitive maps captures how people think and feel about the structure of a subject. In particular, it shows how dimensions, categories, and cognitive taxonomies are grouped. Usually these are used for nomothetic purposes with predetermined elements and constructs, being presented to participants who are asked to show how they are connected, separated, similar, different, etc., depending on the researchers' goals. These can then be compared to show general trends and patterns. A well-known example of this form of mapping is repertory grid analysis (Kelly, 1955), which mechanically and repeatedly presents participants with different combinations of constructs to find underlying patterns.

The second type of data generation cognitive map comes directly from cognitive psychology and seeks to specify people's "schemas, frames and perceptual codes" (Huff, 1990, p. 16). In simpler terms, the goal of this type of map is to "capture" or "represent" someone's thoughts as a graphical pattern (typically like a spidergram) or more lexically as lists of words. The goal of such maps is to unveil the hidden mental map or framework driving cognitive thinking patterns.

The third type of data generation map is called a causal map. It is the most popular mapping technique in the management field (Hodgkinson, 2007). In many ways, it is an enhanced version of the previous type of map showing influence, causality, and system dynamics. The idea is that rather than solely plotting their mental maps, people are asked to identify causal links with the purpose of highlighting the fundamental drivers of actions. A causal map "is a form of cognitive map that incorporates concepts tied together by causality relations" (Weick and Bougon, 1986, p. 106). It is a graphic representation "which consists of nodes and arrows that link them" (Laukkanen, 1994, p. 323). The nodes are the constructs that the person believes are important and the arrows show the relationships between the constructs. Such maps help researchers understand and analyze the underlying mechanisms of a phenomenon and they are a way of ordering and analyzing something that can be fuzzy. It is important to note that, as explained by Eden, Ackermann, and Cropper

(1992), causal maps should not be assumed to be models of cognition as such. Eden (1992, p. 262) explains that "the only reasonable claim that can be made of cognitive maps as an artifact ... is that ... they may represent subjective data more meaningfully than other models." Hence, causal maps can be used simply as a "content and theory free" elicitation technique (Laukkanen, 1998, p. 168) and, as such, they are well suited to idiographic and exploratory research.

Generating maps

In this section we offer broad explanations of how data generation through idiographic and nomothetic research designs differs and some of the key principles within each form.

Idiographic generation. There are several different ways of generating idiographic maps, which broadly break down into lexical and graphical approaches. Lexical approaches involve the elicitation of words from the respondent during interview questioning or the application of a technique such as repertory grid analysis. An example would be Cossette and Audet's (1992) study of Mr Brown, the owner of a lighting systems company, where the authors used in-depth interviews to build a map to gain detailed understanding of how he conducted his business and his vision for it. Lexical approaches use the participant's own language, often through in-depth interviewing, rather than imposing or suggesting preconceived ideas or structures (Eden and Ackermann, 1998a).

Graphical approaches, as the name suggests, employ some form of diagram or pictorial prompt alongside lexical prompts to generate the data for the map. The most common form of graphical map is, as already mentioned, the causal map, which looks like a "spidergram." The process works through spreading activation (Daniels *et al.*, 1995), where the respondent's mention of one relevant factor triggers them to further insights. The basic idea is that people are asked to think about the matter at hand, such as the things influencing their sense of fit. As they think of things, these are recorded on a large sheet of paper (or recorded using mapping software such as Decision Explorer). By doing this, they have the opportunity to "see" their thoughts and in the process new ideas spring to mind. In causal mapping participants are encouraged to think about the factors "causing" or influencing the various factors that initially emerge and link them. This creates a series of causal chains.

Billsberry, Ambrosini, Moss-Jones, and Marsh (2005) specifically looked at idiographic mapping within organizational fit research. They highlighted the importance of the initial prompts used to trigger the elicitation process. These subtly guide the respondents and can greatly alter the data that are generated. Imagine that a researcher wanted to use causal mapping to understand how someone perceives his or her organizational fit. The researcher might begin by writing the word "Fit" in the center of a large piece of paper and then give one of the following instructions to the interviewee: "What factors influence your fit at work?" or "What factors influence your fit to your employer?" or "What factors influence your fit to your organization?" or "What factors influence your fit to your job?" Although the questions look innocuous, the resulting maps may look very different. Such subtle skewing illustrates both the care needed by researchers and the complexity of fit perceptions.

When causal maps are being used graphically for idiographic purposes, the participant sees the map being drawn up in front of him or her. The same is true when groups of people combine to produce a map representing a collective view. This process helps "validate" the map as well as spurring further thoughts. To increase validity further, many researchers who elicit data and construct maps after the interview will show the completed maps to the participants and ask for feedback and to check that the map corresponds to how they think about the subject at hand.

Nomothetic generation. In the field of managerial and organizational cognition, researchers have been striving for some time to build techniques that allow cognitive maps to be used for nomothetic purposes (e.g., Langfield-Smith, 1992; Langfield-Smith and Wirth, 1992; Markóczy and Goldberg, 1995). Frustrated by the difficulty of combining idiosyncratic maps and the "lack of techniques for systematically comparing causal maps in a way that uses all of the information contained in such a map" (Markóczy and Goldberg, 1995, p. 306), the goal has been to develop methods and software that would permit nomothetic generation and comparison.

The method advanced by these researchers is to have a specified pool of constructs from which the participants can choose, rather than allowing the full idiosyncratic generation of multiple constructs. The pool of constructs can be generated either by using pilot studies or by methodically reviewing the literature. Participants are asked to choose a set number of constructs from the pool according to which they find most important or salient to the topic in question, and they are then systematically asked to say whether or how each construct influences the others (Clarkson and Hodgkinson, 2005). This method is effective for use with large numbers of participants because it is possible to use statistical tests to analyze the maps.

Nomothetic map generation is therefore very different from idiographic map generation. Rather than presenting respondents with a blank sheet of paper, literally and figuratively, the researcher presents respondents with an already identified set of constructs. The respondents are asked to "sort" the constructs and show how they link or have meaning. By limiting the respondents to a set of constructs, the researcher is able to combine the maps without dealing with the complexity, messiness, and diversity of idiographically generated maps.

One example of this approach is the aforementioned OCP. As described, 54 values are presented to respondents and they are asked to put these in a predetermined pattern according to how important they find them. An alternative approach is provided by Cognizer (Clarkson and Hodgkinson, 2005). In this method, respondents are presented with the constructs in pairs via a user-friendly piece of software and asked to evaluate them according to a common prompt, such as indicating which of the pair is more important (an example of this method is elaborated later in the chapter). The key feature of this approach is that the content is predetermined by the researcher with the purpose of allowing generalization from the respondents to wider populations.

Analyzing maps

The analysis of causal maps tends to center on two broad approaches: topological analysis and content analysis. The former assesses the features of the map (its nodes, links, heads, tails, loops, clusters, etc.) whereas the latter devotes its attentions to what is contained within the concepts on the map. In a special issue of the *Journal of Management Studies* devoted to causal maps in all their varied forms, Eden, Ackermann, and Cropper (1992) outline the methods that have been used in the analysis of causal maps and provide an overview of how a map's features can be analyzed. These include an analysis of the ratio of links to constructs as a means of obtaining a measure of the cognitive complexity of a map. Depending on the purpose of the mapping, a "domain analysis" might be conducted that assesses the number of arrows in and out of the map's concepts. Elements from social network analysis are also useful. For example, the "nodes"' on the causal map can be weighted according to their distance from a central node. From such an approach, metrics such as betweenness, centrality, closeness, radiality, and reach could focus the analysis. Other ways of analyzing maps include calculating the ratio of head and tail concepts, the Jaccard index, which measures the similarity of datasets (or the Sørensen similarity index, which does a similar thing), and the Jaccard distance, which measures dissimilarity between sets. The shape of the map may also be studied, as may the nature and appearance of causal loops.

Although analyzing the structure and form of a map is often a necessary step in gaining a better perspective on the process, the analysis of the content of the map is often of equal or greater importance. Many of the techniques available for qualitative analysis (e.g., content analysis) can be made relevant to map data.

Having briefly explained how maps can be generated and analyzed, we return to Figure 6.1 and show how mapping can be usefully applied to each of the four research designs.

Box 1: Idiographic analysis of idiographically generated maps. The purpose of this form of map is to understand a particular person, environment, or process using the language and constructs of those involved. Software applications such as Decision Explorer (Eden *et al.*, 1992) and CMAP2 (Laukkanen, 1994) are designed for this particular function and both enable idiographic data generation and analysis (Clarkson and Hodgkinson, 2005). These software programs are designed to aid topological analysis and make the identification of features such as loops and clusters a lot simpler and more rigorous than if the maps are analyzed by hand. In addition, the content of the concepts or nodes can be scrutinized to identify themes. Ennis (1999), for example, in his study of a small firm's growth, used an inductive approach and content analyzed the company owner's causal map to identify five main themes leading to growth and development in the firm. Content analysis of this type allows the researcher to get an in-depth understanding of the factors which play a role for one person or organization. This may result in hypotheses being formed which can subsequently be tested with larger populations, but this would be a by-product and not the purpose of the analysis.

Box 2: Idiographic analysis of nomothetically generated maps. In terms of academic research, as opposed to consultancy or managerial intervention, the idiographic analysis of nomothetically generated maps is an uncommon occurrence. Theoretically, the purpose of constraining the formation of the map would be to explore how the target individual, group, organization, or process compared to theory or a norm. While this is commonly done with the assessment of individuals using questionnaires and similar instruments for recruitment and selection, training, and assessment purposes, it is not clear how maps would specifically help in the process. Nevertheless, if we take a lead from these managerial interventions, it seems that the idiographic analysis of nomothetic maps would focus on difference and similarity of the individual to the group or to a predetermined theory.

Box 3: Nomothetic analysis of nomothetically generated maps. As noted above, the need to be able to study multiple causal maps accurately and efficiently and to be able to analyze them deductively has been recognized for nearly two decades (Fiol and Huff, 1992). Langfield-Smith's (1992) experiment to elicit individuals' shared perceptions, together with her study with Wirth (Langfield-Smith and Wirth, 1992), gave researchers new avenues towards quantitative techniques for developing the means to do this. The use of pools of constructs put forward by Markóczy and Goldberg (1995), using Langfield-Smith and Wirth's (1992) measure of distance ratios, was further developed by Clarkson and Hodgkinson (2005), who made an important contribution in making available a user-friendly piece of software called Cognizer. Previously available computer packages such as Decision Explorer, CMAP2, and Distrat/askmap were not designed, or sufficiently user-friendly, to permit large-scale map comparisons (see Clarkson and Hodgkinson (2005) for a review). Clarkson and Hodgkinson (2005) demonstrated how causal maps can be used with large numbers of participants, exploring front-line call center workers' perceptions of their motivation and performance to assess how these underpin their psychological contracts. They generated 55 constructs from the literature and asked 200 participants in five organizations to create individual causal maps, using these data to illustrate how Cognizer works. The software randomly presents the constructs to the participants, who are asked to select those which they feel are most important (up to a maximum of 13). Pair-wise comparison is used; participants are presented with two constructs and are asked whether one influences the other and, if so, if this is a positive or negative influence. Participants are further probed as to the strength of the influence (strong (± 3), moderate (± 2), or slight (± 1)). The pairs of constructs are presented to the participants on-screen, and they then work their own way through the process systematically. When the process is complete, individuals are able to look at and comment upon the resulting causal map.

Causal maps elicited through the use of Cognizer can, like other causal maps, be analyzed according to their content or structure, the difference being that the analysis is faster and the potential for human error (such as coding error) is vastly reduced. As the constructs are already known, it is the relative strength of influence of each of the constructs that is of interest. To measure this, the "indegree" and "outdegree" values are calculated. The indegree value indicates the extent to which each construct is influenced by other constructs; the outdegree value shows the influence a construct has on others. Clarkson and Hodgkinson (2005) combined the 200 maps into a single composite map before they calculated the constructs' indegree and outdegree values. In addition, they also composed composite maps for each of the five participating organizations, showing that there were key differences between the organizations.

The use of an application like Cognizer would be valuable in the field of organizational fit, where it is possible to generate a theoretically cohesive pool of constructs. For example, the 54 values of the OCP could be mapped by multiple people with the intention of showing the complex network of relationships between the values. Alternatively, researchers studying multidimensional fit might be interested in mapping how the various dimensions of fit relate to each other. If we were to produce a taxonomy of factors influencing fit (or misfit), causal mapping could help us move away from linear lists of factors to a rich picture: a web of nodes showing how the factors are interconnected and influence each other.

As well as calculating relationships between constructs and showing the relative salience to people, Cognizer also facilitates the comparison of similarities and differences between people (using Langfield-Smith and Wirth's (1992) Distance Formula 12 or Markóczy and Goldberg's (1995) measure of difference). It is possible to "systematically link cause maps to a variety of exogenous variables reflecting individual and organizational characteristics" (Clarkson and Hodgkinson, 2005, p. 331). In PE fit studies, this would enable researchers to assess whether differences in fit perceptions are affected by such variables as length of service and involvement in organizational socialization, which are thought to affect the degree of fit. It would also allow the exploration of factors that individuals consider salient at any one time.

Clarkson and Hodgkinson (2005) also note that Cognizer can be used for longitudinal studies. Longitudinal studies are uncommon in the organizational fit literature, but have the great potential to understand our constructs better (Judge, 2007; Kristof-Brown and Guay, 2010). Looking at how individuals' and groups' fit changes over time would offer new insight and greatly increase our understanding of the temporal nature of fit.

Box 4: Nomothetic analysis of idiographically generated maps. Returning to our earlier argument, the nomothetic analysis of idiographically generated causal maps reflects the desire to capture the richness of individuals while still being able to draw generalizable conclusions. The challenge that has frustrated many researchers is how to analyze idiographically developed maps in ways that overcome their diversity. Actively encouraging people to speak in-depth and at length about their perceptions of a situation will generate a wealth of qualitative data but can also lead to analytical headaches. The analysis of multiple idiographic cognitive maps has received some considerable attention, perhaps most notably by Eden and Ackermann (1998b). They caution that comparing idiographic maps is fraught with difficulties, given that people attach different meanings to the words that they use in constructing maps. We believe, however, that this warning should pose a challenge rather than an obstacle to researchers, as there are many ways of analyzing the content and topology of multiple idiographically developed maps and drawing testable propositions.

In addition to the analysis methods described at the start of this section, there are some interesting organizational fit-related techniques that might be usefully applied to multiple idiographic causal maps. Talbot and Billsberry (2010) undertook exploratory work using idiographic causal maps to examine the similarities and differences in the ways that people perceive their fit and misfit. They asked their respondents to describe the factors influencing both their sense of fit and their sense of misfit on one causal map. At the end of the data-gathering process they had 38 causal maps, each containing two heads, fit and misfit, and, in total across the maps, 2,904 concepts. They coded these concepts by assigning them to different forms of fit (i.e., person–organization (PO), person–job (PJ), person–group (PG), person–vocation (PV), person–supervisor (PS), or person–individual (PI)), demographic categories, job embeddedness categories, or emergent categories. As 70% of the concepts could be coded according to the different forms of fit, they demonstrated that map data are amenable to traditional coding methods. Once coded in this way, many of the techniques described for the nomothetic analysis of nomothethically generated maps (box 3) become relevant. In addition, the greater richness of these maps allows for more complex and fine-grained analysis. Talbot and Billsberry (2010), for example, analyzed the content of causal chains and differences in causation of fit and misfit. In addition, by using content analysis, they noticed differences in the way that the interviewees described PO fit: people who fit described values, mission, and other high-level abstractions, whereas people calling themselves misfits talked about the things that their organization did to them, such as poor management practice including bullying, lack of communication, and the imposition of petty and pointless rules. This analysis also showed that when people described themselves as misfits, it was negative and undesired.

Talbot and Billsberry (2010) also demonstrated that nomothetic topological analysis can be conducted on idiographically generated maps. They were able to look at similarities and differences in the length and complexity of causal chains leading to fit and misfit, and they analyzed how unified around a single dimension causal chains were. These forms of nomothetic analysis were generated to address specific research questions and appear to be just the tip of the iceberg in terms of the possibilities.

Taking the route of comparing idiographic causal maps is not to be recommended unless there are compelling reasons to do so. It is a laborious process and issues of validity and reliability are serious problems. However, we suggest that in the organizational fit field, the extra work involved may well yield dividends, particularly because the lack of idiographic research in the field means that we have relatively little understanding of people's day-to-day experience of fit and misfit at work.

Conclusion

In this chapter we have argued that the collection of data should be separated from the manner in which they are analyzed. Doing so allows researchers to achieve different goals. Perhaps the most interesting of these for a book entitled *Organizational Fit: Key Issues and New Directions* is the combination of idiographic data gathering and nomothetic analysis. This approach may provide fit researchers with an avenue to find new theory, new propositions, and new hypotheses.

References

Barber, A. E., and Wesson, M. J. (1998) Using verbal protocol analysis to assess the construct validity of an empirical measure: An examination of the OCP. In J. A. Wagner III (ed.), *Advances in Qualitative Organization Research* (Vol. 1, pp. 67–104). Greenwich, CT: JAI Press.

Billsberry, J. (2007) Attracting for values: An empirical study of ASA's attraction proposition. *Journal of Managerial Psychology*, 22 (2), 132–149.

Billsberry, J., Ambrosini, V., Moss-Jones, J., and Marsh, P. J. G. (2005) Some suggestions for mapping organizational members' sense of fit. *Journal of Business and Psychology*, 19, 555–570.

Cable, D. M., and Edwards, J. R. (2004) Complementary and supplementary fit: A theoretical and empirical integration. *Journal of Applied Psychology*, 89, 822–834.

Cable, D. M., and Judge, T. A. (1997) Interviewers' perceptions of person–organization fit and organizational selection decisions. *Journal of Applied Psychology*, 82 (4), 546–561.

Chatman, J. A. (1989) Improving interactional organizational research: A model of person–organization fit. *Academy of Management Review*, 14 (1), 333–349.

Chatman, J. (1991) Matching people and organizations: Selection and socialization in public accounting firms. *Administrative Science Quarterly*, 36, 459–484.

Clarkson, G., and Hodgkinson, G. (2005) Introducing Cognizer™: A comprehensive computer package for the elicitation and analysis of causal maps. *Organization Research Methods*, 8 (3), 317–341.

Cossette, P., and Audet, M. (1992) Mapping of an idiosyncratic schema. *Journal of Management Studies*, 29 (3), 325–347.

Daniels, K., de Chernatony, L., and Johnson, G. (1995) Validating a method for mapping managers' mental models of competitive industry structures. *Human Relations*, 48, 975–991.

Eden, C. (1990) Strategic thinking with computers. *Long Range Planning*, 23 (6), 35–43.

Eden, C. (1992) On the nature of cognitive maps. *Journal of Management Studies*, 29 (3), 261–265.

Eden, C., and Ackermann, F. (1998a) Analysing and comparing idiographic causal maps. In C. Eden and J. C. Spender (eds.) *Managerial and Organizational Cognition: Theory, Methods and Research* (pp. 192–209). London: Sage.

Eden, C., and Ackermann, F. (1998b) *Making Strategy*. London: Sage.

Eden, C., Ackermann, F., and Cropper, S. (1992) The analysis of cause maps. *Journal of Management Studies*, 29 (3), 309–324.

Eden, C., Jones, S., Sims, D., and Smithin, T. (1981) The intersubjectivity of issues and issues of intersubjectivity. *Journal of Management Studies*, 18 (1), 37–47.

Edmondson, A. C., and McManus, S. E. (2007) Methodological fit in management field research. *Academy of Management Review*, 32, 1155–1179.

Ennis, S. (1999) Growth and the small firm: Using causal mapping to assess the decision-making process. *Qualitative Market Research*, 2 (2), 147–160.

Fiol, C. M., and Huff, A. S. (1992) Maps for managers: Where are we? Where do we go from here? *Journal of Management Studies*, 29, 267–285.

Glaser, B. G., and Strauss, A. L. (1967) *The Discovery of Grounded Theory: Strategies for Qualitative Research*. New York: Aldine.

Grice, J. W., Jackson, B. J., and McDaniel, B. L. (2006) Bridging the idiographic–nomothetic divide: A follow-up study. *Journal of Personality*, 74, 1191–1218.

Harrison, D. A. (2007) Pitching fits in applied psychological research: Making fit methods fit theory. In C. Ostroff and T. A. Judge (eds), *Perspectives on Organizational Fit* (pp. 389–416). New York: Lawrence Erlbaum Associates.

Hodgkinson, G. (2007) The cognitive perspective. In M. Jenkins and V. Ambrosini with N. Collier (eds), *Advanced Strategic Management: A Multiple Perspective Approach* (pp. 152–172). London: Palgrave.

Huff, A. S. (1990) Mapping strategic thought. In A. S. Huff (ed.), *Mapping Strategic Thought* (pp. 1–49). Chichester: John Wiley & Sons, Ltd.

Huff, A., and Jenkins, M. (2002) *Mapping Strategic Knowledge*. London: Sage.

Hughes, W., Lavery, J., and Doren, K. (2010) *Critical Thinking: An Introduction to the Basic Skills*. Calgary: Broadview.

Judge, T. A. (2007) The future of person–organization fit research: Comments, observations, and a few suggestions. In C. Ostroff and T. A. Judge (eds), *Perspectives on Organizational Fit* (pp. 419–445). New York: Lawrence Erlbaum Associates.

Kelly, G. (1955) *The Psychology of Personal Constructs*. Vols I and II. New York: Norton.

Krahé, B. (1992) *Personality and Social Psychology: Towards a Synthesis*. London: Sage.

Kristof-Brown, A. L., and Guay, R. P. (2010) Person–environment fit. In S. Zedeck (ed.), *Handbook of Industrial and Organizational Psychology* (Vol. 3, Chapter 1). Washington, DC: American Psychological Association.

Kristof-Brown, A. L., Zimmerman, R. D., and Johnson, E. C. (2005) Consequences of individuals' fit at work: A meta-analysis of person–job, person–organization, person–group, and person–supervisor fit. *Personnel Psychology*, 58, 281–342.

Langfield-Smith, K. (1992) Exploring the need for a shared cognitive map. *Journal of Management Studies*, 29, 340–368.

Langfield-Smith, K. M., and Wirth, A. (1992) Measuring differences between cognitive maps. *Journal of the Operational Research Society*, 43, 1135–1150.

Larsson, R. (1993) Case survey methodology: Quantitative analysis of patterns across case studies. *Academy of Management Journal*, 36, 1515–1546.

Larsson, R., and Finkelstein, S. (1999) Integrating strategic, organizational and human re-source perspectives on mergers and acquisitions: A case survey of synergy realization. *Organization Science*, 10, 1–26.

Laukkanen, M. (1994) Comparative cause mapping of organizational cognitions. *Organization Science*, 5 (3), 322–343.

Laukkanen, M. (1998) Conducting causal mapping research. In C. Eden and J. C. Spender (eds), *Managerial and Organisational Cognition* (pp. 168–191). London: Sage.

Luthans, F., and Davis, T. R. V. (1982) An idiographic approach to organizational behavior research: The use of single case experimental designs and direct measures. *Academy of Management Review*, 7, 380–391.

Markóczy, L., and Goldberg, J. (1995) A method for eliciting and comparing causal maps. *Journal of Management*, 21, 305–333.

O'Reilly, C. A., Chatman, J., and Caldwell, D. F. (1991) People and organizational culture: A profile comparison approach to assessing person–organization fit. *Academy of Management Journal*, 34 (3), 487–516.

Ravlin, E. C., and Meglino, B. M. (1989) The transitivity of work values: Hierarchical preference ordering of socially desirable stimuli. *Organizational Behavior and Human Decision Processes*, 44, 494–508.

Sarros, J. C., Gray, J., Densten, I. L., and Cooper, B. (2005) The Organizational Culture Profile revisited and revised: An Australian perspective. *Australian Journal of Management*, 30 (1), 159–182.

Schneider, B., Smith, D. B., Taylor, S., and Fleenor, J. (1998) Personality and organizations: A test of the homogeneity of personality hypothesis. *Journal of Applied Psychology*, 83 (3), 462–470.

Talbot, D. L., and Billsberry, J. (2010) Empirically distinguishing misfit from fit. Paper presented at the Academy of Management annual meeting, Montréal, Canada.

Tsoukas, H. (1989) The validity of idiographic research explanations. *Academy of Management Review*, 14 (4), 551–561.

Turban, D. B., and Keon, T. L. (1993) Organizational attractiveness: An interactionalist perspective. *Journal of Applied Psychology*, 78, 184–193.

Van den Brink-Budgen, R. (2000) *Critical Thinking for Students* (3rd edn). Oxford: How To Books.

Weick, K. E., and Bougon, M. G. (1986) Organizations as cognitive maps. In H. P. Sims (ed.), *The Thinking Organization* (pp. 102–135). San Francisco: Jossey-Bass.

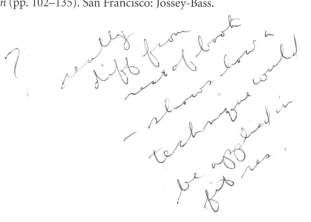

Part 2

New Directions for the Fit Paradigms

7

The Construal of Person–Organization Fit during the ASA Stages: Content, Source, and Focus of Comparison

Annelies E. M. Van Vianen
Department of Psychology, University of Amsterdam

J. W. Stoelhorst
Amsterdam Business School, University of Amsterdam

Marije E. E. De Goede
Department of Psychology, University of Amsterdam

Introduction

The main person–environment (PE) fit theories that have dominated research in organizational psychology – Holland's (1985) model of vocational personality types, Dawis and Lofquist's (1984) Theory of Work Adjustment (TWA), and Schneider's (1987) Attraction-Selection-Attrition (ASA) framework – share some fundamental assumptions. First, people have a basic need to fit their environments and therefore seek out environments that match their own characteristics. This means that person–environment fit theory is basically a theory of human choice (Van Vianen, 2001). Secondly, the degree of fit between people and their work environment is positively related to important individual outcomes, such as work satisfaction, health, and career decisions.

People are confronted with a wide variety of elements that constitute their environment, and PE fit theories hold that they will seek out those that best fit their personal characteristics. The organizational literature has suggested a multitude of domains that concern people's fit experiences, such as their vocation (person–vocation fit), job (needs–supplies fit and demands–abilities fit), work team

Organizational Fit: Key Issues and New Directions, First Edition.
Edited by Amy L. Kristof-Brown and Jon Billsberry.

(person–team fit), supervisor (person–supervisor fit), and organization (person–organization fit). People seem to be able to distinguish among the different domain fits, and they connect these various fits to specific types of outcome (Cable and DeRue, 2002). In this chapter, we exclusively focus on people's person–organization (PO) fit, which has been conceptualized as the congruence between a person and an organization's culture. More specifically, this congruence has typically been understood as the match between people's own values and those of the organization (Kristof-Brown et al., 2005; Verquer et al., 2003).

There are two reasons why PO fit is a particularly intriguing type of fit to study. First, PO fit experiences are among the strongest predictors of people's affective reactions, such as their organizational commitment, and career-related decisions, such as withdrawal cognitions (Kristof-Brown et al., 2005; Van Vianen, 2005). Second, its components (the person and the organization) are arguably more difficult to define than the components of most other types of fit. For example, individuals will find it easier to specify the demands of their job than precisely to portray an organization's values and culture. This is not surprising, as even researchers still struggle to define the various dimensions of organizational culture comprehensively. In fact, despite the many PO fit studies conducted in recent decades, as yet very little is known about how an organization's culture is represented in the minds of individuals when they assess their fit. As a result, studies have used markedly different approaches to assess an organization's culture when assessing people's PO fit, or have simply left it to respondents to decide what the organization's culture and their fit with this culture is. These various operationalizations and methods have led to a rather fragmented picture of PO fit effects, while leaving open the question of what is actually being measured (e.g., Edwards et al., 2006).

The purpose of this chapter is to identify fruitful new directions in organizational fit research through a theoretical reflection on the nature of the PO fit concept. The starting point for this reflection is Schneider's (1987) seminal ASA framework.

The central proposition of the ASA framework is that homogeneity of people within an organization defines the structures, processes, and culture of that organization. Because individual employees were attracted to, selected by, and have stayed with an organization that matches their personal characteristics, people within a specific organization share their needs, values, and personalities. This homogeneity in employee characteristics in turn defines the organization, or in other words: people make the place. One of the attractive features of ASA theory is its emphasis on the different stages of PO fit formation. However, there is a substantial lack of detailed knowledge about how people's PO fit perceptions arise, before, during, and after being selected for a new job. This is unfortunate, because if the process of PO fit formation remains largely unknown, little can be said about how PO fit can be promoted and how misfit can be avoided. Based on Construal Level Theory (CLT; Liberman et al., 2002; Trope and Liberman, 2003), we will argue that psychological distance to an organization affects people's mental representation of this organization and, thus, their PO fit perception. The central idea underlying our elaboration of the nature of the PO fit concept in this chapter is that because people's psychological distance to an organization will change over the course of the ASA cycle, the nature of their PO fit assessments will change as well.

We make two contributions to the PO fit literature. First, we argue that people's PO fit assessments not only depend on the particular *content* of the P and O components, but are also affected by the *focal reference* for the comparison between the components (does the comparison proceed from the characteristics of the person to those of the organization, or vice versa?) and the *source* from which the O component is derived (the organization or the people in it). We derive an explicitly dynamic ASA model that specifies the changing nature of content, source, and reference of PO fit assessments over the different stages of the ASA model.

Second, ASA's dictum that "people make the place" emphasizes that organizations are "social" environments, and that in seeking fit with an organization, people are essentially seeking fit with other people. In this chapter, we embrace this view. However, building on evolutionary and social identity theories, we will argue that some organizational members affect people's fit perceptions more than others. In particular, when people have entered the organization they use prototypical organizational members, who embody the organization and its values, as the main source of their PO fit experiences. This leads to the important qualification that, in terms of PO fit perceptions, *some* people make the place.

In the next section, we will first elaborate on the question of why PO fit is so important to people. The purpose is to develop a more fundamental understanding of the basic function of people's PO fit need, so that we will have a stronger basis for our further propositions about the processes underlying people's PO fit perceptions.

The Need to Fit: The Need to Belong

People have a fundamental need to belong (e.g., Deci and Ryan, 2000) and it is from this need that they compare themselves with other people in the social environment. There are two theoretical lines of thinking that provide an explanation for this human need to belong: one that is based on evolutionary approaches and one that is based on more cognitive psychological approaches towards human behavior.

Over the last three decades, a number of evolutionary perspectives on human behavior have been developed (for an overview, see Laland and Brown, 2002). In this chapter, we build on two evolutionary perspectives in particular: evolutionary psychology (e.g., Barkow, Cosmides, and Tooby, 1992) and gene-culture co-evolution (Boyd and Richerson, 1985; Richerson and Boyd, 2005). What these two perspectives share is the view that humans, as an animal species among many others, face external selection pressures, and that many of our behaviors can be understood as adaptations to these pressures. One crucial adaptation is our capacity to cooperate with others (cf. Nowak, 2006). A capacity to sustain collaborative relationships with others is likely to have given our evolutionary ancestors a reproductive advantage, so that, over many generations, a genetic predisposition towards emotions and behaviors that would help sustain collaboration could spread among the species (Cronin,

1991). This explains why humans have the evolved motivation (and capacity) to be accepted by their fellows, and a profound need to belong (Baumeister and Leary, 1995). This biologically anchored need to belong has been supported by research that shows that social exclusion activates those parts of the brain that are associated with physical pain (Eisenberger, Lieberman, and Williams, 2003). This explains why individuals feel deeply hurt when other people exclude them from their group.

As has been well documented in research on group formation (Brewer and Harasty, 1996; Dasgupta *et al.*, 1999; De Cremer, 2004; Gaertner and Schopler, 1998), a feeling of belonging is most likely when individuals perceive that they share characteristics with others in their social environment. Research has shown that people unconsciously respond to subtle (facial) similarity markers with feelings of familiarity and trust. Humans apparently have a strong tendency to assess their similarities with others, which may stem from a past adaptation to assess genetic relatedness (Tooby and Cosmides, 1989) that enabled behaviors to increase an organism's so-called "inclusive fitness" (i.e., increasing the frequency of copies of one's own genes in the next generation by furthering the reproductive success of kin; Hamilton, 1964). In addition to the tendency to collaborate with genetically related others, individuals also favor collaboration with others if their relationship is based on reciprocity (Axelrod, 1984; Fehr and Fischbacher, 2003; Trivers 1971). Reciprocity is more easily achieved when two people are similar to each other than when they are dissimilar (Lusk *et al.*, 1998). This symmetry-based reciprocity (i.e., directing favors to kin or to others with similar features) has been extensively documented in primates, the species that are our closest genetic relatives (Brosnan and De Waal, 2002), as well as in humans (Knudsen, 2003). Furthermore, perceptions of similarity with others lead to perspective taking – that is, imagining others' feelings (Preston and De Waal, 2002) – higher expectations of others' cooperative behaviors, and enhanced expectations of reward division (e.g., De Waal and Davis, 2003). Thus, given their strong biological roots, similarity assessments are thought to be easily activated and functionally related to sustaining cooperation.

Psychological theories have taken a more cognitive stance towards the human tendency to categorize others as being similar or not. Festinger's (1954) theory of social comparison, Heider's "balanced state" theory (Byrne, 1971; Lott and Lott, 1965), Steele's self-affirmation theory (1988), and Byrne's (1971) similarity–attraction hypothesis all argue that people are drawn to similar others because they seek validation of their opinions and want to maximize the consistency among elements of their belief system. Extant research supports the notion that people like those who hold similar attitudes and opinions more than those with dissimilar attitudes (Byrne *et al.*, 1986; Condon and Crano, 1988; Shaikh and Kanekar, 1994). Furthermore, it has been postulated that humans categorize their social world (into similar or dissimilar) to reduce cognitive overload, to control their world and their place within it, and to preserve the integrity of their self-image (Tajfel, 1969). People strive for certainty about aspects of life that are important to them. This certainty is particularly challenged by the social context – that is, the beliefs, attitudes, and behaviors of others (e.g., Hogg, 2000) – and can thus be increased when people agree with each other. According to this logic, the primary function of people's similarity assessments is uncertainty reduction.

Both evolutionary and psychological theories emphasize the human drive to fit the social environment as rooted in a need to seek out similar others. Although prevalent cognitive psychological theories may suffice as a basis for fit theories in organizational psychology, evolutionary theories stress the additional point that human cooperative behavior is channeled by basic and often unconscious mechanisms. Hence, similarity assessments are likely to be universal and automatic; people are hardwired to establish a fit with social environments, such as organizations. Furthermore, given the emphasis on environmental selection pressures, evolutionary theories seem to suggest that the social environment is the focal reference from which people assess their fit: the self is compared to the salient characteristics of the environment. In contrast, psychological theories seem to suggest that people take the self as the focal reference: the environment is compared to the salient characteristics of the self. In the next section we will further address these and other issues related to people's PO fit assessments.

The Establishment of PO Fit

Person–organization fit can be understood as the match between people's own values and those of the organization (e.g., Kristof-Brown *et al.*, 2005). Values represent conscious desires held by individuals and encompass preferences, interests, motives, and goals, and they are seen as relatively enduring and fundamental to self-identity (Chatman, 1991). Moreover, values touch upon the fundamental assumptions that comprise an organization's culture (Schein, 1992). People seek organizations that fit their values and, when they are on the job, they feel attached to and intend to stay in their organization to the extent that their values match those of the organization (e.g., Cable and DeRue, 2002; Cable and Judge, 1996; Lauver and Kristof-Brown, 2001).

Of the various fit dimensions and operationalizations, people's PO fit experiences are among the strongest predictors of their attitudes and behaviors, which is why researchers have often employed subjective rather than objective measures to assess PO fit (e.g., Edwards and Cable, 2009). PO fit has been measured by asking people to assess their own values, as well as the values of the organization (e.g., Judge and Cable, 1997; Van Vuuren *et al.*, 2008). Surprisingly, the calculated PO fit index that results from comparing these subjective P and O assessments is only moderately related to people's reported PO fit experiences (De Goede *et al.*, 2009; Kristof-Brown and Guay, 2010). In addition, calculated PO fit indices relate less strongly to many individual outcomes than individuals' PO fit perceptions (Kristof-Brown and Guay, 2010; Kristof-Brown *et al.*, 2005). Apparently, people do not make the (calculative) comparison between their own values and those of the organization that PO fit theories suggest. These findings bring us back to the central question raised in the introduction of this chapter: what do people have in mind when assessing their PO fit? We discuss three factors that may explain the modest validity of calculated PO fit indices. These factors are the *content, source,* and *focal reference* of people's PO fit assessments.

The *content* of PO fit assessments has been exclusively determined by researchers rather than lay persons (Billsberry *et al.,* 2005). Researchers have aimed to capture those value dimensions of the person and the organization that they thought to be relevant to both individuals and organizations, and that vary among individuals and organizations. They have derived the P and O components from theories and instruments about individual values (P), such as the basic values as distinguished by Schwartz (1994), which were then transposed to organizations (O), or they have derived these components from theories and instruments regarding organizational cultures (O), such as the Organizational Culture Profile (OCP; O'Reilly *et al.,* 1991), which were then transposed to individuals (P).

In using these methods, researchers assumed that P and O are commensurate and have the same psychological meaning to individuals. Yet, as far as we know, the equivalence of the commensurate P and O constructs has never been tested. Nominal equivalence (P and O are described with similar terms; see Edwards and Shipp, 2007) does not necessarily go together with equivalence of meaning. Mental models that are associated with personal constructs (for example, personal aggressiveness) may be different from the ones that are associated with organizational constructs (for example, organizational aggressiveness). In that case, P and O cannot be compared and combined into a fit index. In addition, the dimensions as selected by researchers may not be the ones that individuals actually take into consideration when assessing their fit. Also, people seem not to have the holistic view about the self and the organization's culture that fit theory seems to imply. Instead, they weigh only specific cultural value dimensions, such as those P dimensions they rate as highly important to the self and those O dimensions that are omnipresent in the organization (e.g., Van Vianen, 2005). Indeed, research on cognitive processing has indicated that people are simply not equipped with the capacity to process large amounts of information. They use only a restricted amount of cues that can be easily detected and/or that are salient to them (e.g., Dijksterhuis, 2004). To our knowledge, there is no research that has first asked individuals to describe the cultural features that are salient to them and then asked them to report their own preferences with regard to these features (or the reverse). The resulting PO fit estimates of such studies may well be more strongly associated with people's PO fit perceptions than is the case with prevailing researcher-driven methods. Furthermore, they are likely to explain more variance in individual affective outcomes since important characteristics of the environment are no longer excluded.

Also the *sources* that individuals use for assessing organizational characteristics and PO fit are not yet clear. Do they derive their impressions about an organization's values and culture from organizational practices and espoused values, and are these practices and communications the sources for assessing their fit? Organizational culture is a rather abstract and complex phenomenon to grasp. The question is how people process perceptions of this complexity. Most likely, they will focus on few informational cues derived from sources they view as reliable. In addition, in keeping with evolutionary and cognitive theories' emphasis on similarity with others as being central to social inclusion, individuals may focus on concrete persons rather than abstract cultures. As we will argue below, they are particularly likely to focus on those organizational members who are most successful, because these members can be seen as best representing the characteristics that fit the organization's culture.

The *focal reference*, or perspective from which individuals assess their PO fit, may make a difference for the resulting PO fit experience as well. The perspective that people take when making a decision, for instance taking the self or the other as the focal referent, significantly impacts decision processes and outcomes (Kahneman, 2003; Kahneman *et al.*, 1982). For this reason, it is unlikely that individuals equally balance sets of personal and organizational attributes against each other. Individuals may take the self – that is, their own core attributes and values – as a reference to assess whether the organization matches the self. Alternatively, they may take the salient attributes and values of the organization as the main reference for establishing their fit. As we noted above, psychological theories emphasize the importance of the person, whereas evolutionary theories point to the environment as the focal reference.

In addition, the content and source of people's PO fit assessments may differ depending on the *stage* of the PO relationship in which they are assessed: that is, during attraction or selection, or after organizational entry (Edwards and Billsberry, 2011; Jansen and Kristof-Brown, 2006). The few studies that included more than only one stage employed similar measures for assessing individuals' PO fit in each of the (two or three) stages (Cable and Parsons, 2001; Cooper-Thomas *et al.*, 2004). In other words, these studies assumed that the constructs of P, O, and PO fit remain the same throughout the ASA cycle. In contrast, in the next section we will argue that there are reasons to believe that the stage in which PO fit is assessed influences the content, source, and reference of the PO fit construct.

ASA: Content, Source, and Reference of PO Fit Perceptions

Although the ASA framework is plausible and research has provided some evidence for homogeneity of personalities in organizations (e.g., Giberson *et al.*, 2005; Ployhart *et al.*, 2006; Schaubroeck *et al.*, 1998; Schneider *et al.*, 1998) there is no research that has investigated the ASA cycle longitudinally, with a within-person design following individuals and their self-selection decisions through all stages of the ASA process. As a result, little is known about the way in which people's organizational fit perceptions emerge, to what extent these perceptions may change, and whether they remain based on the same types of P and O comparisons. One way in which the ASA stages are obviously different is in terms of people's knowledge about the organization, particularly for external applicants. Their PO fit perceptions during attraction and selection concern an organization that is not yet intimately known, whereas PO fit perceptions when employed in the organization concern an organizational environment that is highly familiar.

PO fit with the unknown

In addition to instrumental motives such as pay, opportunities for advancement, career opportunities, location, and company reputation (Cable and Graham, 2000; Lievens *et al.*, 2001; Turban and Cable, 2003), applicant attraction to an organization seems to be based on repeated exposure to an organization's name (Turban *et al.*, 2001) and attractive traits people ascribe to organizations, such as innovativeness, competence, friendliness, and style (Lievens and Highhouse, 2003; Slaughter and Greguras, 2009; Slaughter *et al.*, 2004). Previous studies have examined the images that people hold about organizations that were already somewhat familiar to them: that is, study participants had some general impressions of these organizations based on facts, beliefs, and feelings. These studies found that a positive organizational image leads to an incremental preference for that organization as a potential employer (Allen *et al.*, 2007; Cober *et al.*, 2003; Collins and Stevens, 2002; Turban and Cable, 2003). Most organizations, however, do not have a general reputation or image to rely upon. Instead, job-seekers possess only limited information about these organizations and have to draw inferences from the incomplete and "managed" information that is available to them through sources such as websites, products, and service interactions. These sources of information may activate mental models that encompass impressions of an organization's values and culture (Cable *et al.*, 2000; Rynes *et al.*, 1991; Turban, 2001).

Clearly, job seekers are not only attracted to organizations because of their general attractive features, but – if possible – they also choose organizations on the basis of perceived congruence between their own characteristics and those of the organization (e.g., Cable and Judge, 1994; Rentsch and McEwen, 2002). However, extant studies that examined the relationship between PO fit perceptions and organizational attractiveness have provided job seekers with ready items that reflect personal and organizational characteristics. This raises the question of whether these items bear a resemblance to the mental models that people would spontaneously have in mind when searching for a fitting job. To our knowledge, there is no research that examined job seekers' spontaneous mental representations of themselves in relation to the prospective organizational environment. Nor are we aware of research that has studied if these initial mental representations are similar to those that people have once they are in extended contact with the organization.

Construal Level Theory (CLT) suggests that the content of people's mental models will change as their distance to the actual organization is reduced. This theory proposes that temporal distance changes the way in which people mentally represent events. The greater the distance, the more likely it is that events are represented in relatively few dimensions, and in abstract features rather than detailed ones (Liberman *et al.*, 2002; Trope and Liberman, 2003). When choosing an organization, job seekers will develop a mental model for a temporally distant event, the anticipated organization. They will construct rather abstract representations of possible organizations: for example, based on their products and services and the typical employee they expect to find in this type of company (Devendorf and Highhouse, 2008).

Research on CLT has shown that global personality traits are more abstract, while specific traits, beliefs, and motives are more concrete inferences. Global personality characteristics carry more weight in predicting the distant future than the near future. Also, global values are more likely to be of high weight for the distant future (Eyal *et al.*, 2009; Trope and Liberman, 2003). Therefore, job seekers may think of an organization as a Gestalt, using broad personality terms and broad categories of basic human values. Only in this way are they able to associate their proximal concrete self with their distal and abstract representations of organizations and to establish their prospective PO fits. Consequently, the weak relationship between calculated PO fit indices and job seekers' own PO fit perceptions may be the result of P and O operationalizations that do not reflect job seekers' construal level.

That being said, calculated PO fit indices remain weak predictors of PO fit perceptions when job seekers are explicitly asked to elaborate on their own cultural preferences and to compare these specific preferences to the perceived culture of a prospective organization. De Goede, Van Vianen, and Klehe (2009) conducted a policy-capturing study in which job seekers provided their own cultural preferences (using the OCP) which the researchers subsequently used for creating a unique (within-person) set of organizational profiles that job seekers had to rate on perceived fit and attractiveness. They found that job seekers distinguished between the cultural aspects they liked, labeled as attractive cultural values, and cultural aspects they disliked, the unattractive cultural values. PO fit on the attractive values was weighed more heavily than PO fit on the unattractive values in making their PO fit assessments. The researchers concluded that job seekers attend to what they want rather than to what they do not want when assessing their future employer. This information-processing strategy results in an overall fit impression that is one-sidedly fed by information about cultural aspects that people seek in their future job. Consequently, the content of job seekers' PO fit perceptions depends on their information-processing strategy. Note that by using job seekers' own cultural preferences for constructing the organizational profiles, the researchers used the person and not the organization as the reference. Theoretically, this makes sense since the object of comparison (the future organization) is not yet tangible and job seekers will, thus, use their own salient preferences as the main source for appraising organizations.

The specific content of the P and O dimensions that are processed in the attraction stage may also depend on the types of outcome that job seekers foresee gaining in their future job. These outcomes may be different from the ones that researchers expect to play a dominant role in this stage. Deliberations about a distant future mostly concern thoughts about cognitive[1] future outcomes, such as outcomes one typically associates with jobs in general (e.g., career opportunities, workload). In contrast, deliberations about a near future (such as a concrete work day) also tend to be associated with possible affective outcomes, such as the amount of stress or satisfaction that one will experience (Metcalfe and Mischel, 1999). Furthermore, thoughts about cognitive outcomes carry more weight than affective outcomes for making a decision about the (distant) future (Loewenstein et al., 2001). Hence, while elaborating on their PO fit and attraction towards the organization, job seekers may put less weight on their future affective outcomes.

Altogether, our discussion suggests that deliberations about a prospective organization as a good place to work are at a relatively general and abstract level, and probably portrayed in broad and personalized terms. We expect people to take their own characteristics as a reference for evaluating the organization and establishing PO fit, because the organization is still relatively unknown at this stage of the relationship. Finally, it can be expected that people's fit assessments during the attraction stage are more strongly associated with thoughts about future cognitive outcomes than with thoughts about future affective outcomes, because the distance to the organization at this stage is still large. The more this distance is reduced, the more individuals are able to imagine how they may feel in a (mis)fitting job.

The next step in the ASA cycle concerns the selection of applicants by organizations. Existing research about this stage has mostly been focused on recruiter perceptions of applicant PO fit. Recruiters' assessments of applicant fit tend to stem from intuitive impressions of applicants' knowledge skills, abilities, and personality (Kristof-Brown, 2000; Van Dam, 2003). Recruiters seldom recognize applicants' actual fit, but rather base their PO fit judgment on perceptions of interpersonal similarity (García et al., 2008; Howard and Ferris, 1996) and personal liking (e.g., Cable and Judge, 1997), while also being influenced by applicants' verbal and nonverbal impression management tactics (Higgins and Judge, 2004; Kristof-Brown et al., 2002).

Applicants make intuitive PO fit assessments as well. According to signaling theory (Rynes, 1991), applicants interpret recruiter behavior during the selection interview as a signal of organizational attributes. Although this has been shown to be true (Chapman and Webster, 2006; Turban et al., 1998), applicant attraction to the organization is largely determined by their pre-interview attraction to the organization. In addition, it has also been found that the perceived fairness of the selection procedure affects applicant reactions toward the organization (Gilliland, 1993, 1994), as it is a signal of an organization's fairness values. Hence, existing research has shown that applicant PO fit perceptions in later stages of selection are initiated by their early PO fit impressions, recruiter behavior, and perceived organizational fairness. To date, we do not know what the precise contribution of each of these factors is to applicants' PO fit perceptions during selection since there are no studies that have examined them simultaneously.

PO fit with the known

Abundant research, using different methods and measures, has examined employees' PO fit (perceptions) at work. PO fit has mostly been connected to employees' affective outcomes, such as job satisfaction and affective organizational commitment (see Kristof-Brown *et al.*, 2005). These outcomes do, indeed, seem relevant. First, feelings of value similarity with the organization elicit affective reactions towards the organization. Secondly, as argued above on the basis of Construal Level Theory, nearby concrete events are naturally linked to affective reactions, such as feelings of satisfaction and attachment (Loewenstein *et al.*, 2001).

As mentioned earlier, although people at this stage of the ASA cycle have many opportunities to assess their organization's culture, calculated PO fit indices are only modestly related to people's reported fit experiences (e.g., Kristof-Brown and Guay, 2010). Hence, in this stage of the ASA cycle, it is still unclear what people have in mind when assessing their PO fit. Later we delve into the way in which employees may develop their PO fit impressions immediately following organizational entry. Impressions about the organization that are formed in the first 4 to 6 months seem crucial in establishing PO fit (e.g., Cooper-Thomas *et al.*, 2004). We propose that organizational newcomers utilize a selected group of organizational members as the focal reference for their PO fit assessment. Whereas an organization's physical features, tangible supplies (e.g., an organization's HR practices), and demands are significant sources for perceptions of needs–supplies fit (Piasentin and Chapman, 2006) and demands–abilities fit (Wanous, 1992), we argue that characteristics of the organization's salient members, rather than its general culture, are the ultimate source of PO fit perceptions.

Some people make the place

The ASA framework proposes that organizational cultures are created through the characteristics of organizational members: that is, homogeneity in people's characteristics forms an organization's culture. In general, evolutionary theories seem to support this view: environments select organisms with individual characteristics that fit, and, hence, organisms that fit a particular environment will share many of their basic features. However, gene-culture co-evolution theory (Boyd and Richerson, 1985; Richerson and Boyd, 2005) modifies this general perspective by arguing that it is not just individuals expressing genetically transmitted genes who are selected, but also groups of individuals expressing culturally transmitted ideas and behaviors. While gene-culture co-evolution theory agrees with evolutionary psychology that universal genetic dispositions may go a long way in explaining broad categories of human behavior such as cooperation, it also holds that such dispositions cannot explain cultural differences between groups and postulates that cultural group selection works through such mechanisms as conformity to the behavior of the majority (Boyd and Richerson, 1985). In other words, this evolutionary approach suggests that organizational cultures are primarily the result of homogeneity in behaviors rather than homogeneity in traits.

Recent developments in evolutionary research point to selection mechanisms that support both the behavioral and trait view on the development of homogeneous organizational cultures. First, stable group differences in behavior do exist because of people's tendency to conform to and imitate others (see McElreath *et al.*, 2003). When individuals move from one group to another they tend to adopt the behavioral norms of the new group (Richerson and Boyd, 2005). This explains the human proclivity to conformity (Henrich and Boyd, 1998), docility (Simon, 1990), and imitation, which creates behavioral homogeneity within groups. People's copying behaviors are inherently adaptive, because they allow for efficient control of and adaptation to new environments. Hence, social learning by imitation is the cornerstone of cultural transmission.

Second, although imitation in general is adaptive, indiscriminate imitation is not. Social learning by imitation only increases the mean fitness of individuals if the model from which the behavior is copied produces reliable information. Research in biology has shown that imitating the successful (i.e., those with the highest payoff) is typically a good survival strategy (Laland, 2004). This is consistent with the finding that behaviors with a high payoff, in particular, spread within groups through imitation (Boyd *et al.*, 2003). Natural selection has also favored cognitive abilities to rank potential models according to their payoffs in humans (Henrich and Gil-White, 2001). Furthermore, experimental economic research that used multi-round market and investment games has shown that individuals tend to mimic the beliefs and decisions of successful players in particular, even if all individuals have similar information necessary for making a decision (Henrich, 2004; Offerman and Sonnemans, 1998). Altogether, these studies suggest that people copy the behaviors of successful others, and these shared behaviors create the culture of a group.

Third, the literature on cultural evolution also suggests that although organizational cultures are mainly characterized by homogeneity of behavior, the processes that support conformity to these behaviors may also increase the degree of trait homogeneity. While imitation of successful models is likely, when the model is very different from the imitator, the model's success may not translate into success in the imitator's own circumstances (Boyd and Richerson, 1987). Therefore, individuals preferentially copy successful similar others (Laland, 2004; Swaney *et al.*, 2001). The likelihood that individuals adopt local behavior would therefore also depend on the extent to which organizational members perceive similarity with specific characteristics of the successful models. This is in line with evolutionary theorists like Wilson and Dugatkin (1997) who argue that, although optimal similarity within groups will never be achieved, interactions that are based on mutual attraction (referred to as *assortative interactions* in evolutionary theories) could still contribute to nonrandom groupings (i.e., lower within-group variances as compared to between-group variances). Such arguments are consistent with studies that examine homogeneity in organizations (e.g., Schneider *et al.*, 1998), and find significant but weak indicators of lower within-organization as compared to between-organization variances in personalities and values.

Altogether, we would expect that organizational cultures are rooted, first, in behavior and, second, in the characteristics of organizational models. In other words, some people make the place. Organizational members differentially adopt the behavior of those successful members of the organization whom they perceive as being similar to themselves. Based on such a view, attrition would be the result of an individual's perception that successful organizational models are too dissimilar to themselves to be able to imitate the behaviors that would lead to successful inclusion in the organization.

Fit with prototypical models

Employees perceive and define social environments in the form of prototypes; they have an image of characteristics that are associated with prototypical members in the work environment (Hogg and Terry, 2000). Prototypical members are individuals "in good standing" (Tyler and Blader, 2002). New employees identify prototypical members by means of prestige and the deference they receive from other people in the organization (Henrich, 2004). It may seem that prototypicality is linked to hierarchical position, with organizational leaders being the prototypical members. However, employees who do not occupy a formal leadership position can also be recognized as prototypical members.

Social identity theory (e.g., Tajfel and Turner, 1986) argues that people feel included within their social environment if they match the attributes of prototypical members. Employees make intra-group comparisons in order to assimilate the self to the in-group prototype and to become more group prototypical (Hogg, 2000). In particular, "self-categorization in terms of a well-defined, consensual, and clearly prescriptive in-group prototype" is a means to reduce uncertainty (Hogg, 2000, p. 233).

The proposition that employees' PO fit perceptions mainly stem from prototype-similarity perceptions has not been tested yet. The fit literature has mainly addressed people's fit with co-workers in the group (or interpersonal compatibility among team members), referred to as person–team fit (e.g., Kristof-Brown *et al.*, 2005). We would expect that person–prototype fit and person–team fit are different constructs, because team members are not necessarily prototypical. Moreover, we would expect person–prototype fit and to a lesser extent person–team fit to relate to people's PO fit perceptions.

The specific set of characteristics that people take into account when assessing their similarity with the prototype will mainly depend on the type of reference they use: the self or the prototype. On the one hand, it has been suggested that individuals use the self as an anchor to generate judgments about others (Cadinu and Rothbart, 1996) and, thus, focus on characteristics that are highly relevant to their self-concept (e.g., Otten, 2002; Otten and Epstude, 2006; Simon and Hastedt, 1999). On the other hand, it has been argued that people "seem to base their feelings about one another on perceived similarity on prototypical dimensions only" (Hogg and Terry, 2000, p. 174). In that case, they will focus on features that are distinctive for the prototype and are shared by other prototypes. Similarly, from an evolutionary point of view it can be reasoned that, since environments are selective, the features of the prototypical member are the most likely basis for a similarity assessment.

When entering an organization, people are concerned about their acceptance by other organizational members. This increases their sensitivity to social information and cues that point to future chances of acceptance (Gardner *et al.*, 2000). Precisely which set of prototypical characteristics constitutes the core content of people's fit assessments has yet to be examined. Previous research that investigated the relationship between similarity and interpersonal attraction included similarity of attitudes (e.g., Tan and Singh, 1995), similarity of values (e.g., Johnson, 1989), and similarity of personality (e.g., Moskowitz and Coté, 1995). Studies on attitude and value similarity showed the most unequivocal results: people like those who hold similar attitudes and opinions more than those with dissimilar attitudes (Shaikh and Kanekar, 1994). These results suggest that the attitudes and values of prototypical members are the focal variables for newcomers' PO fit assessments.

Of course, organizational environments may differ in the extent to which they signal clear cues: that is, some organizations may have a clear prototype whereas other organizations may lack such an exemplar. Organizations that have clearly defined prototypes can be referred to as "high entitativity" organizations. Campbell (1958) coined the term "entitativity perception" to refer to the perception of an aggregate of individuals as a group that possesses common attributes. Newcomers begin with observing group behavior, recognize similarities and common goals, and infer common characteristics in prototypical group members. Similarities among prototypical members foster perceptions of entitativity, which, in turn, will lead to the transfer of attributes to the larger whole (Crawford *et al.*, 2002; Ip *et al.*, 2006; Lickel *et al.*, 2001).

Overall, we propose that people's PO fit perceptions after organizational entry are mainly based on the comparison that employees make between the characteristics of prototypical organizational members and their own characteristics. The values and attitudes of prototypical members are used as the main reference to assess one's fit with the prototype. Hence, the specific content of people's prototype fit perceptions depends on salient and shared features of prototypical members. In addition, people's prototype fit perceptions will be strongly linked to their PO fit perceptions. Lower levels of fit with the prototype make it more difficult for people to shape their behavior to conform to the norm of the organization, which will lead to perceptions of organizational misfit and feelings of social exclusion. Higher levels of fit with the prototype, on the other hand, will make adaptation to the organization relatively easy, which causes perceptions of PO fit and feelings of social inclusion.

Table 7.1 summarizes how the content, source, and reference of PO fit perceptions may change across the ASA stages. The content of PO fit perceptions changes from

Table 7.1   PO fit assessments during attraction and selection, and after entrance

Stage	Content	Organizational sources	Main reference
Attraction	Global personality Global attractive values Factual outcomes	Organizational facts Organizational image Types of employee	Self
Selection	Global personality Global attractive values Factual outcomes Fairness Recruiter liking	Organizational facts Organizational image Types of employee Recruiter	Self and other
After entrance	Prototypical attitudes and values Affective outcomes	Prototypical employee	Other

global personalities and attractive values, and projected cognitive outcomes, towards prototypical attitudes and values, and experienced affective outcomes. The organizational source of PO fit perceptions changes as well. In the attraction stage, people derive their organizational perceptions from facts (e.g., an organization's size), an organization's image (if available), and the types of employee they associate with an organization. However, after organizational entry, PO fit perceptions will be largely based on features of prototypical members.

The main reference that people use to establish their fit probably changes from the self (P) to the other (O). Because individuals often have only sparse information about organizations during the attraction stage, at this stage they are likely to take their own personality, values (that they find attractive), and preferred outcomes as the main referent and assess the likelihood that the organization fits the self. In contrast, when becoming more familiar with the organization during selection, but particularly after entrance, they will shift their attention to the features of the environment in order to assess their ability to adapt successfully to the local norms and behaviors as represented by prototypical organization members.

Conclusions and Avenues for Future Research

In this chapter, we have posited that people's PO fit need stems from an evolved need to belong. In order to develop collaborative relationships with others, become socially included, and be able to adapt to the group norm, people seek out social contexts in which they share characteristics with others. We have noted that despite abundant PO fit research, relatively little is known about the constituent elements of people's fit perceptions and the processes underlying the formation of these perceptions. We have addressed three distinct yet related factors that influence the PO fit construct: its content, source, and focal reference. Furthermore, we have discussed these factors for each stage of the ASA cycle and argued that the PO fit construct changes across these stages. In the remainder of this chapter, we summarize our main propositions and suggest some directions for future PO fit research.

Research suggests that when job seekers reflect on their possible fit with a distant and often unfamiliar organization in the attraction stage, they are mostly concerned whether the values they find attractive match those of the organization. They are less focused on the values they find unattractive (De Goede *et al.*, 2009). When entering an organization, people's reference is likely to shift from the self to the organization. Employees try to make sense of their new work environment by observing the behavior, attitudes, and values of prototypical members. Because these members are usually an excellent match with the organization, focusing on the attributes of prototypical members seems like an efficient and successful strategy to establish one's own fit. Moreover, mimicking the prototypical behavior will lead to successful assimilation into the organization. In this stage, the content of people's fit perceptions is likely to shift towards prototypical attributes instead of personal attributes.

These shifts in reference and content of people's PO fit perceptions should be tested in future research, since they have major implications for individuals as well as organizations. After arriving on the job, individuals who initially had high expectations about their fit with the organization (as based on their attractive values) may discover that they do not fit the organization's prototypical attributes. These prototypical attributes may include, for example, aspects that the individual finds unattractive yet did not attend to when applying for the job. Moreover, as opposed to the way in which information is weighed in the attraction stage, people may put more weight on unattractive rather than attractive (prototypical) attributes when they are in the organization. In other words, the presence of unattractive prototypical attributes may have a stronger impact on their reactions towards the organization than the absence of attractive prototypical attributes, even when both would reflect similar amounts of objective misfit. We realize that this latter proposition is somewhat speculative and requires further investigation. Yet, there are some preliminary findings from other fields of research that point in this direction. Recent research on intimate relationships has shown that the goals that people wish to be supported in a relationship change: from promotion-focused goals before marriage to prevention goals after marriage (Molden *et al.*, 2009). A similar phenomenon might hold for employees, namely the types of attribute that should fit may change from attractive attributes before organizational entry to unattractive attributes after organizational entry.

Individuals tend to be biased in their assessments of others by initially assuming that others are similar to them. This has been referred to as "false consensus" (e.g., Tan and Singh, 1995) or social projection (Robbins and Krueger, 2005). This bias seems to suggest that the self is always the main reference of comparison. This would contradict our proposition that people in organizations use the prototype as the focal reference when assessing their fit. However, for the reasons developed in the previous section, we would argue that people use the prototype as the reference and that the consensus bias may result in a focus on prototypical attributes that deviate from people's similarity expectations. This would mean that over time employees tend to focus on their areas of misfit instead of how they fit (Edwards and Billsberry, 2011). Future research could examine whether misfits have a greater contribution to individual affective reactions than attributes that fit and whether misfits on unattractive attributes carry more weight than misfits on attractive attributes.

In addition, we believe that PO fit theory and research could benefit from studies that examine the phenomenology of fit. As fit is not a lay construct (see Harrison, 2007), it should be measured in ways that correspond to people's mental processes and models. Research has shown that different fit measures are only weakly related to each other (Edwards *et al.*, 2006). Exact correspondence between people's PO fit perceptions and calculated fit indices will probably never be reached due to the fact that people's decisions and affective responses often involve unconscious processes. However, if researchers aim to make valid predictions from their *a priori* specified fit constructs, these constructs should reflect people's mental models of fit as much as possible. Edwards *et al.* (2006) found that a discrepancy fit measure (the rated discrepancy between perceived and desired environment) had some overlap with perceived fit. This indicates that, as fit theories assume, people tend to think in terms of discrepancies between themselves and the environment. Furthermore, it was found that the discrepancy measure was mostly determined by the person's assessment of the environment, which corroborates our proposition that people use the organizational environment rather than the self as the focal reference point.

Extant PE fit theories share several basic assumptions (Edwards, 2009), but it has been argued that a comprehensive person–environment fit theory does not exist (e.g., Harrison, 2007). Indeed, we have theorized about PO fit from a social inclusion perspective and this perspective seems hardly appropriate as a basis for other types of fit, such as needs–supplies fit and demands–abilities (DA) fit. However, we think that Self-Determination Theory (SDT) may be well suited as a macro theoretical basis for integrating important fit domains. SDT distinguishes three fundamental human needs: autonomy, competence, and relatedness (e.g., Deci and Ryan, 2000). Whereas people's PO fit motive stems from a relatedness need, other fit motives may originate in the human needs of autonomy and competence. We encourage PE fit researchers to elaborate on the basis of separate fit domains. This may provide better fit operationalizations and stronger predictions regarding the outcomes of specific types of fit. As we have argued in this chapter, the PO fit construct should take into account characteristics of specific, prototypical people rather than abstract descriptions of organizational environments, and PO fit's natural outcomes can be defined in terms of relatedness and social inclusion.

We have emphasized people's need to belong as the theoretical basis of PO fit. However, other literatures have argued that people also have a need to be somewhat distinctive from others (Brewer, 1991; Hornsey and Jetten, 2004). These contrasting needs may well co-exist and be fulfilled if people are socially included while also being unique. Social inclusion and uniqueness can both be reached if people experience fit with the organizational environment on some but not all attributes. This would mean that general measures of PO fit, such as profile similarity indices, will be weaker predictors of individual work attitudes than more specific types of fit measure. We have argued that individuals will experience fit with the organization if there is fit on salient prototypical attributes. Consequently, in order to be distinctive, individuals may want to experience some misfit on non-prototypical attributes. Future research should investigate these and possible other combinations of fit and misfit. Given the many different variables relevant to fit, most people will at any given time experience some degree of misfit (Talbot, 2010). Some instances of not fitting an environment will lead to serious negative consequences for people's well-being, while others will not. The prototypicality of those attributes may be the determining factor in the severity of the outcomes.

In this chapter, we have used Construal Level Theory (CLT), among others, for developing our propositions about the content of people's fit perceptions. CLT throws another light on applicant attraction to organizations as compared to the theories that have been used in this field of research to date: signaling theory, image theory, and the heuristic–systematic model (Ehrhart and Ziegert, 2005). Signaling theory suggests that job seekers use information about an organization as signals for its culture. Image theory argues that job seekers are selective in how they weigh specific types of information that affect their perceptions of prospective fit. The heuristic–systematic model proposes that job seekers' fit perceptions depend on the degree to which they process information about the organization in a systematic or heuristic manner. Organizational information that is specific and personally relevant will be processed in a more systematic manner, whereas more general information will be processed in a heuristic manner. CLT argues that job seekers use abstract terms rather than concrete cultural dimensions to assess their fit and that they tend to process organizational information in a heuristic manner. Future research could competitively test these theories by examining how job seekers label organizational information, what types of future outcome they imagine, and how they arrive at their final decision.

Finally, we would like to note that, although we have discussed PO fit perceptions in terms of perceived fit on prototypical attributes, an organization's culture is comprised of more than the attributes of prototypical members. Moreover, as extant PO fit research shows, people are also able to assess their organization in terms of, for instance, its competitiveness, cohesion, or innovativeness. Nevertheless, in this chapter we have argued that the basic values underlying an organization's culture are primarily manifested in the characteristics of a subset of organizational members. In other words, some people make the place, and it is these prototypical people whom employees have in mind when they assess their fit with the organization.

Note

1. Several authors (e.g., Trope and Liberman, 2003) describe the values of outcomes as being cognition based ("cool") or affect based ("hot"). For example, the value of a meal depends on its nutritious (cognitive) value and on its tastiness (affect).

References

Allen, D. G., Mahto, R. V., and Otondo, R. F. (2007) Web-based recruitment: Effects of information, organizational brand, and attitudes toward a website on applicant attraction. *Journal of Applied Psychology*, 92, 1696–1708.

Axelrod, R. (1984) *The Evolution of Cooperation.* New York: Basic Books.

Barkow, J.H., Cosmides, L., and Tooby, J. (1992) *The Adapted Mind: Evolutionary Psychology and the Generation of Culture.* Oxford: Oxford University Press.

Baumeister, R. F., and Leary, M. R. (1995) The need to belong: Desire for interpersonal attachment as a fundamental human motivation. *Psychological Bulletin*, 117, 497–529.

Billsberry, J., Ambrosini, V., Moss-Jones, J., and Marsh, P. J. G. (2005) Some suggestions for mapping organizational members' sense of fit. *Journal of Business and Psychology*, 19, 555–570.

Boyd, R., and Richerson, P. J. (1985) *Culture and the Evolutionary Process.* Chicago: University of Chicago Press.

Boyd, R., and Richerson, P. J. (1987) The evolution of ethnic markers. *Cultural Anthropology*, 2, 65–79.

Boyd, R., Gintis, H., Bowles, S., and Richerson, P. J. (2003) The evolution of altruistic punishment. *Proceedings of the National Academy of Sciences*, 100, 3531–3535.

Brewer, M. B. (1991) The social self: On being the same and different at the same time. *Personality and Social Psychology Bulletin*, 17, 475–482.

Brewer, M. B., and Harasty, A. S. (1996) Seeing groups as entities: The role of perceiver motivation. *Handbook of Motivation and Cognition*, 3, 347–370.

Brosnan, S. F., and De Waal, F. B. M. (2002) A proximate perspective on reciprocal altruism. *Human Nature*, 13, 129–152.

Byrne, D. (1971) *The Attraction Paradigm.* New York: Academic Press.

Byrne, D., Clore, G. L., and Smeaton, G. (1986) The attraction hypothesis: Do similar attitudes affect anything? *Journal of Personality and Social Psychology*, 51, 1167–1170.

Cable, D. M., and DeRue, S. D. (2002) The convergent and discriminant validity of subjective fit perceptions. *Journal of Applied Psychology*, 87, 875–884.

Cable, D. M., and Graham, M. E. (2000) The determinants of job seekers' reputation perceptions. *Journal of Organizational Behavior*, 21, 929–947.

Cable, D. M., and Judge, T. A. (1994) Pay preferences and job search decisions: A person–organization fit perspective. *Personnel Psychology*, 47, 317–348.

Cable, D. M., and Judge, T. A. (1996) Person–organization fit, job choice decision and organizational entry. *Organizational Behavior and Human Decision Processes*, 67, 294–311.

Cable, D. M., and Judge, T. A. (1997) Interviewers' perceptions of person–organization fit and organizational selection decisions. *Journal of Applied Psychology*, 82, 546–561.

Cable, D. M., and Parsons, C. K. (2001) Socialization tactics and person–organization fit. *Personnel Psychology*, 54, 1–23.

Cable, D. M., Aiman-Smith, L., Mulvey, P. W., and Edwards, J. R. (2000) The sources and accuracy of job applicants' beliefs about organizational culture. *Academy of Management Journal*, 43, 1076–1085.

Cadinu, M. R., and Rothbart, M. (1996) Self-anchoring and differentiation processes in the minimal group setting. *Journal of Personality and Social Psychology*, 70, 661–677.

Campbell, D.T. (1958) Common fate, similarity, and other indices of the status of aggregates of persons as social entities. *Behavioral Science*, 3, 14–25.

Chapman, D. S., and Webster, J. (2006) Toward an integrated model of applicant reactions and job choice. *International Journal of Human Resource Management*, 17, 1032–1057.

Chatman, J. A. (1991) Matching people and organizations: Selection and socialization in public accounting firms. *Administrative Science Quarterly*, 36, 459–484.

Cober, R. T., Brown, D. J., Levy, P. E., Cober, A. B., and Keeping, L. M. (2003) Organizational web sites: Web site content and style as determinants of organizational attraction. *International Journal of Selection and Assessment*, 11, 158–169.

Collins, C. J., and Stevens, C. K. (2002) The relationship between early recruitment-related activities and the application decisions of new labor-market entrants: A brand equity approach to recruitment. *Journal of Applied Psychology*, 87, 1121–1133.

Condon, J. W., and Crano, W. D. (1988) Inferred evaluation and the relation between attitude similarity and interpersonal attraction. *Journal of Personality and Social Psychology*, 54, 789–797.

Cooper-Thomas, H. D., Van Vianen, A. E. M., and Anderson, N. (2004) Changes in person–organization fit: The impact of socialization tactics on perceived and actual P–O fit. *European Journal of Work and Organizational Psychology*, 13, 52–78.

Crawford, M. T., Sherman, S. J., and Hamilton, D. L. (2002) Perceived entitativity, stereotype formation, and the interchangeability of group members. *Journal of Personality and Social Psychology*, 83, 1076–1094.

Cronin, H. (1991) *The Ant and the Peacock*. Cambridge: Cambridge University Press.

Dasgupta, N., Banaji, M. R., and Abelson, R. P. (1999) Group entitativity and group perception: Associations between physical features and psychological judgment. *Journal of Personality and Social Psychology*, 77, 991–1003.

Dawis, R. V., and Lofquist, L. H. (1984) *A Psychological Theory of Work Adjustment*. Minneapolis, MN: University of Minnesota Press.

De Cremer, D. (2004) The closer we are, the more we are alike: The effect of self–other merging on depersonalized self-perception, *Current Psychology*, 22, 316–324.

De Goede, M. E. E., Van Vianen, A. E. M., and Klehe, U.-C. (2009) Job-seekers' perceived person–organization fit: Appetitive, aversive, or holistic fit. Paper presented at the 24th annual meeting of the Society for Industrial/Organizational Psychology, New Orleans, LA.

De Waal, F. B. M., and Davis, J. M. (2003) Capuchin cognitive ecology: Cooperation based on projected returns. *Neuropsychologia*, 41, 221–228.

Deci, E. L., and Ryan, R. M. (2000) The "what" and "why" of goal pursuits: Human needs and the self-determination of behavior. *Psychological Inquiry*, 11, 227–268.

Devendorf, S. A., and Highhouse, S. (2008) Applicant-employee similarity and attraction to an employer. *Journal of Occupational and Organizational Psychology*, 81, 607–617.

Dijksterhuis, A. (2004) Think different: The merits of unconscious thought in preference development and decision making. *Journal of Personality and Social Psychology*, 8, 586–598.

Edwards, J. A., and Billsberry, J. (2011) Testing a multidimensional theory of person–environment fit. *Journal of Managerial Issues*, 22 (4), 476–493.

Edwards, J. R., and Cable, D. M. (2009) The value of value congruence. *Journal of Applied Psychology*, 94, 654–677.

Edwards, J. R., and Shipp, A. J. (2007) The relationship between person–environment fit and outcomes: An integrative theoretical framework. In C. Ostroff and T. A. Judge (eds), *Perspectives on Organizational Fit* (pp. 209–258). New York: Lawrence Erlbaum Associates.

Edwards, J. R., Cable, D. M., Williamson, I. O., Schurer Lambert, L., and Shipp, A. J. (2006) The phenomenology of fit: Linking the person and environment to the subjective experience of person–environment fit. *Journal of Applied Psychology*, 91, 802–827.

Ehrhart, K. H., and Ziegert, J. C. (2005) Why are individuals attracted to organizations? *Journal of Management*, 31, 901–915.

Eisenberger, N. I., Lieberman, M. D., and Williams, K. D. (2003) Does rejection hurt? An fMRI study of social exclusion. *Science*, 302, 290–292.

Eyal, T., Sagristano, M. D., Trope, Y., Liberman, N., and Chaiken, S. (2009) When values matter: Expressing values in behavioral intentions for the near vs distant future. *Journal of Experimental Social Psychology*, 45, 35–43.

Fehr, E., and Fischbacher, U. (2003) The nature of human altruism. *Nature*, 42, 785–791.

Festinger, L. (1954) A theory of social comparison processes. *Human Relations*, 7, 117–140.

Gaertner, L., and Schopler, J. (1998) Perceived ingroup entitativity and intergroup bias: An interconnection of self and others. *European Journal of Social Psychology*, 28, 963–980.

García, M. F., Posthuma, R. A., and Colella, A. (2008) Fit perceptions in the employment interview: The role of similarity, liking, and expectations. *Journal of Occupational and Organizational Psychology*, 81, 173–189.

Gardner, W. L., Pickett, C. L., and Brewer, M. B. (2000) Social exclusion and selective memory: How the need to belong influences memory for social events. *Personality and Social Psychology Bulletin*, 26, 486–496.

Giberson, T. R., Resick, C. J., and Dickson, M. W. (2005) Embedding leader characteristics: An examination of homogeneity of personality and values in organizations. *Journal of Applied Psychology*, 90, 1002–1010.

Gilliland, S. W. (1993) The perceived fairness of selection systems: An organizational justice perspective. *Academy of Management Review*, 18, 694–734.

Gilliland, S. W. (1994) Effects of procedural and distributive justice on reactions to a selection system. *Journal of Applied Psychology*, 79, 691–701.

Hamilton, W. D. (1964) The genetical evolution of social behavior I and II. *Journal of Theoretical Biology*, 7, 1–16; 17–52.

Harrison, D. A. (2007) Pitching fits in applied psychological research: Making fit methods fit theory. In C. Ostroff and T. Judge (eds), *Perspectives on Fit in Organizations* (pp. 389–416). New York: Lawrence Erlbaum Associates.

Henrich, J. (2004) Cultural group selection, coevolutionary processes and large-scale cooperation. *Journal of Economic Behavior and Organization*, 53, 3–35.

Henrich, J., and Boyd, R. (1998) The evolution of conformist transmission and the emergence of between-group differences. *Evolution and Human Behavior*, 19, 215–241.

Henrich, J., and Gil-White, F. J. (2001) The evolution of prestige: Freely conferred deference as a mechanism for enhancing the benefits of cultural transmission. *Evolution and Human Behavior*, 22, 165–196.

Higgins, C. A., and Judge, T. A. (2004) The effect of applicant influence tactics on recruiter perceptions of fit and hiring recommendations: A field study. *Journal of Applied Psychology*, 89, 622–632.

Hogg, M. A. (2000) Subjective uncertainty reduction through self-categorization: A motivational theory of social identity processes. *European Review of Social Psychology*, 11, 223–255.

Hogg, M. A., and Terry, D. J. (2000) Social identity and self-categorization processes in organizational contexts. *Academy of Management Review*, 25, 121–140.

Holland, J. L. (1985) *Making Vocational Choices: A Theory of Vocational Personalities and Work Environments*. Englewood Cliffs, NJ: Prentice Hall.

Hornsey, M. J., and Jetten, J. (2004) The individual within the group: Balancing the need to belong with the need to be different. *Personality and Social Psychology Review*, 8, 248–264.

Howard, J., and Ferris, G. (1996) The employment interview context: Social and situational influences on interviewer decisions. *Journal of Applied Social Psychology*, 26, 112–136.

Ip, G. W-m., Chiu, C-y., and Wan, C. (2006) Birds of a feather and birds flocking together: Psychical versus behavioral cues may lead to trait- versus goal-based group perception. *Journal of Personality and Social Psychology*, 90, 368–381.

Jansen, K. J., and Kristof-Brown, A. L. (2006) Toward a multidimensional theory of person–environment fit. *Journal of Managerial Issues*, 18, 193–212.

Johnson, M. A. (1989) Variables associated with friendship in an adult population. *Journal of Social Psychology*, 129, 379–390.

Judge, T. A., and Cable, D. M. (1997) Applicant personality, organizational culture, and organization attraction. *Personnel Psychology*, 50, 359–394.

Kahneman, D. (2003) A perspective on judgment and choice: Mapping bounded rationality. *American Psychologist*, 58, 697–720.

Kahneman, D., Slovic, P., and Tversky, A. (1982) *Judgment under Uncertainty: Heuristics and Biases*. New York: Cambridge University Press.

Knudsen, T. (2003). Simon's selection theory: Why docility evolves to breed successful altruism. *Journal of Economic Psychology*, 24, 229–244.

Kristof-Brown, A. L. (2000) Perceived applicant fit: Distinguishing between recruiters' perceptions of person–job and person–organization fit. *Personnel Psychology*, 53, 643–671.

Kristof-Brown, A. L., and Guay, R. P. (2010) Person–environment fit. In S. Zedeck (ed.), *APA Handbook of Industrial and Organizational Psychology* (Vol. 3). Washington, DC: American Psychological Association.

Kristof-Brown, A., Barrick, M. R., and Franke, M. (2002) Applicant impression management: Dispositional influences and consequences for recruiter perceptions of fit and similarity. *Journal of Management*, 28, 27–46.

Kristof-Brown, A. L., Zimmerman, R., and Johnson, E. (2005) Consequences of individuals' fit at work: A meta-analysis of person–job, person–organization, person–group, and person–supervisor fit. *Personnel Psychology*, 58, 281–342.

Laland, K. N. (2004) Social learning strategies. *Learning and Behavior*, 32, 4–14.

Laland, K. N., and Brown, G. R. (2002). *Sense and Nonsense: Evolutionary Perspectives on Human Behavior*. Oxford: Oxford University Press.

Lauver, K. J., and Kristof-Brown, A. (2001) Distinguishing between employees' perceptions of person–job and person–organization fit. *Journal of Vocational Behavior*, 59, 454–470.

Liberman, N., Sagristano, M. D., and Trope, Y. (2002) The effect of temporal distance on level of mental construal. *Journal of Experimental Social Psychology*, 38, 523–534.

Lickel, B., Hamilton, D. L., and Sherman, S. (2001) Elements of a lay theory of groups: Types of groups, relation styles, and the perception of group entitativity. *Personality and Social Psychology Review*, 5, 129–140.

Lievens, F., and Highhouse, S. (2003) The relation of instrumental and symbolic attributes to a company's attractiveness as an employer. *Personnel Psychology*, 56, 75–102.

Lievens, F., Decaesteker, C., and Coetsier, P. (2001) Organizational attractiveness for prospective applicants: A person–organization fit perspective. *Applied Psychology: An International Review*, 50, 30–51.

Loewenstein, G. F., Weber, E. U., Hsee, C. K., and Welch, N. (2001) Risk as feelings. *Psychological Bulletin*, 127, 267–286.

Lott, A. J., and Lott, B. E. (1965) Group cohesiveness as interpersonal attraction: A review of relationships with antecedent and consequent variables. *Psychological Bulletin*, 64, 259–309.

Lusk, J., MacDonald, K., and Newman, J. (1998) Resource appraisals among self, friend and leader: Implications for an evolutionary perspective on individual differences. *Personality and Individual Differences*, 24, 685–700.

McElreath, R., Boyd, R., and Richerson, P. J. (2003) Shared norms and the evolution of ethnic markers. *Current Anthropology*, 44, 122–129.

Metcalfe, J., and Mischel, W. (1999) A hot/cool-system analysis of delay of gratification: Dynamics of willpower. *Psychological Review*, 106, 3–19.

Molden, D. C., Lucas, G. M., Finkel, E. J., Kumashiro, M., and Rusbult, C. (2009) Perceived support for promotion-focused and prevention-focused goals. Associations with well-being in unmarried and married couples. *Psychological Science*, 20, 787–793.

Moskowitz, D. S., and Coté, S. (1995) Do interpersonal traits predict affect? A comparison of three models. *Journal of Personality and Social Psychology*, 69, 915–924.

Nowak, M. A. (2006) Five rules for the evolution of cooperation. *Science*, 314, 1560–1563.

Offerman, T., and Sonnemans, J. (1998) Learning by experience and learning by imitating successful others. *Journal of Economic Behavior and Organization*, 43, 559–575.

O'Reilly, C. A., Chatman, J., and Caldwell, D. F. (1991) People and organizational culture: A profile comparison approach to assessing person–organization fit. *Academy of Management Journal*, 34, 487–516.

Otten, S. (2002) "Me and us" or "us and them"? The self as a heuristic for defining minimal ingroups. *European Review of Social Psychology*, 13, 1–33.

Otten, S., and Epstude, K. (2006) Overlapping mental representations of self, ingroup, and outgroup: Unraveling self-stereotyping and self-anchoring. *Personality and Social Psychology Bulletin*, 32, 957–969.

Piasentin, K. A., and Chapman, D. S. (2006) Subjective person–organization fit: Bridging the gap between conceptualization and measurement. *Journal of Vocational Behavior*, 69, 202–221.

Ployhart, R. E., Weekley, J. A., and Baughman, K. (2006) The structure and function of human capital emergence: A multilevel examination of the attraction-selection-attrition model. *Academy of Management Journal*, 49, 661–677.

Preston, S. D., and De Waal, F. B. M. (2002) Empathy: Its ultimate and proximate bases. *Behavioral and Brain Sciences*, 25, 1–72.

Rentsch, J. R., and McEwen, A. H. (2002) Comparing personality characteristics, values, and goals as antecedents of organizational attractiveness. *International Journal of Selection and Assessment*, 10, 225–234.

Richerson, P. J., and Boyd, R. (2005) *Not by Genes Alone: How Culture Transformed Human Evolution*. Chicago: University of Chicago Press.

Robbins, J. M., and Krueger, J. I. (2005) Social projection to ingroups and outgroups: A review and meta-analysis. *Personality and Social Psychology Review*, 9, 32–47.

Rynes, S. L. (1991) Recruitment, job choice, and post-hire consequences: A call for new research directions. In M. D. Dunnette and L. M. Hough (eds), *Handbook of Industrial and Organizational Psychology* (2nd edn, Vol. 2, pp. 399–444). Palo Alto, CA: Consulting Psychologists Press.

Rynes, S. L., Bretz, R. D., and Gerhart, B. (1991) The importance of recruitment in job choice: A different way of looking. *Personnel Psychology*, 44, 487–521.

Schaubroeck, J., Ganster, D. C., and Jones, J. R. (1998) Organization and occupation influences in the attraction-selection-attrition process. *Journal of Applied Psychology*, 83, 869–891.

Schein, E. H. (1992) *Organizational Culture and Leadership*. San Francisco: Jossey-Bass.

Schneider, B. (1987) The people make the place. *Personnel Psychology*, 40, 437–453.

Schneider, B., Smith, D. B., Taylor, S., and Fleenor, J. (1998) Personality and organizations: A test of the homogeneity of personality hypothesis. *Journal of Applied Psychology*, 83, 462–470.

Schwartz, S. H. (1994) Beyond individualism/collectivism: New cultural dimensions of values. In U. Kim, H. C. Triandis, C. Kagitcibasi, S-C. Choi, and G. Yoon (eds), *Individualism and Collectivism: Theory, Method, and Applications* (pp. 85–119). Thousand Oaks, CA: Sage.

Shaikh, T., and Kanekar, S. (1994) Attitudinal similarity and affiliation need as determinants of interpersonal attraction. *Journal of Social Psychology*, 134, 257–259.

Simon, B., and Hastedt, C. (1999) Self-aspects as social categories: The role of personal importance and valence. *European Journal of Social Psychology*, 29, 479–487.

Simon, H. A. (1990) A mechanism for social selection and successful altruism. *Science*, 250, 1665–1668.

Slaughter, J. E., and Greguras, G. J. (2009) Initial attraction to organizations: The influence of trait inferences. *International Journal of Selection and Assessment*, 17, 1–18.

Slaughter, J. E., Zickar, M. J., Highhouse, S., and Mohr, D. C. (2004) Personality trait inferences about organizations: Development of a measure and assessment of construct validity. *Journal of Applied Psychology*, 89, 85–103.

Steele, C. M. (1988) The psychology of self-affirmation: Sustaining the integrity of the self. *Advances in Experimental Social Psychology*, 21, 261–302.

Swaney, W., Kendal, J., Capon, H., Brown, C., and Laland, K. N. (2001) Familiarity facilitates social learning of foraging behavior in the guppy. *Animal Behavior*, 62, 591–598.

Tajfel, H. (1969) Cognitive aspects of prejudice. *Journal of Social Issues*, 25, 79–97.

Tajfel, H., and Turner, J. C. (1986) The social identity theory of inter-group behavior. In S. Worchel and L. W. Austin (eds), *Psychology of Intergroup Relations* (pp. 7–24). Chicago: Nelson-Hall.

Talbot, D.L. (2010) Organisational fit and misfit: An empirical study of similarities and differences. Unpublished doctoral thesis. Coventry University.

Tan, D. T. Y., and Singh, R. (1995) Attitudes and attraction: A developmental-study of the similarity–attraction and dissimilarity–repulsion hypotheses. *Personality and Social Psychology Bulletin*, 21, 975–986.

Tooby, J., and Cosmides, L. (1989) Evolutionary psychology and the generation of culture. Part I: Theoretical considerations. *Ethology and Sociobiology*, 10, 29–49.

Trivers, R. L. (1971) The evolution of reciprocal altruism. *Quarterly Review of Biology*, 46, 35–57.

Trope, Y., and Liberman, N. (2003) Temporal construal. *Psychological Review*, 110, 403–421.

Turban, D. B. (2001) Organizational attractiveness as an employer on college campuses: An examination of the applicant population. *Journal of Vocational Behavior*, 58, 293–312.

Turban, D. B., and Cable, D. M. (2003) Firm reputation and applicant pool characteristics. *Journal of Organizational Behavior*, 24, 733–751.

Turban, D. B., Forret, M. L., and Hendrickson, C. L. (1998) Applicant attraction to firms: Influences of organization reputation, job and organizational attributes, and recruiter behaviors. *Journal of Vocational Behavior*, 52, 24–44.

Turban, D. B., Lau, C. M., Ngo, H. Y., and Chow, I. H. S. (2001) Organizational attractiveness of firms in the People's Republic of China: A person–organization fit perspective. *Journal of Applied Psychology*, 86, 194–206.

Tyler, T. R., and Blader, S. L. (2002) Autonomous vs comparative status: Must we be better than others to feel good about ourselves? *Organizational Behavior and Human Decision Processes*, 89, 813–838.

Van Dam, K. (2003) Trait perception in the employment interview: A five-factor model perspective. *International Journal of Selection and Assessment*, 11, 43–55.

Van Vianen, A. E. M. (2001) Person–organization fit: The match between theory and methodology. Introduction to the special issue. *Applied Psychology: An International Review*, 50, 1–4.

Van Vianen, A. E. M. (2005) A review of person–environment fit research: Prospects for personnel selection. In A. Evers, O. Voskuijl, and N. Anderson (eds), *Handbook of Selection* (pp. 419–439). Boston: Blackwell.

Van Vuuren, M., Veldkamp, B. P., De Jong, M. D. T., and Seydel, E. R. (2008) Why work? Aligning foci and dimensions of commitment along the axes of the competing values framework. *Personnel Review*, 37, 47–65.

Verquer, M. L., Beehr, T. A., and Wagner, S. H. (2003) A meta-analysis of relations between person–organization fit and work attitudes. *Journal of Vocational Behavior*, 63, 473–489.

Wanous, J. P (1992) *Organizational Entry: Recruitment, Selection, and Socialization of Newcomers* (2nd edn). Reading, MA: Addison-Wesley.

Wilson, D. S., and Dugatkin, L. A. (1997) Group selection and assortative interactions. *The American Naturalist*, 149, 336–351.

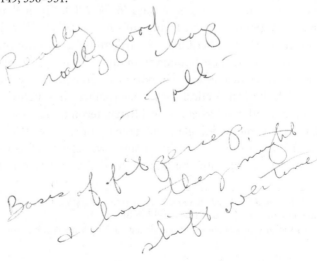

8

Exploring the Middle Range of Person–Environment Fit Theories through a Conservation of Resources Perspective

Anthony R. Wheeler
University of Rhode Island

Jonathon R. B. Halbesleben
University of Alabama

Kristen Shanine
University of Alabama

Edwards (2008) summarized the state of PE fit theories, finding that PE fit scholars have applied more than a dozen theories to ground the construct across five distinct research contexts; yet these theories do not sufficiently satisfy the tenets of good theory. This poses problems for the study of PE fit, as theory serves a critical role in the studies of social sciences (Bacharach, 1989). Social science theorists define theory as explaining four crucial aspects of any phenomenon: what, how, when, and why (Bacharach, 1989; George and Jones, 2000; Mitchell and James, 2001; Sutton and Staw, 1995). A good theory informs social scientists by identifying the phenomenon (what), describing the intra- and inter-relationships of the phenomenon (how), establishing the boundary conditions of the phenomenon (when), and, most importantly, elucidating the importance of the phenomenon (why).

The lack of theoretical clarity has resulted in a highly disparate body of PE fit literature, with researchers using different terminology, operationalizations, research designs and methodologies, and analytic procedures (Cable and Edwards, 2004). For the sake of brevity in this chapter, we refer to all conceptualizations of fit as PE fit. More critically, the lack of good theory has stifled the growth of PE fit

Organizational Fit: Key Issues and New Directions, First Edition.
Edited by Amy L. Kristof-Brown and Jon Billsberry.
© 2013 John Wiley & Sons, Ltd. Published 2013 by John Wiley & Sons, Ltd.

research (Edwards, 2008), called into question the validity of the construct (Judge and Ferris, 1992), and led some researchers to subsume portions of the construct as a component of other constructs (e.g., job embeddedness; Mitchell *et al.*, 2001). To add further confusion to the construct, PE fit researchers have earnestly begun to examine the concept of misfit (e.g., Billsberry, 2009; Talbot, 2010; Wheeler *et al.*, 2007) but cannot agree if misfit simply represents low levels of PE fit or represents an entirely distinct construct (Harrison, 2007). Without a solid theoretical grounding, researchers cannot even satisfy the most basic tenet of research and define what "fit" is.

In the present chapter, we seek to harmonize PE fit-based theories by taking a middle-range (Merton, 1968) theoretical perspective. Middle-range theories "lie between the minor but necessary working hypotheses that evolve in abundance during day-to-day research and the all-inclusive systematic efforts to develop a unified theory that will explain all the observed uniformities" of behaviors (Merton, 1968, p. 39). A middle-range theory does not negate other theory as much as it allows researchers to integrate multiple theories while not taking a level of abstraction that prohibits empirical testing. Our goal is not to judge existing PE fit theories as better or worse in comparison to each other or to add some newly adopted theoretical perspective. We seek not to replace existing theories but to integrate theories. We utilize conservation of resources theory (COR; Hobfoll, 1998, 1989) as a middle-range theory to understand the construct of PE fit inclusive of misfit. COR can provide much needed integrative clarity that not only explains extant fit literatures but also provides a useful framework for undertaking future studies of the construct, including misfit, longitudinal, and multilevel research.

We will not summarize the massive extant PE fit literature, as a recent edited book (Ostroff and Judge, 2007) and a succinct *Academy of Management Annals* monograph (Edwards, 2008) have already covered this ground. We cite several extensive reviews of the PE fit literatures (e.g., Edwards, 2008; Ostroff, 2012) when making points that have been established over the past two decades. We do this not to neglect any researchers' work but simply to reduce the sheer number of citations found in this chapter. We use Edwards' (2008) review of PE fit theories, which included recommendations for developing better theory to ground PE fit, as a guide for this chapter. Edwards argues that any theory applied to PE fit must (1) satisfy 'good theory' requirements delineated by theory builders (e.g., Bacharach, 1989; Sutton and Staw, 1995), (2) have the construct of PE fit as central to the theory, and (3) accommodate the five identified streams of research (i.e., job satisfaction, job stress, vocational choice, recruitment and selection, and culture and climate) that have flowed from PE fit research over the past century. Although we use Edwards' (2008) review as a touchstone, we conceptually depart from his review in one substantial way. COR is not a PE fit theory, so PE fit as a construct is not necessarily at the heart of the theory. We view PE fit as an assessment of whether or not an individual has the personally valued resources, defined as "objects, personal characteristics, conditions, or energies that are valued by the individual" (Hobfoll, 1989, p. 516), to meet the demands of the total work environment. These resources can be found within the person, the environment, or a combination thereof. Like many PE fit researchers (e.g., Cable and Edwards, 2004; Jansen and Kristof-Brown, 2006), we view PE fit as a subjective personal assessment.

Our view of PE fit in terms of resources might strike discordant notes among PE fit purists. However, as none of the theories reviewed by Edwards satisfies the criteria for strong theory, we suggest that PE fit might benefit from a novel approach that integrates existing PE fit-based theories. To alleviate what Edwards (2008) calls the stagnation of fit, we first describe the two principles and four corollaries of COR, which allows us to define PE fit inclusive of its seemingly myriad conceptualizations, describe the nomological PE fit network, elucidate the logic of that nomological network, and incorporate the contextual issues that any good theory should address. These contextual issues include the impact of moderators, levels of analysis, and time. Second, we discuss the implications of grounding PE fit in terms of resources for research on the topic of misfit, as we believe that a good PE fit theory should explain misfit as well as fit. Finally, we highlight the research implications of utilizing COR to ground future PE fit research. Taken together, the present chapter answers Edwards' call for better theory in the study of PE fit.

Conservation of Resources Theory

We begin our chapter by summarizing COR and integrating this theory with the construct of PE fit. Hobfoll (1988, 1989, 1998, 2001) conceived COR as a general motivation theory predicated on the protection, investment, and replenishment of personal resources. Individuals accumulate, protect, and invest resources into the environment to meet the demands of their daily lives, whether at or outside of work. As seen in Hobfoll's definition of resources, resources from a COR perspective have a broader scope than a needs–supply conceptualization of PE fit, where our reading of this literature leads us to conclude that PE fit researchers typically describe resources in compensation-based terms (e.g., Cable and Edwards, 2004). Hobfoll (2001) documented a non-exhaustive list of 74 resources through his research, which includes both work and non-work resources. Some of these resources can be found within the person, like a "sense of pride in myself," "feelings that I am accomplishing my goals," and the "ability to organize tasks." Some of these resources can also be found in the work environment, like the "necessary tools for work," "acknowledgement of my accomplishments," and "support from co-workers." We also note that many of the resources directly map onto operationalizations of PE fit. Resources such as the "necessary tools for work," "role as a leader," and the "ability to communicate well" map onto person–job (PJ) fit, while resources such as "understanding from my employer/boss," "involvement in organizations with others who share similar interests," and "people I can learn from" speak to aspects of person–organization (PO) fit. Moreover, resources such as a "sense of humor," "self-discipline," and "positive feelings about myself" could reflect the personality-driven aspects of person–vocation (PV) fit, while resources such as "financial assets," "stable employment," and "medical insurance" link to needs–supply (NS) fit.

COR has two fundamental principles to explain how and why individuals behave as a function of resources. First, individuals experience greater distress and anxiety when facing the potential or actual loss of resources (termed "primacy of resource loss") than they feel relief and satisfaction when gaining resources. For example, if an individual accepts a job offer that requires relocation, that individual will probably focus more on the loss of personal resources (e.g., proximity to friends and family) with the move than on what will be gained with the new job (e.g., career opportunity, salary, benefits). When individuals experience the threat or actual loss of resources they feel stress, which they are motivated to alleviate (Hobfoll, 1988, 1989).

Second, individuals have a strong motive to invest current resources in order to gain more resources, to protect against resource loss, and to recover from resource losses (termed "resource investment"). Because individuals constantly expend resources to meet the demands of their lives, they constantly seek to replenish resources. For example, an employee will invest time and effort into his or her job as a means to earn a salary, which is then used to acquire other resources (e.g., suitable housing, food, etc.) that are important in satisfying life demands. Taken together, these two principles describe individual motivation as a constant and cyclical process of protecting, investing, and replenishing their resources that, in and of itself, requires employees to invest resources (Hobfoll, 2001). The inability to manage this resource process or the inability to replenish resources results in stress, which, if chronic, leads to a host of deleterious outcomes like increased burnout, turnover, and ruinous physical and mental health problems (e.g., heart attacks, depression, suicidal tendencies, etc.) as well as decreased satisfaction, commitment, and performance. In PE fit terms, when an individual, for example, lacks or loses the values and interests that are the resources indicative of PO fit, COR predicts that this individual will experience stress. If this PO fit-based stress is left unmitigated, COR predicts that this individual will experience the same negative outcomes described above. The preponderance of PE fit evidence demonstrates that these outcomes do occur when a person has low levels of fit (see Edwards, 2008; Kristof, 1996). Conversely, individuals who ably manage this resource process experience many benefits, including increased satisfaction, commitment, and performance, and decreased stress-related outcomes (for a review of stress-based COR research, see Halbesleben and Buckley, 2004). In PE fit terms, when an individual again, for example, feels sufficient PO fit, this individual will feel good about his or her work environment. COR predicts that this person will have ample personal resources to invest into their work environment, maybe in the form of increased organizational citizenship behaviors (OCBs). COR also predicts that this person would want to continue working in this environment and not want to sacrifice the positive outcomes associated with high levels of fit by leaving the employer. Investment of fit resources allows for new, excess, or replenished resources to be gained. As with the negative outcomes associated with low PE fit, overwhelming PE fit evidence exists to support the notion that high levels of fit result in the positive outcomes described above (see Arthur *et al.*, 2006; Kristof-Brown, Zimmerman, and Johnson, 2005).

Hobfoll (2001) attached four corollaries to the second principle of COR. The first corollary affirms that individuals with more resources are less vulnerable to resource loss and more prone to resource gain. A primary way individuals seek to gain resources is through relying upon available pools of social support, and individuals rely on this support as a form of resources. These social support resources can come from both work and non-work sources, but the support most effectively helps employees manage the COR process to the extent that the context of the support and the context in which the resources are being managed match (Halbesleben, 2006; Hobfoll, 2001). For example, support that comes from an organizational system like formal socialization programs best assists an individual who expends resources to meet the demands of work. An organization-based support resource (the human resource management (HRM) practice of formal socialization) develops the organization-bound resource of PO fit, which is consistent with PE fit research on the topic of socialization (Cable and Parsons, 2001). However, the same sources of support resources can also threaten an individual's existing resources (Song, 2009). Just as a company's HRM systems can provide valuable PE fit resources for employees to perform their jobs, a company's HRM systems can just as easily threaten these PE fit resources and cause negative outcomes. Complaints about HRM inhibiting employee performance and increasing employee turnover abound (e.g., Holtom *et al.*, 2008).

The second corollary of COR is that individuals seek to manage resources through hoarding excess resources (Hobfoll, 2001). Because individuals seek to invest initial resources as a means to gain resources, the more resources they have, the more they can invest with the hopes of greater returns. Hobfoll (2001) called this process a "resource gain spiral," where resource gains beget more resource gains. Further, individuals who possess an excess of one resource can bundle that resource with other related resources to form a meta-resource that the individual can invest back into the environment for even greater returns. For example, conscientiousness, agreeableness, and previous training and experience could increase the likelihood of success in an attempt to gain more PE fit-based resources, such as a promotion and a pay raise at work. Hobfoll (2001) termed this process a "resource caravan."

Conversely, the third corollary of COR states that the fewer resources an individual has to invest, the less the individual will be able to recoup the minimal resource investment, which leads to a reinforcing cycle of resource loss. For example, if one were to lose his or her job, and as a result lose his or her health benefits, the lack of a job might lead to illness (Jin *et al.*, 1995), which without insurance could lead to financial strain (Himmelstein *et al.*, 2005) that could increase family or marital strain (Gudmunson *et al.*, 2007). Hobfoll (2001) called this process a "resource loss spiral," where resource losses beget more resource losses. Finally, the fourth corollary of COR asserts that those who lack resources are likely to adopt defensive resource conservation strategies (Hobfoll, 2001). For example, if someone lacked appropriate knowledge, skills, and abilities (KSAs) to perform a redesigned or changing job, it is likely that this person will concentrate his or her dwindling resources into behaviors that will yield the highest rates of return as possible. This might entail investing personal resources into relationships with co-workers (e.g., OCB-I), who presumably can provide immediate assistance, as opposed to investing resources into behaviors directed at general organizational well-being (e.g., OCB-O; Halbesleben and Bowler, 2007).

From a theoretical standpoint, COR is an interactional motivation theory, explaining how the interaction between resources found within the person and in the environment motivate individual behavior. Moreover, this interaction affects both individual and environmental outcomes (Hobfoll, 2001). A person can invest a resource such as conscientiousness to increase an external resource like a raise in compensation, and a person can invest an environmental resource such as co-worker support to enhance a resource such as feeling good about him or herself. To date, COR has seen extensive conceptual and empirical investigation in the context of stress and burnout (see Halbesleben and Buckley, 2004), which has, by and large, supported the primacy of loss principle of the theory (Hobfoll, 2001). The resource investment principle has also received empirical support in the stress and burnout literatures; albeit most of this research occurs in the context of resource loss, so that the four corollaries of the theory have yet to see comprehensive testing (Halbesleben and Buckley, 2004; Hobfoll, 2001). Conceptualizing COR as a middle-range PE fit theory should help researchers to examine the benefits of resource gain, abundance, and investment. This type of COR-grounded research on the topic of job embeddedness (Mitchell *et al.*, 2001), which describes the psychological forces (including PE fit) that enmesh an individual within the organization and non-work community, has framed that construct as a resource caravan that individuals invest into participating in their jobs (Halbesleben and Wheeler, 2008). Further, the PE fit aspect of job embeddedness can be viewed as the excess resources around which the other embeddedness components are built, but this supposition needs further development, which we now attempt to address.

The Construct of PE Fit

While consistently operationalizing PE fit has proved problematic for researchers (e.g., PO fit, PJ fit, etc.), a general definition of the construct has emerged. PE fit is the "congruence, match, or similarity between the person and environment" (Edwards, 2008, p. 168). PE fit describes when the individual "supplements, embellishes, or possesses characteristics which are similar to other individuals" (e.g., supplementary PE fit; Muchinsky and Monahan, 1987, p. 269) or when a "weakness or need in the environment is offset by the strength of the individual, or vice versa" (Muchinsky and Monahan, 1987, p. 271). Furthermore, PE fit can be viewed objectively (e.g., the actual absence or presence of characteristics of the person or environment) or subjectively (e.g., an individual's perception of their fit into the environment). Verquer, Beehr, and Wagner's (2003) meta-analysis suggests that subjective perceptions of PE fit most strongly relate to general work attitudes. Original conceptualizations of PE fit contained two forms of fit, one describing the congruence between rewards in the environment and rewards needed by the individual (*needs–supply fit*; French *et al.*, 1982) and one describing congruence between the demands of the environment and the abilities of the individual (*demands–ability fit*; French *et al.*, 1982). These forms of fit explain the process by which individuals fit.

Subsequently, however, other PE fit researchers have more narrowly defined, and in the process operationalized PE fit to identify contexts within which individuals fit, including the congruence between personal and organizational values (PO fit; Chatman, 1989), individual personality and personality types found in the vocational environment (PV fit; Holland, 1985), individuals and their work groups or teams (PG fit; Judge and Ferris, 1992; Kristof, 1996), and individual knowledge, skills, abilities (KSAs) and KSAs required by the job itself (PJ fit; Caldwell and O'Reilly, 1990; Edwards, 1991). These more narrow operationalizations or dimensions of PE fit have spawned robust, yet empirically overlapping literatures and within each of these literatures researchers provide different mechanisms describing how and why individuals assess fit. By taking a middle-range theoretical approach, we believe that COR integrates the PE fit dimensions and helps explain how the dimensions nomologically overlap. Meta-analytic research demonstrates that many of the dimensions of PE fit share similar nomological networks. The most comprehensive meta-analysis of multiple PE fit dimensions (Kristof-Brown *et al.*, 2005) reports remarkably consistent patterns of relationships across PJ, PO, and PG fit with general work attitudes, intentions to and actual turnover, and job performance. Assouline and Meyer (1987) report similar meta-analytic results with PV fit and general work attitudes. While these meta-analytic results do not provide conclusive evidence that the dimensions come from the same psychological source or state of mind, the results suggest that these dimensions are related and appear to result in similar outcomes. Edwards (2008) also summarizes the extent to which PE fit researchers have used the same theories across dimensions to explain the relationships with antecedents and outcomes. Like the children's poem "Humpty Dumpty," the construct of PE fit has fractured into many pieces; and PE fit researchers have attempted to play the role of "the king's horses and men" to put the construct back together through integrative theory-building efforts.

Theories of Multidimensional Fit

In this section, we will summarize two theoretical models of multidimensional PE fit, and do so to demonstrate that PE fit researchers have sought to find a common process that underlies how people assess PE fit across more than one dimension. We hope to show that the motivation processes described by COR can integrate these two theories.

Jansen and Kristof-Brown (2006) postulate that PE fit, as a whole, is an additive construct comprised of multiple dimensions, which represent distinct aspects of a person's environment. People can find a dimension more or less salient than other dimensions, but the dimensions interact to predict important outcomes. They argue that because a person might find a particular dimension salient, the salient dimension becomes that person's focal point in assessing fit. As a result, it becomes important to understand individual difference characteristics, environmental differences, and stage of employment differences that might predict dimension saliency. For example, they propose that traits such as agreeableness relate to the saliency of dimensions that are social in nature (e.g., PG fit); whereas a strong organizational culture relates to the increased saliency of the PO fit dimension, during the recruitment stage of employment, PJ fit dimensions increase in saliency. Based on the factors influencing the saliency of the dimensions, people make their assessments of fit on one or multiple dimensions of fit to form a global perception of PE fit.

Jansen and Kristof-Brown's (2006) multidimensional theory of PE fit highlights the temporal factors involved in assessing PE fit and the importance of saliency for the sake of reserving cognitive resources in fit assessments, and argues that the distinct dimensions exist within the same nomological network of antecedents and outcomes. Fit on the most salient dimension that drives the global assessment of PE fit leads to the typical outcomes found in the extant PE fit literatures (e.g., increased general work attitudes and retention for higher levels of PE fit). If we integrate their work with COR, their argument about saliency of specific dimensions of PE fit is similar to Hobfoll's (2001) notion of a resource caravan. The most salient dimension reflects the most abundant fit resource that the individual has, and the remaining fit resources are then bundled around that excess resource. Moreover, their rationale that the most salient dimension of fit drives the global assessment of fit across multiple dimensions for cognitive efficiency purposes mirrors Hobfoll's assertions that resources are limited and that managing resources requires resources. In essence, using the most salient dimension around which other assessments are made is both a resource protection mechanism and a strategic investment that provides the best return on the investment. Basing global assessments of fit on the most salient dimension saves cognitive resources; moreover, such a process constitutes a strategic resource investment that provides the individual with the best probability of gaining a return on that investment.

We might also extrapolate from Jansen and Kristof-Brown's (2006) model that higher levels of resources create a resource caravan, which leads to increased percep-tions of global PE fit and creates a resource gain spiral of PE fit. First, Hobfoll (2001) construes a caravan as being additive, which Jansen and Kristof-Brown (2006) the-orize about multidimensional fit. Second, because an individual experiences high levels of PE fit, that individual is likely to have surplus resources to invest into the environment, which will then lead them to gain more resources and increased per-ceptions of their PE fit. In fact, Kristof-Brown, Jansen, and Colbert (2002, p. 989) provide evidence for our extrapolation. They conclude that "the combination of high fit across all aspects of the work environment generates more positive evaluations than would be expected than by a simple additive combination of each type of fit." The contextual factors they identified (e.g., individual differences, environmental differences, temporal change) can influence this process. Although Jansen and Kristof-Brown (2006) did not address PE misfit, we think it is likely that misfit on a salient dimension would create a resource loss spiral where the lack of resources (i.e., misfit) would trigger the individual to invest remaining resources into the environment to increase fit on other dimensions. In other words, if the most salient type of fit was PG fit, and group composition changed such that greater PG misfit was experienced, this might give rise to questions about PJ misfit or PO misfit, and then to questions about PV misfit as well. If I don't fit the group, do I also not fit the job, culture, or even vocation? Or do these dimensions become more salient to me? The employee might not be able to rectify the PG misfit but could invest resources into fitting other aspects of the environment.

Wheeler *et al.* (2005) propose that the multiple conceptualizations of PE fit relate to how individuals describe their self-concepts. This explains the differential salience or importance of the PE fit dimensions across individuals. They argue that such a mapping of PE fit onto the self-concept allows individuals to expand or collapse their self-concepts relative to fit such that individuals can experience fit on salient dimensions (and experience the benefits thereof) and compartmentalize misfit on other dimensions (to minimize the costs therein). This process allows individuals to maximize feeling good about themselves (e.g., self-esteem) and preserve cognitive resources that might otherwise be spent on thinking about whether or not they fit and what to do about it. We note that Wheeler *et al.* also conceptualize PE fit as a supplementary match between individuals and environments (e.g., matching the environment). However, the focus on fit and misfit led Wheeler *et al.* (2005) to propose an outcome model of PE misfit to explain the behavioral actions that an individual might take to alleviate misfit. This model of PE misfit is largely a complementary conceptualization of fit, as they describe "misfit behaviors" as attempts to influence or bring new characteristics to the environment. Unfortunately, their model of PE misfit does not necessarily follow from their theoretical development of what they called "multidimensional fit," which we consider a major shortcoming of their work. If PE fit and misfit are opposite ends of a continuum, their theory of multidimensional PE fit and misfit should share similar theoretical underpinnings.

We can also integrate Wheeler *et al.*'s (2005) multidimensional theory of PE fit into COR terms along the same lines as Jansen and Kristof-Brown's (2006) theory. Employees feel good about their abilities to meet the demands of their lives to the extent that they can find personal or environmental resources to meet those demands. Employees' preferences for certain fit resources are based on which resources are threatened. For example, if value-based resources are at risk due to a company merger, PO fit becomes the most salient dimension of fit. Misfits lack resources to meet work demands, so they invest their remaining resources into behaviors they think will net the largest return on those investments. For example, lacking value-based resources could trigger employees into investing resources to gain more skills, which can be leveraged into getting a new job or transferring into a part of the company where better value fit might occur. Hence, COR can account for both multidimensional PE fit and misfit.

Although researchers have examined the joint effects of at least two combinations of established dimensions of PE fit, little empirical evidence has accumulated that tests the theoretical tenets of either Jansen and Kristof-Brown's (2006) or Wheeler *et al.*'s (2005) theories of multidimensional PE fit. In the most direct test of either theory, Edwards and Billsberry (2011) found little support for the additive effects of multiple dimensions of PE fit as outlined by Jansen and Kristof-Brown (2006). Instead, Edwards and Billsberry (2011) reported that the discrete dimensions of PE fit (e.g., PO fit, PJ fit, etc.) did not appear to add together to form a higher-order PE fit construct, but that some dimensions appeared to independently yet differentially predict general work attitudes and turnover intentions. While PO fit more strongly predicted organizational commitment and turnover intentions compared to PJ fit, PJ fit more strongly predicted job satisfaction than did PO fit. In lieu of additive effects, they found strong positive correlations among the multiple dimensions of PE fit. Edwards and Billsberry (2011) did not specifically measure saliency of the dimensions, nor did they test the individual, environmental, or temporal aspects of Jansen and Kristof-Brown's theory, but their results resemble the findings of Scroggins' (2007) test of multiple dimensions of fit. Scroggins (2007) found, too, that dimensions of PE fit differentially predicted outcomes. While Scroggins did not specifically comment on the idea that one or more dimension would be more salient than others in predicting general work attitudes, an examination of the analyses suggests that the needs–supply and PJ fit dimensions accounted for much of the variability of the outcomes. Taking Edwards and Billsberry (2011) and Scroggins (2007) together, we might infer that PO fit and PJ fit are the salient dimensions around which others might caravan. The third test of multiple dimensions of PE fit (Kristof-Brown *et al.*, 2002) found that individuals develop preferences for PE fit dimensions based upon demographic characteristics. These preferences for PE fit dimensions predict job satisfaction, and they also found that individuals can form additive multidimensional perceptions of PE fit to predict job satisfaction as well. Regarding the empirical multidimensional PE fit research, we note that the researchers utilize different theories to ground their studies (e.g., Dawis *et al.*, 1964; Lewin, 1935). The mixed and matched utilization of different theories again speaks to the lack of clear theory regarding PE fit. Are the different PE fit-based theories chosen to explain outcomes of interest, or are the theories chosen to explain the process through which PE fit is experienced or occurs? In total, we see that the lack of theoretical clarity around PE fit has muddled exactly what anyone means when they say "PE fit."

PE Fit and COR

Here we define PE fit in terms of COR. PE fit reflects the presence of personal resources that individuals need to meet the demands of their work environment. From a resource perspective, PE fit can be seen in terms of matching the environment (e.g., supplementary) or adding something new to the individual or environment (e.g., complementary) because the key is whether or not individuals have sufficient

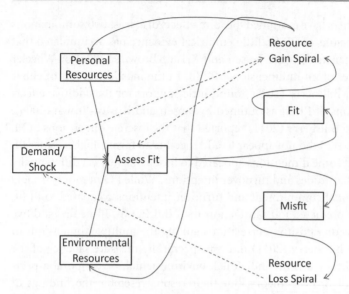

Figure 8.1 A conservation of resources perspective of PE fit

resources to meet the demands of the environment and vice versa. So matching the environment, for instance, might signal available co-worker resource support, whereas complementing the environment might signal resources specific to an individual being able to utilize his or her unique knowledge skills and abilities. Resources can be found in the person, in the environment, or a combination of both. We present Figure 8.1 to describe a COR-based PE fit process pictorially. When individuals do not have sufficient resources or feel that their resources are threatened (e.g., a resource shock), they will assess whether or not they have resources available, which might be found in the person or environment, to meet this resource threat. If individuals do not possess the resources to meet the resource loss, they will report lower levels of PE fit and commensurate decreased levels of general work attitudes, intentions to remain, and organizational citizenship behaviors. Over time, if poorly fitting employees fail to mitigate the resource loss (e.g., continue to feel PE misfit), the resource drain inevitably leads to stress, burnout, and turnover (accompanied by the negative outcomes above). Resource drain becomes an environmental demand, which reinforces the assessment of PE misfit and the resource drain. Conversely, if individuals experience resource threat and perceive adequate or excess levels of resources, they are likely to experience PE fit. Continued assessments of positive PE fit lead to increases in positive general work attitudes, intentions to remain, and organizational citizenship behaviors. Future resource demands are then assessed in the context of having surplus resources, so individuals with PE fit resources are more resilient to resource loss.

Over the past decade, PE fit researchers have grappled with the differences between the supplementary and complementary views of PE fit (e.g., Cable and Edwards, 2004; Ostroff, 2012; Ostroff and Schulte, 2007). In short, PE fit researchers want to understand if, how, when, and why these views interact. While Cable and Edwards

(2004) found support for a theoretical model that suggested independence between supplementary and complementary PE fit, a COR view of PE fit might suggest a more nuanced explanation of this relationship. First, as we previously stated, COR defines resources more broadly than does most PE fit research. Values–interests resources, which PE fit researchers usually examine in terms of supplementary PE fit, are considered the same as needs–supply resources, which PE fit researchers usually examine in terms of complementary fit. The resource investment principle of COR stipulates that people invest resources to get more resources. While the context of the gained resources should match the context in which the resources will be spent, COR makes no distinction between one type of resource and another being invested to gain a specific other resource. Resources are simply resources.

What COR might suggest about supplementary and complementary PE fit is that the saliency or importance of specific resources changes based upon specific environments (Hobfoll, 2001). For instance, a recent college graduate might place more importance on compensation-based resources because that graduate needs to start paying back student loans. We would say this graduate views PE fit from a complementary perspective (i.e., what can the company provide me that I don't have?). However, once the company meets that individual resource need and assuming it is not threatened, other resource needs become salient. For instance, this graduate might have taken a job to satisfy traditional complementary PE fit needs, only to find that he or she does not share similar values or interests with his or her co-workers, which PE fit researchers typically view through a supplementary PE fit lens. We now see this graduate's values–interests resources being threatened, which motivates the graduate to rectify the threat of resource loss. In this example, we can see how supplementary PE fit needs mediate the complementary PE fit; it is an outcomes relationship. However, we could also envision a situation where the complementary–supplementary order changes. People have been known to prefer working for organizations with which they share a strong social value mission, and the compensation issues inherent in the employment contract cause the values–interests resources to become threatened. Indeed, motivation research demonstrates that external rewards can sometimes decrease a person's intrinsic motivation to perform (e.g., Deci *et al.*, 1999). What someone used to view as being personally fulfilling can be dampened when external rewards are introduced. In a sense, the supplementary–complementary PE fit distinction becomes blurred in COR because COR describes a very person-based resource motivation process.

The specific context of the environment and what resources the person needs at that specific point in time matter in COR. The environment might require both supplementary personal resources (i.e., sharing similar values, traits, and KSAs with co-workers, to develop a strong culture) and complementary personal resources (i.e., sharing different KSAs with co-workers to facilitate role specialization). Furthermore, the environment will help integrate those resources and generate beneficial outcomes. For example, two researchers might share similar values regarding the quality of what journals to send their research to, but these two researchers might have different skill sets that combine to produce research that is published in high-quality academic journals. The environment, in this case a research-oriented university, helps to integrate the resources that each brings to work.

COR suggests that individuals can invest their resources into the environment as a means to alter the environment in ways that provide returns on those investments (e.g., more resources). The distinction between dimensions of PE fit represents the immediate saliency of different types of resources that individuals require to meet the demands of their work lives. Individuals can possess these resources or can find these resources in the environment, and employees' beliefs that resource needs are met, whether from personal resources, environmental resources, or a combination of the two, is what we call "fit." In the following section, we describe PE fit's nomological network in terms of COR. Much of the existing research on PE fit's nomological network can be explained as a function of COR's primacy of loss principle. That is, the positive outcomes we typically associate with PE fit occur because individuals feel that they have sufficient resources to meet the demands of their work environments, and the negative outcomes we typically associate with the lack of PE fit occur because individuals feel the threat or actual loss of fit-based resources. However, we believe that COR's resource investment principle and its four corollaries provide a suitable theoretical framework to understand behaviors that might result when someone experiences PE misfit.

The Nomological Network of PE Fit

As mentioned earlier, Edwards (2008) argues that any PE fit theory must explain the findings of five distinct streams of PE fit research: job stress, job satisfaction, vocational choice, recruitment and selection, and culture and climate. The fact that five streams of research have grown within PE fit, each with its own or multiple theoretical groundings, suggests to us that a middle-range theoretical explanation might help to integrate this vast literature. We start with job stress, as this research has already been subsumed into the COR-based stress and burnout literatures (Halbesleben and Buckley, 2004).

PE fit research on stress suggests that the lack of congruence between the demands of the environment and the abilities of the employee creates stress. Moreover, the further lack of congruence between the resources supplied by the company and the employees' needs creates stress (for a review, see Edwards, 2008). Hence, PE fit stress research is predicated on resources (French *et al.*, 1982). Edwards (2008) notes that some of these PE fit stress theories propose that excess resources can lead to stress because the resources should match the environment, and that psychologically managing resources can in and of itself create a demand. Hobfoll (2001) proposes the same contention: managing resources requires resources. Edwards summarizes the strengths and shortcomings of PE fit stress theories, highlighting that while the theories clearly define the person, environment, and their relationship to strain and strain's downstream consequences (e.g., job satisfaction, job performance, etc.), the theories fail to define resources clearly and sometimes have contradictory internal logic. For instance, Edwards (2008) highlights French, Kaplan, and Harrison's (1982) PE fit theory of stress as offering alternative constructs to reduce stress other than PE fit congruence, which allows researchers to expand this theory to the point of limiting researchers' abilities to either support or refute basic tenets of the theory. To some extent, COR has the same shortcoming in terms of defining resources. However, COR extends our understanding of stress because the theory is a general motivation theory and explains why someone is experiencing stress and how they think or behave as a result. COR's investment processes not only capture stress and burnout processes but can also integrate the other streams of PE fit research, such as explaining how job applicants respond to resource signals included in organizational recruitment materials (Rynes, 1991).

The second stream of PE fit research identified by Edwards (2008) focuses on job satisfaction to describe the congruence between the person and the environment. Edwards (2008, p. 175) summarizes PE fit theories in this realm as operating on "the premise that job satisfaction results from the comparison between what the job provides and what the employee needs, wants, or desires from the job." Discrepancy theories, as job satisfaction PE fit theories are termed, appear similar to the PE fit stress theories in that the satisfaction theories focus on the needs–supply dimension of PE fit (Edwards, 2008). The greater the discrepancy between the individual's needs and what the job supplies (e.g., resources), the less satisfied that individual becomes. Interestingly, these discrepancy PE fit theories include not just KSA-type resources but also values as individual needs that the job can satisfy. Edwards concludes that, while clear in defining components of PE fit, causes and outcomes of discrepancies, and the inclusion of values, these theories include circular internal logic that makes it almost impossible to test them empirically. Interestingly and relevant to COR, the roots of discrepancy theories are in resources, whether actual or perceived.

The third stream of PE fit research focuses on an individual's vocational preferences as a function of the match between an individual's "needs, interests, and abilities ... and the reinforcers and requirements of different occupations, vocations, and careers" (Edwards, 2008, p. 191). Within PE fit vocational theories (e.g., Dawis and Lofquist, 1984; Holland, 1985), individuals have profiles that overlap with profiles of others found within occupations. These theories predict that individuals have strong predispositions to self-select into certain occupations that generally satisfy their needs. Individual profiles consist of almost every type of conceptualization of PE fit to include values and goals of PO fit, KSAs and needs of PJ fit, and personality traits. Edwards (2008) suggests that the broad conceptualization of PV fit is a main shortcoming of vocational preference PE fit models. The ambiguity of this conceptualization makes testing the theory difficult. COR might help to clarify this ambiguity. The personality-based resources listed by Hobfoll (2001) might predispose people to select into work environments that they perceive as having resources to support or enhance their existing personality-based resources. For example, research on need for achievement has found that people who possess high levels of that trait appear to self-select out of highly bureaucratic and hierarchical organizations, such as government, because these environments do not allow high need for achievement individuals to demonstrate their successes (Chusmir and Azevedo, 1992; Elder, 1968). Someone who seeks the resource of "feeling that I am accomplishing my goals" might seek to enter an environment where that resource is more readily available or more easily invested.

The fourth stream of PE fit research, recruitment and selection, has also utilized PE fit rationales to explain how organizations and individuals mutually select to meet each other's needs. PE fit models in this context emphasize the match between individuals and organizations as leading to increased positive work attitudes, retention, and job performance. The PE fit recruitment and selection literature takes an active view of PE fit as organizations and individuals can manipulate perceptions of PE fit. For example, organizations transmit PE fit-related information through recruitment materials in order to attract applicants (Dineen et al., 2002; Rynes, 1991), and research has indicated that organizations might only present positive information (Phillips, 1998; Wanous, 1992). Disconnects between what organizations transmit during recruitment and selection and what applicants actually encounter once hired have been linked to a host of outcomes. For instance, research suggests that when applicants' pre-hire expectations about PE fit are unmet post-hire, individuals feel less positive about their jobs and organizations (Cable and Judge, 1996), which has been linked to increased turnover intentions and actual turnover (Kristof, 1996). Conversely, Kristof-Brown, Barrick, and Franke (2002) have found that applicants engage in impression management tactics on resumés and during interviews as a means to improve recruiter and interviewer perceptions of applicant PE fit, leading to negative outcomes as well.

From a COR perspective, these findings make a great deal of sense. Because individuals seek sources of support to accumulate, protect, and replenish resources, the fit-related signals companies transmit during recruitment and selection (Rynes, 1991; Spence, 1973) are meant to indicate resource availability to applicants. When companies do not disclose the negative aspects of the environment that typically induce stress, employees are unprepared to cope with the loss of these promised resources. On the other hand, applicants can signal the extent to which they will add resources to the company. In the event that applicants manipulate recruiter or interviewer perceptions of applicant resources, decision makers in the organization are likely to feel that these applicants drain more organization resources than the organization expected. Thus, decision makers in the organization will see a negative return on their investment decision and seek to mitigate the resource drain.

It is in the PE fit research on recruiting and selection that one can see examples of how COR can account for the interplay between the supplementary and complementary distinctions within PE fit. Applicants can be attracted to the supplementary PE fit signaled by organizations through culture messaging in recruitment materials, but recruiters in organizations might initially be attracted to the complementary PE fit signaled by applicants in their resumés. On the other hand, applicants might be initially attracted to the complementary NS fit information presented in recruiting materials (Rynes, 1991), while companies might primarily assess supplementary PO fit in the interviewing process (Judge et al., 2000). The importance of resources to both applicants and organizations that COR implies ties the supplementary and complementary views together, which COR can explain and integrate with other PE fit theories.

The last segment of PE fit research identified by Edwards, which we think closely resembles the arguments above on the recruiting and selection research, examines the interaction between individuals' values, goals, and beliefs and the culture or climate of organizations. This stream of research draws upon interactional psychology theories such as Lewin's (1943) field theory and Schneider's (1987) attraction-selection-attrition (ASA) framework. Schneider (1987) postulates that individuals and decision makers within organizations are differentially attracted to each other based on congruence, and when mutual attraction exists they will select each other. Should either the individual or organization become unattractive to the other, the relationships will voluntarily or involuntarily end (attrition). Thus, PE fit culture and climate theories describe congruence in terms of mutual attraction of similar values, norms of behavior, and beliefs. Like PE fit recruitment and selection research, PE fit culture and climate research takes an interactional view of congruence. Chatman's (1989) conceptualization describes how HRM functions like selection and socialization alter individuals' perceptions of congruence, and her conceptualization speaks to the potential influence that the person has on the environment. While the PE fit culture and climate research generally predicts the positive outcomes we traditionally find in most PE fit research (e.g., increased positive work attitudes, extra-role performance, retention) and also includes contextual or boundary conditions that affect PE fit (e.g., personality traits, organizational structures and systems, etc.), this research often describes the lack of PE fit in terms of turnover. For the research in this stream of research that utilizes the ASA framework, the terminal point of PE misfit is turnover (attrition).

The PE fit culture and climate research can be integrated with the other PE fit research through a COR perspective. Mutual attraction and selection occur as a function of resources, which individuals and organizations signal to each other during recruiting and selection. Furthermore, the socialization process within organizations continues the signaling of resources between individuals and organizations as well as providing new employees with some of the resources (e.g., knowledge of the job) to complete tasks. The lack of resources triggers both parties to assess whether resource needs are being met and, if they are not met, where or how they might be better met. While turnover might occur due to lack of resources, COR's investment principle and four corollaries predict that individuals can engage in activities designed to increase returns on resource investments and by doing so can increase fit.

Time and PE Fit

Time plays an important, if unspecified, role in the ASA framework, with Schneider and his colleagues (Schneider, 1987; Schneider *et al.*, 1995) suggesting that the assessment of PE fit occurs on a continuous basis. We might interpret that to mean two different things. The assessment of PE fit occurs through stages of employment (e.g., during recruitment, selection, socialization, etc.) or literally on a continuous basis (e.g., hourly, daily, weekly, monthly, or yearly). We, however, find it unlikely that individuals literally assess PE fit on a continuous basis (e.g., hourly, daily). Jansen and Kristof-Brown (2006) and Wheeler *et al.* (2005) theorize that such continuous assessments would require individuals to expend their limited cognitive resources. The notion that the assessment of PE fit requires cognitive resources closely aligns with COR, and COR probably precludes this level of assessment intensity. Recall that COR stipulates that individuals are motivated to protect, invest, and replenish resources. An individual will be motivated to assess PE fit to the extent that resource needs are not met, and the investment of cognitive resources to assess PE fit would require individuals to replenish those spent resources. Continuous or even frequent assessment of PE fit would require the individual to expend resources continually, which would create stress. COR would consider the frequent assessment of fit to be poor return on investment behavior. Wheeler, Gallagher, Brouer, and Sablynski (2007) and COR suggest that it is more likely that environmental events trigger the assessment of PE fit. This view is consistent with Lee and Mitchell's (1994) unfolding model of turnover, which postulates that expected (e.g., promotion) or unexpected (e.g., layoffs, mergers, co-worker turnover, etc.) events, termed "shocks," cause individuals to assess their current fit. These shocks activate the threat of resource loss and cause individuals to reevaluate the extent to which they or the environment hold enough resources to meet the demands of their jobs. Resource shocks make individuals think about PE fit.

Levels of Analysis, Fit, and COR

Recent research on the ASA framework examines aspects of fit across multiple levels of an organization. Ployhart, Weekley, and Baughman (2006) argue that the ASA framework and the shared perceptions of personality across levels of the organization, in this case the job and organization levels, influenced individuals' job satisfaction and motivated job performance. Employees form perceptions of group homogeneity in terms of the personality traits they ascribe to people working in certain jobs or in parts of the organization. The shared perceptions of personality create a supportive environment that explains these multilevel relationships. So there is evidence, consistent with the idea of resources, that fit creates a supportive environment that is conducive to individuals meeting the demands of their jobs. Wheeler, Halbesleben, and Harris (2012) synthesize COR with Barney's (1991) resource-based view of the firm (RBV) as a means to generate multilevel hypotheses, and their synthesis might help future PE fit researchers to tie PE fit research to strategic human resource management research. As resources underlie both COR and RBV, Wheeler, Halbesleben, and Harris (2012) argue that employee-level resources, which are developed through work-related sources of support like effective HRM systems, increase employee motivation to participate in their jobs (e.g., motivated, performing, and likely to remain). Moreover, as organizational support facilitates the development of human capital, organizations can leverage that capital to meet strategic goals and increase firm productivity.

In terms of PE fit, the synthesis of COR and RBV as an explanation of how resources affect individuals and organizations has multilevel implications for the assessment of PE fit and misfit. When individuals feel that they have the salient resources needed to meet their job demands, they will perceive PE fit and experience the beneficial outcomes typically associated with PE fit (e.g., job satisfaction, organizational commitment, organizational citizenship, intention to remain, etc.). The resources can be personal (e.g., personality traits) or environmental (e.g., social support). This, in turn, should lead to increased contextual and task performance, as well as decreased turnover. Thus, the organization stands to benefit financially through increased PE fit. Organizations can choose to invest resources, through activities like mentoring, training, or performance management, to increase their unique human capital and will expect a return on that investment. After all, we note that PE fit researchers examine how efficient recruiting, selection, and socialization alter individuals' perceptions of fit to benefit organizations in terms of retention, while strategic HRM scholars often find that efficient HRM systems lead to increased organizational financial performance (e.g., Huselid, 1995).

PE Misfit

One of the more recent avenues of research within PE fit is misfit. As we previously described, most of the extant PE fit research assumes that the lack of fit results in employee turnover. For instance, the ASA framework (Schneider, 1987) underpins much of the PO fit research on recruiting, selection, and culture/climate, and this framework explicitly theorizes that misfit results in turnover. Similarly, PE fit stress and job satisfaction theories posit that turnover is the terminal point of misfit (Edwards, 2008). PE misfit might indeed eventually result in turnover, but no current PE fit theories explain the behaviors that misfitting employees engage in on their way to exit. Empirically, we know that the lack of PE fit, or misfit as we have been discussing it, predicts minimal actual variance in turnover, because fewer people decide to leave their jobs than those who think about leaving. For example, Kristof-Brown, Zimmerman, and Johnson's (2005) meta-analysis found correlations between PJ fit and PO fit and actual turnover of -0.07 and -0.13, respectively. Although PE fit strongly predicts *intentions to turnover*, it does not strongly predict actual turnover. So what are misfitting employees doing?

Several non-PE-fit-related streams of research provide clues as to how PE misfits might behave. Turnover researchers find that dissatisfied employees who do not leave might exhibit greater absenteeism or tardiness (Harrison, Newman, and Roth, 2006) or engage in counterproductive work behaviors (Rusbult *et al.*, 1988). Similarly, organizational commitment researchers have found that less committed employees might exert minimal efforts to meet the basic tenets of the job. Leader–member exchange (LMX) researchers also shed light on how misfits might behave. Employees in poor-quality relationships with their supervisors often seek less feedback from their supervisors, which often decreases their extra role behaviors (Chen *et al.*, 2007). Furthermore, employees in low-quality LMX relationships often become noninstrumental complainers, meaning they complain about issues unrelated to specific tasks or goals but about general issues like not being welcomed (Heck *et al.*, 2005). While these streams of research do provide insights, an extensive search of misfit reveals that very few models of PE misfit exist.

Perhaps the best known of these misfit models is one we developed to explain the behaviors in which misfits might engage (Wheeler *et al.*, 2005; Wheeler *et al.*, 2007) that we will integrate with COR. Our model shows five potential outcomes for individuals who experience PE misfit once that assessment has been made. First, misfits, if willing and able, can adapt to fit the organization, job, or vocation. If unwilling or unable to adapt, misfits have choices to make contingent upon viable job alternatives. They might choose to leave if suitable job options exist, become vocal about the source of the misfit as a means to potentially change the environment, engage in passive–aggressive behaviors designed to hide their misfit, such as impression management, or simply ignore the misfit and continue to work as best they can. We later empirically tested a small portion of this model, finding that turnover intentions increased as levels of PO misfit and job dissatisfaction increased. However, turnover intentions for those with limited perceived job mobility, even when dissatisfied and lacking PO fit, decreased. This suggests to us that PO misfit, and its resulting impact on job satisfaction, does not necessarily increase turnover intentions. Although our theoretical model and very limited empirical testing do provide some insights as to the complexity of behaviors resulting from PE misfit, we find that our previous research lacked important theoretical grounding. We think a COR framework provides a suitable theoretical lens to consider the causes and outcomes of PE misfit.

Any true interactional theory must account not just for the impact of the environment on the person but also for the impact of the person on the environment (Chatman, 1989). A COR framing would suggest that PE misfits might engage in some type of resource investment with the hope of increasing fit. To this point, Kohn and Schooler (1978) found that, over time, individuals with high cognitive abilities alter their jobs to suit their interests. Similarly, Miner (1987) found that individuals with unique KSAs have their job descriptions incrementally change to suit their unique KSAs. A nascent body of literature on the concept of *job crafting* (Wrzesniewski and Dutton, 2001) describes "individuals at work, at virtually any level of an organization, who make unsupervised, spontaneous changes in their job" (Lyons, 2008, p. 25). Job crafting occurs because employees seek more satisfaction, fulfillment, and identification with their jobs (Lyons, 2008). Job crafting occurs because employees want better congruence between themselves and their work environments. From a COR perspective and consistent with the second principle of the theory, PE misfits would invest their resources into changing what they see as the cause of their lack of fit. PE misfits might see this as their best potential for return on investment, as COR suggests that individuals seek to maximize their best chances of gaining returns (Baltes, 1997; Baltes and Baltes, 1990). From a PE fit perspective, this type of activity would look like complementary PE fit behavior. The PE misfit hopes to change the environment to suit his or her own resource needs.

On the other hand, job crafting could take the form of supplementary PE fit behaviors. Take the example of a faculty member who no longer feels he or she fits with her present position because his or her new department chair has begun emphasizing service over research and teaching. He or she could reassess which dimension of fit is most important, for example evaluating whether PJ fit (which would now require greater service) or PV fit is more important. Or, he or she could craft the job to address the new values of the chair without compromising his or her fit (e.g., by performing service in a research-focused area, such as reviewing internal grant applications or mentoring students on research projects).

COR predicts that the threat to resources associated with the newly perceived misfit (not fitting with the chair's new emphasis) would create the need to reevaluate one's options and invest remaining resources in the option that seems most likely to yield positive results. So, in the case of our faculty member, if reevaluating the dimensions of fit leads to the conclusion that PV fit is a higher priority than PJ fit, he or she may be more likely to leave the job to find a job that fits with his or her preferred resources (e.g., an environment supportive of research). On the other hand, if leaving the job would require a large sacrifice in resources, the faculty member may instead craft the job so that he or she could meet the new environmental demands with the resources he or she already has.

Being vocal about the source of PE misfit also has complementary–supplementary PE fit implications. For instance, an employee might believe in the value of practicing environmentally sustainable business practices, which his or her employer does not currently value. The lack of congruence on this value, depending on the saliency and intensity of the value, could create a sense of supplementary PE misfit for the employee. The employee might become vocal about the value of environmentally sustainable practices and make the business case for these practices, while the organization might create a committee to investigate the value of "going green." In this instance, being vocal is a complementary PE misfit behavior designed to increase supplementary PE fit. Interestingly, the remaining two PE misfit paths of engaging in impression management and simply ignoring the misfit might appear to be supplementary PE misfit behaviors. These behaviors in essence are attempts to hide the misfit and give the appearance that the misfit matches the environment. On the whole, a COR framework might suggest that impression management and ignoring the misfit are poor returns on investment behaviors because the person is not actually doing anything to rectify the misfit. These behaviors are likely to create a resource drain, while the more active behaviors of job crafting or being vocal might represent behaviors that give misfits a chance to rectify the source of misfit. We venture to state that the active PE misfit behaviors are more likely to stave off turnover, but the passive PE misfit behaviors probably more quickly lead to turnover.

Benefits of COR View of PE Fit

Given the scattered nature of the PE fit literature, it is natural to ask how yet another theory adds clarity, even if the theory can explain a continuum of PE fit through misfit. First, COR satisfies the "good theory" requirements. The theory specifically defines what resources are (Hobfoll, 2001), which we have applied to the construct of PE fit. PE fit reflects the extent to which individuals perceive or actually have the resources, whether in their possession or available in the environment, to meet the demands of their work environments. COR also allows us to explain how and why constructs within PE fit's nomological network relate to each other. Contextual variables represent support found in the environment, and the presence of resources across levels of the organization predicts individual- and organization-level outcomes. Moreover, COR provides important boundary conditions to explain the timing of when PE fit assessment occurs.

Second, while COR may not have previously been tied to the PE fit literature, we believe that PE fit is central to COR theory. In essence, COR argues that people want to maintain their desired level of resources relative to what is available in their environment. The integrative advantage of COR is that it goes further in arguing what conditions would cause perceptions of lack of fit (or misfit) and the general motivational processes used to resolve lack of fit.

Finally, as we have identified above, COR theory can address all five streams of research that have evolved from the PE fit literature. Moreover, it offers an integrated view of them, through its accommodation of multidimensional fit theories (e.g., Wheeler et al., 2005), that brings more structure to the literature than had existed before. Combined, COR offers suitable middle-range theory to integrate the PE fit literatures and offer insights into PE misfit behaviors.

Conclusion

This chapter provides a new direction for theoretically grounding the construct of PE fit. The view of fit as a resource might address the lack of integration and coherence among current theoretical constructions of what we call "fit." Our chapter also contributes to the COR literature, especially related to the resource investment tenet of the theory. Unlike the stress and burnout empirical research that examines outcomes in the context of resource loss, much of the PE fit research examines outcomes in the presence of fit not misfit. Our chapter provides a bridge to understanding both fit and misfit as a function of resource investment or loss, respectively.

References

Arthur, W. A., Jr, Bell, S.T., Villado, A. J., and Doverspike, D. (2006) The use of person–organization fit in employment decision making: An assessment of its criterion-related validity. *Journal of Applied Psychology*, 91, 786–801.

Assouline, M., and Meir, E. I. (1987) Meta-analysis of the relationship between congruence and well-being measures. *Journal of Vocational Behavior*, 31, 319–332.

Bacharach, S. B. (1989) Organization theories: Some criteria for evaluation. *Academy of Management Review*, 14, 496–515.

Baltes, M. M., and Baltes, P. B. (1990) Psychological perspectives on successful aging: The model of selective optimization with compensation. In P. B. Baltes and M. M. Baltes (eds), *Successful Aging: Perspectives from the Behavioral Sciences* (pp. 1–34). New York: Cambridge University Press.

Baltes, P. B. (1997) On the incomplete architecture of human ontogeny: Selection, optimization, and compensation as foundation of development theory. *American Psychologist*, 52, 366–380.

Barney, J. B. (1991) Firm resources and sustained competitive advantage. *Journal of Management*, 17, 9–120.

Billsberry, J. (2009) Fit as wellness, misfit as illness. Paper presented at the Academy of Management annual meeting, Chicago, IL.

Cable, D. M., and Edwards, J. R. (2004) Complementary and supplementary fit: A theoretical and empirical integration. *Journal of Applied Psychology*, 89, 822–834.

Cable, D. M., and Judge, T. A. (1996) Person–organization fit, job choice decisions, and organizational entry. *Organizational Behavior and Human Decision Process*, 67, 294–311.

Cable, D. M., and Parsons, C. K. (2001) Socialization tactics and person–organization fit. *Personnel Psychology*, 54, 1–23.

Caldwell, D. F., and O'Reilly, C. A., III (1990) Measuring person–job fit with a profile comparison process. *Journal of Applied Psychology*, 75, 648–657.

Chatman, J. (1989) Improving interactional organizational research: A model of person–organization fit. *Academy of Management Review*, 14, 333–349.

Chen, Z., Lam, W., and Zhong, J. A. (2007) Leader–member exchange and member performance: A new look at individual-level negative feedback-seeking behavior and team-level empowerment climate. *Journal of Applied Psychology*, 92, 202–212.

Chusmir, L. H., and Azevedo, A. (1992) Motivation needs of sampled Fortune 500 CEOs: Relations to organization outcomes. *Perceptual and Motor Skills*, 75 (4), 595–612.

Dawis, R. V., and Lofquist, L. H. (1984) *A Psychological Theory of Work Adjustment*. Minneapolis, MN: University of Minnesota.

Dawis, R. V., England, G. W., and Lofquist, L. H. (1964) A theory of work adjustment. *Minnesota Studies in Vocational Rehabilitation* (whole no. 15).

Deci, E. L., Koestner, R., and Ryan, R. M. (1999) A meta-analytic review of experiments examining the effects of extrinsic rewards on intrinsic motivation. *Psychological Bulletin*, 125, 627–668.

Dineen, B. R., Ash, S. R., and Noe, R. A. (2002) A web of applicant attraction: Person–organization fit in the context of web-based recruitment. *Journal of Applied Psychology*, 87, 723–734.

Edwards, J. A., and Billsberry, J. (2011) Testing a multidimensional theory of person–environment fit. *Journal of Managerial Issues*, 22 (4), 476–493.

Edwards, J. R. (1991) Person–job fit: A conceptual integration, literature review, and method-ological critique. *International Review of Industrial/Organizational Psychology* (Vol. 6, pp. 283–357). London: John Wiley & Sons, Ltd.

Edwards, J. R. (2008) Person–environment fit in organizations: An assessment of theoretical progress. *Academy of Management Annals*, 2, 167–230.

Elder, G. H., Jr (1968) Achievement motivation and intelligence in occupational mobility: A longitudinal analysis. *Sociometry*, 31 (4), 327–354.

French, J. R. P., Jr, Kaplan, R. D., and Harrison, R. V. (1982) *The Mechanisms of Job Stress and Strain*. London: John Wiley & Sons, Ltd.

George, J. M., and Jones, G. R. (2000) The role of time in theory and theory building. *Journal of Management*, 26, 657–684.

Gudmunson, C. G., Butler, I. F., Israelsen, C. L., McCoy, J. K., and Hill, E. J. (2007) Linking financial strain to marital instability: Examining the roles of emotional distress and marital interaction. *Journal of Family and Economic Issues*, 28, 357–376.

Halbesleben, J. R. B. (2006) Sources of social support and burnout: A meta-analytic test of the conservation of resources model. *Journal of Applied Psychology*, 91, 1134–1145.

Halbesleben, J. R. B., and Bowler, W. M. (2007) Emotional exhaustion and job performance: The mediating role of motivation. *Journal of Applied Psychology*, 91, 93–106.

Halbesleben, J. R. B., and Buckley, M. R. (2004) Burnout in organizational life. *Journal of Management*, 30, 859–880.

Halbesleben, J. R. B., and Wheeler, A. R. (2008) The relative roles of engagement and em-beddedness in predicting job performance and intention to leave. *Work and Stress*, 22, 242–256.

Harrison, D. A. (2007) Pitching fits in applied psychological research: Making methods fit theory. In C. Ostroff and T. A. Judge (eds), *Perspectives on Organizational Fit* (pp. 389–416). New York: Lawrence Erlbaum Associates.

Harrison, D. A., Newman, D. A., and Roth, p. L. (2006) How important are job attitudes? A meta-analytic comparison of integrative behavioral outcomes and time sequences. *Academy of Management Journal*, 49, 305–325.

Heck, A. K., Bedeian, A. G., and Day, D. V. (2005) Mountains out of molehills? Test of the mediating effects of self-esteem in predicting workplace complaining. *Journal of Applied Social Psychology*, 35, 2262–2289.

Himmelstein, D. U., Warren, E., Thorne, D., and Woolhandler, S. (2005) Illness and injury as contributors to bankruptcy. *Health Affairs*, 24, w63–w73.

Hobfoll, S.E. (1988) *The Ecology of Stress*. New York: Hemisphere.

Hobfoll, S. E. (1989) Conservation of resources: A new attempt at conceptualizing stress. *American Psychologist*, 44, 513–524.

Hobfoll, S. E. (1998) *Stress, Culture, and Community*. New York: Plenum Press.

Hobfoll, S.E. (2001) The influence of culture, community, and the nested self in the stress pro-cess: Advancing conservation of resources theory. *Applied Psychology: An International Review*, 50, 337–370.

Holland, J. L. (1985) *Making Vocational Choices: A Theory of Careers* (2nd edn). Englewood Cliffs, NJ: Prentice Hall.

Holtom, B. C., Mitchell, T. R., Lee, T. W., and Eberly, M. B. (2008) Turnover and retention research: A glance at the past, a closer review of the present, and a venture into the future. *Academy of Management Annals*, 2, 231–274.

Huselid, M. A. (1995) The impact of human resource management practices on turnover, productivity, and corporate financial performance. *Academy of Management Journal*, 38, 635–672.

Jansen, K. J., and Kristof-Brown, A. (2006) Toward a multidimensional theory of person–environment fit. *Journal of Managerial Issues*, 18, 193–212.

Jin, R. L., Shah, C. P., and Svoboda, T. J. (1995) The impact of unemployment on health: A review of the evidence. *Canadian Medical Association Journal*, 153, 529–540.

Judge, T. A., and Ferris, G. R. (1992) The elusive criterion of fit in human resources staffing decisions. *Human Resource Planning*, 15, 47–68.

Judge, T. A., Higgins, C. A., and Cable, D. M. (2000) The employment interview: A review of recent research and recommendations for future research. *Human Resource Management Review*, 10, 383–406.

Kohn, M., and Schooler, C. (1978) The reciprocal effects of the substantive complexity or work and intellectual flexibility: A longitudinal assessment. *American Journal of Sociology*, 84, 24–52.

Kristof, A. L. (1996) Person–organization fit: An integrative review of its conceptualizations, measurement, and implications. *Personnel Psychology*, 49, 1–49.

Kristof-Brown, A. L., Barrick, M. R., and Franke, M. (2002) Applicant impression management: Dispositional influences and consequences for recruiter perceptions of fit and similarity. *Journal of Management*, 28, 27–46.

Kristof-Brown, A. L., Jansen, K. J., and Colbert, A. E. (2002) A policy capturing study of the simultaneous effects of fit with jobs, groups, and organizations. *Journal of Applied Psychology*, 87, 985–993.

Kristof-Brown, A. L, Zimmerman, R. D., Johnson, E. C. (2005) Consequences of individuals' fit at work: A meta-analysis of person–job, person–organization, person–group, and person–supervisor fit. *Personnel Psychology*, 58, 281–342.

Lee, T. W., and Mitchell, T. R. (1994) An alternative approach: The unfolding model of voluntary employee turnover. *Academy of Management Review*, 19, 51–89.

Lewin, K. (1935) *A Dynamic Theory of Personality: Selected Papers*. New York: McGraw-Hill.

Lewin, K. (1943) Defining the "field at a given time." *Psychological Review*, 50, 292–310.

Lyons, P. (2008) The crafting of jobs and individual differences. *Journal of Business Psychology*, 23, 25–36.

Merton, R. K. (1968) *Social Theory and Social Structure*. New York: The Free Press.

Miner, A. (1987) Idiosyncratic jobs in formal organizations. *Administrative Science Quarterly*, 32, 327–351.

Mitchell, T. R., and James, L. R. (2001) Building better theories: Time and the specification of when things happen. *Academy of Management Review*, 26, 530–547.

Mitchell, T. R., Holtom, B. C., Lee, T. W., Sablynski, C. J., and Erez, M. (2001) Why people stay: Using job embeddedness to predict voluntary turnover. *Academy of Management Journal*, 44, 1102–1121.

Muchinsky, P. M., and Monahan, C. J. (1987) What is person–environment congruence? Supplementary versus complementary models of fit. *Journal of Vocational Behavior*, 31, 268–277.

Ostroff, C., and Judge, T. A. (eds) (2007) *Perspectives on Organizational Fit*. Mahwah, NJ: Lawrence Erlbaum Associates.

Ostroff, C. (2012) Person–environment fit in organizations. In S. W. J. Kozlowski (ed.), *Handbook of Organizational Psychology* (Vol. 1, pp. 373–408). Oxford: Oxford University Press.

Ostroff, C., and Schulte, M. (2007) Multiple perspectives of fit across levels of analysis. In C. Ostroff and T. Judge (eds), *Perspectives on Organizational Fit*. Mahwah, NJ: Lawrence Erlbaum Associates.

Phillips, J. M. (1998) Effectiveness of realistic job previews on multiple organizational outcomes: A meta-analysis. *Academy of Management Journal*, 41, 673–690.

Ployhart, R. E., Weekley, J. A., and Baughman, K. (2006) The structure and function of human capital emergence: A multilevel examination of the attraction-selection-attrition model. *Academy of Management Journal*, 49, 661–677.

Rusbult, C. E., Farrell, D., Rogers, G., and Mainous, A. G. (1988) Impact of exchange variables on exit, voice, loyalty, and neglect: An integrative model of responses to declining job satisfaction. *Academy of Management Journal*, 31, 599–627.

Rynes, S. L. (1991) Recruitment, job choice, and post-hire consequences: A call for new research directions. In M. D. Dunnette and L. M. Hough (eds), *Handbook of Industrial and Organizational Psychology* (2nd edn). Palo Alto, CA: Consulting Psychologists Press.

Schneider, B. (1987) People make the place. *Personnel Psychology*, 40, 437–453.

Schneider, B., Goldstein, H. W., and Smith, D. B. (1995) The ASA framework: An update. *Personnel Psychology*, 48, 747–773.

Scroggins, W. A. (2007) An examination of the additive versus the convergent effects of employee perceptions of fit. *Journal of Applied Social Psychology*, 37, 1649–1665.

Song, F. (2009) Intergroup trust and reciprocity in strategic interactions: Effects of group decision-making mechanisms. *Organizational Behavior and Human Decision Processes*, 108, 164–173.

Spence, M. (1973) Job market signaling. *Quarterly Journal of Economics*, 87, 355–373.

Sutton, R. I., and Staw, B. M. (1995) What theory is not. *Administration Science Quarterly*, 40, 371–384.

Talbot, D. L. (2010) Organisational fit and misfit: An empirical study of similarities and differences. Unpublished PhD thesis. The Open University, Buckingham.

Verquer, M. L., Beehr, T. A., and Wagner, S. H. (2003) A meta-analysis of the relations between person–organization fit and work attitudes. *Journal of Vocational Behavior*, 63, 473–489.

Wanous, J. P. (1992) *Organizational Entry*. Reading, MA: Addison-Wesley.

Wheeler, A. R., Buckley, M. R., Halbesleben, J. R., Brouer, R. L., and Ferris, G. R. (2005) "The elusive criterion of fit" revisited: Toward an integrative theory of multidimensional fit. *Research in Personnel and Human Resources Management*, 24, 265–304.

Wheeler, A. R., Gallagher, V. C., Brouer, R. L., and Sablynski, C. J. (2007) When person–organization (mis)fit and (dis)satisfaction lead to turnover: The moderating role of perceived job mobility. *Journal of Managerial Psychology*, 22, 203–219.

Wheeler, A. R., Halbesleben, J. R. B., and Harris, K. J. (2012)The influence of job-level HRM effectiveness on employee intent to turnover and workarounds in hospitals. *Journal of Business Research*, 65, 547–554.

Wrzesniewski, A., and Dutton, J. E. (2001) Crafting a job: Revisioning employees as active crafters of their work. *Academy of Management Review*, 26, 179–201.

9

A Review and Agenda for Incorporating Time in Fit Research

Karen J. Jansen
University of Virginia

Abbie J. Shipp
Texas A&M University

One of the widely shared beliefs in organizations is that the fit or congruence between a person and the environment predicts important outcomes such as satisfaction, adjustment, and turnover. However, as prolific as person–environment (PE) fit research has been in addressing these topics (cf. Kristof-Brown *et al.*, 2005), relatively little research has addressed the role of time in PE fit. For example, perceived PE fit research, in particular, has remained largely contemporaneous for more than a quarter of a century (cf. Brousseau, 1983; Caplan, 1983), primarily focusing on fit in the current moment, despite renewed interest in temporal perceptions across the field of management (e.g., Ancona *et al.*, 2001; Bluedorn, 2002; George and Jones, 2000; Mitchell and James, 2001).

We argue that such a contemporaneous view limits our ability to thoroughly and accurately understand fit experiences. Indeed, early fit research recognized that the assessment of congruence between a person and a characteristic of the work environment occurs in a temporal context (Lewin, 1943, 1951; Murray, 1938). For example, Murray (1938, p. 49) states that "man [sic] is not a mere creature of the moment ... what he does is related not only to the settled past but also to shadowy preconceptions of what lies ahead." Therefore, our goal in this chapter is to reinforce the notion that fit is far from "static" (Ostroff *et al.*, 2002). Rather, we view fit as temporally situated within the past and future, and changing over time when individuals and aspects of their environments change (Jansen and Kristof-Brown, 2006). When this temporal context is ignored, we neglect the important role that context plays in defining experience (Johns, 2006; Kozlowski, 2009; Rousseau and

Organizational Fit: Key Issues and New Directions, First Edition.
Edited by Amy L. Kristof-Brown and Jon Billsberry.
© 2013 John Wiley & Sons, Ltd. Published 2013 by John Wiley & Sons, Ltd.

Fried, 2001). As a result, we are unable to understand fully the reality of individual interpretations and reactions to fit over time.

In this chapter, we provide the first detailed review of PE fit research from a temporal perspective. By examining the existing literature for any reference to time (whether explicit or implicit), we provide a history of temporal fit research as well as a road map to guide future research. First, we define temporal fit based on three components (context, impact, and process). Next, we use these three components as an organizing framework for reviewing relevant literature in the fit domain. Finally, we develop a research agenda for pushing temporal fit research forward in terms of theory, research, and practice.

A Temporal Review of Fit Research

Person–environment (PE) fit is defined as the degree of compatibility between a person and various aspects of the environment (Kristof, 1996; Kristof-Brown et al., 2005). PE fit is thus a broad construct, incorporating both subjective and objective experience, multiple levels[1] of the environment (e.g., individuals, jobs, groups, organizations), and a wide array of dimensions upon which comparisons are made (e.g., values, personality, needs, abilities, or vocational interests). Interestingly, most research emphasizes the fit between the person and the environment at a given point in time. However, as suggested by the earliest fit researchers (Lewin, 1943; Murray, 1938), we believe that time plays an important role in how fit exists, is perceived or experienced, and influences outcomes. As Murray's quote above suggests, individuals make sense of the present by referring to the past and future. This makes time a critical consideration in developing theory and designing empirical studies in this domain.

In keeping with the broad definition of PE fit above, we conceptualize temporal fit not as a particular type of fit (e.g., supplementary versus complementary; Muchinsky and Monahan, 1987) or even as specifying a particular time horizon (e.g., past, present, or future fit; Caplan, 1983). Rather, our view of *temporal fit* is one that incorporates time on at least one of three conceptual dimensions: *context* (i.e., the temporal setting in which fit is perceived or experienced), *impact* (i.e., the temporal effects of fit on outcomes), and *process* (i.e., how fit unfolds over time and influences subsequent fit or outcomes).

We used these conceptual dimensions to guide our review of the literature, intentionally casting a wide net for research that incorporated time in the study of fit. We identified articles by conducting a search across several online databases (i.e., Proquest, Psycinfo, and Google Scholar), using a variety of keywords (i.e., fit, time, temporal, process, change). Given that a clearly defined label of "temporal" fit research does not exist, we augmented the database search by revisiting the pioneering articles on fit, drawing on our own knowledge of the discipline, and consulting reviews of the literature (e.g., Edwards, 1991; Kristof, 1996; Kristof-Brown et al., 2005). In addition, we made several decisions regarding inclusion as we encountered particular articles. For example, we included articles in our review that considered aging or adjustment as implicitly temporal in nature (e.g., French, Rogers, and Cobb, 1974; Kristof-Brown *et al.*, 2002), but excluded papers that simply separated the measurement of fit from its outcomes (e.g., Cable and DeRue, 2002; Fricko and Beehr, 1992), as we believe these studies were merely a methodological choice to avoid common method bias rather than an attempt to study temporal fit. In addition, we excluded research examining time as a content dimension of congruence (e.g., preferred polychronicity) because it did not consider the temporal context of current fit, or the process by which fit changes or impacts outcomes over time. For example, research on polychronic fit has demonstrated that various outcomes depend upon the congruence between how much multitasking an individual prefers and how much is supplied by the environment (Bluedorn *et al.*, 1999; Hecht and Allen, 2005; Slocombe and Bluedorn, 1999). Similarly, research on the congruence between an individual's time urgency and that of their work group has demonstrated that satisfaction and helping behaviors are highest when individual and group hurriedness are congruent (Jansen and Kristof-Brown, 2005). With these exclusions in mind, we review the fit literature below using the criteria of context, impact, and process to characterize the state of temporal fit research and determine what remains to be done.

The temporal context of fit

As shown in Figure 9.1, we focus on two primary aspects of the temporal context of fit: *clock time*, defined as any evolution in fit with the actual passage of time (Bluedorn and Denhardt, 1988; McGrath and Rotchford, 1983), and *psychological*

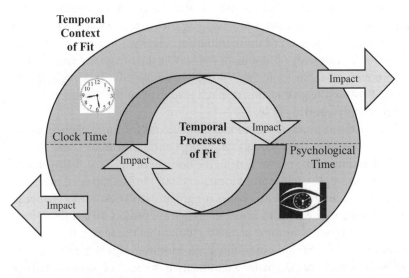

Figure 9.1 The context, processes, and impact of temporal fit

time, defined as the perception of past and future fit in the current moment (Lewin, 1943, 1951; Murray, 1938). Consistent with most western thought, clock time represents the objective and linear passage of time that can be measured (Bluedorn and Denhardt, 1988; McGrath and Rotchford, 1983). Clock time characterizes the present as preceded by the past and followed by the future, such that time flows linearly in one direction. In contrast, psychological time represents a subjective view of relative time that is cognitively accessible at any moment and in which the meaning of a particular experience depends upon the past, present, and future circumstances surrounding it (Rousseau and Fried, 2001). With psychological time, individuals can mentally "time travel" using retrospection and anticipation (George and Jones, 2000; Wheeler *et al.*, 1997).

Clock time. Both the person and the environment are likely to change across clock time, as is the resulting congruence between them. For example, person change can occur as the individual learns, grows, changes priorities, or experiences the atrophy of skills over time (e.g., Brousseau, 1983; Caspi *et al.*, 2005; Feldman and Vogel, 2009; Harrison and Martocchio, 1998; Kahneman, 1999; Smola and Sutton, 2002; Tesluk and Jacobs, 1998; Vaidya *et al.*, 2002). Environment change also occurs as organizations respond to the external environment, shift strategic direction, or experience a change in key leadership or group composition (e.g., Cable and Judge, 1997; Fried *et al.*, 2007; Schneider, 1987a).

Fit research incorporating clock time can be categorized as either implicitly or explicitly temporal. We considered fit research as implicitly addressing clock time if it inherently recognized actual time passing, but was not explicit as to the temporal drivers or influence that time played. For example, age, tenure, and work experience are frequently used as implicit proxies for actual time passing (e.g., Feldman, 2002; Kristof-Brown *et al.*, 2002; Schneider, 1987b). In addition, Ryan and Schmit (1996) developed the Organizational Fit Index, not explicitly to account for the role of time, but as a tool to identify opportunities for changing the person or the environment and to measure the effectiveness of those initiatives. Finally, some fit research has examined whether assessments of fit remain stable over time (e.g., Chatman, 1991; Roberts and Robins, 2004; Taris and Feij, 2001), but we consider this implicit with respect to time because the goal of this research is to explain the validity of the fit concept rather than dynamism per se.

Alternatively, some authors have responded to the call for more explicit incorporation of clock time into their models (cf. George and Jones, 2000), and a more nuanced understanding of the role of time in the domain of fit (Kristof-Brown and Jansen, 2007). For example, DeRue and Morgeson (2007) utilize repeated measures of person–group fit (operationalized as values congruence) to assess actual change in fit from the beginning to the end of a semester-long team project. In a similar study of fit on academic interests, Schmitt *et al.* (2008) found that changes in fit over time led to changes in satisfaction and other outcomes. However, direct measures of fit were used in both of these studies, making it difficult to discern the source of change (i.e., whether the P or E prompted the change). Other articles have incorporated explicit feedback loops over time into their theories of fit (e.g., Ellis and Tsui, 2007; Kammeyer-Mueller, 2007; Ostroff *et al.*, 2002), such as examining how a change in people's interests may lead them to change jobs in search of better person–vocation fit (Ostroff *et al.*, 2002). These feedback loops are rooted in emerging theory about why individuals and environments change (e.g., Caldwell *et al.*, 2004; Ostroff and Schulte, 2007), and how the various aspects of fit may become more or less salient over time (Jansen and Kristof-Brown, 2006).

Psychological time. As stated earlier, psychological time implies that an individual can mentally "time travel" (Wheeler *et al.*, 1997) to experience fit at another point in time by reliving past fit or "pre-living" future fit (Shipp and Jansen, 2011). Interestingly, the vast majority of fit research overlooks the importance of psychological time. Caplan (1983) is one of the few to address the role of psychological time in the fit domain by introducing the concepts of retrospected and anticipated fit, and outlining general predictions about their effects on strain. He highlighted the much neglected dynamic aspects of fit theory, particularly French, Rodgers, and Cobb's (1974) two adjustive techniques: coping, as individuals respond to a change in objective fit, and defense, as individuals subjectively change their perceptions of fit in the absence of objective change. He developed a rather detailed theory incorporating objective and subjective fit at three points in time, temporal comparison effects, and a consideration of change being either person- or environment-initiated. In the only direct empirical test of his theory, Caplan, Tripathi, and Naidu (1985) found independent effects for subjective retrospected, current, and anticipated fit on strain among students preparing for examinations. Based on their obtained results, they speculated that subjectively uncontrollable dimensions of fit are more salient in the past, while subjectively controllable dimensions of fit are more salient in the future. Although these early fit researchers acknowledged the importance of the perceived past and anticipated future, a consideration of psychological time has remained virtually ignored in the developing fit research.

Recently we have argued for a revitalization of fit research relating to psychological time by recognizing that individuals are not "mere creatures of the moment" (Murray, 1938), but instead carry "temporal baggage" (i.e., perceptions of past and future fit) that impacts their current fit experiences (Shipp, 2006; Shipp and Edwards, 2005). As a result, we have further expanded upon these ideas by developing theory to explain how individuals craft fit narratives to help them temporally synthesize and react to their past, present, and future fit experiences (Shipp and Jansen, 2011). In our model depicted in Figure 9.2, individuals craft and recraft stories of fit over psychological time based on perceived changes in the person, changes in the environment, or various individual and situational factors. By explicitly addressing psychological time, this stream of research offers new directions for exploring the concepts of retrospected and anticipated fit, the importance of understanding current fit only as it is embedded within the context of these periods of temporal fit, and the possibility for additional views of fit as an ever-changing story rather than a static snapshot of fit.

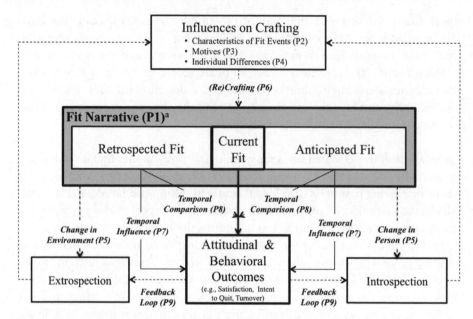

^a Current fit represents the current moment in time, connected by longer periods of retrospection and anticipation.

Figure 9.2   A temporal model of fit narratives

Summary. In terms of context, we found that explicit work on clock time has been the source of most of the recent developments, which primarily appeared within one edited book (e.g., Ellis and Tsui, 2007; Kammeyer-Mueller, 2007; Kristof-Brown and Jansen, 2007). These recent and concurrently published articles provide a unique opportunity to synthesize, cross-fertilize, and expand upon clock time aspects of fit. In addition, we were surprised to find that clock time considerations such as age, tenure, and experience were infrequently measured or specified as important for fit, despite the fact that these temporal variables can be easily used (even implicitly) to address time (Avolio *et al.*, 1990; Tesluk and Jacobs, 1998). Finally, we found the least amount of research on context in psychological time, despite these ideas dating back to the beginning of fit research. Although recent work has been revitalizing the early position that retrospections and anticipations matter (Shipp and Jansen, 2011), more empirical study is needed to determine the degree to which psychological time matters for current fit and outcomes.

The temporal impact of fit on outcomes

The second dimension of temporal fit in our model is represented by the straight arrows in Figure 9.1, in which fit impacts outcomes under the context of clock or psychological time.

Clock time. The upper right arrow represents the impact that fit has on traditional outcomes (e.g., satisfaction, strain, citizenship behavior, turnover) with the actual passage of time. Research in this vein considers how outcomes relate to changes in fit, duration of fit, and the salience of fit. For example, Saks and Ashforth (2002) studied whether pre-entry person–job and person–organization fit continued to influence job attitudes after organizational entry. Cable and Parsons (2001) investigated how socialization led to changes in values before and after organizational entry. In addition, Caplan's (1983) research recognized the important role of duration, an implicit clock time aspect of fit. This research suggested that the longer a fit experience lasts, the stronger its impact on outcomes and the more likely it is that individuals will eventually reach the point where they are no longer willing to tolerate misfit (Caplan, 1983; Kristof-Brown and Jansen, 2007). Finally, in a review of the fit literature by temporal stage, Jansen and Kristof-Brown (2006) noted that fit researchers have primarily examined the impact of fit on outcomes during organizational entry (e.g., recruitment and selection, job choice, socialization) or organizational exit, as shown in Figure 9.3. They developed theory to predict how multiple aspects of fit combine or become salient at various times over the course of an individual's work experience. Edwards and Billsberry (in press) conducted an empirical test of Jansen and Kristof-Brown's (2006) model, but the focus was on the multidimensionality of fit rather than the temporal salience of various dimensions.

Psychological time. The bottom-left arrow in Figure 9.1 highlights the temporal impact of fit within psychological time (i.e., retrospected and anticipated fit) on various outcomes. Shipp and Jansen (2011) highlighted two ways in which retrospected and anticipated fit relate to current attitudinal and behavioral outcomes: temporal influence and temporal comparison. First, *temporal influence* describes how a retrospected or anticipated fit experience influences current outcomes through the vicarious effects of reliving the past or the future (cf. Elster and Loewenstein, 1992; Markman and McMullen, 2003; Tversky and Griffin, 1991). Whether nostalgia, regret, savoring, or dread, the effects of retrospected and anticipated fit are considered vicarious because the individual experiences fit as if it is happening in the current moment. For example, recalling a previous job in which an employee perceived that he had a distinctive set of skills to meet the demands of the job (e.g., positive demands–abilities fit) may continue to influence current outcomes, even without the same degree of current congruence. In this case, the nostalgia of the past continues to be satisfying, above and beyond what the current job offers. Thus, a temporal fit perspective recognizes that fit outside of the current moment may influence current reactions, a point which previous research had not considered.

A second way in which fit over psychological time influences outcomes is by *temporal comparison*, the means by which current fit is contrasted against retrospected or anticipated fit, such that individuals will be better off to the extent that current fit represents an improvement as compared to the recollected past or the anticipated future (Shipp and Jansen, 2011). For example, individuals may be more satisfied with current needs–supplies fit for pay if it represents an increase from past needs–supplies pay fit. However, if an individual has accepted a new job where future pay is more congruent with her needs, current satisfaction may be reduced because current

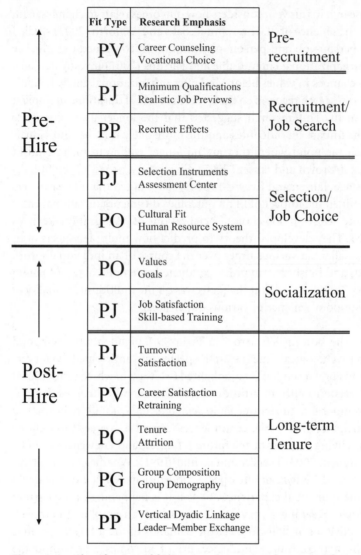

Figure 9.3   Classification of fit literature by temporal stage and fit assessed

fit on pay looks more dismal against the anticipated pay standard (e.g., Loewenstein, 1988). As is evident from our examples, temporal comparison implies that current fit does not lead to current outcomes in a vacuum; rather, current fit is evaluated within the context of retrospected and anticipated fit. Therefore, the outcome of current fit depends upon retrospected and anticipated fit.

Summary.   Considering the impact of temporal fit on outcomes, we identified empirical research that has examined aspects of fit change and duration, and fairly recent theoretical research on salience and temporal comparison and influence processes. We suggest that future research build more theory around the impact of fit change and duration on outcomes in response to recognition that stronger theory in the fit domain is needed (Edwards, 2008). Conversely, the recent theoretical advances in the areas of salience and psychological time require empirical testing to improve our understanding of how these emerging concepts influence outcomes in organizational settings.

The temporal process of fit(ting)[2]

To this point, we have discussed the temporal context and impact of fit in both clock time and psychological time, noting that there has been little fit research that moves beyond a static view of fit (i.e., taking "snapshots" of fit at particular instances in time). In contrast, the consideration of "fitting" processes highlights a dynamic view of fit (i.e., a "movie" of fit over time; Weisbord, 1988) and provides answers to questions about how fit changes. As such, the final dimension of a temporal perspective on fit complements the content research (e.g., Pettigrew, 1992) reviewed in the previous two sections by considering the evolutionary processes by which fit evolves or changes over time (cf., Van de Ven, 1992; Van de Ven and Huber, 1990) and how these processes impact outcomes. By emphasizing the processes of fitting, we are suggesting that there may be a natural evolution or progression of fit over time that may be discernible only by employing a process lens (cf. Poole *et al.*, 2000).

Clock time. As shown in Figure 9.1, these temporal processes can evolve across clock time, psychological time, or a combination of both. As we suggested earlier, some fit research has focused on fit changing over clock time, though only a few of these studies have included theory about how this change occurs. For example, Van Vianen, DePater, Kristof-Brown, and Johnson (2004) examined surface- and deep-level cultural differences in expatriate adjustment. They extended theory originally developed by Harrison, Price, and Bell (1998), who proposed that surface-level (i.e., demographic) differences in groups become less salient with interaction over time, while deep-level (i.e., attitudinal) differences become more salient. Van Vianen, DePater, Kristof-Brown, and Johnson (2004) found that surface-level differences (e.g., cuisine, climate, housing conditions) were related to general adjustment, but that deeper values (universalism and benevolence) were related to interaction and work adjustment. Although neither of these studies specifically examined the temporal evolution of these differences per se, their conceptual arguments highlight important process considerations for fit research: when and how fit matters.

Other fit research has hinted at underlying process explanations for a variety of fit relationships, such as how individuals are selected and socialized into a new organization (e.g., Bretz *et al.*, 1993; Cable and Parsons, 2001; Cooper-Thomas *et al.*, 2004; Rynes and Gerhart, 1990) or respond to organizational changes (e.g., Caldwell *et al.*, 2004). Others have viewed fit as potentially changing through the processes of coping and adaptation in response to misfit, which implicitly identifies clock time through feedback loops. Feedback loops suggest that individuals experience misfit and change the environment, themselves, or their perceptions to restore fit (e.g., Edwards, 1992; French et al., 1974). Additionally, researchers have encouraged us to view fit as an evolving concept, such as Chatman's (1989) conclusion that individuals sometimes change to fit an organization and other times change the organization, and Schneider's work on the Attraction-Selection-Attrition framework, in which people "make" the place (ASA; Schneider, 1987a; Schneider et al., 1995). These studies marked an important departure from a contemporaneous view of fit to one that began to consider how and when fit evolves.

In contrast, ideas about fit processes evolving over clock time have become more explicit in recent years. We believe that two process theories outside of the fit domain, but clearly related to fit, have contributed to an expansion in fit process research. First, the theory of work adjustment (TWA; Dawis and Lofquist, 1984; Dawis et al., 1968) considers the process of mutual adjustment between an individual and their work environment. The TWA can inform the processes by which an individual's fit changes from pre-entry, through socialization, and into long-term tenure. Second, Wrzesniewski and Dutton (2001) introduce the concept of job crafting to describe how individuals take action to shape their jobs in physical, cognitive, and relational ways to reflect their interests and talents and create meaning from their work. This concept highlights the sense-making process inherent in individuals' work lives, and allows for an examination of how individuals construct meaning regarding their fit over time. Combined, these process theories provide a powerful lens for examining similar temporal processes in individuals' experience of fit.

Several recent process approaches within the fit domain have been based upon these process theories. For example, Ostroff, Shin, and Feinberg (2002) applied the TWA to an examination of how early-career individuals achieve career success through repeated efforts to assess and modify person–organization, person–job, and person–occupation fit. Kammeyer-Mueller (2007) examined how newcomers and environments mutually adjust over time based on organizational tactics, individual dispositions, and social interactions. In addition, he proposed several empirical approaches that may be useful for examining adjustment as well as several specific suggestions for exploring fit dynamics. Ellis and Tsui (2007) took a different approach by focusing on demographic homogeneity (i.e., demographic fit), particularly examining the evolutionary process by which individuals and organizations may adapt to each other. They proposed four stages of outcomes (i.e., affective, cognitive, behavioral, survival) as well as adaptive and nonadaptive responses that operate throughout the process. Finally, Ostroff and Schulte (2007) took an even broader view by drawing upon the TWA and the ASA model to build a multilevel model that explains how fit evolves over time based on the principles of composition and compilation. Although these articles represent an important first step in understanding fit processes over time, they also recognize that these ideas "are only the tip of the iceberg in terms of dynamic fit possibilities" (Kammeyer-Mueller, 2007, p. 116).

Psychological time. Other recent research has focused on fit processes in psychological time, such as our theory (Shipp and Jansen, 2011) about how and when individuals craft narratives of fit. In that paper we suggest that when individuals begin their first jobs, they craft initial fit narratives composed of both current fit and anticipated fit. As they gain more experience, they continue to add more fit experiences to their story, selecting those that are more intense (i.e., a high point or a low point), of longer duration, recent, consistent with the overall narrative theme, and embedded in the period of time on which an individual focuses. We further propose that fit narratives are likely to be recrafted when individuals and environments change (particularly if those changes are substantial; i.e., a turning point), and when individuals are open to change, whether dispositionally (e.g., openness to experience or learning goal orientation) or because the fit story is not particularly strong. As we discuss in the next section, these fit narratives lead to attitudinal and behavioral outcomes, which further reinforce changes in fit narratives.

Impact of temporal processes on fit. Just as we reviewed the temporal impact of fit on outcomes, so the temporal processes we just described may also have an impact on fit, both in clock time and in psychological time. However, to date, very little consideration has been given to these ideas. The impact of clock time processes on fit, depicted by the upper curved arrow in Figure 9.1, is addressed in Kristof-Brown and Jansen's (2007) chapter, which details two processes by which one aspect of fit could impact other aspects of fit over time. First, spillover draws on the work-life literature (Rice *et al.*, 1980) to describe how a highly salient aspect of fit (e.g., strong person–group fit) is likely to influence or change less important or discrepant fit assessments over time (e.g., adjusting the perception of low person–job fit to better match strong person–group fit). Second, spirals describe how a high correspondence among fit assessments over time can result in deviation-amplifying spiraling effects (e.g., Fredrickson, 2003; Lindsley *et al.*, 1995), such that good fit gets better and poor fit gets worse. For example, to the extent an individual sees herself as a misfit, she may selectively perceive experiences that contribute to further misfit, which is likely to spiral towards turnover. A similar spiraling process was proposed by Quick, Nelson, Quick, and Orman (2001), who extended theory of person–environment fit and strain by first developing a hypothesis about certain environmental (i.e., decision latitude, uncertainty, social support) and individual factors (i.e., control expectancy, tolerance for ambiguity, self-reliance) likely to lead to increased strain. They then made several corollary predictions about how these factors may dynamically follow a process of mutual accommodation. They outlined several corollaries for upward spirals of accommodation as individuals respond to changes in themselves (i.e., adaptation strategy) or in response to a changing environment (ecological strategy).

   The impact of psychological processes on fit is depicted by the lower curved arrow at the center of Figure 9.1. This idea captures the notion that the way individuals think about the past, present, and future can change their perceptions of fit. For example, because individuals vary in temporal focus (i.e., how much they think about the past, present, and future; Shipp *et al.*, 2009), we have proposed that individuals will pay more attention to periods of fit that are consistent with their temporal focus profile (Shipp and Jansen, 2011). For example, highly past-focused individuals should craft stories of fit that are more heavily weighted with retrospected fit experiences whereas highly future-focused individuals may craft stories of fit that are more heavily weighted with anticipated fit experiences. These individuals frequently live in the past of "the way things were" or they may be constantly scanning the horizon for how future fit will be impacted by job or organization changes. Thus, the fit story one tells depends upon the period(s) of time on which one focuses. In addition, culture is a broad influence on the time periods that individuals consider (e.g., Hofstede and Bond, 2001; McGrath and Tschan, 2004), such as how North Americans tend to be more current focused whereas Chinese individuals tend to be more past focused (e.g., Ji, Guo *et al.*, 2009). In addition, Sekiguchi (2006) provides evidence that human resource practices and national cultures influence different types of fit. For example, in comparing US and Japanese approaches to fit, he observed that individuals in Japan tend to move around within organizations to establish better fit, while Americans tend to move across organizations. Thus, we believe that the temporal focus profile of an individual and the culture in which he or she is embedded can play an important role in determining how individuals respond to a variety of fit experiences over time.

Summary. Recent articles have made important in-roads in understanding fit processes (e.g., Ellis and Tsui, 2007; Kammeyer-Mueller, 2007; Ostroff and Schulte, 2007; Ostroff *et al.*, 2002; Shipp and Jansen, 2011). However, each of these authors also recognizes that much more remains to be done. As Ostroff and Schulte (2007, p. 59) point out, "only in the past 15 years or so have we witnessed a rigorous and consistent exploration of the fit process in organizational domains." We encourage researchers to expand upon this body of research and to draw more specifically on TWA and ASA to incorporate concepts about individual and organizational change/adjustment. Further, a combination of qualitative and quantitative approaches may be beneficial for work on temporal processes of fit in psychological time. By creating more opportunities to test these processual ideas (e.g., spillover and spirals), particularly with rich qualitative data, we stand to gain a deeper understanding of the concept of fit itself.

Implications

Taken as a whole, our review of the literature left us with three conclusions about the state of temporal research on fit. First, temporal initiatives in the fit domain could benefit from developing a more systematic research agenda under each of the three categories we outlined, not only to build upon recent theoretical advancements, but also to conduct much needed empirical studies (both quantitative and qualitative). Second, we noted that the extant research has been applied to a variety of topical areas, although there seemed to be a slight emphasis on research applied to pre- and post-entry socialization. Perhaps this should not be too surprising given that the socialization process is a temporal phenomenon (cf., Ashforth *et al.*, 2007) and one that can be easily examined as new employees join an organization. Yet, we suggest that other topical areas may be ripe for research with temporal fit. For example, another natural context for exploring temporal fit is organizational change efforts, yet this topical domain has only recently been leveraged (cf. Caldwell *et al.*, 2004). Finally, we note that very little temporal research has incorporated two or more of our categories simultaneously (context, process, and impact). This is an issue, given that we see process and impact as subsumed within temporal context. The nature of process or impact differs depending upon whether clock time or psychological time is the overarching context. Because existing research has not examined these three elements in a systematic fashion, it may not have fully considered the importance of concurrently considering process or impact within temporal context. Further, we note here that research that takes a broader and more integrative view of time across the three categories will promote understanding and further development of the role of time in fit research. Therefore, in the next section, we develop more specific suggestions for future research within and across these three categories.

Developing an Agenda for Temporal Fit Research

As reviewed above, the scattered nature of the theoretical and empirical research on temporal issues related to fit highlights a major challenge for fit researchers: the need for improving our understanding of temporal fit context, impact, and processes, while ensuring that this research is relevant and useful for management practice. In this section, we outline specific agendas for advancing temporal fit research in these domains. Our recommendations are more focused than exhaustive, providing a starting place to begin to build a body of theoretical and empirical research. Overall, we believe the time is right to push fit research further into the temporal domain, and to create a community of scholars broadly interested in temporal ideas related to fit.

An agenda for temporal context research

As reviewed above, the temporal context of fit highlights the temporal setting in which fit is either perceived or experienced. As such, research focusing on temporal context can extend existing research by asking two key questions: when fit changes (both in clock time and in psychological time), and when perceptions of past and future fit matter (in psychological time).

When fit changes. Much of the fit literature has emphasized the early stages of person and environment adjustment during organizational entry and socialization processes. However, there are many more opportunities to study naturally occurring P or E change. For example, considering clock time, the actual experience of fit may change after a person attends a training program, experiences a significant life event, or begins the transition to retirement. Similarly, fit may change after large-scale organizational change, job redesign, or a promotion. In addition, when considering psychological time, actual changes in fit may or may not be reflected in people's perceptions, retrospections, and anticipations (Caplan, 1983; Shipp, 2006; Shipp and Jansen, 2011). These questions highlight the importance of understanding the variety of events that trigger fit change, those that do not, and the timing and perception of any change in fit.

When perceptions of past and future fit matter. Because extant fit research only measures current fit, we have not yet specifically delineated a conceptual or empirical distinction between past fit, present fit, and future fit. For example, measuring person–job or person–organization fit prior to entry is actually an assessment of anticipated fit, whereas measuring them post-entry may be an assessment of current fit (perhaps mixed with anticipated fit). Individuals often accept job offers based on the anticipated level of fit along such dimensions as anticipated career opportunities, anticipated demands, and anticipated characteristics of the organization (Harrison, 1978; London, 1983; Schoenfelder and Hantula, 2003). Although these dimensions are currently perceived, their referent is in the future because the individual has not yet joined the company. Thus, extant recruitment and selection research may focus on "current" person–job or person–organization fit leading to job choice, but the appropriate referent is more likely to be anticipated fit.

As another example, using measures of fit that do not specify the time period for a fit experience could capture reports of current fit, but they also may include aspects of retrospected fit: that is, memories of fit at one's current organization or current job. When individuals are asked to report their perceptions of fit, they may retrieve memories of defining moments such as beginnings, endings, peaks, and valleys related to fit (Shipp and Jansen, 2011). These experiences of fit tend to be more vivid and long-lasting cognitions (Pillemer, 2001). They can also be more emotionally charged, and thus more likely to remain in a person's memories (Fredrickson, 2000; Fredrickson and Kahneman, 1993; Holmes, 1970; Kahneman *et al.*, 1993; Lucas, 2007; McAdams, 2001). As a result, rather than reporting perceptions of current fit at a moment in time, individuals may additionally draw upon cognitions of these meaningful moments when deciding how well they fit at the present moment. Thus, a report of the degree of current fit without a specified temporal period may be more appropriately viewed as a mixture of retrospected and current fit perceptions.

An agenda for temporal impact research

The temporal effects or impact of fit on outcomes will be partly and naturally addressed when examining temporal context and temporal process, as researchers will continue to measure important fit outcomes such as satisfaction, strain, and turnover. In this section, we propose more specific research relating to the impact of fit on outcomes in both clock time and psychological time.

Clock time effects of fit on outcomes. We recommend that researchers adopt a more holistic view of fit across time and stages of employment to better learn when fit is particularly salient (e.g., Jansen and Kristof-Brown, 2006) and/or more influential on outcomes. For example, it could be that fit is only salient when something significant has changed either in the person or in the work environment. When business is as usual, it is possible that fit is not salient at all. Research on job embeddedness (cf. Mitchell *et al.*, 2001) may be a useful lens to apply to a consideration of when fit matters in predicting outcomes such as turnover. The embeddedness research demonstrates how fit has an impact upon turnover by making it harder to leave an organization or a community, but when fit would be most salient in the course of events has not been explored.

A contextual factor that may influence when fit becomes salient is the historical or temporal context of the study: that is, the setting and current events surrounding a piece of research (Rousseau and Fried, 2001), such as the economic environment. We propose that the economy may be both a boundary condition and a meaningful influence of fit perceptions on outcomes in three respects. First, one or more types of fit may be less salient when alternative jobs are unavailable (Jansen and Kristof-Brown, 2006) because one's current job may be the best (or only) option in a poor economy (Fricko and Beehr, 1992). For example, when receiving a paycheck is of utmost importance (e.g., needs–supplies fit), other types of fit may be compromised (e.g., value congruence or demands–abilities fit). Thus, the economy may change the effect of fit on outcomes such that certain types of fit matter more when the economic environment is stronger and less when the economic environment is weaker. Second, individuals typically no longer expect long-term employment at a single firm due to changes in employment relationships (Baker, 2009; Leana, 2002) and the increasing use of contingent employment (Rousseau, 1997). As a result, the importance of person–organization fit may be less of a priority than getting the right "stepping stones" over time. Finally, because younger individuals expect more jobs in their careers and tend to focus more on the present moment than the past or future (Zimbardo and Boyd, 1999), they may consider fit in a different way than older, more traditionally career-focused individuals. Given that the current labor market is the only one young employees have known, fit researchers need to be prepared to adapt their research to a different meaning of fit (Chao and Gardner, 2008) with potentially different implications for turnover intentions or satisfaction.

Psychological time effects of fit on outcomes. We believe that the timing of P or E change may influence how strongly perceptions of retrospected and anticipated fit impact current outcomes. For example, retrospected fit may be more important immediately after an organizational change as individuals initiate natural comparisons between past and current fit. In fact, Talbot and Billsberry (2010) found that perceived misfit is most often triggered by a change in the organization. However, anticipated fit may be important before the change (e.g., What can I expect?) as individuals naturally consider future experiences to some degree. In addition, an individual's tendency to focus on a particular time period (i.e., temporal focus) may play an important role when forming or changing perceptions of fit. Generally speaking, we have more to learn about when past fit or future fit is likely to be more influential on outcomes. In other words, time may play a role as a moderator of the relationship between fit and outcomes. Clearly, there is no single theory of time, nor any other research stream that is very explicit about the role of time as a moderator (Mitchell and James, 2001). However, we need more theoretical development on this issue to know exactly when we should capture fit and when we can anticipate impact from good or poor fit.

An agenda for temporal process research

Our final set of recommendations for future research focuses on temporal processes of fitting in terms of how fit evolves over time, as well as the mechanisms by which these processes influence subsequent fit or outcomes. In this section, we propose research agendas for both clock time and psychological time processes of fit by considering three "how" questions: how long fit endures, how fit progresses, and how fit changes.

How long (mis)fit endures. A process perspective raises theoretical and empirical considerations regarding the duration of fit experiences. Kristof-Brown and Jansen (2007) highlighted several research questions for which a process perspective is well suited. For example, how long will an individual or organization tolerate misfit before a change is made? Further research is needed to examine the timing of coping and defense processes in response to misfit (French *et al.*, 1974), such as when these processes are initiated and when one predominates over the other (e.g., changing the actual environment versus changing perceptions to alleviate pain). In addition, even though research has recognized that misfit may not be defended against or coped with in some circumstances (e.g., Kristof, 1996; Schneider, 1987a), more research is needed that examines when (and for how long) misfit provides a valuable opportunity to innovate and learn (e.g., wild ducks; Billsberry, 2009; Geber, 1990). Research findings also suggest that individuals who switch jobs frequently versus those who remain with one organization for a long time may differentially experience fit (Kristof-Brown *et al.*, 2002), so it is conceivable that these different paths may influence an individual's tolerance of misfit. As a result, it is possible that long-enduring fit experiences have differential impact on outcomes if experienced early versus later in one's career. In addition, recent research provides evidence that other variables, in this case job mobility, are likely to play a role in predicting the relationship between misfit and turnover (Wheeler *et al.*, 2007). By considering questions such as these, we can shed light on the process by which individuals choose to remain in or leave poorly fitting work situations (e.g., Schneider, 1987a).

How fit progresses. Given the broader changes in the employment context (e.g., Leana, 2002; Rousseau, 1997) and the realization that individuals adapt their skills and abilities in response to these shifting circumstances (e.g., Agnew *et al.*, 1997; Hill and Elias, 2006), it becomes important to examine how P change, E change, or fit change occurs, and how these progressions influence outcomes. For example, we encourage attention to be paid to the circumstances under which P change is characterized as gradual and moving forward, as opposed to punctuated, cyclical, or staged. Building upon the work done in the socialization literature (e.g., Louis, 1980), there may be common progressions or cycles in work situations (i.e., E change) that could potentially affect fit, such as adjusting to new leadership or transitioning to retirement.

In the shorter time horizon, there may also be different rhythms to an individual's experience of his job (e.g., does an accountant perceive fit differently during tax season than at other times?). For example, there may be rhythms to the day, week, or month in which people report different levels of fit (e.g., perhaps perceiving worse fit on Mondays, but better fit around the end of the day, around pay time, or around holidays). Methodological approaches such as case studies, qualitative methods, or experience sampling methodology (ESM)[3] may enable us to examine these progressions. For example, ESM may find that fit derives from daily rhythms of workload and strain (cf., Fuller *et al.*, 2003; Ilies *et al.*, 2010), which would have implications for how people perceive fit on a more day-to-day basis. In examining individual character using a "lived day" approach (Craik, 1991), it became apparent that ordinary conduct in a typical day is less than noteworthy and therefore may be overlooked when individuals assess their work. Craik (1993) points out that there is value to be gained from attending to these routine versus nonroutine events. From a fit perspective, this may help us to understand when and how often individuals actually consider fit as they navigate their daily work environments.

Finally, we can consider progressions of fit over time. One way to study these would be to build upon the narrative idea presented in Shipp and Jansen (2011), by tracing common story progressions. Researchers have proposed a variety of such story progressions, including redemption (i.e., a story that starts poorly but improves over time), contamination (i.e., a story that worsens over time), and tragedy (i.e., a story that is consistently poor) (Gergen and Gergen, 2004; McAdams, 1993). For example, employees may prefer stories of redemption, in which fit improves over time, because they expect this upward trajectory of employment (Fried *et al.*, 2007; Shipp and Jansen, 2011). Such an investigation may shed light on common themes people use to construct their evolving stories of fit.

How fit changes. A third area for process research is to study how fit changes. For example, one line of research can consider whether certain types of fit are more susceptible to the passage of time than others. We surmise that needs–supplies fit may change more frequently than demands–abilities fit or values congruence. Given that needs reflect preferences or desires (French, Rodgers, and Cobb, 1974), needs may change simply because a person changes his or her mind. In contrast, abilities may require training or attrition to invoke changes (Harrison and Martocchio, 1998; Tesluk and Jacobs, 1998). Values may require even longer to change given that they are relatively stable (Rokeach and Ball-Rokeach, 1989) but may change as individuals age (e.g., Smola and Sutton, 2002), experience organizational socialization (e.g., Hazer and Alvares, 1981), or experience major life events such as the terrorist attacks on September 11th (e.g., Verkasalo *et al.*, 2006). Other dimensions of fit may be even more temporally independent, such as vocational fit, which can endure despite job or organizational changes.

In terms of psychological changes in fit, we propose that certain aspects of fit could be more prone to temporal influence effects versus temporal comparison effects. For example, person–job fit is often focused on progression over time (e.g., improvement in abilities over time relative to demands, or increasing pay over time relative to increasing needs). Thus, people may naturally compare present fit to past fit. As such, person–job fit may demonstrate temporal comparison effects more frequently than person–organization fit, which may highlight temporal influence due to the nostalgia of past values congruence or the hope of future values congruence. Finally, a qualitative lens can be employed to shed light on the process by which individuals psychologically craft and utilize fit narratives. For example, Lovelace and Rosen (1996) employed a critical incident technique to reveal that individuals consider different incidents when they appreciate fit than when they question it. A similar approach can be used to understand the process by which narratives are constructed and reconstructed over time.

An agenda for practice: What is fit and when does it matter?

It may seem rather late in the timeline of fit research to consider the question, "What is fit?" However, we believe there is knowledge to gain about how employees conceptualize and understand fit in practice and over time. Therefore, we recommend that researchers observe patterns in how fit ebbs and flows in actual experience (e.g., as a theory-in-use) rather than how it might be touted to be in theory (e.g., espoused theory) (Argyris and Schon, 1974). Further, we may consider that fit may not mean the same thing for employees and managers. This can be the case during recruitment as recruiting managers and potential employees may refer to different aspects of fit (e.g., person–job fit versus person–organization fit). What we do not know is what happens to that understanding and practice over time. As time passes, some employees may think more about misfit and others about fit. The narrative perspective pushes us in this direction, but more can be done to understand how managers can leverage fit narratives. For example, individuals may respond differently to managers helping them recraft their stories by painting a particular picture of future fit (akin to a realistic job preview) or introducing an enlarged conceptualization of fit (akin to job enlargement). These approaches may be considered helpful or they may be considered downright manipulative by employees. Future research into individual or cultural differences that may lead people with particular characteristics to approach fit differently over time is warranted.

The second important practical question is: when does fit matter? For example, during secondary or post-secondary education, person–vocation fit may be most salient to individuals because they are contemplating careers. After graduation, person–job and person–organization fit may matter for both organizational entry and exit. Although some preliminary theoretical work has been done to address the question of when fit matters (Jansen and Kristof-Brown, 2006), we know less about whether there is some implied order to or temporal dependencies among different types of fit. For continued employment in an organization, person–job, person–group, and person–supervisor fit may be the strongest predictors of outcomes as these day-to-day experiences are the most salient experiences. However, we know very little about how these types of fit interact over time. For example, socioemotional selectivity theory (Carstensen, 2006; Carstensen *et al.*, 1999) suggests that as individuals approach endings (e.g., graduation, job transfer, retirement), they move closer to social interactions and away from novel or developmental experiences. So during periods of endings (e.g., changing jobs, retirements, closing offices), person–group and person–supervisor fit may matter more than person–job or person–organization fit.

These questions have important implications for managers. For example, aspects of fit with one's job and one's manager are strong drivers of the decision to stay or quit, as evidenced by a recent Gallup survey (Robinson, 2008). Thus, to maximize recruiting and retention of the right individuals, managers may want to focus on progressions in person–job or person–supervisor fit over time rather than person–organization fit. For example, because employees are more likely to quit their supervisors than their organizations (Robinson, 2008), managers could focus their attention more on improving person–supervisor fit than person–organization fit in order to reduce unwanted turnover.

In addition, in terms of psychological time, there may be times when past fit and future fit are more or less influential. Although we suggested above that retrospected and anticipated fit have the potential to influence current outcomes, there may be times when only past or future "E" matters (e.g., what supplies were or will be received, or what demands were or will be made) rather than past or future fit. For example, individuals with low private self-consciousness (i.e., individuals who engage in self-reflection and insight infrequently; Grant *et al.*, 2002) may be less aware of their past needs and future needs and instead focus on what they actually received or experienced in the environment. As a result, "fit" at other points in time may not matter because the person standard of comparison against which the past or future environment is compared no longer exists to these individuals. Instead, what is relevant to current well-being is only the level of environment the individual retrospects or anticipates (cf., Cable and Edwards 2004; Edwards and Harrison, 1993; Edwards and Rothbard, 1999).

Conclusion

Just a few years ago, Kristof-Brown and Jansen (2007) acknowledged that temporal fit research was still in its infancy, even though the founding concepts date back to the pioneers of PE fit research (Lewin, 1943; Murray, 1938). In reviewing the fit literature for this chapter, our goal was to recognize that there is a small but growing body of temporal research that has begun to incorporate time and PE fit at some level, albeit not yet in a systematic way. Therefore, as our research agenda suggests, there are many challenging and intriguing questions that remain both conceptually and empirically. By providing a review of what has been done and outlining what remains to be done, we hope that research on temporal fit will continue to grow and provide us greater insight into the temporal issues surrounding fit.

Notes

1. For a more in-depth consideration of levels, as well as fit across levels, see Ostroff and Schulte (2007).
2. See Jansen and Kristof-Brown (2002), which plays off of Weick's (1979) purposeful use of the term "organizing" to refute Katz and Kahn's (1966) use of the term "organization" as an explicit means of highlighting process rather than a static end state.
3. Experience sampling methodology is an approach to data collection that repeatedly captures individuals' reactions at a moment in time (Larson and Csikszentmihalyi, 1983; Stone and Shiffman, 1994), such as random measurements throughout a work day or over the course of a week. This approach focuses on repeated measures on a frequent basis to highlight the importance of real-time, within-person cognitions and behaviors.

References

Agnew, A., Forrester, P., Hassard, J., and Procter, S. (1997) Deskilling and reskilling within the labour process: The case of computer integrated manufacturing. *International Journal of Production Economics*, 52 (3), 317–324.

Ancona, D. G., Okhuysen, G. A., and Perlow, L. A. (2001) Taking time to integrate temporal research. *Academy of Management Review*, 26 (4), 512–529.

Argyris, C., and Schon, D. (1974) *Theory in Practice*. San Francisco: Jossey-Bass.

Ashforth, B. E., Sluss, D. M., and Harrison, S. H. (2007) Socialization in organizational contexts. In G. P. Hodgkinson and J. K. Ford (eds), *International Review of Industrial and Organizational Psychology* (Vol. 22, pp. 1–70). Chichester: John Wiley & Sons, Ltd.

Avolio, B. J., Waldman, D. A., and McDaniel, M. A., (1990) Age and work performance in nonmanagerial jobs: The effects of experience and occupational type. *Academy of Management Journal*, 33 (2), 407–422.

Baker, T. B. (2009) Towards a new employment relationship model: Aligning the changing needs of individual and organization. *Leadership and Organization Development Journal*, 30 (3), 197–223.

Billsberry, J. (2009) Fit as wellness, misfit as illness. Paper presented at the Academy of Management annual meeting, Chicago, IL.

Bluedorn, A. C. (2002) *The Human Organization of Time: Temporal Realities and Experience.* Stanford, CA: Stanford Business Books.

Bluedorn, A. C., and Denhardt, R. B. (1988) Time and organizations. *Journal of Management,* 14 (2), 299–320.

Bluedorn, A. C., Kalliath, T. J., Strube, M. J., and Martin, G. D. (1999) Polychronicity and the Inventory of Polychronic Values (IPV): The development of an instrument to measure a fundamental dimension of organizational culture. *Journal of Managerial Psychology,* 14 (3), 205–230.

Bretz, R. D., Jr, Rynes, S. L., and Gerhart, B. (1993) Recruiter perceptions of applicant fit: Implications for individual career preparation and job search behavior. *Journal of Vocational Behavior,* 43, 310–327.

Brousseau, K. R. (1983) Toward a dynamic model of job–person relationships: Findings, research questions, and implications for work system design. *Academy of Management Review,* 8, 33–45.

Cable, D. M., and DeRue, D. S. (2002) The convergent and discriminant validity of subjective fit perceptions. *Journal of Applied Psychology,* 87 (5), 875–884.

Cable, D. M., and Edwards, J. R. (2004) Complementary and supplementary fit: A theoretical and empirical integration. *Journal of Applied Psychology,* 89, 822–834.

Cable, D. M., and Judge, T. A. (1997) Interviewers' perceptions of person–organization fit and organizational selection decisions. *Journal of Applied Psychology,* 82 (4), 546–561.

Cable, D. and Parsons, C. (2001) Socialization tactics and person–organization fit. *Personnel Psychology,* 54, 1–23.

Caldwell, S. D., Herold, D. M., and Fedor, D. B. (2004) Toward an understanding of the relationships among organizational change, individual differences, and changes in person–environment fit: A cross-level study. *Journal of Applied Psychology,* 89 (5), 868–882.

Caplan, R. D. (1983) Person–environment fit: Past, present, and future. In C. L. Cooper (ed.), *Stress Research* (pp. 35–78). New York: John Wiley & Sons, Inc.

Caplan, R. D., Tripathi, R. C., and Naidu, R. K. (1985) Subjective past, present, and future fit: Effects on anxiety, depression and other indicators of well-being. *Journal of Personality and Social Psychology,* 48 (1), 180–197.

Carstensen, L. L. (2006) The influence of a sense of time on human development. *Science,* 312, 1913–1915.

Carstensen, L. L., Isaacowitz, D. M., and Charles, S. T. (1999) Taking time seriously: A theory of socioemotional selectivity. *American Psychologist,* 54 (3), 165–181.

Caspi, A., Roberts, B. W., and Shiner, R. L. (2005) Personality development: Stability and change. *Annual Review of Psychology,* 56, 453–484.

Chao, G. T., and Gardner, P. D. (2008) Young adults at work: What they want, what they get, and how to keep them. White paper prepared for Monster.com.

Chatman, J. A. (1989) Improving interactional organizational research: A model of person–organization fit. *Academy of Management Review,* 14 (3), 333–349.

Chatman, J. A. (1991) Matching people and organizations: Selection and socialization in public accounting firms. *Administrative Science Quarterly,* 36 (3), 459–484.

Cooper-Thomas, H. D., Van Vianen, A., and Anderson, N. (2004) Changes in person–organization fit: The impact of socialization tactics on perceived and actual P–O fit. *European Journal of Work and Organizational Psychology,* 13, 52–78.

Craik, K. H. (1991) The lived day of an individual: A person environment perspective. Invited address to the Division of Population and Environmental Psychology at the annual meeting of the American Psychological Association, San Francisco.

Craik, K. H. (1993) Accentuated, revealed, and quotidian personalities. *Psychological Inquiry*, 4 (4), 278–281.

Dawis, R. V., and Lofquist, L. H. (1984) *A Psychological Theory of Work Adjustment*. Minneapolis: University of Minnesota Press.

Dawis, R. V., Lofquist, L. H., and Weiss, D. J. (1968) A theory of work adjustment (revision). *Minnesota Studies in Vocational Rehabilitation* (No. XXIII, 1–14). Minneapolis: University of Minnesota, Industrial Relations Center.

DeRue, D. S., and Morgeson, F. P. (2007) Stability and change in person–team and person–role fit over time: The effects of growth satisfaction, performance, and self-efficacy. *Journal of Applied Psychology*, 92, 1242–1253.

Edwards, J. A., and Billsberry, J. (in press) Testing a multidimensional theory of person–environment fit. *Journal of Managerial Issues*.

Edwards, J. R. (1991) Person–job fit: A conceptual integration, literature review, and methodological critique. In C. L. Cooper and I. T. Robertson (eds), *International Review of Industrial and Organizational Psychology* (Vol. 6, pp. 283–357). Chichester: John Wiley and Sons, Ltd.

Edwards, J. R. (1992) A cybernetic theory of stress, coping, and well-being in organizations. *Academy of Management Review*, 17 (2), 238–274.

Edwards, J. R. (2008) Theories of person–environment fit: An assessment of theoretical progress. *Academy of Management Annals*, 2, 167–230.

Edwards, J. R., and Harrison, R. V. (1993) Job demands and worker health: Three-dimensional reexamination of the relationship between person–environment fit and strain. *Journal of Applied Psychology*, 78 (4), 628–648.

Edwards, J. R. and Rothbard, N. P. (1999) Work and family stress and well-being: An examination of person–environment fit in the work and family domains. *Organizational Behavior and Human Decision Processes*, 77, 85–129.

Ellis, A. D. and Tsui, A. S. (2007) Survival of the fittest or the least fit? When psychology meets ecology in organizational demography. In C. Ostroff and T. A. Judge (eds), *Perspectives on Organizational Fit* (pp. 287–351). Mahwah, NJ: Lawrence Erlbaum.

Elster, J. and Loewenstein, G. (1992) Utility from memory and anticipation. In J. Elster and G. Loewenstein (eds), *Choice over Time.* (pp. 213–234). New York: Russell Sage Foundation.

Feldman, D. C. (2002) Stability in the midst of change: A developmental perspective on the study of careers. In D. C. Feldman (ed.), *Work Careers: A Developmental Perspective* (pp. 3–26). San Francisco: Jossey-Bass.

Feldman, D. C., and Vogel, R. M. (2009) The aging process and person–environment fit. In S. G. Baugh and S. E. Sullivan (eds), *Maintaining Focus, Energy, and Options over the Career* (pp. 1–27). Charlotte, NC: Information Age Publishing.

Fredrickson, B. L. (2000) Extracting meaning from past affective experiences: The importance of peaks, ends, and specific emotions. *Cognition and Emotion*, 14 (4), 577–606.

Fredrickson, B. L. (2003) Positive emotions and upward spirals in organizations. In K. S. Cameron, J. E. Dutton, and R. E. Quinn (eds), *Positive Organizational Scholarship: Foundations of a New Discipline*. San Francisco: Berrett-Koehler.

Fredrickson, B. L., and Kahneman, D. (1993) Duration neglect in retrospective evaluations of affective episodes. *Journal of Personality and Social Psychology*, 65 (1), 45–55.

French, J. R. P., Jr, Rodgers, W., and Cobb, S. (1974) Adjustment as person–environment fit. In G. Coelho, D. Hamburg and J. Adams (eds), *Coping and Adaptation* (pp. 316–333). New York: Basic Books.

Fricko, M. A., and Beehr, T. A. (1992) A longitudinal investigation of interest congruence and gender concentration as predictors of job satisfaction. *Personnel Psychology*, 45 (1), 99–117.

Fried, Y., Grant, A. M., Levi, A. S., Hadani, M., and Slowik, L. H. (2007) Job design in temporal context: A career dynamics perspective. *Journal of Organizational Behavior*, 28, 911–927.

Fuller, J. A., Stanton, J. M., Fisher, G. G., Spitzmuller, C., Russell, S. S., and Smith, P. C. (2003) A lengthy look at the daily grind: Time series analysis of events, mood, stress, and satisfaction. *Journal of Applied Psychology*, 88 (6), 1019–1033.

Geber, B. (1990) How to manage wild ducks. *Training*, 27 (5), 29–36.

George, J. M., and Jones, G. R. (2000) The role of time in theory and theory building. *Journal of Management*, 26 (4), 657–684.

Gergen, K. J., and Gergen, M. M. (2004) Narratives of the self. In L. P. Hinchman and S. K. Hinchman (eds), *Memory, Identity, Community: The Idea of Narrative in the Human Sciences* (pp. 161–184). New York: State University of New York Press.

Grant, A. M., Franklin, J., and Langford, P. (2002) The self-reflection and insight scale: A new measure of private self-consciousness. *Social Behavior and Personality*, 30 (8), 821–835.

Harrison, D. A., and Martocchio, J. J. (1998) Time for absenteeism: A 20-year review of origins, offshoots, and outcomes. *Journal of Management*, 24 (3), 305–350.

Harrison, D. A., Price, K. H., and Bell, M. P. (1998) Beyond relational demography: Time and the effects of surface- and deep-level diversity on work group cohesion. *Academy of Management Journal*, 41 (1), 96–107.

Harrison, R. V. (1978) Person–environment fit and job stress. In C. L. Cooper and R. Payne, *Stress at Work* (pp. 175–205). New York: John Wiley & Sons, Inc.

Hazer, J. T., and Alvares, K. M. (1981) Police work values during organizational entry and assimilation. *Journal of Applied Psychology*, 66 (1), 12–18.

Hecht, T. D., and Allen, N. J. (2005) Exploring links between polychronicity and well-being from the perspective of person–job fit: Does it matter if you prefer to do only one thing at a time? *Organizational Behavior and Human Decision Processes*, 98, 155–178.

Hill, L. A., and Elias, J. (2006) Retraining midcareer managers: Career history and self-efficacy beliefs. *Human Resource Management*, 29 (2), 197–217.

Hofstede, G., and Bond, M. H. (2001) The Confucius connection: From cultural roots to economic growth. *Organizational Dynamics*, 16 (4), 5–21.

Holmes, D. S. (1970) Differential change in affective intensity and the forgetting of unpleasant personal experiences. *Journal of Personality and Social Psychology*, 15 (3), 234–239.

Ilies, R., Dimotakis, N., and De Pater, I. E. (2010) Psychological and physiological reactions to high workloads: Implications for well-being. *Personnel Psychology*, 63 (2), 407–436.

Jansen, K. J., and Kristof-Brown, A. L. (2002) Beyond "fit happens": A temporal theory of fitting at work. Symposium presented at the Academy of Management annual meeting, Denver, CO.

Jansen, K. J., and Kristof-Brown, A. L. (2005) Marching to the beat of a different drummer: Examining the impact of pacing congruence. *Organizational Behavior and Human Decision Processes*, 96, 93–105.

Jansen, K. J., and Kristof-Brown, A. (2006) Toward a multidimensional theory of person–environment fit. *Journal of Managerial Issues*, 18 (2), 193–212.

Ji, L. J., Guo, T., Zhang, Z., and Messervey, D. (2009) Looking into the past: Cultural differences in perception and representation of past information. *Journal of Personality and Social Psychology*, 96 (4), 761–769.

Johns, G. (2006) The essential impact of context on organizational behavior. *Academy of Management Review*, 31 (2), 386–408.

Kahneman, D. (1999) Objective happiness. In D. Kahneman, E. Diener, and N. Schwarz (eds), *Well-being: The Foundations of Hedonic Psychology* (pp. 3–25). New York: Russell Sage Foundation.

Kahneman, D., Fredrickson, B. L., Schreiber, C. A., and Redelmeier, D. A. (1993) When more pain is preferred to less: Adding a better end. *Psychological Science*, 4, 401–405.

Kammeyer-Mueller, J. D. (2007) The dynamics of newcomer adjustment: Dispositions, context, interaction, and fit. In C. Ostroff and T. A. Judge (eds), *Perspectives on Organizational Fit*, SIOP Organizational Frontiers Series (pp. 99–122). Mahwah, NJ: Lawrence Erlbaum.

Katz, D., and Kahn, R. L. (1966) *The Social Psychology of Organizations.* New York: John Wiley & Sons, Inc.

Kozlowski, S. W. J. (2009) Editorial. *Journal of Applied Psychology*, 94 (1), 1–4.

Kristof, A. L. (1996) Person–organization fit: An integrative review of its conceptualizations, measurement, and implications. *Personnel Psychology*, 49 (1), 1–49.

Kristof-Brown, A. L., and Jansen, K. J. (2007) Issues of person–organization fit. In C. Ostroff and T. Judge (eds), *Perspectives on Organizational Fit*, SIOP Organizational Frontiers Series (pp. 123–153). Mahwah, NJ: Lawrence Erlbaum.

Kristof-Brown, A. L., Jansen, K. J., and Colbert, A. (2002) A policy-capturing study of the simultaneous effects of fit with jobs, groups, and organizations, *Journal of Applied Psychology*, 87 (5), 985–993.

Kristof-Brown, A. L., Zimmerman, R. D., and Johnson, E. C. (2005) Consequences of individuals' fit at work: A meta-analysis of person–job, person–organization, person–group, and person–supervisor fit. *Personnel Psychology*, 58 (2), 281–342.

Larson, R., and Csikszentmihalyi, M. (1983) The experience sampling method. *New Directions for Methodology of Social and Behavioral Science*, 15, 41–56.

Leana, C. R. (2002) The changing organizational context of careers. In D. C. Feldman (ed.), *Work Careers: A Developmental Perspective.* New York: John Wiley & Sons, Inc.

Lewin, K. (1943) Defining the "field at a given time." *Psychological Review*, 50, 292–310.

Lewin, K. (1951) *Field Theory in Social Science: Selected Theoretical Papers.* Westport, CT: Greenwood Press.

Lindsley, D. H., Brass, D. J., and Thomas, J. B. (1995) Efficacy–performance spirals: A multilevel perspective. *Academy of Management Review*, 20 (3), 645–678.

Loewenstein, G. F. (1988) Frames of mind in intertemporal choice. *Management Science*, 34 (2), 200–214.

London, M. (1983) Toward a theory of career motivation. *Academy of Management Review*, 8, 620–630.

Louis, M. R. (1980) Surprise and sensemaking: What newcomers experience in entering unfamiliar organizational settings. *Administrative Science Quarterly*, 25, 226–251.

Lovelace, K., and Rosen, B. (1996) Differences in achieving person–organization fit among diverse groups of managers. *Journal of Management*, 22, 703–722.

Lucas, R. E. (2007) Adaptation and the set-point model of subjective well-being: Does happiness change after major life events? *Current Directions in Psychological Science*, 16 (2), 75–79.

Markman, K. D., and McMullen, M. N. (2003) A reflection and evaluation model of comparative thinking. *Personality and Social Psychology Review*, 7 (3), 244–267.

McAdams, D. P. (1993) *Personal Myths and the Making of the Self.* New York: Guilford Press.

McAdams, D. P. (2001) The psychology of life stories. *Review of General Psychology*, 5, 100–122.

McGrath, J. E., and Rotchford, N. L. (1983) Time and behavior in organizations. *Research in Organizational Behavior*, 5, 57–101.

McGrath, J. E., and Tschan, F. (2004) Time and the research process. In J. E. McGrath and F. Tschan (eds), *Temporal Matters in Social Psychology: Examining the Role of Time in the Lives of Groups and Individuals* (pp. 141–154). Washington, DC: American Psychological Association.

Mitchell, T. R., and James, L. R. (2001) Building better theory: Time and the specification of when things happen. *Academy of Management Review*, 26 (4), 530–547.

Mitchell, T. R., Holtom, B. C., Lee, T. W., Sablynski, C. J., and Erez, M. (2001) Why people stay: Using job embeddedness to predict voluntary turnover. *Academy of Management Journal*, 44 (6), 1102–1121.

Muchinsky, P. M., and Monahan, C. J. (1987) What is person–environment congruence? Supplementary versus complementary models of fit. *Journal of Vocational Behavior*, 31, 268–277.

Murray, H. A. (1938) *Explorations in Personality: A Clinical and Experimental Study of Fifty Men of College Age.* New York: Oxford University Press.

Ostroff, C., and Schulte, M. (2007) Multiple perspectives of fit across levels of analysis. In C. Ostroff and T. Judge (eds), *Perspectives on Organizational Fit*, SIOP Organizational Frontiers Series (pp. 3–69). Mahwah, NJ: Lawrence Erlbaum.

Ostroff, C., Shin, Y., and Feinberg, B, (2002) Skill acquisition and person–occupation fit. In D. Feldman (ed.), *Work Careers: A Developmental Perspective* (pp. 63–92). San Francisco: Jossey-Bass.

Pettigrew, A. M., (1992) The character and significance of strategy process research. *Strategic Management Journal*, 13, 5–16.

Pillemer, D. B. (2001) Momentous events and the life story. *Review of General Psychology*, 5 (2), 123–134.

Poole, M. S., Van de Ven, A. H., Dooley, K., and Holmes, M. E. (2000) *Organizational Change and Innovation Processes.* New York: Oxford University Press.

Quick, J. C., Nelson, D. L., Quick, J. D., and Orman, D. K. (2001) An isomorphic theory of stress: The dynamics of person–environment fit. *Stress and Health*, 17, 147–157.

Rice, R. W., Near, J. P., and Hunt, R. G. (1980) The job satisfaction/life satisfaction relationship: A review of empirical research. *Basic and Applied Social Psychology*, 1, 37–64.

Roberts, B. W., and Robins, R. W. (2004) Person–environment fit and its implications for personality development: A longitudinal study. *Journal of Personality*, 72 (1), 89–110.

Robinson, J. (2008) Turning around employee turnover. *Gallup Management Journal*, May 8. Accessed June 8, 2010, http://gmj.gallup.com/content/106912/.

Rokeach, M., and Ball-Rokeach, S. J. (1989) Stability and change in American value priorities, 1968–1981. *American Psychologist*, 44 (5), 775–784.

Rousseau, D. M. (1997) Organizational behavior in the new organizational era. *Annual Review of Psychology*, 48, 515–546.

Rousseau, D. M., and Fried, Y. (2001) Location, location, location: Contextualizing organizational research. *Journal of Organizational Behavior*, 22, 1–13.

Ryan, A. M., and Schmit, M. J. (1996) An assessment of organizational climate and P–E fit: A tool for organizational change. *International Journal of Organizational Analysis*, 4 (1), 75–95.

Rynes, S., and Gerhart, B. (1990) Interviewer assessments of applicant "fit": An exploratory investigation. *Personnel Psychology*, 43 (1), 13–35.

Saks, A. M., and Ashforth, B. E. (2002) Is job search related to employment quality? It all depends on the fit. *Journal of Applied Psychology*, 87 (4), 646–654.

Schmitt, N., Oswald, F. L., Friede, A., Imus, A., and Merritt, S. (2008) Perceived fit with an academic environment: Attitudinal and behavioral outcomes. *Journal of Vocational Behavior*, 72, 317–335.

Schneider, B. (1987a) The people make the place. *Personnel Psychology*, 40, 437–453.

Schneider, B. (1987b) E = f (P, B): The road to a radical approach to person–environment fit. *Journal of Vocational Behavior*, 31, 353–361.

Schneider, B., Goldstein, H., and Smith, D. B. (1995) The ASA framework: An update. *Personnel Psychology*, 48, 747–773.

Schoenfelder, T. E., and Hantula, D. A. (2003) A job with a future? Delay discounting, magnitude effects, and domain independence of utility for career decisions. *Journal of Vocational Behavior*, 62, 43–55.

Sekiguchi, T. (2006) How organizations promote person–environment fit: Using the case of Japanese firms to illustrate institutional and cultural influences. *Asia Pacific Journal of Management*, 23, 47–69.

Shipp, A. J. (2006) The moving window of fit: Extending person–environment fit research with time. Unpublished doctoral dissertation. University of North Carolina.

Shipp, A. J., and Edwards, J. R. (2005) Recollected, current, and anticipated person–environment fit within the present moment. Symposium presented at the Academy of Management annual meeting, Honolulu, HI.

Shipp, A. J., and Jansen, K. J. (2011) Reinterpreting time in fit theory: Crafting and recrafting narratives of fit *in medias res*. *Academy of Management Review*, 36(1), 76–101.

Shipp, A. J., Edwards, J. R., and Lambert, L. S. (2009) Conceptualization and measurement of temporal focus: The subjective experience of past, present, and future. *Organizational Behavior and Human Decision Processes*, 110 (1), 1–22.

Slocombe, T. E., and Bluedorn, A. C. (1999) Organizational behavior implications of the congruence between preferred polychronicity and experienced work-unit polychronicity. *Journal of Organizational Behavior*, 20, 75–99.

Smola, K. W., and Sutton, C. D. (2002) Generational differences: Revisiting generational work values for the new millennium. *Journal of Organizational Behavior*, 23, 363–382.

Stone, A. A., and Shiffman, S. (1994) Ecological Momentary Assessment (EMA) in behavioral medicine. *Annals of Behavioral Medicine*, 16 (3), 199–202.

Talbot, D., and Billsberry, J. (2010) Empirically distinguishing misfit from fit. Paper presented at the Academy of Management annual meeting, Montreal, Canada.

Taris, R., and Feij, J. A. (2001) Longitudinal examination of the relationship between supplies–values fit and work outcomes. *Applied Psychology: An International Review*, 50, 52–80.

Tesluk, P. E., and Jacobs, R. R. (1998) Toward an integrated model of work experience. *Personnel Psychology*, 51 (2), 321–355.

Tversky, A., and Griffin, D. (1991) Endowment and contrast in judgments of well-being. In F. Strack, M. Argyle, and N. Schwarz (eds), *Subjective Well-being: An Interdisciplinary Perspective. International Series in Experimental Social Psychology* (Vol. 21, pp. 101–118). Elmsford, NY: Pergamon Press.

Vaidya, J. G., Gray, E. K., Haig, J., and Watson, D. (2002) On the temporal stability of personality: Evidence for differential stability and the role of life experiences. *Journal of Personality and Social Psychology*, 83, 1469–1484.

Van de Ven, A. H. (1992) Suggestions for studying strategy process. *Strategic Management Journal*, 13, 169–188.

Van de Ven, A. H., and Huber, G. P. (1990) Longitudinal field research methods for studying processes of organizational change. *Organization Science*, 1 (3), 213–219.

Van Vianen, A. E. M., De Pater, I. E., Kristof-Brown, A. L., and Johnson, E. C. (2004) Fitting in: Surface- and deep-level cultural differences and expatriates' adjustment. *Academy of Management Journal*, 47 (5), 697–709.

Verkasalo, M., Goodwin, R., and Bezmenova, I. (2006) Values following a major terrorist incident: Finnish adolescent and student values before and after September 11, 2001. *Journal of Applied Social Psychology*, 36 (1), 144–160.

Weick, K. E. (1979) *The Social Psychology of Organizing* (3rd edn). Reading, MA: Addison-Wesley.

Weisbord, M. R. (1988) Towards a new practice theory of OD: Notes on snapshooting and moviemaking. In W. Pasmore, and R. W. Woodman (eds), *Research in Organizational Change and Development* (Vol. 2, pp. 59–96). Greenwich, CT: JAI Press.

Wheeler, A. R., Gallagher, V. C., Brouer, R. L., and Sablynski, C. J. (2007) When person–organization (mis)fit and (dis)satisfaction lead to turnover: The moderating role of perceived job mobility. *Journal of Managerial Psychology*, 22 (2), 203–219.

Wheeler, M. A., Stuss, D. T., and Tulving, E. (1997) Toward a theory of episodic memory: The frontal lobes and autonoetic consciousness. *Psychological Bulletin*, 121 (3), 331–354.

Wrzesniewski, A., and Dutton, J. (2001) Crafting a job: Revisioning employees as active crafters of their work. *Academy of Management Review*, 26, 179–201.

Zimbardo, P. G., and Boyd, J. N. (1999) Putting time in perspective: A valid, reliable individual-differences metric. *Journal of Personality and Social Psychology*, 77 (6), 1271–1288.

10

Fitting Person–Environment Fit Theories into a National Cultural Context

Yih-teen Lee
IESE Business School, Barcelona

Aarti Ramaswami
ESSEC Business School, Paris

Practitioners and researchers have long recognized that fit with a job, group, organization, supervisor, and colleagues is crucial to the success of individuals, groups, and organizations (Arthur *et al.*, 2006; Billsberry *et al.*, 2005; Hoffman and Woehr, 2006; Kristof, 1996; Kristof-Brown *et al.*, 2005; Ostroff and Judge, 2007; Verquer *et al.*, 2003). While numerous reviews and meta-analyses have helped us make sense of the person–environment (PE) fit phenomenon, many unresearched areas fortunately still remain. We say "fortunately" because unanswered questions and unexplored topics help invigorate the field, rejuvenate fit researchers, and ultimately energize their efforts. In this chapter we deal with one such unexplored area: an area with potential to expand and take the PE fit literature forward. In particular, we want to look at the role of societal/national cultures in PE fit.

Edwards (2008) notes that PE fit theory lacks adequate consideration of boundary conditions. Boundary conditions refer to "limits beyond which the theory does not apply" (Edwards, 2008, p. 172). In this chapter we explore culture as the boundaries within and beyond which the heretofore known understanding of PE fit, as well as its relationships with certain outcomes, may vary. We would like to state upfront that from here on "culture" in this chapter, unless otherwise specified, refers to societal/national cultures. While we include "national" culture under the broad blanket of "culture," we are mindful of intra-cultural variance within countries (Au, 1999), and hence also include "regional" or "societal" culture. In essence, our

Organizational Fit: Key Issues and New Directions, First Edition.
Edited by Amy L. Kristof-Brown and Jon Billsberry.
© 2013 John Wiley & Sons, Ltd. Published 2013 by John Wiley & Sons, Ltd.

references to culture pertain in general to the community to which an individual belongs, be it societal, regional, or national.

With the increase in organizational diversity and international collaborations, it has become rather a cliché to state that a cultural understanding of organizational behavior and human resource topics is imperative (Gelfand *et al.*, 2007; Tsui *et al.*, 2007). Several authors (Gomez-Mejia and Welbourne, 1991; Hofstede, 1980; Ramamoorthy and Carroll, 1998) have suggested that human resource practices are culture specific. However, the study of culturally embedded PE fit has been scarce. Although scholars have started to study the PE fit phenomenon in non-US societies (see, e.g., Erdogan *et al.*, 2004; Nyambegera *et al.*, 2001; Parkes *et al.*, 2001; Turban *et al.*, 2001; Vandenberghe, 1999; also see Gelfand *et al.*, 1997, and Kristof-Brown and Guay, 2010, for a more comprehensive list and review of such studies), most of the studies remain cross-sample replications or validations. Few have adopted a systematic approach to expand the PE fit theory to integrate cultural variables, and efforts to provide a cultural perspective on fit have been rather scant or invisible (Gelfand *et al.*, 2007).

Recent PE fit studies started to detect variation of the PE fit phenomenon across cultures (Hult, 2005; Lee and Antonakis, in press; Ramaswami and Dreher, 2009; Van Vianen *et al.*, 2004; Westerman and Vanka, 2005). For example, it is found that in high power distance societies, individuals' preference may become less relevant in determining their attitudinal and behavioral outcomes (see Lee and Antonakis, in press; Westerman and Vanka, 2005). Another cross-cultural study found that different types of mentor–protégé fit, measured as similarity on various facets, relate differently to mentoring outcomes depending on the culture's level of gender egalitarianism, collectivism, and individualism (Ramaswami and Dreher, 2009). Such results highlight the importance of cultural values in understanding fit dynamics, which might have implications for attracting, selecting, and retaining talented individuals in organizations. To provide more visibility into this important and unexamined area, we put on our cultural glasses and look at PE fit through the lens of cultural values and norms to understand the cultural boundary conditions that influence PE fit processes and outcomes better. To that end, this chapter answers Edwards' (2008) call for developing PE fit theory by considering its boundary conditions. We offer an initial explanation of how culture may influence PE fit by dealing with the following questions: (1) Why is culture relevant to understanding PE fit? (2) Which cultural values, at the individual or societal level, may be relevant in explaining variation in individuals' interpretation of, and response to, fit (or misfit) across countries?

We structure the chapter in the following order. First, we offer a brief overview of culture and explain why and how culture may influence the phenomenon of PE fit. Second, we explain how various cultural values influence the interpretation of and response to PE fit and misfit by considering their implications for PE fit dynamics and human resource practices before and after organizational entry. At the end, we discuss the theoretical, research, and practical implications of considering the role of culture in PE fit, and suggest promising avenues for future research.

National Culture and Person–Environment Fit

Concept and dimensions of culture

In this section we provide a brief overview of the concept of culture and key cultural dimensions that we believe are most theoretically relevant to PE fit. Following this we discuss how culture may influence people's interpretation of and response to PE fit and misfit. According to Kroeber and Kluckhohn (1952, p. 357), "Culture consists of patterns, explicit and implicit, of and for behavior acquired and transmitted by symbols, constituting the distinctive achievement of human groups, including their embodiment in artifacts; the essential core of culture consists of traditional (i.e., historically derived and selected) ideas and especially their attached values; culture systems may, on the one hand, be considered as products of action, on the other as conditioning elements of further action." In a more concise way, culture can be defined as the "the collective programming of the human mind that distinguishes the members of one human group from those of another" (Hofstede, 1980, p. 25). Hence, culture is the "crystallisation of history in the thinking, feeling and acting of the present generation" (Hofstede, 1993, p. 5), such that its variations reflect the distinctive traditions, values, attitudes, and historical experiences of different societies.

In order to render this complexity of culture accessible, it has been common to conceptualize and measure culture through various value dimensions (e.g., Hofstede, 1980, 2001; Schwartz, 1994; Trompenaars and Hampden-Turner, 1997). Although reducing the concept of culture to a limited set of value dimensions is not without controversy, this approach allows for scrutinizing cultural differences on certain key aspects. This prevents loss of focus and facilitates cross-cultural comparisons on similar dimensions.

To date, the most widely accepted framework is that of Hofstede (1980, 2001), which postulates individualism/collectivism, power distance, uncertainty avoidance, masculinity/femininity, and long-term versus short-term orientation as the key cultural dimensions. Very briefly, *individualism/collectivism* refers to the central unity of human activity: whereas individualism values independence and puts the self at the center in viewing the world, collectivism emphasizes interdependence between the self and one's group or community (Triandis, 1985). *Power distance* is the extent to which the less powerful members of institutions and organizations within a society expect and accept that power is distributed unequally (Hofstede, 1991). *Uncertainty avoidance* refers to the extent to which the members of a culture feel threatened by uncertain or unknown situations. *Masculinity/femininity* reflects the attitude toward achievement: whereas masculine cultures are characterized by an emphasis on financial achievement and performance, feminine cultures reflect values that emphasize quality of life, the environment, and protection of the weak. Finally, the meaning of *long-term versus short-term orientation* is more straightforward: long-term orientation indicates the importance attached to tradition and the prescription of long-term commitment, whereas short-term orientation tends to focus on more immediate benefits and results (see Hofstede (2001) for more details). These dimensions have received a significant amount of attention in cross-cultural research and may help us decipher how the PE fit phenomenon varies across cultures.

In addition to the dimensions suggested by Hofstede (2001), certain other cultural dimensions may also help us understand variation in PE fit. For example, *universalism versus particularism* (Trompenaars and Hampden-Turner, 1997), defined as the degree to which a society emphasizes rules (universalism) or relations (particularism), may be highly relevant to our discussion. More specifically, people with a universalist value believe that rules or laws can be applied to everyone. On the other hand, particularism refers to the belief in placing emphasis on friendships, and looking at the situation for guidance on what is right or ethically acceptable; deals are made based upon relationships and friendships. In sum, these cultural values may have considerable influence on how people interpret and respond to fit. We will discuss such influence with concrete examples in the following sections.

Effects of culture on individuals' interpretation of and response to fit

Our primary thesis is that cultural values influence: (1) the way in which individuals conceptualize the person and the environment, (2) the emphasis placed on the person and the environment fitting each other, and (3) ways in which fit and misfit are tolerated and managed. We will begin by briefly discussing how culture influences people's conceptualization of person and environment in this section. Then, in the main body of the present chapter, we focus on the process of fit *interpretation* and *response.*

Culture is a kind of mental programming or frame of reference that shapes the way people make sense of the world (Hofstede, 1980; Kluckhohn and Strodtbeck, 1961). Such influence happens mainly through culture's impact on social information processing: that is, how individuals scan, select, and interpret information from the environment (Salancik and Pfeffer, 1978). Thus, culture shapes one's conceptualization of the E component of PE fit. Culture also manifests itself in how people in different societies conceive of "self" (Markus and Kitayama, 1991): that is, of the P component of PE fit. We contend that the culturally influenced sense making of the P and E components will in turn affect how individuals *interpret* and *respond* to fit and misfit.

PE fit essentially involves an evaluative process in which persons (as individuals or as representatives of organizations) assess the degree of congruence, compatibility, and match between the P and E components. Such evaluations, like all other social information processes, are in some way constrained by culture (Erez and Earley, 1993; Miller, 1984). It has been demonstrated that people of different cultures describe the social world in very different ways. For example, Kashima, Kashima, Kim, and Gelfand (2006) found that English speakers, as compared to Korean speakers, have a greater tendency to objectify and decontextualize descriptions of self, of interpersonal relationships, and of groups. A more contextualized frame may lead people to include a wider variety of factors and considerations in assessing the P and

E components and their fit. Hence, we may reasonably assume that the way PE fit is perceived and interpreted is also conditioned by cultural frames.

The *process* by which P and E are evaluated and combined to assess fit may also vary based on cultural values. Fit is a multidimensional construct, and generally requires simultaneous assessment of various aspects of P and E for understanding their individual and joint effects on specific outcomes (Jansen and Kristof-Brown, 2006; Kristof-Brown and Guay, 2010; Ostroff *et al.*, 2005). For example, Harrison (2007, p. 391) described fit as "a state of compatibility of joint values of one or more attribute, a, b, c, ... , j, of a focal entity (P), and a commensurate set of attribute values, a, b, c, ... , j of the entity's environment (E), expressed as [(P$_a$, P$_b$, P$_c$, ... , P$_j$) ∩ (E$_a$, E$_b$, E$_c$, ... , E$_j$)]." Culture may play a role in such compatibility assessment as Nisbett and colleagues (Nisbett and Miyamoto, 2005; Nisbett, Peng, Choi, and Norenzayan, 2001) indicate: "Asian people tend to use a holistic style of cognition, whereas Westerners are more likely to use an analytical approach, meaning 'paying attention primarily to the object and the categories to which it belongs and using rules, including formal logic, to understand its behavior' " (Nisbett *et al.*, 2001, p. 291). Consequently, we expect culture to influence: (1) which aspects of P and E would be included in this PE fit joint assessment (in terms of the number of attributes taken into consideration and their contents), and (2) the relative weight of each aspect.

Furthermore, we argue that people's *response* to fit and misfit may also vary across cultures. Viewing culture as a shared knowledge structure, it would result in "decreased variability in individual response to stimuli" (Erez and Earley, 1993, p. 23). A recent empirical study by Greguras and Diefendorff (2009) has shown that different types of fit satisfy different needs, which in turn leads to attitudinal and behavioral outcomes such as commitment and performance. As the needs and motivation of people vary across cultures (Erez, 2008; Erez and Earley, 1993; Iyengar and Lepper, 1999), each type of fit may also lead to different outcomes for people of diverse cultural origins. This implies that needs–supplies fit may be on different dimensions for people from different cultures. Furthermore, such difference in basic needs can even lead to the acceptance of some needs not being met. For example, people in high power distance and collectivistic cultures might want lesser autonomy on the job and would be more comfortable with directives from supervisors than are those in less power distant and more individualistic cultures. Consequently, people in high power distant cultures might be more tolerant to not having their autonomy needs met due to normative cultural constraints on hierarchical interactions with supervisors (e.g., Lee and Antonakis, in press). The variation in responses to fit can also be understood by cultural differences in the degree of tolerance for misfit or incongruence (Heine and Lehman, 1997; Suh, 2002). Such differences may make people react differently to their own perceived misfit in terms of both attitudes and behaviors. For example, cultural norms differ in whether and how choices and (negative) emotions are expressed (Kim and Sherman, 2007). Also, people with diverse cultural orientations may vary in their willingness to adapt themselves to suit the environment (Chatman and Barsade, 1995).

Taken together, we expect culture to influence the way people interpret and respond to fit and misfit. In the next section, we will apply this lens to examine how such cultural variations in fit interpretation and response may happen in three stages of employees' entry in organizations – specifically, *before* organizational entry, *during* organizational entry and employment, and at organizational exit.

Cultural Variations of Fit in Organizational Entry and Exit

Influence of culture on fit perceptions *before* organizational entry

In light of the previous discussion, we expect certain cultural values to influence PE fit interpretation before organizational entry. From the job-seekers' perspective, the dimension of individualism/collectivism could influence *how attracted* candidates feel to an organization or a job position – that is, one may observe different weights given to the several types of fit during the attraction process in individualist and collectivist cultures. For example, people in individualist cultures may focus more on person–job (PJ) fit because they will feel attracted to a job or an organization where the job content, design, and compensation are in line with their needs. In contrast, those in collectivist cultures may tend to place more weight on value congruence as well as individual or group attraction (i.e., person–organization (PO), person–supervisor (PS), and person–group (PG) fit) as a result of an emphasis on personal relationships and obligations.

Such phenomena can be explained by the relative foci of instrumental and expressive motives of individualists and collectivists (Chen *et al.*, 1998; Triandis, 1995). As suggested by Chen, Chen, and Meindl (1998), while individualists and collectivists are both likely to have instrumental and expressive motives, individualism and collectivism determine the different foci of these motives – individual for individualists, and the collective for collectivists. Individualists are likely to emphasize the instrumentality of their efforts for fulfillment of self-interest, whereas collectivists evaluate the instrumentality of individual efforts for fulfillment of collective interests. Likewise, the expressive motives of individualists are a reflection of their true individual potential, whereas collectivists' expressive motives are reflected in the dedication of the self to the collective good, as expressed by loyalty, solidarity, and so forth. These differential foci of motives (individual versus group) may also be reflected in recruitment and selection practices of individualists and collectivists. Given the group-oriented bias of collectivists, their emphasis on demographic similarity and shared social identity between candidates and recruiters may be stronger (Goldberg, 2003; Turban *et al.*, 1998), hence contributing to a heightened weight of PS and PG fit on mutual attraction in recruiting processes. Furthermore, Turban *et al.* (2001) found that PO fit based on value congruence plays a role in job-seekers' application decisions in Mainland China. In such contexts, people may recommend friends for employment because of PO fit considerations rather than PJ fit criteria because the latter essentially emphasizes the satisfaction of individual goals (Sue-Chan and Dasborough, 2006).

Similarly, because a person's job or career decision is likely to be influenced by significant others (Phillips *et al.*, 2001), we argue that such influence will be more pronounced in collectivist cultures. Given the emphasis on interdependence in such cultures, one can expect that parental and family influences are stronger in collectivist contexts. Consequently, the influence of significant others in such sociocultural contexts is more likely to determine how attractive certain jobs and organizations are (Fouad and Byars-Winston, 2005). In this sense, fit consideration is no longer individual-centered (i.e., not whether this job fits *me*, but whether this job fits *me as defined by my relevant others*). In a different but somewhat related context, Zhang and Kline (2009) found that the influence of networks on intentions to marry and on relational commitments in general is enhanced for the Chinese, as compared to American people. Such findings show how the interpretation of fit and attraction, illustrated here by the choice of dating or marital partner, can be culture bound.

In a related vein, some culturally indigenous concepts may also influence how fit is assessed by candidates and employers before organizational entry, such as during the attraction stage (Schneider, 1987a, 1987b). One of the best-known indigenous concepts in Chinese culture is *guanxi*, defined as relational ties between an individual and others that are developed through shared social experiences (e.g., going to the same school, being born in the same place, being a relative or former boss or student, to name a few) with implied reciprocal social exchanges (Chen *et al.*, 2004; Farh *et al.*, 1998). Equivalents, such as *jan-pehchan* and *sambandh* in India (Zhu *et al.*, 2005), can be found in other collectivist cultures. These relationship-based concepts may affect business connections, interpersonal attraction, as well as selection processes (Chen and Francesco, 2000; Zhu *et al.*, 2005). The literature brings to light possible cultural variations in fit and attraction, such that in collectivist cultures it is the quality of the existing relationship or exchanges between P and E that influences "fit" and its consequences on attraction, rather than the exact matching of P and E characteristics, that counts. That is, in collectivistic cultures where *guanxi* or *jan-pehchan* are central, PS, PG, or PO forms of fit are implicitly important, whereas other types of fit, such as PJ fit, will matter less.

In addition to individualism/collectivism, long-term versus short-term time orientation may also shape one's perception and interpretation of fit in the attraction stage. The weight people place on current or immediate fit versus long-term or future fit may influence whether or not one is attracted to, or will stay with, a current job or organization. Specifically, people in cultures with short-term orientation may find organizations and jobs that they perceive to be an immediate fit in terms of job design or compensation package to be more appealing, whereas those in cultures with a long-term orientation may prefer positions which lack immediate fit but can potentially fit in the longer run. While individuals may want both short-term and long-term fit, we suggest that the emphasis placed on these will differ by culture.

In sum, we argue that cultural dimensions such as individualism/collectivism and time orientation will cast non-negligible impacts on the interpretation of fit prior to organizational entry.

Influence of culture on fit perceptions *during* organizational entry and employment

Existing research has shown recruitment and selection practices to be culture bound (e.g., Huo *et al.*, 2002; Phillips and Gully, 2002; Ramamoorthy and Carroll, 1998; Ryan *et al.*, 2009). The cultural values of individualism/collectivism (and the related *guanxi*), universalism/particularism, and uncertainty avoidance may shed some light on the cultural variations in how PE fit influences the selection process from an organizational or recruiters' perspective.[1]

From the recruiters' perspective, hiring decisions are based on selection criteria that may differ in individualist and collectivist cultures. Specifically, individualism/collectivism and associated values may influence the weights placed on PJ, PG, PO, and PS fit during selection. Collectivistic cultures, given their orientation towards group harmony and group goals, would probably place more emphasis on PG, PO, and PS fit rather than PJ fit, which in turn may be emphasized in more individualistic cultures (Ramamoorthy and Carroll, 1998; Sekiguchi, 2004; Sinha and Sinha, 1990). Selection practices that emphasize individual rights, individual interests, and job compatibility as the sole criteria of selection (which is more common in individualistic societies) would result in hiring on the basis of PJ fit rather than other types of fit (Ramamoorthy and Carroll, 1998). Moreover, in collectivistic cultures, PG or PS fit may signal more than just fitting the group or supervisor in complementary or supplementary ways. PS and PG forms of fit may be interpreted as *guanxi* or reference from relevant others. Research suggests that in India organizations rely on internal recruitment, based on word-of-mouth advertising and recommendations for selection (Budhwar and Khatri, 2001). In other words, fitting with key individuals (and thus with the overall values of the organization) seems to play a major role in selection decisions in such a cultural context, suggesting an emphasis on PS and PG forms of fit rather than PJ fit.

Empirical research generally concurs with our argument. For example, Sue-Chan and Dasborough (2006) found that particularistic ties, defined as the friendship-based relationship between individuals, positively influence hiring decisions in the Hong Kong Chinese cultural context but not in the Australian cultural context. In a similar vein, Xin and Pearce (1996) suggest that *guanxi* helps reduce "transaction costs" in social exchange situations in collectivistic cultures such as China. Applied to the selection process, this would imply that organizations in eastern cultures where *guanxi* exerts normative influence on behavior, applicants' shared social capital, or social ties with interviewers and employers might be a convenient cultural heuristic that influences selection processes and outcomes. Furthermore, in cultures with higher levels of uncertainty and relatively weak legal frameworks or requirements for defensible selection practices, the importance of *guanxi* and *jan-pehchan* is heightened (e.g., Xin and Pearce, 1996). In such cultures, *guanxi*-based connections may provide access to reliable and accurate information about an individual applicant in a quick and efficient manner (Chen and Francesco, 2000; Millington *et al.*, 2006; Yang, 2002).

Providing further support, Steiner and Gilliland (2001) note that individualistic cultures tend to prefer equity rules for recruitment and selection (arising from an emphasis on performance), whereas collectivistic countries emphasize group harmony and therefore prefer equality and consider the specific needs of the target group. They also note that the extent to which hiring through personal or family contacts is viewed as accepted, fair, or just is a function of the relative emphasis placed on special needs versus equity by a particular culture (e.g., Gilliland, 1995). In collectivistic cultures, hiring on the basis of social integration facilitators such as PG, PO, and PS fit may be more valued as they encourage higher employee compatibility and lower employee turnover and attrition, thereby compensating for any potential deficiencies of not hiring on the basis of PJ fit (Gomez-Mejia and Welbourne, 1991).

In addition, cultural values such as universalism/particularism, uncertainty avoidance, and achievement (performance) orientation may also influence the selection process during organizational entry. Based on a review of the extant literature, Aycan (2005) suggests that recruitment and selection in cultures high on performance orientation or universalism are based on hard criteria such as job-related knowledge and technical skills (i.e., PJ fit), whereas in cultures low on performance orientation, emphasizing ascribed status or particularistic ties, soft criteria such as relational skills or social class affiliation (i.e., PS and PG fit) are favored. Moreover, societies that strongly hold an individualistic orientation, masculinity values, and internal locus of control may be highly sensitive to equity and hence would favor selection based on PJ fit: that is, one that focuses on qualifications and hard, measurable selection criteria. On the other hand, societies with a strong collectivistic orientation, femininity values, and a sense of fatalism or external locus of control may be less equity-sensitive and more comfortable with ambiguous selection criteria.

Finally, cultural values may also influence whether or not fit is considered in a global or piecemeal fashion. We suggest that such cultural difference will impact upon the degree to which ambiguity in information about a candidate, or ambiguity in the selection process in general, is tolerated. In cultures of high uncertainty avoidance, employers will make larger efforts to ensure fit in the selection process. For example, more extensive selection procedures and a greater variety of selection tests are used in countries high on uncertainty avoidance (Ryan, McFarland, Baron, and Page, 1999). Conversely, collectivism and traditionalism are negatively related to the preference for test-based selection systems (Ramamoorthy and Carroll, 1998). In sum, who fits, and even how fit is defined, will differ across cultures (as shown in the procedural preference variations during the selection process) because cultural values may change (1) which aspects of P and E matter, (2) the process by which fit is evaluated, and (3) the consequences of fit and misfit.

Influence of culture on fit perceptions affecting organizational exit

A key factor leading to attrition is the perception and response to fit and misfit from the perspective of both the employers and the employees. Unhappy employees may voluntarily leave organizations, and organizations will encourage exit for those they consider to be misfits, which blurs the distinction between voluntary and involuntary turnover. Again we expect that cultural values will affect these attrition processes. First, the types of fit predicting turnover may differ across cultures. The commitment and attachment of collectivists to an organization may be more strongly influenced by satisfaction with supervisors and colleagues (Wasti, 2003). Such relationship orientation may lead collectivists to pay more attention to PS and PG fit (Pelled and Xin, 1997). Likewise, the commitments of individualists tend to be associated more closely with work or promotion. Such task orientation makes them care more about PJ fit with respect to attrition decisions. In support of this view, empirical evidence in a cross-cultural study on job embeddedness among call-center agents in the USA and India has shown that PO fit and organizational links explain turnover better in India, due to the stronger identification of individuals with organizational values in a collectivistic culture. On the other hand, PJ fit is more important in predicting turnover in the USA, a country representing an individualistic culture (Ramesh, 2007).

More fundamental cultural differences reside, nevertheless, in the interpretation of fit and misfit, and in how people respond to these studies. In a series of studies on self-construal, researchers consistently found that compared to the American subjects, Japanese subjects have a more interdependent self-concept, and have higher tendencies toward self-criticism and self-improvement in response to normative pressures (Kanagawa *et al.*, 2001; Kitayama *et al.*, 1997). In contrast, Americans, who embrace individualist values, are more likely to emphasize self-enhancement. Given these distinct perspectives, when the P and E components do not match, it is likely that the behavioral consequences will differ across cultures. People in collectivist cultures will focus on the P side of the equation (i.e., oneself) and may try to adjust themselves to the E component (i.e., to "improve oneself") so as to achieve fit (Suh, 2002). As a result, unlike individualists, collectivists are less likely to "blame" the environment for creating a misfit. In a similar vein, Thomas, Au, and Ravlin (2003) argue that collectivists have a higher overall threshold for psychological contract violation than individualists do. As a result, compared to individualists, it is less likely that collectivists will consider a job or an organization a "misfit."

Furthermore, the level of tolerance for misfit also differs considerably across cultures. In other words, people across cultures may respond to the presence of perceived misfit in very different ways. Generally, as employees, collectivists are more loyal to organizations than are individualists, and will not choose to leave immediately in the presence of misfit. In other words, they tend to tolerate misfit more if their company needs them or if they feel attached to their colleagues. For example, it is found that job satisfaction is a stronger predictor of turnover intentions in the

USA than in Mexico (Posthuma *et al.*, 2005). Such results suggest that in collectivist cultures, such as Mexico, low job satisfaction (implying perceived misfit with job or organization) is less likely to lead to voluntary turnover, compared to individualist cultures such as the USA. Similarly, Ng, Sorensen, and Yim (2009) found that the job satisfaction–job performance relationship is stronger in individualistic (versus collectivistic) cultures. Such results suggest that people in collectivist cultures may have a higher level of tolerance of misfit.

In the same vein, in a class simulation Chatman and Barsade (1995) found that students with cooperative or collectivist dispositions adjusted their behavior to fit with the culture of organizations better, whereas individualist students may not be able or willing to be as malleable. As a result, whereas misfit can be a reliable predictor of voluntary turnover for individualists, collectivists may have very different responses to misfit in terms of attrition. Such differences can also be understood by the cross-cultural variations in the general tendency to be a *maximizer* versus a *satisficer*. According to Hwang and Chang (2009, p. 1027), maximizers can be defined as "persons who are always looking for the best, whereas satisficers are satisfied once the threshold of acceptability, based on their intrinsic values, is crossed." Under the influence of Buddhism, Asian people are more likely to embrace the attitude of a satisficer (Hwang and Chang, 2009). Consequently, Asians may have a wider margin in their assessment of fit – as long as the E components get close enough to the P components, they may feel that fit is achieved. This can be understood in terms of a higher tolerance for less "objective" fit. On the contrary, Europeans or Americans are more likely to be maximizers, emphasizing more exact fit.

In conjunction with previous discussions, the cultural dimension of uncertainty avoidance can also be a contributing factor to the differential interpretation and response to fit and misfit. Logically, uncertainty avoidance will influence the extent to which people are willing to accept ambiguity in fit in order to stay in a position or an organization. While people with high uncertainty avoidance tend to make every effort, even by resorting to attrition, to minimize ambiguity of fit, people with low uncertainty avoidance may tolerate such ambiguity better and react differently. Like the processes of organizational entry discussed earlier, organizational exit (and consequently the fit processes underlying it) is highly susceptible to culture's influence.

From the perspective of employers as well, culture may influence the link between PE fit and attrition. For instance, in collectivist cultures where family and other relational ties are extremely important, managers may be reluctant to let employees go (or force them to leave), even if they do not perform well on the job (i.e., have low PJ fit). Consequently, collectivist employers are more likely to reciprocate employee loyalty by accommodating misfitting individuals and not firing them immediately. We thus expect organizations in collectivistic cultures to focus on loyalty and permanent employer–employee relationships, thereby promoting employment security and commitment to the organization (i.e., valuing longer-term PO fit regarding attrition). Organizations in individualist cultures may focus on promotion and career decisions based on employee achievement, and hence may be more likely to fire employees who do not fit or meet performance expectations (Gomez-Mejia and Welbourne, 1991; Ramamoorthy and Carroll, 1998).

To conclude, we argue that culture will influence people's interpretation of and response to fit and misfit during the different stages of organizational entry as well as exit, as demonstrated by the conceptual arguments and empirical evidence mentioned above.

Implications and Directions for Future Research

As noted at the start of the chapter, Edwards (2008) says that one of the challenges for the development of PE research and practice is a better understanding of the boundary conditions of its theoretical assumptions. A culturally grounded under-standing of PE fit can promote theoretical and empirical advances in this important stream of research because it considers the cultural boundaries that have been pre-viously neglected in this literature. Although recently some scholars have started to examine the effect of culture on PE fit (e.g., Lee and Antonakis, in press; Lee, Reiche, and Song, 2010; Westerman and Vanka, 2005), such endeavors are only at their initial stage at best and can still be categorized as exceptions. Systematic efforts are needed to make PE fit theory more culture sensitive and complete. Below we provide recommendations for future research on areas that have received insufficient attention so far.

On the theory side, our chapter underscores the need to reconceptualize and re-define PE fit from a cultural perspective. We also revisit the western assumptions that underlie the PE fit phenomenon, which, as we have shown using examples and extant studies from other literature streams, do not hold universally. This chapter therefore highlights contextual and cultural boundary conditions that influence PE fit and its outcomes, including but not limited to cultural values and norms. There seems to be no articulated theory on the role of culture in fit conceptualizations, processes, and outcomes. This chapter underscores the need for future theoretical work in this area. For example, some questions that might be addressed in future research include: How do cultural values influence the conceptualization of the person, the environ-ment, and their match? How does culture influence the notion of fit being fixed versus dynamic over time? Are there cultural differences in the importance placed on the person versus the environment? And relatedly, what cultural factors influence the way in which both the person and the environment change, if at all, in the case of misfit? What cultural contexts recognize, tolerate, or even encourage misfit?

In addition to the conceptual development of culture-sensitive theories of PE fit, a systematic approach to examine fit phenomena across cultural contexts is needed. Scholars have started to study PE fit in non-US societies (see Kristof-Brown and Guay, 2010). We encourage more comparative work that clearly spells out the role of culture in PE fit. Moreover, we strongly encourage qualitative studies, which can help uncover a more indigenous notion of PE fit. In fact, to address some of the theoretical questions noted above, researchers will have to move away from traditional quantitative research paradigms, and build PE fit theory from the bottom up. To achieve this, future research could focus on gathering data from more nonwestern and non-US populations, with a clear cultural frame in mind. Furthermore, we suggest that, rather than use the cultural lens only when data are collected from non-US samples, researchers should understand the fit phenomenon from a cultural and contextual perspective. This would help us critically evaluate hypothesized fit relationships with antecedents and outcomes, as well as the base arguments for our hypotheses, in a more enriched theoretical framework.

Furthermore, it is not entirely clear that misfit is universally avoided or that the benefits of fit can be realized under all cultural conditions. The role of cultural values at the individual, group, organizational, and societal levels in the relationship between different types of fit (and misfit) and outcomes must be examined. Testing some of the ideas outlined earlier may be a good start. To that end, collaborations with researchers from and with multiple cultural backgrounds would be invaluable, thereby sowing the seeds of global contributions to the study of PE fit (Billsberry and De Cooman, 2010).

Finally, some managerial and practical implications of a culturally sensitive understanding of PE fit must also be noted. Examining PE fit with a cultural lens would benefit organizations that either have a highly diverse workforce or are looking to expand their operations in other cultures. By increasing their cultural sensitivity and knowledge of cross-cultural interfaces (Gelfand *et al.*, 2007), managers and practitioners would better recognize the cultural influences on organizational entry and exit of employees, and may be more tolerant and appreciative of the diversity of sometimes invisible influences on standard human relations (HR) practices. Organizational justice, equity, commitment, and psychological contract perceptions are a few of the many organizational outcomes that could be better anticipated and managed with an understanding of how culture infuses HR decisions related to fit. Given the ever-increasing number of expatriates and cross-cultural employee exchanges, there is a high chance that the interviewer and interviewee are not from the same cultural or ethnic background. Consequently, applicants, as well as recruiters, need to be aware of what the other party considers important in its evaluations of fit with the supervisor, job, group, and organization, and where there are overlaps in fit perceptions. Furthermore, a cultural perspective of PE fit would provide material for expatriate training on international HR practices, interpersonal relationships, and role expectations.

Conclusion

Fit is a more useful construct for management, including cross-cultural management, if one takes a contextual approach to understanding it. As an initial effort to demonstrate cultural differences in the interpretation of and response to fit and misfit, this chapter paves the way for future research to advance our understanding of PE fit in different cultures.

In this chapter, we primarily considered the role of national, regional, and societal cultural values and norms, and how variations in PE fit underlying organizational entry and exit processes may be explained by a set of such cultural dimensions. We acknowledge that a cultural perspective of PE fit may not be sufficient to understand completely the contingencies that impinge upon individuals' employment processes. Legal systems or policies regarding recruitment and selection could also influence these processes (e.g., clear hiring policies based on job descriptions, access to legal recourse in case of perceived violation of policy and/or discrimination, etc.). Apart from legal systems, sociopolitical structures and political processes (e.g., having a quota system) may equally influence the effect of fit (and its weight) on recruitment, selection, and attrition stages of organizational life. Group norms, organizational cultures, labor market, and economic conditions will also play a role. Nevertheless, given the purposes of this chapter, our limited focus on culture seems justified. With such research it should be possible to predict the salient aspects of fit for a particular individual or a particular culture, depending on their position on various cultural dimensions. We hope that the ideas presented in this chapter will stimulate future research in this long-neglected area, producing PE fit knowledge that is more intellectually complete and practically useful.

Note

1. Although it is also likely that job-seekers' decision to join an organization would be influenced by cultural factors, we assume that such influence has been captured by the perceived attractiveness of a job/organization. Because such a perspective is well covered in the preceding section on cultural influences on fit before organizational entry, where we address the issues mainly from applicants/job-seekers' point of view, in this section we focus on how organizations make selection decisions for organizational entry.

References

Arthur, W., Bell, S., Villado, A. J., and Doverspike, D. (2006) The use of person–organization fit in employment decision making: An assessment of its criterion-related validity. *Journal of Applied Psychology*, 9, 786–801.

Au, K. Y. (1999) Intra-cultural variation: Evidence and implications for international business. *Journal of International Business Studies*, 30, 799–812.

Aycan, Z. (2005) The interplay between cultural and institutional/structural contingencies in human resource management practices. *International Journal of Human Resource Management*, 16 (7), 1083–1119.

Billsberry, J. and De Cooman, R. (2010) Definitions of fit and misfit in northern Europe: Insights from a cross-national research collaboration. Paper presented at the 4th Global e-Conference on Fit. www.fitconference.com/2010/thu01.pdf.

Billsberry, J., Ambrosini, V., Moss-Jones, J., and Marsh, P. (2005) Some suggestions for mapping organizational members' sense of fit. *Journal of Business and Psychology*, 19, 555–570.

Budhwar, P. S., and Khatri, N. (2001) A comparative study of HR practices in Britain and India. *International Journal of Human Resource Management*, 12 (5), 800–826.

Chatman, J. A., and Barsade, S. G. (1995) Personality, organizational culture, and cooperation: Evidence from a business simulation. *Administrative Science Quarterly*, 40, 423–443.

Chen, C. C., Chen, X.-P., and Meindl, J. R. (1998) How can cooperation be fostered? The cultural effects of individualism–collectivism. *Academy of Management Review*, 23, 285–304.

Chen, C. C., Chen, Y.-R., and Xin, K. (2004) Guanxi practices and trust in management: A procedural justice perspective. *Organization Science*, 15 (2), 200–209.

Chen, Z. X., and Francesco, A. M. (2000) Employee demography, organizational commitment, and turnover intentions in China: Do cultural differences matter? *Human Relations*, 53, 869–887.

Edwards, J. R. (2008) Person–environment fit in organizations: An assessment of theoretical progress. *Academy of Management Annals*, 2, 167–230.

Erdogan, B., Kraimer, M. L., and Liden, R. C. (2004) Work value congruence and intrinsic career success: The compensatory roles of leader–member exchange and perceived organizational support. *Personnel Psychology*, 57, 305–32.

Erez, M. (2008) Social-cultural influences on work motivation. In R. Kanfer, G. Chen, and R. D. Pritchard (eds), *Work Motivation: Past, Present, and Future* (pp. 501–538). Mahwah, NJ: Lawrence Erlbaum Associates.

Erez, M., and Earley, C. P. (1993) *Culture, Self-Identity, and Work*. New York: Oxford University Press.

Farh, J.-L., Tsui, A. S., Xin, K., and Cheng, B.-S. (1998) The influence of relational demography and guanxi: The Chinese case. *Organization Science*, 9 (4), 471–488.

Fouad, N. A., and Byars-Winston, A. M. (2005) Cultural context of career choice: Meta-analysis of race/ethnicity differences. *Career Development Quarterly*, 53, 223–233.

Gelfand, M. J., Erez, M., and Aycan, Z. (2007) Cross-cultural organizational behavior. *Annual Review of Psychology*, 58 (1), 479–514.

Gilliland, S. W. (1995) Fairness from the applicants' perspective: Reactions to employee selection procedures. *International Journal of Selection and Assessment*, 3, 11–19.

Goldberg, C. B. (2003) Applicant reactions to the employment interview: A look at demographic similarity and social identity theory. *Journal of Business Research*, 56 (8), 561–571.

Gomez-Mejia, L. R., and Welbourne, T. (1991) Compensation strategies in a global context. *Human Resources Planning*, 14, 29–42.

Greguras, G. J., and Diefendorff, J. M. (2009) Different fits satisfy different needs: Linking person–environment fit to employee commitment and performance using self-determination theory. *Journal of Applied Psychology*, 94 (2), 465–477.

Harrison, D. A. (2007) Pitching fits in applied psychological research: Making fit methods fit theory. In C. Ostroff and T. A. Judge (eds), *Perspectives on Organizational Fit* (pp. 389–416). New York: Lawrence Erlbaum Associates.

Heine, S. J., and Lehman, D. R. (1997) Culture, dissonance, and self-affirmation. *Personality and Social Psychology Bulletin*, 23, 389–400.

Hoffman, B. J., and Woehr, D. J. (2006) A quantitative review of the relationship between person–organization fit and behavioral outcomes. *Journal of Vocational Behavior*, 68, 389–399.

Hofstede, G. (1980) *Culture's Consequences: International Differences in Work-Related Values*. Beverly Hills, CA: Sage.

Hofstede, G. (1991) *Cultures and Organizations*. London: Harper Collins.

Hofstede, G. (1993) Intercultural conflict and synergy in Europe: Management in western Europe. In D. J. Hickson (ed.), *Society, Culture and Organization in Twelve Nations* (pp. 1–8). New York: de Gruyter.

Hofstede, G. (2001) *Cultures Consequences: Comparing Values, Behaviors, Institutions, and Organizations across Nations* (2nd edn). Thousand Oaks, CA: Sage.

Hult, C. (2005) Organizational commitment and person–environment fit in six western countries. *Organization Studies*, 26 (2), 249–270.

Huo, Y. P., Huang, H. J., and Napier, N. K. (2002) Divergence or convergence: A cross-national comparison of personnel selection practices. *Human Resource Management*, 41 (1), 31.

Hwang, K.-K., and Chang, J. (2009) Self-cultivation: Culturally sensitive psychotherapies in Confucian societies. *The Counseling Psychologist*, 37 (7), 1010–1032.

Iyengar, S. S., and Lepper, M. R. (1999) Rethinking the value of choice: A cultural perspective on intrinsic motivation. *Journal of Personality and Social Psychology*, 76, 349–366.

Jansen, K. J., and Kristof-Brown, A. (2006) Toward a multidimensional theory of person–environment fit. *Journal of Managerial Issues*, 18 (2), 193–214.

Kanagawa, C., Cross, S. E., and Markus, H. R. (2001) "Who am I?" The cultural psychology of the conceptual self. *Personality and Social Psychology Bulletin*, 27 (1), 90–103.

Kashima, Y., Kashima, E. S., Kim, U., and Gelfand, M. (2006) Describing the social world: How is a person, a group, and a relationship described in the East and the West? *Journal of Experimental Social Psychology*, 42 (3), 388–396.

Kim, H. S., and Sherman, D. K. (2007) "Express yourself": Culture and the effect of self-expression on choice. *Journal of Personality and Social Psychology*, 92 (1), 1–11.

Kitayama, S., Markus, H. R., Matsumoto, H., and Norasakkunkit, V. (1997) Individual and collective processes in the construction of the self: Self-enhancement in the United States and self-criticism in Japan. *Journal of Personality and Social Psychology*, 72 (6), 1245–1267.

Kluckhohn, F. R., and Strodtbeck, F. L. (1961) *Variations in Value Orientations*. Evanston, IL: Row, Peterson & Co.

Kristof, A. L. (1996) Person–organization fit: An integrative review of its conceptualizations, measurement, and implications. *Personnel Psychology*, 49, 1–49.

Kristof-Brown, A. L., and Guay, R. P. (2010) Person–environment fit. In S. Zedeck (ed.), *APA Handbook of Industrial and Organizational Psychology* (pp. 3–50). Washington, DC: American Psychological Association.

Kristof-Brown, A. L., Zimmerman, R. D., and Johnson, E. C. (2005) Consequences of individuals' fit at work: A meta-analysis of person–job, person–organization, person–group, and person–supervisor fit. *Personnel Psychology*, 58, 281–342.

Kroeber, A., and Kluckhohn, C. (1952) *Culture*. New York: Meridian Books.

Lee, Y.-t., and Antonakis, J. (in press) Satisfaction and individual preference for structuring: What is fit depends on where you are from. *Journal of Management*.

Lee, Y.-t., Reiche, B. S., and Song, D. (2010) How do newcomers fit in? The dynamics between person–environment fit and social capital across cultures. *International Journal of Cross Cultural Management*, 10 (2), 153–174.

Markus, H. R., and Kitayama, S. (1991) Culture and the self: Implications for cognition, emotion, and motivation. *Psychological Review*, 98, 224–253.

Miller, J. G. (1984) Culture and the development of everyday social explanation. *Journal of Personality and Social Psychology*, 46 (5), 961–978.

Millington, A. I., Eberhardt, M. E., and Wilkinson, B. (2006) Supplier performance and selection in China. *International Journal of Operations and Production Management*, 26 (2), 185–201.

Ng, T. W. H., Sorensen, K. L., and Yim, F. H. K. (2009) Does the job satisfaction–job performance relationship vary across cultures? *Journal of Cross-Cultural Psychology*, 40 (5), 761–796.

Nisbett, R. E., and Miyamoto, Y. (2005) The influence of culture: Holistic versus analytic perception. *Trends in Cognitive Sciences*, 9 (10), 467–473.

Nisbett, R. E., Peng, K., Choi, I., and Norenzayan, A. (2001) Culture and systems of thought: Holistic vs analytic cognition. *Psychological Review*, 108 (2), 291–310.

Nyambegera, S. M., Daniels, K., and Sparrow, P. (2001) Why fit doesn't always matter: The impact of HRM and cultural fit on job involvement of Kenyan employees. *Applied Psychology*, 50, 109–140.

Ostroff, C., and Judge, T. A. (2007) *Perspectives on Organizational Fit*. New York: Lawrence Erlbaum Associates.

Ostroff, C., Shin, Y., and Kinicki, A. J. (2005) Multiple perspectives of congruence: Relationships between value congruence and employee attitudes. *Journal of Organizational Behavior*, 26 (6), 591–623.

Parkes, L. P., Bochner, S., and Schneider, S. K. (2001) Person–organisation fit across cultures: An empirical investigation of individualism and collectivism. *Applied Psychology: An International Review. Special Issue: Person–Organisation Fit*, 50 (1), 81–108.

Pelled, L. H., and Xin, K. R. (1997) Birds of a feather: Leader–member demographic similarity and organizational attachment in Mexico. *Leadership Quarterly*, 8 (4), 433–450.

Phillips, J. M., and Gully, S. M. (2002) Fairness reactions to personnel selection techniques in Singapore and the United States. *International Journal of Human Resource Management*, 13 (8), 1186–1205.

Phillips, S. D., Christopher-Sisk, E. K., and Gravino, K. L. (2001) Making career decisions in a relational context. *The Counseling Psychologist*, 29 (2), 193–214.

Posthuma, R. A., Joplin, J. R. W., and Maertz, C. P., Jr (2005) Comparing the validity of turnover predictors in the United States and Mexico. *International Journal of Cross Cultural Management*, 5 (2), 165–180.

Ramamoorthy, N., and Carroll, S. J. (1998) Individualism/collectivism orientations and reactions toward alternative human resource management practices. *Human Relations*, 51 (5), 571–588.

Ramaswami, A., and Dreher, G. F. (2009) A cross-cultural examination of the relationship between mentor–protégé similarity and mentor behavior in India and the US. Academy of Management annual meeting, Chicago, IL.

Ramesh, A. (2007) Replicating and extending job embeddedness across cultures: Employee turnover in India and the United States. University of Maryland.

Ryan, A. M., Boyce, A. S., Ghumman, S., Jundt, D., Schmidt, G., and Gibby, R. (2009) Going global: Cultural values and perceptions of selection procedures. *Applied Psychology: An International Review*, 58 (4), 520–556.

Ryan, A. M., McFarland, L., Baron, H., and Page, R. (1999) An international look at selection practices: Nation and culture as explanations for variability in practice. *Personnel Psychology*, 52 (2), 359–392.

Salancik, G. R., and Pfeffer, J. (1978) A social information processing approach to job attitudes and task design. *Administrative Science Quarterly*, 23 (2), 224–253.

Schneider, B. (1987a) E = f(P,B): The road to a radical approach to person–environment fit. *Journal of Vocational Behavior*, 31, 353–361.

Schneider, B. (1987b) The people make the place. *Personnel Psychology*, 40, 437–453.

Schwartz, S. H. (1994) Beyond individualism/collectivism: New cultural dimensions of values. In K. Uichol, C. Kagitcibasi, H. C. Triandis, and G. Yoon (eds), *Individualism and Collectivism: Theory, Method, and Applications* (pp. 85–119). Thousand Oaks, CA: Sage.

Sekiguchi, T. (2004) The role of different types of person–organization fit in Japanese recruiters' judgments of applicant qualifications: An experimental policy capturing investigation. *Japanese Association of Industrial/Organizational Psychology Journal*, 17, 51–63.

Sinha, J. B. P., and Sinha, D. (1990) Role of social values in Indian organizations. *International Journal of Psychology*, 25, 705–714.

Steiner, D. D., and Gilliland, S. W. (2001) Procedural justice in personnel selection: International and cross-cultural perspectives. *International Journal of Selection and Assessment*, 9, 124–137.

Sue-Chan, C., and Dasborough, M. T. (2006) The influence of relation-based and rule-based regulations on hiring decisions in the Australian and Hong Kong Chinese cultural contexts. *International Journal of Human Resource Management*, 17 (7), 1267–1292.

Suh, E. M. (2002) Culture, identity consistency, and subjective well-being. *Journal of Personality and Social Psychology*, 83, 1378–1391.

Thomas, D. C., Au, K., and Ravlin, E. C. (2003) Cultural variation and the psychological contract. *Journal of Organizational Behavior*, 24 (5), 451–471.

Triandis, H. C. (1995) *Individualism and Collectivism*. Boulder, CO: Westview Press.

Trompenaars, F., and Hampden-Turner, C. (1997) *Riding the Waves of Culture: Understanding Cultural Diversity in Business* (2nd edn). London: McGraw-Hill.

Tsui, A. S., Nifadkar, S. S., and Ou, A. Y. (2007) Cross-national, cross-cultural organizational behavior research: Advances, gaps and recommendations. *Journal of Management*, 33, 426–478.

Turban, D. B., Forret, M. L., and Hendrickson, C. L. (1998) Applicant attraction to firms: Influences of organization reputation, job and organizational attributes, and recruiter behaviors. *Journal of Vocational Behavior*, 52 (1), 24–44.

Turban, D. B., Lau, C.M., Ngo, H. Y., Chow, I. H. S., and Si, S.X. (2001) Organizational attractiveness of firms in the People's Republic of China: a person–organization fit perspective. *Journal of Applied Psychology*, 86, 194–206.

Van Vianen, A. E. M., De Pater, I. E., Kristof-Brown, A. L., and Johnson, E. C. (2004) Fitting in: Surface- and deep-level cultural differences and expatriates' adjustment. *Academy of Management Journal*, 47, 697–709.

Vandenberghe, C. (1999) Organizational culture, person–culture fit, and turnover: A replication in the health care industry. *Journal of Organizational Behavior*, 20, 175–184.

Verquer, M. L., Beehr, T. A., and Wagner, S. H. (2003) A meta-analysis of relations between person–organization fit and work attitudes. *Journal of Vocational Behavior*, 63, 473–489.

Wasti, S. A. (2003) The influence of cultural values on antecedents of organizational commitment: An individual-level analysis. *Applied Psychology: An International Review*, 52 (4), 533–554.

Westerman, J. W., and Vanka, S. (2005) A cross-cultural empirical analysis of person–organisation fit measures as predictors of student performance in business education: Comparing students in the United States and India. *Academy of Management Learning and Education*, 4 (4), 409–420.

Xin, K. R., and Pearce, J. L. (1996) Guanxi: Connections as substitutes for formal institutional support. *Academy of Management Journal*, 39 (6), 1641–1658.

Yang, M. M.-h. (2002) The resilience of guanxi and its new deployments: A critique of some new guanxi scholarship. *China Quarterly*, 170 (1), 459–476.

Zhang, S., and Kline, S. L. (2009) Can I make my own decision? A cross-cultural study of perceived social network influence in mate selection. *Journal of Cross-Cultural Psychology*, 40 (1), 3–23.

Zhu, Y., Bhat, R., and Nel, P. (2005) Building business relationships: A preliminary study of business executives' views. *Cross Cultural Management*, 12 (3), 63–84.

Index